Latin America today

D1593125

Note to the reader from the UNU

Latin America Today grew out of a United Nations University project concerned with the current situation in Latin America. Entitled "Perspectivas de América Latina" (PAL; Latin American Perspectives), the project was aimed at identifying and analysing the major trends influencing economic, social, political, and cultural development in Latin America. It was also directed at promoting a rigorous exchange among Latin American social scientists on subjects they perceive as crucial to the region. The 10 main subject areas covered by the project were: (1) theory and practice of the state; (2) social movements; (3) political systems and political parties; (4) the state, civil society, and crisis; (5) political processes and institutional change; (6) culture, politics, and power; (7) emerging democracy; (8) conflicts and the crisis; (9) future studies; and (10) regional synthesis in Latin America in the present combination of circumstances. In addition to this English volume, a number of reports and some 20 books in Spanish have been produced, constituting a rich library of information and Latin American perspectives on the region today.

Latin America Today provides a synthesis of these efforts and offers the reader an aggregate image of the current situation in the region. It constitutes an exceptional study of the unity and diversity that are Latin America today and is essential reading for the understanding of the contemporary Latin American scene.

Latin America today

Edited by Pablo González Casanova

United Nations
University Press
TOKYO • NEW YORK • PARIS

First published in Spanish in 1990 as *América Latina, hoy*.

Translated from the Spanish by Anne Bar Din and Margarita Montalvo.

United Nations University Press
The United Nations University, 53-70, Jingumae 5-chome,
Shibuya-ku, Tokyo 150, Japan
Tel.: (03) 3499-2811   Fax: (03) 3499-2828
Telex: J25442   Cable: UNATUNIV TOKYO

Typeset by Asco Trade Typesetting Limited, Hong Kong
Printed by Permanent Typesetting and Printing Co., Ltd.,
Hong Kong
Cover design by Apex Production, Hong Kong

TWWD-2/UNUP-819
ISBN 92-808-0819-2
United Nations Sales No. E.92.III.A.6
04500P

Contents

Introduction

Pablo González Casanova

At the end of 1982, an investigation into Latin America's outlook for the future was begun, sponsored by the United Nations University and the Institute for Social Research of the Universidad Nacional Autónoma de México (UNAM). This research was part of a larger project dedicated to the study of Africa, the Middle East, Asia, and Latin America. Dr Kinhide Mushakoji, Vice-Rector at the United Nations University and director of the overall project, from the very beginning endowed the project with what might be called "a new epistemological style." Rather than fixing it within a previously established theoretical framework, or tying it to a previously formulated problem, Mushakoji began by encouraging questioning and prioritization, conjecture and hypothesis, which in turn determined the actual form in which the work was approached.

For the study on the prospects for Latin America (PAL), a consultant board was established that included several specialists in the social sciences: Daniel Camacho, Theotonio Dos Santos, Carlos Tello, Agustín Silva Michelena, Jorge Graciarena, Enzo Faletto Verné, Lorenzo Meyer, Gérard Pierre-Charles, and Hugo Zemelman. This board was the first of a series of work groups that collectively, but with different types of individual contributions, carried out a series of seminars, round-table discussions, and workshops on subjects that had until then received relatively little attention, subjects such as social movements, especially popular ones; theories and practices of the state; emergent democratic phenomena running through Latin America and the Caribbean with many variants and innovations; the systems and political parties of the 20 Latin American nations; political culture and power; political conflicts and institutional change, with their limits and possibilities at the domestic as well as the international level in different circumstances and conjunctures. In addition, several in-depth studies were made of the crisis and its impact on civil society and state, as well as a series of complementary bibliographical and statistical studies. Many of these works took the nation as their unit of analysis; others the whole of Latin America. Of course, studies were also undertaken on smaller units – provinces, towns, groups. The editorial plan for these works envisages several volumes, many of which have already been published.

The decentralized and autonomous nature of PAL, the geographic diversity of its components, which were spread all over Latin America, as well as the theoretical and academic pluralism of the research teams, all played an important part in the novelty of the empirical and theoretical contributions of both narrowly focused studies and synthesizing studies – national, regional, international.

PAL was to become one of the greatest social science research projects of our time. That is thanks not only to the United Nations University's support and its respect for freedom of research and academic freedom, but also to the support of the UNAM, and many other national, state, and provincial universities, as well as to direct contributions and support from three important social science organizations: CLACSO (Latin American Council of Social Sciences), FLACSO (Latin American School of Social Sciences), and ALAS (Latin American Association of Sociology). With their help, PAL was able to organize one or more research teams in each Latin American country, and in the larger regional networks, in the Caribbean, Mexico–Central America, and South America. In Mexico and Brazil, PAL planned for a research team for each province, but this could not be done in Brazil because of a lack of economic resources. In the end research teams were organized in the 32 federative entities of Mexico. This was so successful that we hope to implement the same system in the future, not only in Brazil and Latin America but also in other areas so as to encourage study of provinces and federative entities in the present world.

In terms of methodology, our point of departure was the decision that it was preferable to lose comparability and gain creativity. The teams were given considerable theoretical and empirical freedom in their research. To that end, detailed research designs were rejected in favour of manuals that were enhanced during the seminars and work groups. These seminars sharpened and sometimes even determined the theoretical framework, its main hypotheses, concepts, and variables. Generalization and explanation were controlled by varying the works' level of abstraction, and by systematically comparing case-studies and synthesizing studies.

The establishment of a network of seminars and groups in each area of study that brought together different sides or dimensions of the same issues permitted us to accumulate a file of works. Consulting and integrating these works not only helps us to link analyses and facts that were disconnected before, but allows us to study the sociology of knowledge in the social sciences.

A total of 1,028 studies embracing historical, political, and social analysis has accumulated on each country and its history, from the end of World War II, and from the crisis of the 1970s to the present day. There are more than 300 studies on social movements, 169 on emergent democratic phenomena, 43 on the theory of the state and political parties, 43 on the present crisis, 34 on political culture and power, 32 on current conflicts and struggles, etc.

In the realm of facts, numerous signs indicate a new social, political, and cultural structure. Among them we might draw attention to:
(1) a phenomenon we have called "emergent democracy," in which political struggle and struggle for power or social struggle are combined with the struggle for a new everyday democratic culture,
(2) the appearance and development of new influences and trends, supporting pluralistic and dialogical thought that is neither doctrinaire nor typological,
(3) new civil structures and what could be called informal politics, which modify the old categories of "formal country–real country" and "political country–real country,"
(4) new social and popular movements that are not linked to existing party politics,
(5) the rise of new power structures or coalitions,
(6) the rise of new forms of social and diplomatic negotiation,
(7) a restructuring of the domestic and the international in the whole of the state, civil society, and culture,
(8) a new significance for world peace of social revolution and social reforms that compel us to reconsider the diplomatic and political problems that would make the presence of the United Nations effective, through a reinforcement of the principles of non-intervention and self-determination of nations not only in the field of law, but also in those of economics, technology, society,

culture, education, and politics, as the only agenda that might ensure peace and world survival.

The strong ideological and programmatic nature of these issues
poses a question that is central to the social sciences. It constitutes
what Myrdal would call the present dilemma of the world's nations:
how to reconcile the values of the Modern Age with the mass democratic project at the centre of Latin America's struggle.

The authors of the papers in this volume coordinated seminars in
their fields of specialization. They later met to put this volume
together: it is therefore the result of a collective effort. The last chapter on Latin American conflicts is a product of close collaboration
between specialists on their respective countries, especially Agustín
Cueva, Jorge Cardena Roa, Pablo Mariñez, Jorge Lara, Rafael Ver-
gara, and Beatriz Stolovicz. We thank them, as well as María Beatriz
Reina, technical secretary of PAL, Elke Köppen, who organized the
system of documentation and archives of PAL, George Aseniero,
and many others whose perseverance and enthusiasm contributed to
bringing this work to fruition. We are greatly indebted to Dr Kinhide
Mushakoji, whose greatest contribution was knowing how to encourage the first study on the third world undertaken by third world researchers.

1
Economy and crisis

Pedro Vusković

I. The signs of the crisis

1. Recent evolution of Latin American economies

It is now generally acknowledged that the economic crisis affecting Latin America, which became evident at the beginning of the 1980s, is the most serious the region has had to face since the 1930s, and according to some analysts the effects of the current economic crisis might surpass those of the earlier one. This would put Latin American nations on the verge of a momentous historical transition and face them with the necessity of implementing transformations that presuppose fundamental changes, as much in the patterns of their internal development as in their economic relations with the external world. Even if the most visible manifestations of this process can be identified in its economic scope, its essential nature is being projected onto a larger body of social and political phenomena.

Information about the depth of the crisis, as well as on its extent and duration, confirms these suppositions. In fact, for the region as a whole, the years since the beginning of the 1980s have been ones of unmitigated adversity. The resulting decline has affected all

The central theses expounded in this synthesis are developed further by the author in his paper "Latin America in front of the challenges of the crisis: report on the crisis"; also prepared for the United Nations University and finished in February 1988. In that paper, a greater effort at identifying national peculiarities within the world framework of the crisis will also be found, which is referred to here more generally in so far as Latin America is concerned. It is also important to point out that the majority of the analysis does not apply to socialist Cuba and, to a great extent, it does not apply to Nicaragua either.

Latin American countries, with the exception of Cuba, with varying intensity.

According to the latest available estimates, the domestic gross national product per capita in the region as a whole registered a continual decline in 1981, 1982, and 1983. It showed a modest recovery during the three following years, with an almost imperceptible increase in 1987. Its cumulative variation over the years 1980–1987 worked out negative for almost all countries, with the exception, once again, of Cuba, which showed a substantial increase, and of Brazil, Colombia, and Panama, which showed small increases. For some countries, the 1980–1987 period represented a regression to levels of 10 or 15 years earlier.

Other indicators, such as those related to consumption, investment, or foreign trade, portray the same general picture of adverse circumstances. In addition, they characterize a Latin American situation that is less favourable than that of other large areas of the underdeveloped world.

Negative production trends were manifested also in financial disequilibrium, and particularly in inflationary pressures. The latter grew in intensity from 1981, and reached a climax in 1985: weighting national indices for the corresponding population, the regional consumer price index was then 275 per cent. In 1986, influenced by antiinflationary policies, it dropped to less than 65 per cent, but in 1987, in spite of these policies, it acquired a renewed intensity and rose to 187 per cent.

Inflation and the recessionary effects of the policies used in an attempt to check it helped in turn to accentuate the regressive distribution of income. Of the 11 countries for which information on the evolution of the urban real minimum wage is available, 6 show 1987 levels to be lower than those recorded in 1980. The loss of real income for this group of workers was at this time close to 40 per cent in Mexico, Peru, and Ecuador, and in the order of 30 per cent in Chile and Brazil.

To decreases in real wages were added losses of employment opportunities relative to the size of the economically active population. Data from the Economic Commission for Latin America (ECLA) for 15 countries, and relating only to urban unemployment, reveal rates of unemployment that are conspicuously higher than those of 1980, and, in nine countries, indices of urban open unemployment higher than 10 per cent.

These trends in both income and employment, whose consequences were felt with relatively greater intensity among the working classes, eventually affected the basic standard of living of the general population quite severely, particularly if one takes into account the effects of public spending reductions in the social services. Various indices relating to nutrition, the incidence and causes of morbidity and mortality, and access to schooling also reflected dangerous retrogressive tendencies.

In another manifestation of the crisis, impoverishment and the lack of productive job opportunities led to alarming levels of delinquency and corruption.

The obvious impossibility – until now – of checking these trends, of halting the crisis and opening the way to new strategies of development, also compromises the outlook for any kind of political evolution. In general, no coherent economic plan has been proposed and maintained that might be able to sustain hopes of recovery and strengthen the social goal of democratic coexistence. On the contrary, attempted moves in this direction will soon have to recognize their vulnerability in the face of such a profound economic crisis.

2. Outward characteristics of the region's economic relations

Strictly speaking, some of the most obvious expressions of the economic crisis in Latin America first appeared in the region's trade and financial relations.

A drastic change in the international economic climate occurred within a short space of time. The 1970s were characterized, in fact, by a significant dynamism in world trade and an exceptional flow of foreign loans to Latin America. At the beginning of the 1980s, economic recession in large capitalist countries considerably weakened the demand for Latin American export products, which seriously affected export prices. The rapid growth of the external debt and the sudden increase in interest rates led to the "debt crisis," which was typified by unsustainable debt service payments in relation to their current income. This put pressure on the indebted countries to cut imports drastically.

After marked fluctuations and in spite of a considerable recovery in 1987, the dollar value of regional exports of goods still remained lower than that recorded for 1981. At the same time, payments of capital gains and interest more than doubled between 1980 and 1982. The positive contribution of net capital movements fell abruptly during 1982 and showed very slight growth during the next few years. A

3

Pedro Vusković

sharp contraction of imports was enforced with consequences for economic activity levels: from a value close to $100,000 million in 1981, imports fell to less than $80,000 million in 1982 and to less than $60,000 million during each of the following years, barely recovering to $65,500 million in 1987.

The imbalance between the external debt services and current export income became so great that successive negotiations were necessary to delay payments. Nevertheless, and in spite of a severe reduction in imports, the absolute amount of the debt kept increasing: it went from $288,000 million in 1981 to $410,000 million towards the end of 1987.

The eloquence of the figures suggests that "external" factors have played a determining role in the suddenness of the Latin American crisis. But it would be wrong to conclude from this a strict correspondence between the evolution of Latin America's economy and the world economy. Developed capitalist countries recorded relatively high rates of economic growth until the end of the 1970s. Their dynamism weakened in 1979, and 1980 marked the beginning of a severe recession that lasted until 1982. The parallelism stops in 1983: then the developed world's gross product increased by 2.6 per cent and that of North America in particular grew by 3.6 per cent. The phenomenon was more marked in 1984 when US GNP rose 6.4 per cent and that of all capitalist developed countries rose 4.7 per cent. During the next few years they maintained variable patterns, but they were all positive.

One might observe that Latin America has a record of crisis situations that are much more intense and prolonged than the recessionary phenomenon exhibited by the capitalist developed economies. At the same time, the recent economic deterioration of the region is relatively more intense than that experienced by other third world countries. The recovery and expansion of the capitalist developed economies are not inducing comparable processes of recovery in Latin American economies. On the contrary, they seem to explain part of the sluggishness of the latter's progress. In any case, recognizing that external factors played a decisive role in triggering Latin America's economic crisis is not sufficient to explain the nature of this crisis; it is necessary also to recognize its domestic origins. These may be more remote and less visible, but they are no less significant. In addition, one must not fail to note that the factors that appear as "external" not only respond to "exogenous" causes, but are also in part the result of factors of a predominantly domestic nature.

4

3. Internal processes in the Latin American crisis

As a part of the evolution that could be considered to be domestic, and from the perspective of a larger time-frame, some trends that continually threaten Latin American development can be readily observed. These trends show themselves either by threatening the continuity of global economic growth, or by increasing basic disequilibriums in the workings of the economic system, or by sharpening the social and political tensions they provoke.

Although national experiences vary significantly, Latin American development in general reveals a series of characteristic features. Among them, it is possible to identify a pattern of unstable growth within a long-term tendency to stagnation. Almost all the economies of the region have experienced, at various times, phases of considerable dynamism during which their income levels rose notably, their productive structures diversified to some degree, and they enjoyed a period of modernization and urbanization. But at the same time these economies had to face increasing problems in sustaining this economic growth as they neared the limits of, among other things, the absolute magnitude of respective national economies.

The pattern that this growth assumes has also shown exceptional characteristics. Rather than the productive units already in existence being modernized and provided with the latest technology, new units have been superimposed on the existing ones, making them relatively weaker. The "structured heterogeneity" of Latin American economies took shape and became progressively emphasized in this way. This process produces inequality and differentiation of productivity between productive sectors and strata, which became an obstacle on the road to higher levels of development.

It is necessary to mention also the inability to resolve basic problems of living standards for large sectors of national populations, even during phases of relatively rapid growth.

Income distribution, which is extremely concentrated for the benefit of a privileged few, and its counterpart, the scanty participation of the poorer social sector, have shown remarkable stability. Processes of urbanization and industrialization did not automatically result in a somewhat fairer distribution of the fruits of increased growth. Policies of redistribution, through which an attempt was made to compensate for the absence of this spontaneous improvement, had only limited and short-term effects. In turn, this abnormal income distribution had an effect upon the formation of the productive structure

5

that grew out of it. This productive structure favours the demands of those with a higher share of purchasing power. This eventually generated a sort of "dynamic of inequality" which is generally typical of all Latin American development experiences, and to whose social limits can be added corresponding economic limits. It is probably now, in this phase of its historical evolution, that these limits are being approached, particularly if one takes into account the fact that the crisis itself and the policies intended to end it have done nothing but accentuate these inequalities even more. In fact, the working masses of the Latin American nations are absorbing nearly all the costs of the crisis, in part because the loss of employment and the reduction in real wages have been much more acute recently than the fall in the gross national product or the increasing "transfers" of income abroad.

Yet another common feature is the insufficient domestic integration of Latin American national economic systems, which prolongs and reinforces external dependence and the inability to generate dynamic autonomous growth. Essentially, we are dealing with an industrializing scheme that was only weakly geared towards the production of capital goods (with the partial but significant exception of Brazil) and that was oriented more towards exportation, when feasible, and towards the various consumption demands of the social groups that benefited from income concentration. To be sure, there are also important differences of degree among the various economies of the region, influenced as they are by individual mean levels of development and differing absolute sizes. But essentially this phenomenon is present throughout Latin America. In any case, one of its consequences is to subordinate domestic growth to the fluctuations of import capacity, as can be seen time and again within the framework of the present crisis. Seen in this light, the crisis in Latin America ultimately assumes the character of a culmination of complex external or domestic factors, of either short- or long-term gestation.

The very longevity of the crisis reveals another dimension. Antecedents of various origins suggest that it had been latent for several years and that this explains policies that tried to hold it off, by at least temporarily prolonging the existing developmental patterns. It could even be said that, towards the end of the 1950s, in some cases, and during the 1970s in others, the limitations of this mode of development were already visible, and that it was this basic insight that motivated various projects searching for other courses of development (the Cuban Revolution, and, later, the attempts in several countries to take "non-capitalist routes," with their most eloquent expression in the process of Popular Unity in Chile). Later, in the mid-1970s, the extraordinary dynamism of world trade and the unprecedented levels of foreign loans once again postponed the reality of the crisis. But when these external factors reversed their course at the beginning of the 1980s, the crisis exploded with the full force of this historical significance.

II. Interpretation of the crisis

1. Different approaches

Notwithstanding the absolute certainty of the crisis, its intensity, and its duration, it has provoked and still provokes a variety of interpretations of its essential nature and, consequently, of the policies necessary to confront it effectively. Explicitly or implicitly, the crisis has initiated an unresolved controversy in which various points of view, tendencies, or "bodies of thought" can be identified.

The angles of main interest differ particularly when an analysis of the crisis is planned, in part as a result of the position from which these analyses are undertaken – from the point of view of developed or underdeveloped economies, from the point of view of managers or of workers, etc. Theoretical or ideological backgrounds have an influence too, depending on whether they use Marxist or non-Marxist categories of analysis, for example. All this leads to very different appraisals of the historical significance of the crisis, its chronology, the relative influence of external and internal factors, and the possibility and content of a characteristically Latin American response.

Some basic differences arise from conflicting perceptions of the contemporary crisis: whether it should be understood as a world phenomenon of universal magnitude, or one that comprises at least the whole of the capitalist system and that happens to be *projected* on to Latin America, or, on the other hand, to what extent it should be necessary to identify some "Latin American particularities" or a "Latin American crisis" that has to be understood in terms of the particular features of its own pattern of development. Furthermore, this would not preclude very important differences within one or the other of these criteria. It is therefore clear that it is not easy to propose a synthetic classification of the crisis or its observers, and that any attempt at global characterizations has inevitably to accept a significant degree of arbitrary simplification.

Now that the danger has been acknowledged, there follows a

7

selection of the approaches, both personal and institutional, that are considered representative of the various currents of thought. This offers an extensive panorama of the points of view, and the controversies motivated by them. For each perspective, an effort is made to summarize very briefly its most characteristic elements.

2. Prebish and the ECLA

In some of his most recent work (1985, 1986), Raúl Prebish locates the peak of the crisis as a contemporary phenomenon, affecting the whole world economy. For him, we are dealing with a "planetary" crisis: a crisis of capitalism as an expression not only of incidental factors but also of fundamental problems, and also a crisis of "concrete socialism." In the first case, the root of the crisis can be found in the discrepancy between the pattern of accumulation and the pattern of spending. In the second case, it is principally a crisis of productivity.

In a specific reference to developed capitalism, he rejects the idea that capitalism has lost the "capacity of expansion" it exhibited during the previous phase of great capital accumulation, and he even suggests that the crisis could be a "consequence of capitalism's vigour, of its increased technological innovations, and of its proven ability to improve the material well-being of great numbers of people." We would then be dealing with new and complex phenomena derived from technical evolution and the contradiction this creates and its consequences for the structure of society and for relations between "the centre and the periphery." For the same reason, "we cannot understand this crisis in the Latin American environment by taking it out of the global context of the system."

The Economic Commission for Latin America's analyses of these questions are generally based on the recognition that Latin America finds itself faced with a particularly serious type of crisis, but the ECLA's reports do not always agree about the essential nature of this phenomenon. Some of the reports arrive at the conclusion that the crisis is much more than just a recessionary phase in a relatively normal cycle in the evolution of the prevailing development model. Rather, the crisis seems to be a manifestation of the model's exhaustion. The reports identify the origins of the crisis in internal and external factors as well as conjunctural ones, to which they nevertheless attribute different degrees of relevance. In fact, the criteria concerning the relevance of some key factors are not very clear in the majority of the texts. There are also some papers that display an obvious bias in favour of external circumstances: "the influence of external factors has been decisive . . ."; "the external factors appear clearly in most of the countries, defining the nature and the scope of the crisis . . ." (ECLA, August 1985).

Maybe this very difference of interpretation in the institutional reports explains why, when attempts are made to extend analysis to a plan of action, ECLA's position would seem to involve the view that in Latin America's present situation it is necessary to face two types of phenomenon: a set of structural problems and breakdowns that have compromised development's continuity, and the crisis itself, which seems to be essentially identified by deteriorating external financial equilibrium and in large measure determined by external factors.

Putting it another way, there is a double challenge: the crisis as an immediate problem and the unresolved task of "correcting" structural breakdowns that had begun to develop previously. This means that two successive economic policy programmes would be required, the first to find a solution to the crisis and the second to initiate the task of structural transformation. The crisis would have accentuated these structural failures, and its resolution would in turn constitute a challenge to redefine development policies in the broader sense of the term.

It is within the framework of this vision that the ECLA evaluates the results of "adjustment policies" and the economic and social costs they involve. At the same time, it anticipates the necessity of opening the way for a new phase of reactivation with the prospect of generating new dynamics of growth. And it is also in this context that it identifies the overwhelming weight of the external debt as one of the greatest obstacles to economic reactivation.

3. The International Monetary Fund

The International Monetary Fund symbolizes what in general could be considered as the neo-liberal interpretation of the crisis. From this point of view, the crisis as it manifests itself in Latin America would appear to be the expression of two groups of problems.

In the first place, it is a question of the consequences for regional economies of the recession suffered by developed countries, which reduced their demand for Latin American products and provoked a severe collapse in the international prices of primary products, while at the same time shrinking the flow of loans and the level of direct

Pedro Vusković

foreign investment. These facts, together with the unprecedented increase in interest rates, had a severe negative impact on the ability of Latin American economies to import, forcing them abruptly to reduce imports. The dimension of the crisis is external and conjunctural, supposedly surmountable to the extent to which the tendencies of the world economy can be reversed.

The diagnosis is not limited to these exogenous and allegedly transitory factors, however. In addition, it identifies as origins of the crisis a series of "excesses" incurred in the domestic management of economic policies, including a disproportionate expansion of workers' social gains, excessive increases in public spending and subsidies, and the expansion of foreign indebtedness without a corresponding strengthening of the capacity to repay. This diagnosis also mentions "hyper-expansion" of state controls, without a corresponding increase in efficiency. The proliferation of public enterprises as substitutes for what are thought to be clearly advantageous private initiatives, the inability to create an economic climate that could halt the capital drain, and the discouragement of greater foreign investment could all be said to have contributed to some of the most noteworthy consequences of this hyper-expansion. In short, it is mostly external and "structural" factors, in the particular sense given to these terms in IMF thinking, that are responsible for the economic state of affairs.

This school of thought sees that the disequilibrium that upsets development originates in the implementation of mistaken policies that stimulate the overvaluation of currencies and in the excesses of global demand, which accelerated the shift of economic relations away from "normalcy." To this conceptualization they add that, taking into account the changes that had occurred in the world economy, and the "monetary theory of the balance of payments" (which attributes a basic role to financial variables), the economic policy that would best allow for long-term external equilibrium in the countries that cannot influence decisions on international prices and interest rates would be a policy of "opening" their economies and standardizing these indicators with corresponding values on the international market. Stability, understood as equilibrium in the balance of payments and absence of pressures on prices, is seen as the paradigm of normalcy in the workings of the economic system.

This is more than just a "pragmatic" approach, as called for by the IMF; this is an apologetic vision of a capitalist market that supposedly achieves an optimum allocation of resources on a national and international scale only if the "free" functioning of the market is not upset. Once the origins of disequilibrium have been identified, the response must take the form of "policies of adjustment," which consider not only the external framework but also the corresponding internal modifications: "adjustment presupposes in general a reduction of total demand, modifications in relative prices of factors and products, and alteration of the distribution of resources" (Tseng, 1984).

The principal source of excess spending – according to the IMF – is the state and its institutions. Policies that reduce this spending and that increase tax receipts and raise public service rates are required in order to put the fiscal deficit on a sound footing. A decrease in monetary and credit expansion would serve the same purpose, while an increase in interest rates would encourage savings and would avoid inflationary distortions with repercussions on the balance of payments. On the other hand, a restrictive wage policy would help reduce private consumption. Various economic policy devices could be implemented to expand exports, such as the elimination of trade controls and the encouragement of "real" exchange rates through devaluation or liberation of monetary control. Some "structural changes" would be enforced in order to reduce state participation in favour of national and foreign private enterprises.

The controversy provoked by such IMF action has to do in part with the theoretical basis of its recommendations. But the controversy also concerns the gravitational pull of interests represented by IMF decisions, and the actual results of the policies it recommends. In relation to the first point, it is already obvious to large sections of Latin American society that the IMF does not equitably represent all of the divergent interests of the international community. On the contrary, it favours the interests of international financial capital and the exporting/banking community in underdeveloped countries. As regards the second point, there is a growing belief that one is dealing, in the final analysis, with programmes bearing a clearly anti-national and anti-populist stamp: national interests are subordinated to external ones, even in the case of foreign debt repayment, and serious damage is inflicted upon the standard of living of large segments of national populations. All this also has political repercussions when, in the name of economic freedom at all costs, democratic liberties are sacrificed.

11

4. Interpretations of Marxist thinking

The theme of the crisis as an expression of the historical evolution of social and economic systems has considerable weight in Marxist thinking. The current Latin American crisis has come to represent a challenge of interpretation and a fertile ground for development of this current of thought. Its contributions – which are not exempt from often significant variation – recognize the diverse origins of institutions, analysts, researchers, organizations, and political actors. And while they locate the area's crisis within a much more comprehensive framework, their analyses rest on classical theoretical sources and on elaborations around the theme of capitalism's general crisis and of capitalism's structural crisis at the present time.

Their point of departure is the idea that modern capitalism's crisis consists of three overlapping critical dimensions: it is a stage in the general crisis of capitalism, that is, in the historical process leading to the disappearance of the system over a lengthy period; it is a slowly growing structural economic crisis that includes the crisis of state monopolist regulation as well as other factors, and is part of a relatively large phase; and it is a highly conjunctural cyclical crisis that springs from the classical anarchy of capitalist production.

Within the area of cyclical movements, the cyclical crisis of 1974–1975 can be seen as resulting from the overproduction of industrial goods and the underproduction of raw materials (foodstuffs and energy) in developed countries. It thus affected underdeveloped countries relatively little, and recovery was achieved through an increasing internationalization of the system, expanding the imports of developed capitalist countries and directing capital into loans and direct investments in the underdeveloped world. On the other hand, the next cyclical crisis, in 1980–1982, arose from a general overproduction of industrial goods and raw materials without an accompanying overproduction of capital, thus manifesting itself in an abrupt contraction of international economic relations.

The evolution of Latin American economies indeed shows indicators whose direction corresponds to this analysis. During the 1970s, general growth was superior to that of industrialized countries and, during the cyclical crisis of 1974–1975, the recession in Latin America was minor, its duration shorter, and the recovery more significant. But in 1980–1982 the area experienced a serious drop in its level of activity, a contraction of the external sector and investments, a net capital outflow, and a deterioration in the general standard of living.

This situation did not significantly change until now, forming what is called "the crisis in a state of repose."

One may note that the recovery after the 1974–1975 crisis was based on an unprecedented expansion of international economic relations, which brought to Latin America a higher level of integration with the international economy. Transnational enterprises occupied key positions, they exercised a decisive influence upon national decision-making centres, and they affected the functioning of entire national economies. During the cyclical crisis of the 1980s, Latin America felt the combined impact of the financial crisis, of credit restrictions, of increased interest rates, of capital withdrawal, and of the pull-out of transnational enterprises. All these factors precipitated the "debt crisis" and the balance-of-payments crisis. During the 1990s, the high levels of hoped for inclusion in the world economy will be incompatible with the objective halt in the process of integration (internationalization) developed by the system during the 1980s.

To deal with the crisis and to fulfil debt-servicing commitments, economic policies that favour exports might be applied when developed capitalist countries contract the volume of their transactions and restrict the placement of capital within their own economies, when Latin America no longer constitutes a zone of investment for loan money or international capital. Consequently, the prolonged slow growth of the system will continue to be a brake on potential recovery at the same time that the development of a new cyclical world market crisis would have, for Latin America, consequences even more serious than those of the previous crisis.

5. Debt and unequal exchange: President Castro's proposal

In the last few years Cuba's President Fidel Castro has taken up the subject first of the external debt, and then of the crisis and the international economic order, and promoted a discussion that involves an uncommon level of social involvement. His acute grasp of the facts and the political boldness of his proposals became the principal points of reference for a debate that has embraced the continent's entire political spectrum.

Strictly speaking, his proposals constitute more than an economic diagnosis and even a political one of the whole situation. They are dominated by the notion that Latin America finds itself at a crossroads in its history, which could become a generalized struggle for its complete economic independence. There exist objective conditions

13

for the union of a wide spectrum of forces and government, and for the mobilization of these forces to generate the indispensable external conditions for the development of the area.

Castro (1985c) ranks the current crisis as "the most serious, profound and most generalized," in part because of the magnitude of the debt. Socio-economic crisis and political crisis overlap to create a situation in which the magnitude and the intensity of the crisis, as well as the political situation they create, oblige Latin America to face a challenge so great that it would objectively call for a joint mobilization of forces unknown since the struggle for political independence.

Coming from a Marxist standpoint, President Castro perceives the crisis as an essential phenomenon of the capitalist system, recognizing at the same time a historical situation in which Latin America's relations with developed capitalist countries assume particular features that spread the crisis in the most ruthless way. Although it is part of the cyclical course of developed capitalist economies, the crisis nevertheless presents some new, exacerbating and complicating features.

Castro's interpretation can be summed up in two basic propositions. The first places the external debt accumulated by third world countries, and particularly by Latin America, at the centre of the current crisis. It holds that external debt has become a decisive factor and, at the same time, has taken on characteristics that make it unpayable, in that there does not exist an adequate policy to deal with the crisis that does not involve the repudiation or cancellation of the debt. The second proposition holds that the debt itself is a manifestation of deeper problems that have their source in the nature of Latin America's external insertion. For this reason, it would be necessary to redress the basis of the unequal exchange and offer a real alternative for a new international economic order.

President Castro invokes in support of his theory the notion that the course of the Cuban Revolution has been marked not only by domestic changes but also by the establishment of different relations with socialist countries generating an environment favourable to development, from which, he suggests, we can see various possibilities for a different international economic order. In the same way he points to the necessity of Latin America's integration: "for Latin America it is not enough just to cancel the debt in order to achieve the New International Economic Order (NIEO). It is also necessary to seek economic integration in the absence of which we could not really develop or survive as independent nations" (1985e).

Together with laying bare the importance of the roots of its dependency, the crisis could at the same time provide a unique historical opportunity for Latin America. A failure to take advantage of it would have not only economic consequences but also political ones; in several countries the crisis has to some extent contributed to the process of democratic opening. But "if the economic problems derived from the debt are not resolved, these democratic processes will inevitably be in crisis too" (1985e).

III. Practical politics under the cloud of the crisis

1. Policies of adjustment: Conception and content

The differing interpretations of the nature of the crisis contrast with the relative uniformity of the policies aimed at dealing with it. These have in general been termed "adjustment policies" whose essential features have been defined by the IMF and incorporated into the national policies of almost all Latin American countries.

The immediate background that motivated the introduction of adjustment policies is the untenable balance-of-payments situation, which resulted from a weakening of foreign demand and the worsening of terms of trade, the rise in interest rates in international financial markets, and the extreme contraction of new flows of financial resources coming from abroad. It is for these reasons that the basic objective of adjustment policies is defined as "eliminating that portion of the deficit in current accounts which could no longer be financed through the net capitation of loans and foreign investment, or through international reserves" (Castro, 1985d).

The matter goes beyond the strict environment of external accounts. In fact, a deficit on the current account implies domestic expenditure (an internal use of goods and services) greater than the product generated (the value of goods and services produced in the country); in other words, excessive expenditure that is financed by external resources (with indebtedness). To the extent that it is no longer possible to dispose of additional foreign financing (or of accumulated reserves of foreign currency), it becomes necessary to modify the relation between imports and exports and to restrain expenditure, "adjusting" in such a way that it no longer puts pressure on the balance of the current account with foreign countries.

For this reason, the "adjustment," or, more precisely, the intention to "adjust," leads to two types of policies: on the one hand,

15

those that try to curb or reduce domestic spending (in more technical terms: "policies of aggregate demand control") through revenue policies, fiscal and public spending, and monetary control; and, on the other, policies that attempt to alter levels and reciprocal relations of exports and imports, changing the relative costs of internationally negotiable goods and those that are not negotiable, through exchange tariffs, export promotion policies, etc.

At the centre of this concern is the disequilibrium in the foreign accounts, so that all efforts concentrate on correcting this by acting both on the properly external variables of the economy and on the domestic processes that have an indirect influence on them. From another angle, it could be said (though it is never phrased thus in the adjustment proposals) that everything possible is attempted in order to keep paying off the external debt in the extremely difficult conditions that prevail. To this central aim is added the simultaneous objective of relieving the pressure on domestic prices and controlling inflationary processes.

This is why the policies that are put into practice express themselves in different and varied areas of economic policy and why they are designed to affect the functioning of the entire economic system.

The same basic principles manifest themselves in distinct forms of expression. Thus, for example, in typical IMF terminology, one talks about two fields of adjustment policies, depending on the cause of the disequilibrium. If it is attributed to excessive domestic demand, fiscal and monetary policies will be required to shrink it to a magnitude corresponding to the level and growth rate of the productive capacity. If the problem originates from structural weaknesses that jeopardize supply and lead to price distortions, it will be necessary to improve resource allocation in order to strengthen the productive base, modifying common situations such as overvalued rates of exchange or low or negative real rates of interest, etc.

Difficulties in managing foreign payments are closely associated with deficiencies in domestic policies, so that "corrective action" is necessary, although this presupposes sacrificing growth and a further deterioration in income distribution. This "corrective" action has as one of its principal aims the modification of the structure of relative prices between goods for external trade and goods for domestic consumption, in such a way as to induce a shift in production towards the former. As in the disequilibrium between supply and demand, the adaptation of supply is a process requiring time for the adjustment to express itself first in a restriction of demand, with the consequent "costs" of lowered consumption and temporary displacement of the workforce.

2. Adjustment, neo-liberalism, and stabilization

The assumptions of adjustment policies and the areas in which they express themselves would seem to identify them with stabilization programmes and neo-liberal policies. They do in fact suggest similar objectives (balancing payments and fighting inflation) and they are indeed somewhat similar in terms of the instrumental areas they touch upon (exchange, fiscal, credit, and wage policies). But in spite of their similarities of form, they involve different restructuring effects on the dynamics of accumulation and economic power relations.

Neo-liberalism, as expressed in the economic programmes put into practice in various Latin American countries during the 1970s, represented a long-term option, a project to found the capitalist societies again at the start of the international crisis. Adjustment programmes, on the other hand, have a short-term perspective, attempting to pave the way for a recovery that will make possible the discussion of further strategies. It is true that the IMF's adjustment proposals incorporate a new element: a greater concern for the "structural" spread of the "distortions" the IMF sees it necessary to correct. But it limits structural elements to what it considers to be the inefficiency of state guidance of the economy.

There is also a curious relation between "adjustment" and "stabilization." The implementation of some of the components of adjustment policies – particularly devaluation, public enterprises, increased tariffs, domestic fuel costs, and interest rate increases – caused an acceleration of inflationary pressures, which created unusual patterns of price increases in several countries. The fall in production levels of basic goods and the extent of speculative phenomena in trade activities occurred in the same way. The control of inflationary processes became as high priority an objective as external balance, leading to the implementation of new packages of economic policies specifically designed to "stabilize."

An example of the latter was the Austral Plan in Argentina, and later the Cruzado Plan in Brazil. Both were called "heterodox programmes," a name at times extended to the economic policy measures attempted in Peru. Appearing within the perspective discussed here nevertheless diminishes substantially the meaning of "heterodoxy." It

17

is true that the programmes represented a temporary retreat from the neo-liberal omission, and that they attempted to intervene actively to contain inflationary tendencies that were becoming uncontrollable. But these measures were always within the framework of crisis management rather than intended to open new horizons for national development, even if this appeared to be the case during the period of the Peruvian proposal.

Analyses of and controversies over the experiences of Argentina and Brazil are still very much alive in scholarly work on Latin America's economy. The initial success of both Argentina and Brazil in their attempts to bring down inflation was spectacular. But because the measures were not accompanied by more far-reaching action, they progressively lost their efficacy and ended up producing tensions and uncertainty comparable to those that existed before the measures were initiated. The economic policy followed in Peru had short-term "reactivating" effects, but it was not applied widely enough to give it continuity, and it too eventually ran out of steam.

3. Results of the adjustment

Meanwhile, whether it is a matter of more or less "classical" or more or less "heterodox" policies, what is certain is that a considerable period of adjustment time has elapsed, and yet the crisis is still hitting the majority of Latin American economies with the same intensity.

It could be said that the adjustment has been successful insofar as its purpose was to reduce external disequilibrium. In fact, there was a spectacular turn over (amounting to $33,000 billion for the whole of Latin America) in the balance of trade of goods between 1981 and 1983. But this resulted exclusively from an extremely violent contraction of imports: for the entire region, they dropped from $98 billion in 1981 to $56 billion in 1983. In Argentina and Chile, imports were halved during the same period; in Venezuela, they dropped 47 per cent in real terms in 1983 alone, in Uruguay 63 per cent (during 1981–1983), and in Mexico 67 per cent (in 1982 and 1983).

It should be noted in passing the remarkable contrast between this import contraction and the relative stability of net interest and profit payments abroad. These remittances reached a peak for Latin America as a whole of almost $39 billion in 1982, and they then oscillated around $35 billion during the next few years.

The contraction of imports and the reduction in domestic spending have negatively affected production and consumption levels, thus aggravating a recessionary and inflationary situation that still lingers on. Indices of open unemployment and underemployment have increased notably. In turn, inflation and unemployment have affected real incomes and have led to a further deterioration in the already skewed income distribution. The exclusion of social groups from economic activity in Latin American societies has increased, as has social inequality. To the unprecedented fall in real wages we can also add the contraction of "indirect income" (represented by public services in education, health, and housing). The same recessionary situation has led to liquidations, mergers, and takeovers of medium and small units of production by large conglomerates. That is to say, it has contributed to the concentration and centralization of capital while giving it an even greater intensity.

Even when we consider specific goals, the results are negative: despite surpluses on commercial balances and the reduction of the public deficit, external disequilibrium persists, fed by the servicing of the external debt and capital flight.

To evaluate critically the significance of these outcomes, it is important to take into account the fact that the design of adjustment policies derives from a particular concept that perceives the crisis as a transitory manifestation of external breakdowns and of distortions in domestic productive systems brought about by state interference, inflated public spending and state apparatuses, and a supposed "excess" in social demands. This understanding of the crisis remains at least implicit in the IMF's formulations. At the same time, the efficacy of the adjustment will depend upon the degree to which this conception actually corresponds to the real nature of the crisis. Only if it is accurate can we hope that adjustment policies will create the conditions necessary for the next step of "reactivation" and lead the way to a full recovery of development as a spontaneous result of the "return to normalcy."

So far, there seems to be no guarantee that this will happen. Rather than being programmes to overcome the crisis, adjustment policies seem barely able to alleviate its effects. Among other things, the social costs of the crisis turned out to be much higher than had been expected, and its supposed brevity seems now to stretch into the unforeseeable future. After a considerable enforcement period, "reactivation" does not seem any closer. The conception of the adjustment seems to be self-defeating: it tries to lower external disequilibrium rapidly, initially acting mainly on imports, a manoeuvre that has recessionary results, which in turn limits the possibility of reassigning resources from non-commercial goods to exports and import substitution. Thus adjustment policies fail to bring about real changes in the structure of production. Yet this is thought to be the key to success.

From another angle, the main objective of guaranteeing the continued servicing of the external debt has been attributed to adjustment polices, to their design and the way in which they are put into practice. The cost of servicing, scarcely reduced by a process of constant renegotiation, constitutes the ineluctable *fact*, in relation to which the remaining so-called *variables* have been adjusted: the level of productive growth, capital formation, real wages. Until now, this purpose was managed with relative efficiency, but not without great national and social costs. In addition, there is no resolution in sight: renegotiation has in every case involved increases in the total amount owed, and the burden of its direct tax is incompatible with any prospective reactivation and the overcoming of the crisis. Moreover, from this angle, economic policies with the stamp of "adjustment" are caught in a circle of interrelated economic phenomena that influence each other and prevent positive solutions. It would seem that only a substantially more favourable external market could offer the basic conditions for positive adjustment. But events do not point in that direction.

The conception of adjustment as the reassignment of resources as a function of external balance appears to presuppose the existence within international markets of sufficient room for exportable Latin American goods. But the recovery of "central" economies has not given any indication that this is the case, and the protectionist barriers are still in place. Instability and restriction continue to exist in financial markets, and attempts are being made to attract foreign capital in circumstances that actually point to a decrease in direct foreign investment flows into Latin America. If this continues, the result will be to sacrifice the present and to put the future under obligations without a real objective expectation of more favourable conditions.

Adjustment policies have two strategies with respect to external equilibrium: on the one side, expanded exports and reactivation of external financial flows, and on the other side contraction of imports. Only the second strategy has been effective, that is to say, that of the restrictive order, which, in the long run, tends to extend the global crisis situation.

The substantiation of these facts dispels the hope that adjustment could bring about the necessary conditions for reactivation and then a chance for new development. On the contrary, what is clear is the dramatic need to design and implement new concepts in economic policies, the efficiency of which will depend on the degree to which they can correspond to the structural roots of the crisis, and not just to its conjunctural ones. It is appropriate to ask what might be the short-term contents of a single global policy of development, one attempting to fulfil reactivation goals that at the same time – and not as an imagined pre-existing condition – undertake the structural changes that are impossible to ignore if we desire a full understanding of the crisis.

IV. External conditioning factors in the future evolution of Latin American economies

1. Likely evolution of external factors

Although the interpretations ostensibly differ in the weight they attribute to external factors as determinants of the Latin American economic crisis, at the very least all interpretations recognize their importance. In fact, the policies of most countries of the area seek, in the improvement of the terms of their external economic relations, a way to recover from the crisis. Nevertheless, the reactivation of the world economy in recent years has not had the positive effects that were once hoped for. It seems that there are trends of a structural order and not only of simple conjuncture. The notion that the crisis arises from the traditional system of Latin America's external economic relations appears to be increasingly confirmed by recent events as well as by medium and long-range forecasts, and involves real trade currents as well as financial relations.

The intensity and even to some extent the direction of foreseeable external changes are nevertheless not entirely obvious. We must remember that since the 1970s there have been signs of a growing "internationalization" of capitalism's economic life at the world level. It has been suggested that tendencies towards "industrial redeployment" seemed to point to a new international division of labour. But these tendencies were paralysed during the 1970s as the recessionary phase of developed capitalist economies began and by the protectionism that became a characteristic trait of their policies. It remained an open question whether these tendencies could be reactivated, or if new circumstances, principally related to the vast technological changes being put into practice, might auger the lasting and more autonomous growth of the developed world with respect to natural resources and the workforces of the underdeveloped countries. This would mean, in turn, limited dynamism in the demand for primary products and greater obstacles to the diversification of Latin America's exports.

Financial relations became completely subordinated to the external debt situation. In the generally restrictive context of new transfers of financial resources towards the underdeveloped countries, as well as of new direct foreign investment (increasingly limited to areas of particular interest to central countries), the new flow of financial resources appeared to be closely conditioned by negotiation of the accumulated debt.

In the light of these trends, widely divergent analyses seemed to indicate the same group of expectations as the central processes shaping the future's external picture:

(1) some cautious forecasts with respect to the strength of future growth for the industrialized economies when they were required to face very important changes in their pattern of accumulation;

(2) the continued maintenance of protectionist policies, as much a result of competition within developed capitalism as because of potential access to their markets by the relatively more advanced countries of the third world;

(3) a greater demand for financial resources within the developed capitalist economies themselves, thus diminishing the availability of funds for allocation abroad; and

(4) powerful technological changes that, among other things, would further weaken Latin America's "comparative advantage" in the international scene, as much in terms of the advantage deriving from lower wages as in terms of Latin America's natural resources, thus limiting still more the potential dynamism of its exports.

2. Export possibilities to capitalist developed countries

In the framework of such prognostications, the significance of the technological changes already put into action acquires a special importance.

Some recent analyses (for example Adam Schaff's *Que futuro nos aguarda?* [What future awaits us?], 1985) point out the implications of the scientific and technological revolutions in microelectronics, biotechnology, and nuclear energy, which constitute a second industrial revolution or a second revolution of science and technology. The first, occurring from the beginning of the eighteenth century, "consisted in substituting for the physical strength of man the strength of machines, first powered by steam and later principally by electricity." This second industrial revolution would consist in the first place "in amplifying man's intellectual power and even substituting robots for it, which would eliminate human labour in production and services with growing success." To this contribution from microelectronics is added microbiology's revolution and its results – genetic engineering, which allows "man to intervene effectively with growing insight in the laws of organic nature's development." In fact, genetic engineering "allows us to alter plants and animals' innate genetic code; and even to deliberately create new codes." The third element, the revolution in energy supplies, would substitute for current sources "new, more powerful and practically inexhaustible sources": solar energy, geothermal and tidal energy, water and wind power, and, most importantly, nuclear energy.

Schaff reflects mostly from the point of view of developed societies, for which the central problem will be how to guarantee the maintenance of an army of structurally unemployed people, unemployed because of the automation of production and services. He admits that in a first period of transition the problem could be dealt with by a reduction in individual working hours, which at any rate would oblige society to reconsider the issue of income distribution: the solution will have to be found in new principles of national revenue distribution. This cannot be done without violating, or at least modifying, property rights as they now exist. Even so, on a long-term basis it would not be possible to keep on reducing the working day. This would produce a situation in which paid work would no longer earn the living of large sections of the population, and the means of consumption would have to be provided by society, independently of the population's work contribution.

Schaff's own brief references to the potential consequences of these processes for the underdeveloped world tend to point to the differences within it. Thus, what he defines as "the group of great and potentially rich Latin American countries, already partially industrialized [Brazil, Mexico, Venezuela and Argentina]" would enter this second industrial revolution at the same time as they find themselves shaken by the social and economic conflicts of the capitalist world induced by a mixture of explosive problems that could lead to a "classic type of revolution."

North African countries such as Algeria and Egypt, which are more industrially advanced than the rest of the third world, would not be rich enough to undertake modern development and the current industrial revolution could prevent the expansion of their traditional industries. The oil-producing countries of the Middle East would have the financial means but "they pull along an underdeveloped political system and old social institutions." The Republic of China could enter the world of the current industrial revolution because it has already carried out the necessary changes in economic formation and it could face the ensuing social changes in an evolutionary and planned way.

For the other countries, which form "the proletariat of the present world and which are characterized by poverty, hunger, absence of objective and subjective opportunities to create modern industries and agriculture," the second industrial revolution could be as disastrous as it could be beneficial. On the one hand, innovations in automation and robotization in industrialized countries could reduce and even "repatriate" their investments abroad and create a situation in which "not even the cheapest workforce could compete with modern robots." On the other hand, the same technological revolution opens the way for attainable prospects of solving basic problems of hunger, lack of water, desertification, etc.

Other approaches (see, for example, the recent work of Gonzalo Arroyo and Miguel Márquez, 1985) also imagine, from a Latin American perspective, the likely effect of new technological developments on the economies of the area. They emphasize the wide applicability biotechnology could have in farming and agri-industry, as well as in the fields of energy, health, and mining. They foresee that, by the mid-1990s, these countries could be making extensive use of new strains of corn, wheat, rice, soya, sugar cane, and cotton. It is already technically possible to substitute the cocoa bean. Corn-based sweeteners are already being manufactured, which partially explains the US's drastic and progressive reduction in sugar-cane imports. New fermentation techniques substantially increase protein production through cultivated micro-organisms. In cattle raising, significant improvements in terms of breeds and animal health are also opening up.

All that has been mentioned suggests the extent to which biotechnology could permit industrialized countries to substitute home-based production of the primary products for the present system of imports they are obliged to use. The development of microelectronics and the automation of productive processes will tend to slow down the transference of production lines, or parts of them, to countries offering the incentive of "cheap manpower." Other technological developments of varying degrees of innovation also point to the substitution of primary products: new varieties of ceramics could replace some metals in the electrical industry, the manufacture of machinery and tools or engines; optic fibres could advantageously replace copper in telecommunications; new plastics and polymer compounds would be cheaper and tougher than steel and lighter than aluminium as materials for the car industry and the manufacture of planes.

The horizon of Latin America's exports to developed capitalist countries is tending to shrink, accelerating a tendency that was already apparent even in the 1970s. The proportion of Latin American exports to developed capitalist countries had decreased as much in terms of the general amount as of each category of products, with the exception of fuel. The export of manufactured articles was affected as much by the continued protectionist policies as by the technological breakthroughs, which will end up damaging even the "maquiladora" industry (small workshops where manual or unitary work is done for factories as part of the production process) and the "tax-free" areas (zonas francas) of production for world markets. Tobacco, coffee, and sugar are the persistent targets of campaigns to reduce their consumption in the great importing countries. And, with the help of technological breakthroughs, these countries are preparing themselves to be increasingly efficient producers of many other basic products.

In short, various objective antecedents, viewed from different angles, have created a very restricted outlook for Latin America's exports to "central" capitalist economies. This would lead one to expect that an exporting strategy seeking to develop within the framework of what had been the predominant pattern of trade relations in the region would have limited objective support.

3. Transnationalization of the international marginalization of Latin America

According to what has been suggested, technological breakthroughs of such potential reach cannot fail to raise serious questions with respect to the future of the commercial exchange schemes that characterized Latin America's economic relations with developed capitalist countries in the past; especially when one adds to this the consequences of the accumulated debt in the area of financial relations.

In its extreme characterization, the uncertainty could be phrased in terms of how far the current forces can continue, the forces that in past years led to a process of rapid internationalization of world capitalism's economic life, of industrial redeployment, of the expansion of "maquiladora" industries, and of export activities to the world market from productive units based in underdeveloped countries; in short, of greater integration of the underdeveloped "periphery" with the "centre" of the system. Or the new technological revolution, although it may make developed capitalist nations more interdependent, could help make irrelevant the underdeveloped world as a depository of natural resources and home of an enormous workforce available at ridiculously low wages. In this last instance, more than in the case of "integration," the outlook would be one of growing "marginalization" of the underdeveloped world, and the "casting off" would be not an option exercised as a decision by the periphery to be self-sufficient but an externally imposed fact, not open to decision-making, which would oblige the periphery to define new strategies of autonomous development.

There is also the possibility – strictly speaking maybe the most probable one – that in the conflict of a global strategy of increased internal inequalities, the "internationalization" would tend to include only and apply itself selectively to the "modern" strata of underdeveloped economies, leaving large sectors of the economy and layers of society in a state of relative marginalization, externally as well as internally.

Whatever the long-term historical outlook may be, the present one is a transitional phase in which Latin America will be obliged to sell at a loss some resources that are still necessary to developed capitalism, and to transfer abroad part of the income generated by this sale to honour the terms of debt servicing – an extremely heavy burden. That is to say, Latin America can expect terms of external economic relations that involve contradictory trends in the course of the crisis: the recovery of developed capitalist nations is conditional upon the continuity of the crisis in Latin America (and the underdeveloped world in general).

The final analysis leads to two basic conclusions. In the first place, a strategy of future development necessarily has to incorporate drastic changes in the prevailing patterns of Latin America's external economic relations. Most probably this would be in the direction of a geographical diversification of these relations, for which there are three possibilities: Latin American economic integration, association with other underdeveloped regions, and a greater link with socialist countries. Secondly, this strategy of future development will probably have to change the weight of the "external sector" in the functioning and development of national economic systems, in order to reduce dependency and increase autonomy.

V. Towards overcoming the crisis: Redefinition of global strategies of development

1. Options and strategies of development

The reality of the crisis as a profound and long-lasting phenomenon, the recognition that "adjustment" measures are inadequate to check it, and the evidence of "structural" roots that worsen its symptoms increasingly make clear the absence of alternative concepts that might lead to positive prospects of a way out of the crisis. This results in greater attention to the theme of "options" and alternative "strategies" of development.

This preoccupation had already been apparent earlier in international institutions: towards the end of the 1960s and during the early years of the 1970s, various agencies of the UN initiated discussion of "development styles," "life quality," and similar topics. The definition of the successive "decades of development" proclaimed by the United Nations was also informed by considerations of this nature. And in the Latin American environment, several national experiences were characterized by the search for alternative patterns of economy and social development.

The "external euphoria" of the mid-1970s, when the region's exports reached, in some cases, extraordinary dimensions, and when the flow of loans coincided in unprecedented magnitude, made one lose sight of these preoccupations. Latin American economies were expanding with relative rapidity and the traditional schemes of external exchange and of internal development seemed to find new horizons of possibilities. But the abrupt reversal of these tendencies and the acceleration of the crisis at the beginning of the 1980s brought the preoccupations up again in urgent and dramatic terms. Moreover, it was becoming increasingly accepted that the crisis expressed not only the adverse consequences of external processes but also the exhaustion of the prevailing pattern of development or, at least, of some of its important components.

The scope of the necessary reconsiderations is nevertheless not evident, nor do they meet with more or less generalized acceptance. The debate still tends to take place around relatively particularized options; for example, "external" growth or "internal" growth, greater integration in the international economy or more autonomous development, expansion of the range of action of the state or transfer of responsibilities to "private enterprise," planning or "market" as the basic source of decision-making in the allocation of resources, the spatial distribution of economic activity, sectoral priorities (hierarchization of the role of agriculture or of industry, or, more generally, concepts of "productivity restructuring" and "industrial reconversion"), attitudes and policies with respect to technological advance (the idea of an "endogenous nucleus of technological dynamization" or, on the other hand, the importance attached to "intermediate technologies"), etc. Other proposals, in contrast, are extremely global in nature, as in suggestions that strategic formulations in the economic realm should express higher decisions of a political order – the idea of a "national plan," for example, to which consistent economic programmes should correspond; or a "democratizing strategy," whose main economic thrust would be wide participation at the various levels of direction and administration of the economy and a fairer distribution of the results of the productive process; or the identification of a new social "consensus," of "agreement" as a basic initial consideration for defining development policies.

2. Diagnosis and strategic formulations

Certainly, we are not dealing with an exercise in option identification in the abstract, and preferences for some of the options. The real options of the future cannot ignore and fail to take into account the "inheritance" from the previous course of development, as well as the new factors that condition the future. Put in another way, the discussion must be based explicitly on the "diagnosis" of the present and its antecedents, and on the revision of the strategy that now seems worn out, of its teachings and its projections.

With this purpose in mind, we must remember that, in general, the predominant pattern of development over the last few decades has essentially reflected a strategy of "substitute industrialization" and of expansion and diversification of exports. In the course of this strategy, two sources of dynamism were identified: foreign demand, whose instability motivated phases of minor or major intensity of growth, and the demand for domestic consumption by the social sector benefiting from income concentration, whose relatively low absolute dimension and its wide diversification imposed the stamp of industrialization. Today, there would be sufficient grounds to support the basic hypothesis that these two main driving forces of the past have lost their capacity to sustain the continuity of development.

As was said earlier, the antecedents lead to the conclusion that the crisis is also a crisis of Latin America's external relations system, in terms as much of trade as of financial relations. The latter appear to be completely conditioned by the debt, which for this reason will continue to represent for a long time to come a burden that will absorb a significant proportion of domestic savings and of export-derived income. To this one must add the prognosis that central countries will tend to keep for their own use the greater part of the financial surplus at their disposal in the future.

Commercial links seem to be dependent upon very intensive transformation processes in developed capitalism, driven by, among other things, great technological advances. At the moment the consequences are unforeseeable, but they will certainly have the effect of diminishing the importance of Latin America's comparative advantages, which have maintained themselves through a cheap labour force and the fact that the countries are sources of great natural resources. In short, it is very likely that external demand will not have any significant role in the future as a dynamic impulse for Latin American development.

The second area of consideration has to do with the dynamics of domestic demand, and all it represents as a reflection of the crucial knot of interrelations between income distribution, the composition of consumption, and the structure of the productive system. In fact, the limitations of domestic markets constituted a constant penury in the process of substitute industrialization and explain the need to search for various expedients that could permit, through economic policy, the overcoming of such limitations: protection, which could shelter national industry in the face of external competition; consumption credit; agrarian reform, which would bring manufactured consumer goods within the reach of the rural masses; plans for regional and subregional Latin American economic integration.

Lastly, the growing productive diversification increased and relied on the demands of high-income sections of the population and on the growing concentration of national wealth. Thus, although concentration was socially reprehensible in the past, it fulfilled a "positive" economic function, that of stimulating overall economic growth, which was to a certain extent transmitted to the whole system. Now, instead, one can maintain that the crisis has created a new situation in which concentration can no longer constitute a dynamizing element for the system as a whole; this function too has become exhausted in the extreme degrees of concentration already reached.

Within the framework of this export/concentration pattern, the great structural breakdowns emerged and grew, including: external disequilibrium, brought about more by "import greed" than by the lack of exports; a productive structure geared to foreign demand and high-income domestic demand, and unable to generate or sustain its own dynamic of development; underutilization of the workforce (unemployment and underemployment), which could in no way correct itself spontaneously with growth; and the increasing accumulation of great "social deficits."

"Adjustment policies," with which an attempt was made to respond to the crisis, did nothing but worsen these structural breakdowns. It is crucial to recognize that they are part of the crisis itself, and, because of this, there is no way out of the crisis if they are not included in a perspective of resolution. Put another way, the discussion of alternative strategies cannot be left until *after* the crisis. The crisis can be satisfactorily overcome only *within the framework* of new strategies that orientate all economic efforts and action from now on.

3. Main options at present

The "reasons for the diagnostic," even if they deserve to be relatively widely acknowledged, of course do not directly determine a unique strategic vision of the future, capable of being expressed in a conceptual plan or in concrete action. Furthermore, the varying interests of nations and social strata will also express themselves in the implementation of strategic projects corresponding to their particularized interests. The contribution of the diagnosis refers rather to the explanation of the requirements of each project, of their economic and political viability, and of the social costs they might involve.

This is what is happening in Latin America today. Despite the notorious absence or inadequacy of technical elaborations that could contribute to giving a precise shape to the various strategic options, the undeniable reality of the situation is itself identifying them with growing clarity. This is how, without denying the high level of arbitrariness this implies, one can identify at least three basic "strategic models" that, implicitly or explicitly, as a whole or only in part, seem to capture in a general sense the essential components of the present proposals.

A "segregation" strategy

One such option, identifiable in practice more than in explicit conceptual formulations, appears to be a type of segregation strategy.

This option is shaped by economic interest factions inside and outside that are currently predominant and which, for that reason, are manifested through the actual actions of the government. Its origin is the implicit recognition that the preservation of these interests can no longer be sustained within the framework of the pattern of development that has prevailed in previous decades, and that it is necessary to accept and undertake important changes. It also involves the equally implicit recognition that there is no possibility of resolving some of the great questions of Latin American development on a truly national scale, in the sense that what is being attempted has the backing of the whole economy and the entire society. The limitations on the resources that can be mobilized, the external conditioning factors and restrictions of all kinds would oblige one to adopt a policy of "selectivity." It is clear that the key to this policy being put into practice will be to gather and locate all possible resources in one part of the economy such that they benefit also one part of society, accepting as a supposedly inevitable side-effect some sort of marginalization of the rest of society.

The transformations that have occurred during the last few years in Chile's economy and society constitute an eloquent illustration of this strategic orientation. It has been obvious there how the policies of a military dictatorship have channelled resources in order to create, in one part of Chile, the necessary conditions for a society of relative abundance sustained by a modern and technologically sophisticated economy. As a side-effect, the rest of Chile is characterized by impoverishment, a regression in the standard of living, unemployment, and at the same time repression and constant control by the police apparatus.

The privileged sector in Chile is closely linked to the world capitalist economy. It is the segment that has "transnationalized" itself and that is principally oriented toward exports, "reconverting" the productive base, modernizing itself, and bringing itself up to date technologically to the greatest possible extent. But transnationalization cannot reach the entire economic system. The greater part of Chilean society does not interest transnational capital, and it remains marginalized from progress, does not receive help or resources, and is essentially left to its own devices; it is merely carefully supervised to prevent it from becoming a threatening source of political opposition.

The severity of the results led some people to try to hide them or apologize for them; including, on the ideological plane, a kind of idealization of the informal economy, as in Mario Vargas Llosa's prologue to an investigation on the subject in Peru (Soto, 1987). Not just damaged by their marginalization for the benefit of others, the members of the informal economy appeared to Llosa as the supposedly lucky ones who did not depend on a bureaucratic and oppressive state apparatus, who solved their own problems, who were "free." And this in circumstances in which what is expected of them (or what is imposed upon them) is that they should accept this supposed freedom and real poverty, that they renounce their legitimate claims and complaints so that the resources they might demand for themselves can be concentrated in the sector receiving the benefits.

One must point out that if a strategy of segregation of this nature is not generally applied today in Latin America in its complete, integral form, as is the case in Chile, in several places elements of it are already quite extensive. The risk is that the very dynamics let loose by this partial application drive increasingly toward segregation and a complete conformation to this strategy.

The economic efficiency of a strategy of this sort as a means of overcoming the crisis and opening up new paths of future development is, to say the least, very questionable. Its main objective is not to resolve the crisis but to protect the interests it represents from the consequences of the crisis. In terms of economic possibilities, it can probably further the development of the favoured area quite a lot, especially as the marginalization and deterioration of the other sectors increase. For the same reason, there is no doubt that its social effects make such a strategy incompatible with any prospects of recovery or advancement of democratic forms of coexistence, so that what is seen in the forefront is the question of its political feasibility in the medium and long term.

A "correcting" strategy

Another strategic perspective, which generally could be called a "correcting" strategy, defines itself in relation to the conditions of "extreme poverty" or "critical poverty" that still affect large sections of Latin American society.

This strategy is promoted principally by international organizations and more specifically by the United Nations, and it rests on the implicit belief that the levels reached by the productive forces in the underdeveloped world – particularly in Latin America – and the possibilities of international cooperation could have the necessary force to eradicate situations of extreme poverty and indigence. Rather than a specific formulation, this is a general orientation with significant hues and differentiations. In the social and political area, these are seen as the requirement to preserve and develop democracy and to mobilize some sort of agreement or "social pact" that would establish political feasibility and would allow reforms to be carried out that would not require great changes. In the economic arena, the various versions tend to promote the harmonization and orientation of "growth toward the domestic area" (as a function of these basic needs), with the ongoing pledge to achieve a greater involvement in the world economy. And they call for more active state participation, as much to support the development of the private sector as to prepare for the direct supply of what is necessary to satisfy some of these basic needs.

The ECLA ranks as one of the more notable proponents of this strategy. Its very specific formulations articulate the importance that such a strategy would have in terms of particularized policies in agricultural or industrial development, or of incorporation or development of technical progress and technological and scientific research. They also examine ways of mobilizing resources to adjust the processes of capital formation and their impact on public consumption and on the private consumption of high- and middle-income sectors of populations.

It is implicit in the ECLA analyses that these are proposals that acquire full validity after the crisis is overcome rather than as means *to overcome* it. So much so that this suggests, among other things, an inability to acknowledge that the interim policies produce results that are the exact opposite of those proposed in a strategy of basic needs.

Considering things from another angle, it can be seen that the specific purpose of correcting extreme poverty, such as it is proposed, without affecting in the essential the actual terms of functioning of economic systems, would not require great political adjustments, to the point where they seem to envision an attainable "social consensus." But as one delves into the roots of these situations and sees the degree to which they depend on the general conditions of unemployment, of deep structural heterogeneity, of acute income concentration, and of the gravitational pull of external interests within national economies, it becomes clear that the demands for change would be much greater. For the same reason, the political requirements would also be greater. There would be a need for a social force able to impose much more drastic policies and actions, in which case they would not limit themselves to moderate final objectives. Put another way: the "correcting" strategy could demand, in order to be effective, a diversity of actions – even the alteration of the current relations and means of production – sufficiently profound that they would work toward much more wide-ranging goals than the mere overcoming of extreme poverty, and which would incorporate other purposes that would be projected onto the entire economic and social life.

A "transforming" strategy

A third view of strategic order – which is even further from practical action or from explicit conceptual formulation than the previous ones – would be a coherent application of the conclusions and the diagnoses sketched in the previous sections. In fact, the two dimensions identified in the present crisis – the crisis of inequality and the crisis of the prevailing system of external economic relations – simultaneously help us to understand its profound nature, and also contribute to the identification of the essential features of the option one could call the "transforming" strategy.

Perhaps the most decisive central point is the acknowledgement that the underlying dynamic of future development will have to move towards the needs and demands of entire populations. The drying up of foreign demand and of demand derived from income concentration does not appear to leave us any other options, thus forcing social desirability and economic needs to coincide. Once again, this would involve a reorientation of growth "toward home," but this time with a very distinct direction – making the needs of all the central objective of economic effort.

Presented in this way, the proposal appears simple and almost unobjectionable. But in fact it presupposes a very fundamental turn-round. In the first place, it involves a radical change in income distribution and, in harmony with this, also a very important remodelling of the productive structure. In fact, distribution is not an "autonomous" variable, nor does it depend only on a policy of incomes (prices and wages). It is also determined by the degree of monopolization in such a way that it affects property questions. It is determined by the inter- and intra-sector heterogeneities. In addition, redistribution acquires real meaning only to the extent that it subsequently alters the composition of the *productive flow* and, at the same time, the structure of *productive capital*, which in turn presupposes other patterns of resource allocation.

With a strategic orientation of this sort, what is at stake is not just resolving the problems of "extreme poverty" or "basic needs" as a complementary part of development, but that *the needs of all constitute the principal objective* from which patterns of investment and the functioning of the entire productive system would be defined. Understood in this way, some economic analyses suggest that the final pattern of development would exhibit decreased saving demands and capital formation, a greater absorption of the workforce and less pressure on imports for every additional unit of production.

The second question to consider has to do with the function that so-called external association ought to perform within the framework of this scheme. Of course, it expresses the theme of export in other terms. It would be a question not so much of what dynamic function exports could have (that is to say, what is the maximum it would be possible to export), but rather of what import capacity would be necessary to sustain the new strategy (that is to say, what is the minimum necessary level of exports). Nor does this scheme entail the subordination of domestic policies to the objective of maintaining or increasing the "comparative advantages" that would lead to more export possibilities, an aim that frequently ends up by halting the growth of real wages or contributing to their deterioration.

None the less, the necessity of disposing of a significant amount of foreign income would persist. Even supposing a positive solution to the debt problem, a considerable volume of imports would be necessary for the expansion and adaptation of the productive structure, as well as to ensure essential supplies. All this leads to the identification of another key strategic path, the *geographic* diversification of external economic relations in three main dimensions: expanded economic relations with the socialist nations, a considerable increase in "South–South" relations, and very decisive progress towards Latin American economic integration. This last dimension has a special relevance, to the point that positive progress towards Latin American economic unification would very probably have to be a central component of any strategy of future development for the region.

It is worth mentioning in passing that a "no exports/no concentration" option also presupposes another view of the technological revolution under way in Latin America. More than the challenge of incorporating technical advances from the international markets, what is most interesting is the possibility raised by the new technologies of resolving problems of internal supply, principally that of food stuffs, which take precedence in the framework of the new strategies of development.

From another angle, it is clear that any outline of economic strategy similar to the ones presented here, which are without doubt very important, would also have to redefine the position and function of the various "agents" of development. In the first place, this strategy proposes, as was said earlier, to tackle the problems of inequality at the roots, including the causes of "heterogeneity" that lead to large differences in the productivity and incomes of the workforce. This implies a re-evaluation of the "strata" that distinguish the very dissimilar positions and levels of productivity in each sector of activity (producing in the farming community, for example, what characterizes "modern" or "capitalist" agriculture on one side and "peasant" agriculture on the other). A less unequal distribution of income at the national level could be achieved only through relatively major progress by the lower strata. In many cases, the contribution of these strata – which is potentially much greater – would be essential to attain the new productive structure presupposed by this strategy. It is clear, too, that an active policy of progressively decreasing "heterogeneity" requires a break with the "global principle" of economic policy: in the face of heterogeneity, discriminatory polices are needed. Global policies in general tend to increase heterogeneity still more.

A new strategy of development could also involve the transfer of some basic activities to a social control system, whether under a kind of state or collective ownership or under some authority coordinating the "social sector of the economy." In any case, it will spur recovery and strengthen the economy's capacity of leadership, the role of the state, including the systematic practice of a continuous process of levelling, particularly if one takes into consideration the foreseeable "heritage" of the crisis and the wear and tear shown by the conventional instruments of economic policies.

In short, what we are seeing is a strategy favouring basic demands ("the needs of all") as the dynamic axis, a strategy pointing to a rapid decrease in inequality, and seeking gradually to surmount the legacy of heterogeneity, a strategy proposing to diversify external economic relations geographically, walking firmly towards Latin America's economic unification, a strategy involved in acceding to the benefits of the technological revolution mainly as a function of its own necessities, and a strategy that develops a system and puts into practice a continuous process of levelling.

All this leaves open the questions of, at least, the "feasibility" of a strategy of this nature, the correlation of social forces capable of impelling it and the route – the short-term policies – between the current crisis and this "image–objective" of the future.

4. The feasibility of a transforming strategy

The discussion on "feasibility"
The design of new strategies of development and the anticipation of an "image–objective" of society in the distant future acquire real meaning only in the measure in which they are economically and politically feasible. Economically, it is essential to know the extent to which an objective basis exists that is at once sufficient and attainable to sustain the strategies with the necessary force to surmount the crisis and reroute economic processes toward another future perspective, and what possible routes exist from the current situation and its prevailing forces to other "dynamics" and another "image–objective" of future society. The political feasibility – at least in so far as it depends upon objective conditions – has a great deal to do with changes in the current position and expectations of the various "agents of development" for the new outlines of the economic strategy.

Looking at things very generally, the "segregation" strategy would not appear to present great obstacles of economic feasibility in the short term. In fact, several of its essential features are incorporated in policies already in practice today, and relatively wide-spread in the region. The accumulation of restrictions and limitations does not invalidate its applicability; what they do is enlarge still more the size of the "segregated" sector. But the segregation strategy certainly does not go so far as to shape an effective response to the crisis, if one hopes for such a response to have a national reach, because in essence it postulates that resources and possibilities be concentrated in one sector of the productive system and for the benefit of only one sector of society. In the political realm, it is obvious that a segregation strategy cannot sustain itself for more than a short time unless it is carried out under authoritarian regimes, able to bend to their will the inevitable resistance of the marginalized sectors. That is to say, this strategy is not viable in a democracy.

The "correcting" strategy, on the other hand, would seem to show the most promising signs of political feasibility. In fact, the declared purpose of trying to solve extreme poverty would receive, at least temporarily, the support of many social strata. And the promise of doing so without profoundly altering the present functioning of the system would neutralize the resistance of other sectors and suggests the possibility of channelling its action in the framework of a broad "social alliance." Problems begin to emerge however, as was noted earlier, when we recognize that its main objective of guaranteeing the satisfaction of "basic needs" is greater than the realm of partial actions that were supposedly sufficient for this purpose. To the extent that things happen in this way, the correcting strategy will tend to lose political support as much from the interests that are not disposed to make major concessions, as from those who would remain frustrated in the hope of resolving urgent problems in their life situation. The most likely result would then be a rift which, depending on the correlation of political forces, would either lead to something very close to a segregated strategy, or tend to identify the strategy with an openly transforming one.

For the transforming strategy, the problems of economic and political feasibility appear greater, notwithstanding the fact – or precisely because of it – that this strategy would more directly and profoundly confront the essential nature of the crisis. There is a growing acknowledgement that, in the face of the magnitude of the crisis, and the factors that incubated it, changes stemming from or forced by increasing instability would be quite insufficient. The transformation of what exists now and the reversal of its tendencies would be inevitable. Among other things, this situation of difficulty and need justifies examining the problems of feasibility of this strategy in greater detail.

Economic feasibility

In any perspective of future events, the identification of problems has to be accompanied by the objective recognition of positive factors that are capable of serving as bases for efforts like the transforming strategy.

Among them one must consider the medium levels of income and productivity that have already been reached. It is well known that

Latin America, taken as a whole, is situated in an intermediate position between one of the most underdeveloped areas and one of the most advanced areas of the world. The level of development of its productive forces does not fail to be significant, as is also – to a lesser degree – its industrial diversification. Some of its greater social problems are better attributed to the extreme concentrations and distributions of income than to the absolute capacity of production of goods and services, and it has great potential in terms of its ability to save, increase fiscal income, or reduce imports. In short, it is a *relative* underdevelopment, which in any case offers a base from which Latin American economies can move toward a higher stage.

There is also enormous productive potential in the high proportion of the workforce at the moment underutilized, especially if one takes into consideration that we are dealing with an experienced and relatively highly evolved workforce. Over and above the evidence of serious problems of employment, is the strategic question of how, in present circumstances, to mobilize this latent productive potential.

In the same situation are the relatively idle reserves of natural resources that place Latin America in an advantageous position. The accumulated capital is not negligible either, whether it is directly productive capital or basic infrastructure – roads and railways, irrigation works and electricity-generating plants, buildings, and means of communication. In any case, a sufficiently large structure is in place to sustain – with better exploitation – a considerably higher level of production. It would be necessary to count as well, as an intangible asset, the accumulated experience of many years of national statehood, formal independence, and the assimilation of lessons concerning problems of leadership in economic matters, the design and practice of economic policies, and even experiences that could help to guide the planning of economic and social development. Contributing to this is the heritage of institutions, as much on the national scale as on that of the region as a whole. In all these areas, the heritage from the past is not irrelevant and it is necessary to value it duly in the face of the magnitude of the challenges that lie ahead. All these constitute support factors that lend economic feasibility to a transforming strategy and to its long-term objectives.

The possibility of an alternative economic policy
What is at issue is not only the "realism" of a few assumptions about some basic conditioning factors for the future, or of the internal coherence of "projections," but also the possible connections be-

tween present situations (usually the diagnosis of "the problems") and the image–objective of the future (usually dressed in idealized features). Put another way, it is necessary to identify what immediate actions and short-term policies can substitute efficiently for those in use at the moment, in such a way that they respond as much to the exigencies of the present as to the progress towards the correction of structural maladjustments and the new patterns of future development. Some additional reflections are justified from this more specific angle.

Of course, it will be necessary to recognize that a fundamental consideration when thinking about an alternative economic policy that, without leaving aside immediate exigencies, shapes a viable route towards the new objectives and patterns of development is the organization of a systematic effort to mobilize, to the greatest extent possible, sources of *potential productivity* already in place. In fact, one of the most aberrant manifestations of the crisis is the contrast between very depressed levels of activity, unmet needs and demands, and wasted resources, idle productive talents, and underutilized workforces.

A second consideration could refer to the necessary recovery of the *productive* function in the face of *speculative* distortions that Latin American economies have shown in general. One of the most obvious requirements of any future policy will have to be the re-establishment of a due ranking of the directly *real* productive processes over *financial* phenomena, reassigning resources and orienting for this purpose all monetary, fiscal and credit-oriented measures, interest rates, etc.

Although these two points are quite obvious, their absence in discussions of alternatives of economic policy is surprising. At the same time, very limited progress has been made towards the elaboration of some sort of alternative programme of economic policy able to fulfil a reactivating function and to place itself in a perspective that would permit it to overcome the crisis effectively and render feasible the initiation of new dynamics of development.

To illustrate the point, one could suggest that an alternative programme of this sort would consider the following:
1. Identify and put into practice a series of "mobilizing projects" founded on a systematic recognition of the current productive potential contained in available but underutilized resources, in already installed but underused productive equipment, and in idle and underemployed qualified workforces.

40

In this context, certain projects would be particularly interesting, namely those with the capacity to reach the entire economy (in order to fulfil their "reactivating" functions to the full), those concerned with production meant to satisfy the needs and demands of the majority of the population, and those that could replace supplies that are currently imported.

2. Design and put into practice a "package" of short-term measures and policies contributing to reactivation and to the initiation of rectifications of some of the structural maladjustments occurring within the crisis itself. This is the case in areas such as the following:

(A) PRICE CONTROL MEASURES AND PROGRAMMES FOR IMPROVING REAL WAGES. The recent increase in inflationary pressures in almost all the Latin American countries obliges the adoption – as has already occurred in several of them – of measures to prevent these pressures from becoming uncontrollable. The problem is what direction these controls should adopt. In fact, the very policies of adjustment have had some negative effects on price levels, and in some cases have led to the implementation of "stabilization programmes" that have put off still further any possibility of reactivation.

Re-establishment of the domestic market – especially that having to do with basic consumption by the whole population as an axis of a new development strategy – demands a gradual but persistent improvement in real wages. In the absence of other measures, this improvement in real wages would most likely be negated by enterprises trying to make up their losses through higher prices. If that happened, a policy of price control would be inevitable; this would in addition induce enterprises to seek the preservation of their benefits through an increase in production or sales volume, which would favour reactivation, and not through an increase in unitary prices for lower production, as has been the predominant practice until now.

(B) REDEFINITION OF FISCAL POLICY AND PUBLIC SPENDING. Public spending is called upon to fulfil a key function in any reactivating policy, as much for its direct effects as for what it can represent as an indirect stimulus on other sectors of activity. If its increase were concentrated in a selective way in some of its components, principally those meant for social services (education, public health, housing), it would contribute at the same time to progress towards the central objectives of the new development patterns.

This presupposes a series of measures of a fiscal order, enabling the public sector to fulfil this dynamic function without undue inflationary effects and without affecting the tax system, which falls most heavily onto salaried workers' wages. Possibilities in this direction appear promising in the majority of Latin American countries, where they would depend more upon political decisions than upon practical and technical procedures.

(C) REASSIGNMENT OF FINANCIAL SURPLUS. In the discouragement of predominantly speculative activities and the transfer of more resources to the strictly productive sphere, the principal role belongs to the banking system: in both its capacity as the capturer of financial surplus and its ability to channel it. There resides the importance of policies that encourage savings and investments, and, particularly, of the adaptation of a credit policy to the needs of the whole of an alternative economic policy.

3. Overcome the limits imposed by the situation of trade and external payments. The present terms of external economic relations constitute a restraint on the reactivation in a short-term perspective as well as on the revival of a stable dynamic of development. From there it follows that actions undertaken in three emphasized areas play a key role:

(A) IN TERMS OF THE EXTERNAL DEBT. The entire present perspective is still one of continuity of some services that absorb enormous proportions of domestic savings and of current export income. Consequently, a comprehensive resolution of this problem continues to be a prerequisite for any immediate policy meant to overcome the crisis, and, even more so, of one seeking to build new dynamics of development.

In the light of the experiences just examined, it is obvious that it will be essential to face the problem with more far-reaching proposals than those that have been presented so far. One possibility, in no way exclusive of others, would be to change the "negotiation scenario," appealing to the fact that the debt is no longer just the problem of some creditors and some debtors, acting individually or collectively; it is a crucial problem for the "international community," in which all are compromised. For this reason, its resolution should be taken up by the correspondingly international institution, the United Nations. It is within its purview that feasible ways could be found for effective, definite solutions, such as the constitution of an international fund to assume the debt of the underdeveloped world made up of contributions from all countries in proportion to their respective national income.

(B) IN TERMS OF EXPORTS. The progressive decrease in demand for primary products by capitalist developed countries, and the regulation they exercise through their protectionist practices on manufactured products from less developed countries, severely restrict the short-term possibilities of exports from Latin America to these countries. On a long-term basis, prospects are even more slender because of the consequences of the gigantic technological change towards which the industrial countries are headed.

Under such conditions, it would be necessary systematically to reorient all efforts to proceed, as was said earlier, with a greater *geographical* diversification of external trade; that is, to intensify the "South–South relation," to increase trading with socialist countries, and, mostly, to rethink new formulas of economic integration for Latin America, beginning with an exhaustive exploration of short-term inter–Latin American cooperation.

(C) IN TERMS OF IMPORTS. Probably one of the most decisive factors determining the success of a reactivation policy, given the present conditions, is the capacity to import external supplies that might become indispensable. The search to overcome these limitations by means of increased exports does not meet with favourable conditions. Consequently, a very important component of an alternative economic policy is related to the necessary adoption of a strict scheme of priorities for the import of goods and services as well as the establishment of an adequate system to control them.

Conditions of political feasibility
If some reflections and lines of work such as the ones that have been suggested earlier seem to demonstrate the economic feasibility of new strategies of development and the possibility of expressing them through some concrete programmes of short-term economic policies, the decisive question of their political feasibility remains at stake.

The uncertainties aroused by the crisis seem to affect, paradoxically, the most reactionary social forces as well as the most progressive ones. The obvious failure of neo-liberal experiences, which had appeared to offer an integrated option with economic and political content, resulted in the project most attractive to the conservative forces. The exhaustion of reformist formulas as they were conceived

43

in the 1960s and the 1970s presented social democratic ideas with a challenge that has not been resolved by its capacity to realize new proposals. Social forces advocating a revolutionary transformation appear to be in retreat, not just because of the repression exercised on their organized expression in various countries, but also because they have been weakened by their dispersal and by the inadequacies of their responses in the face of the ideological exclusion to which they have been subjected.

The crisis manifests itself not only through economic indicators, but also in social development, in the institutions, in cultural assets, and in political hopes. Social constructions representing the effort of many years are undermined by the crisis. The historical frustration that all of this represents is leading to subjective dispositions that do not favour a social will to confront the crisis. Scepticism and despair gain some ground. A sort of "realism" complex reduces any proposals to insignificance. A conservatism has spread that does not correspond to the magnitude of new challenges. Social solidarity diminishes while individualism and opportunism flourish. Any project that contains a glimmer of another perspective is seen as utopian. There is, in sum, a contradiction between the objectives that are called for as a result of the profound reality of the crisis and attitudes that seem to hope to resolve it all through minor adjustments, with, in the end, retrogressive consequences.

It is an extraordinary trait of this Latin American present that we encounter such enormous difficulties in harmonizing economic processes with political ones. There are obvious dissociations that could not go on for very much longer. In some cases, the advance of the democratic reconquest (or the expectation of democracy) coincides with serious regressions and economic obstacles, to the point where the failure to resolve these dissociations becomes the greatest threat to the continuity of this democratic recovery and its deepening. In other cases, the predominance of conservative tendencies is expressed in economic proposals that are insufficient or even useless in relation to their most immediate objectives.

The harmonization of economic and political dimensions in facing the crisis will probably have to emerge from the recognition of the enormous task entailed by the readaptation of the "heritage" left by the previous patterns of development and the crisis itself. Before such a task, the change that could arise from what is added would be completely insufficient: the change to what already exists and the reversal of its tendencies cannot be ignored. In another way the framework of inevitability that tends to seal the fate of Latin America today will not be destroyed by a variety of political options, including the ones predominating now that cannot find corresponding formulas of economic feasibility, or economic requirements for which the conditions of political feasibility do not exist.

The fundamental question posed by all this, in terms of what interaction of social forces, and under what political direction, would be able to take charge of the new tasks, cannot be answered for all of Latin America in one generalized solution; it will depend in large measure on the specific circumstances of each country. What is relatively common are the economic "figures" that form the base: a crisis that is profoundly altering the objective position of various classes and strata of society, and that involves for each of them very suggestive lessons about their past conduct; a crisis that will oblige them to face resolutely the heritage of "structural heterogeneity" motivating today's great differences in productivity and incomes; and, lastly, a crisis that will not find an exit away from the framework of economic and social transformations, which will have to be quite far-reaching.

Bibliography

Abalo, Carlos. "El Plan Austral como mecanismo de ajuste en la economía argentina." Paper submitted to the International Seminar on the Crisis in Latin America, 8–10 June 1987, Mexico, Universidad Autónoma de Puebla, 1987.

Aguilar, Alonso et al. *Naturaleza de la crisis actual*. Mexico: UNAM–Nuestro Tiempo, 1986.

Andean Reserve Fund (ARF). "Las institutiones financieras latinoamericanas y la crisis actual." *Boletín Centro de Estudios Monetarios Latinoamericanos* 30(1) (Mexico, January–February 1984): 21–27.

Aranda, Sergio, Miguel Márquez et al. *América Latina en crisis*. Caracas, Venezuela: Latin American Institute of Social Research (ILDIS), December 1980.

Aranda, Sergio, and Dorothea Mezger, eds. *Crisis sin salida? La economía mundial y América Latina*. Caracas, Venezuela: CENDES, 1982.

Arroyo, Gonzalo et al. *Agricultura y alimentos en América Latina. El poder de las transnacionales*. Mexico: UNAM–ICI, 1985.

Barandiarán Pagador, Luis. "El pacto interno, evaluación posibilidades y limitaciones." In: *Autoafirmación colectiva: una estrategia alternativa de desarrollo, Lecturas* No. 49, selection by E. Oteiza, Mexico: Fondo de Cultura Económica, 1984, pp. 242–266.

Barros de Castro, Antonio. "Ajustement et adaptation structurelle: l'expérience Brésilienne." *Problèmes d'Amérique Latine*, no. 74 (France, 4th quarter 1984): 49–61.

Berzosa, Carlos et al. *La deuda externa*. Madrid: IEPALA Fundamentos.

Bianchi, Andrés et al. "El proceso de ajuste en la América Latina 1981–1986." *El Trimestre Económico* no. 216, 54(4) (Mexico, October–December 1987): 855–911.

Browne, William P., and Don F. Hadwiger. *World Food Policies. Toward Agricultural Interdependence.* Boulder, Colo., USA: Lynne Rienner Publishers, 1986.

Calcáneo A., Raúl, and Edmar L. Bacha. "El milagro y la crisis. Economía brasileña y latinoamericana." *Investigación Económica* no. 179, 46 (Mexico, UNAM, January–March 1987): 301–318.

Carraud, Michel. "L'Intégration Latino-américaine face à la crise." *Amérique Latine*, no. 22 (France, April–June 1985): 18–25.

Castillo, Mario, and Álvaro García. *Cambio estructural e industrialización: análisis de escenarios.* ILO, Regional Employment Programme for Latin America and the Caribbean (PREALC), December 1984.

Castro, Fidel. *La crisis económica y social del mundo. Sus repercusiones en los países subdesarrollados, sus perspectivas sombrías y la necesidad de luchar si queremos sobrevivir.* Report to the VII Summit of Non-Aligned Countries, Havana, Cuba: State Council Publications Department, 1983.

———. *Diálogo sostenido con los delegados a la Conferencia Sindical de los Trabajadores de América Latina y el Caribe sobre la deuda externa, durante la sesión de clausura del evento, el jueves 18 de julio de 1985.* Havana, Cuba: Editora Política, 1985a.

———. *Esta deuda no sólo es impagable, sino que ya, además, es una deuda incobrable.* Speech to the afternoon session, Sunday, 7 July 1985, IV Congress of the Federation of Latin American Journalists (FELAP). Havana, Cuba: Editora Política, 1985b.

———. *La impagable deuda externa de América Latina y del Tercer Mundo, cómo puede y debe ser cancelada y la urgente necesidad del Nuevo Orden Económico Internacional.* Interview granted to the newspaper *El Excélsior* of Mexico. Havana, Cuba: Editora Política, 1985c.

———. *No hay otra alternativa: la cancelación de la deuda o la muerte política de los procesos democráticos en América Latina.* Interview (the part dealing with economic problems) granted to Congressman Mervin Dymally and academic Jeffrey Elliot, both from the United States of America. Havana, Cuba: Editora Política, 29 March 1985d.

———. *Nuestra lucha es la de América Latina y el Tercer Mundo.* Interview granted to the newspaper *El Día*, 8 July 1985. Havana, Cuba: State Council Publications Department, 1985e.

Cataife, Daniel et al. *La fase actual del capitalismo.* Mexico: UNAM–UAM; Iztapalapa: Nuestro Tiempo, 1985.

Centro Tepoztlán-Rial. "Crisis y deuda en América Latina." *Boletín Centro de Estudios Monetarios Latinoamericanos*, 29(5) (Mexico, September–October 1983): 263–266.

Chaponay, Henryane de. "Face aux défis, quel développement pour l'Amérique Latine." *Amérique Latine*, no. 22 (France, April–June 1985): 26–34.

Cline, R. William. "Perspective on the External Debt Situation. International Debt: From Crisis to Recovery?" *American Economic Review* 75(2) (USA, May 1975): 185.

Comercio Exterior, 36(6) Mexico: Banco Nacional de Comercio Exterior S.N.C., June 1986.

Coplamar. *Macroeconomía de las necesidades esenciales en México, situación actual y perspectivas al año 2000*. Mexico: Siglo XXI, 1983.

Córdova, Armando. "Modo de articulación externa y nuevas estrategias de desarrollo en América Latina." Paper submitted to the Seminar on Strategies and Paradigms for Development, organized by the Centre of Development Studies, Caracas, Venezuela, 16–20 November 1981.

Couriel, Alberto. "Pobreza y subempleo en América Latina." *Revista de la CEPAL*, no. 24 (Chile, December 1984): 39–62.

Devlin, Robert. "Deuda externa y crisis en el ocaso de la gestión ortodoxa." *Revista de la CEPAL*, no. 27 (Chile, December 1985): 35–53.

Domínguez Villalobos, Lilia."Las políticas de estabilización: una evaluación crítica." *Investigación Económica*, no. 179, 46 (Mexico, UNAM, January–March 1987): 107–130.

Dornbusch, Rudiger. "El problema mundial de la deuda." *El Trimestre Económico*, no. 216, 54(4) (Mexico, October–December 1987): 805–825.

Economía de América Latina, no. 16 (Forum of Latin American Convergence), Mexico: CIDE, 1987.

Economic Commission for Latin America (ECLA). "La crisis mundial y América Latina." *Sociedad interamericana de planificación* 18(3) (Mexico, July–September 1983): 1–5.

———. *Políticas de ajuste y renegociación de la deuda externa en América Latina*. Chile: *Cuadernos de la CEPAL*, no. 48, 1984.

———. "La crisis en Centroamérica: orígenes, alcances y consecuencias." *Revista de la CEPAL*, no. 22 (Chile, April 1984): 53–80.

———. "La crisis en la América Latina: su evaluación y perspectivas." *El Trimestre Económico*, no. 204, 51(4) (Mexico, October–December 1984): 885–974.

———. "Pasado y presente de la crisis en América Latina: visión de la CEPAL." *Comercio Exterior* 35(7) (Mexico, July 1985): 672–687.

———. "Crisis y desarrollo en América Latina y el Caribe." *Revista de la CEPAL*, no. 26 (Chile, August 1985): 9–57.

———. *Revista de la CEPAL*, no. 32 (Chile, August 1987).

———. *Panorama económico de América Latina 1987. Argentina, Brasil, Colombia, Ecuador, México, Perú, Uruguay, Venezuela*. Santiago, Chile: United Nations, September 1987.

Edwards, Sebastian, and Simon Teitel. "Introduction to Growth, Reform and Adjustment: Latin America's Trade and Macro-economic Policies in the 1970s and 1980s." *Economic Development and Cultural Change* 34(3) (April 1986): 423–431.

Esser, Klaus. "La transformación del modelo de industrialización en América Latina." *Revista de la CEPAL*, no. 26 (Chile, August 1985): 103–115.

Estudios Económicos (special issue). Mexico: El Colegio de México, October 1987.

Faletto, Enzo, and Gonzalo Martner, eds. *Repensar el futuro. Estilos de desarrollo*. Caracas, Venezuela: Nueva Sociedad, UNITAR/PROFAL, 1986.

Felix, David. "How to Resolve Latin America's Debt Crisis." *Challenge* 28(5) (USA, November–December 1985): 44–51.

Ferrer, Aldo. "Dette, souveraineté et démocratie en Amérique Latine." *Problèmes d'Amérique Latine*, no. 74 (France, 4th quarter 1984): 7–21.

Ffrench-Davis, Ricardo. "Dette extérieure, ajustement et développement en Amérique Latine." *Revue Tiers Monde* 28 (France, January–March 1987): 79–94.

————. "Dette extérieure et options de développement en Amérique Latine." *Problèmes d'Amérique Latine*, no. 74 (France, 4th quarter 1984): 29–47.

Foxley, Alejandro. "Las políticas de estabilización neoliberales: lecciones de la experiencia." *El Trimestre Económico*, no. 199 (Mexico, July–September 1983): 1299–1319.

————, ed. *Distribución del ingreso*, Lecturas No. 7, Mexico: Fondo de Cultura Económica, 1974.

Frank, André Gunder. *La crisis mundial. Occidente, países del Este y Sur*. Spain: Bruguera, 1979.

Geller, Lucio. "Del ajuste recesivo al ajuste estructural." *Revista de la CEPAL* (Chile, December 1986): 37–53.

Gilhodes, Pierre. "Les composantes des crises en Amérique Centrale." *Problèmes d'Amérique Latine*, no. 76 (France, 2nd quarter 1985): 26–32.

González, Norberto. "Balance preliminar de la economía latinoamericana en 1985." *Comercio Exterior* 36(2) (Mexico, February 1986): 105–124.

————. "Reactivación y desarrollo: el gran compromiso de América Latina y el Caribe." *Comercio Exterior* 36(6) (Mexico, June 1986): 531–537.

González Casanova, Henrique. "Les classes et la crise." *Amérique Latine*, no. 22 (France, April–June 1985): 50–53.

González de la Rocha, Mercedes. *Los recursos de la pobreza. Familias de bajos ingresos de Guadalajara*. Mexico: El Colegio de Jalisco, CIESAS, SPP, 1986.

González Gómez, Andrés. *Economía política de la crisis. Las contradicciones de la acumulación en el Perú, 1950–1975*. Lima, Peru: Universidad Mayor de San Marcos, Faculty of Social Sciences, 1985.

González Rubí, Rafael. "Encrucijadas de la crisis en América Latina." *Comercio Exterior* 36(7) (Mexico, July 1986): 603–608.

Graciarena, Jorge. *Creación intelectual, estilos de desarrollo y futuro de la civilización industrial*. Japan: United Nations University, 1981.

Ground, Richard. "El sesgo recesivo de las políticas de ajuste del FMI." *El Trimestre Económico*, no. 213, 54(1) (Mexico, March 1987).

Guay, François le. "La crisis internacional y el desarrollo latinoamericano: objetivos e instrumentos." *Revista de la CEPAL*, no. 26 (Chile, August 1985): 129–139.

Guerguil, Martine. "La crisis financiera internacional: diagnóstico y prescripciones." *Revista de la CEPAL*, no. 24 (Chile, December 1984): 149–172.

Guth, Wilfried. "International Debt Crisis: The Next Phase." *The Banker*, no. 689, 133 (UK, July 1983): 25–30.

Gutiérrez R., Roberto. "La espiral del endeudamiento externo de México y sus problemas de renegociación en el contexto de la experiencia latinoamericana." *Investigación Económica*, no. 178, 45 (Mexico, UAM, October–December 1986): 167–203.

Hanson, James A. "Inflation and Imported Input Prices in Some Inflationary Latin American Economies." *Journal of Development Economics* 18 (2–3) (Netherlands, August 1985): 395–410.

Hillcoat, Guillermo. "L'Amérique Latine sous la tutelle du FMI." *Amérique Latine*, no. 13 (France, January–March 1983): 59–64.

Hirschman, Albert O. "La estrategia del desarrollo económico." *El Trimestre Económico*, no. 199 (Mexico, July–September 1983): 1331–1435.

————. "The Political Economy of Latin American Development: Seven Exercises in Retrospection." *Latin America Research Review* 22(3) (USA, 1987): 7–36.

————. "La economía política del desarrollo latinoamericano." *El Trimestre Económico*, no. 216, 54(4) (Mexico, October–December 1987): 769–804.

Hodara, Joseph. "La conducción latinoamericana: perspectivas socioeconómicas." *Comercio Exterior* 35(12) (Mexico, December 1985): 1123–1130.

Ibarra, David. "Crisis, ajuste y política económica en América Latina." *Revista de la CEPAL*, no. 26 (Chile, August 1985): 149–156.

Iguiñiz Echeverría, Javier. "Perú: crisis económica y democracia." *Investigación Económica*, no. 179, 46 (Mexico, UNAM, January–March 1987): 223–254.

Ikonicoff, Moisés. "Endettement et crise des modèles de développement dans le Tiers Monde." *Revue Tiers Monde*, no. 99, 25 (France, July–September 1984): 603–627.

————. "La industrialización del Tercer Mundo en la prueba de los grandes cambios." *El Trimestre Económico*, no. 213 (Mexico, January–March 1987): 3–32.

Institute of Social Studies. *Teoría y diseño de políticas para la satisfacción de las necesidades básicas.* Ecuador: Institute of Social Studies, Ministry of Cooperation for Development, Netherlands, 1987.

Investigación Económica, no. 168, 43. Mexico: UNAM, Faculty of Economics, July–September 1984.

Iturraspe, Francisco, ed. *Participación, cogestión y autogestión en América Latina,* vol. 1, San José, Costa Rica: Nueva Sociedad, 1986.

————, ed. *Participación, cogestión y autoguestión en América Latina,* vol. 2, San José, Costa Rica: Nueva Sociedad, 1986.

Jetin, Bruno. "La culture inflationniste: une présentation du débat sur l'inflation inertielle en Amérique Latine." *Revue Tiers Monde* 28 (France, January–March 1987): 139–156.

Klochkovski, Lev, and Igor Sheremetiev. "El imperialismo y la crisis económica en América Latina." *América Latina* 7(79) (USSR–Mexico, July 1984): 4.

Knox, A. David. "Reanudación del crecimiento en América." *Finanzas y desarrollo* 22(3) (USA, September 1985): 15–18.

Kuznetsov, Viacheslav. "Atenazados por la deuda externa." *América Latina* 10(82) (USSR–Mexico, December 1984): 21.

Latin American Export Bank [BLADEX]. "Ampliación y refuerzo de los mecanismos de cooperación financiera frente a la actual crisis internacional." *Boletín Centro de Estudios Monetarios Latinoamericanos* 29(6) (Mexico, November–December 1983): 283–285.

Laulan, Yves. "A New Approach to International Indebtedness." *The Banker*, no. 688, 133 (UK, June 1983): 25–38.

Leff, Nathaniel H., and Sato Kazuo. "Entrada de capital extranjero, ahorro interno e inversión en América Latina: una historia negativa y precautoria." *El Trimestre Económico*, no. 211, 53(3) (Mexico, July–September 1986): 561–584.

Lejavitzer, Moisés. "Obstáculos al comercio intralatinoamericano y esfuerzos tendientes a su reactivación." *Boletín Centro de Estudios Monetarios Latinoamericanos* 31(4) (Mexico, July–August 1985): 184–200.

Leriche, Cristian, and Enrique Quintana. "Los programas de ajuste latinoamericanos bajo la perspectiva de la transformación del capitalismo a nivel mundial."

Análisis económico 5(9) (UAM U. Azcapotzalco, Mexico, July–December 1986): 139–166.

Lichtensztejn, Samuel. "De las políticas de estabilización a las políticas de ajuste." *Economía de America Latina*, no. 11 (Mexico, CIDE–CET, 1984): 13–33.

Lobo, Félix. "Teoría política del desarrollo económico en el último cuarto del siglo XX. Nuevo Orden Económico Internacional y Estrategia de las Necesidades Básicas." *El Trimestre Económico*, no. 199 (Mexico, July–September 1983): 1507–1535.

Maldonado L., Guillermo. "América Latina y la integración: opciones frente a la crisis." *Revista de la CEPAL*, no. 27 (Chile, December 1985): 51–71.

Mamalakis, Markos. "Una estrategia de desarrollo relacionada con los servicios: algunas consideraciones básicas." *El Trimestre Económico*, no. 199 (Mexico, July–September 1983): 1537–1560.

Márquez Ayala, David. "Deuda externa: explosión o solución." *Investigación Económica*, no. 178, 45 (Mexico, UNAM, October–December 1986): 319–339.

Martner, Gonzalo. "L'Amérique Latine dans l'ordre économique mondial." *Amérique Latine*, no. 16 (France, October–December 1983): 45–56.

———. "La inserción de América Latina en la economía mundial. Una visión del futuro." *El Trimestre Económico*, no. 208, 52(1) (Mexico, October–December 1985): 1021–1048.

———, ed. *Diseños para el cambio. Modelos socioculturales*. Caracas, Venezuela: Nueva Sociedad, UNITAR/PROFAL, 1987.

———, ed. *El desafío latinoamericano*. Caracas, Venezuela: Nueva Sociedad, UNITAR/PROFAL, 1987.

Mendelson, M.S. "International Debt Crisis: The Practical Lessons of Restructuring." *The Banker*, no. 689, 133 (UK, July 1983): 33–38.

Merin, Boris, and Yulia Vizgunova. "La revolución científica y técnica y la situación del proletariado industrial en América Latina." *America Latina* 4(64) (USSR–Mexico, April 1984): 4.

Minian, Isaac, ed. *Transnacionalización y periferia semiindustrializada*, vol. II. Mexico: Libros del CEDE, 1984.

National Institute of Planning. *Distribución del Ingreso 1986*. Lima, Peru: Presidency of the Republic, 1987.

Nueva Sociedad ("Marginalidad del Sector Informal"), Caracas, Venezuela, July–August 1987.

Ocampo, José Antonio, and Santiago Montenegro. *Crisis mundial, producción e industrialización. Ensayos de historia económica colombiana*. Bogotá, Colombia: Fondo Editorial CEREC, 1984.

Ortiz, José Pedro. "El club latinoamericano de deudores: una reevaluación." *Boletín Centro de Estudios Monetarios Latinoamericanos* 31(1) (Mexico, January–February 1985): 38–54.

Pastor, Manuel, Jr. "The Effects of IMF Programmes in the Third World: Debate and Evidence from Latin America." *World Development* 15(2) (UK, 1987): 249–262.

Paz, Pedro. "Alternativas para el desarrollo de América Latina." Buenos Aires, mimeo, 11 November 1987.

Pazos, Felipe. " Qué modificaciones a su política económica deben hacer los países de América Latina?" *El Trimestre Económico*, no. 216, 54(4) (Mexico, October–December 1987): 827–853.

Pinto, Aníbal, "El modelo de desarrollo reciente de América Latina." In: *Desarrollo latinoamericano: ensayos y críticas, Lecturas* No. 6, selection by José Serra, Mexico: Fondo de Cultura Económica, 1974, pp. 29–49.

———. "Notas sobre estilos de desarrollo en América Latina." *Revista de la CEPAL* (Chile, 1st quarter 1976): 97–128.

Prebisch, Raúl. "La periferia latinoamericana en la crisis global del capitalismo." Lecture to the Experts Meeting on Crisis and Development in Latin America and the Caribbean, CEPAL, Santiago de Chile, Conference Room Document No. 19, 25 April 1985.

———. "La crisis del capitalismo y sus consecuencias sobre América Latina." *Investigación Económica*, no. 177, 45 (Mexico, UNAM, July–September 1986): 315–326.

Preeg, Ernest H., ed. *Hard Bargaining Ahead: U.S. Trade Policy and Developing Countries.* U.S.–Third World Policy Perspectives No. 4, New Brunswick, USA, and Oxford, UK: Transaction Books, 1985.

Rama, Germán W. "La juventud latinoamericana entre el desarrollo y la crisis." *Revista de la CEPAL*, no. 29 (Chile, August 1986): 17–39.

Rama, Germán W., and Enzo Faletto. "Sociedades dependientes y crisis en América Latina: los desafíos de la transformación político social." *Revista de la CEPAL*, no. 25 (Chile, April 1985): 127–145.

Rama, Martín. "Uruguay de la croissance à la crise." *Problèmes d'Amérique Latine*, no. 70 (France, 4th quarter 1983): 95–126.

Ramos, Joseph. "Políticas de estabilización y ajuste en el Cono Sur, 1974–1983." *Revista de la CEPAL*, no. 25 (Chile, April 1985): 85–108.

Regional Employment Programme for Latin America and the Caribbean [PREALC]. *El problema del empleo en América Latina: situación, perspectivas y políticas.* Santiago, Chile: ILO, 1976.

———. *Empleo y salarios.* Santiago, Chile: ILO, 1983.

Reiter, A.R.M. "La crisis de la deuda latinoamericana: causas, efectos y perspectivas." *Comercio Exterior* 37 (Mexico, January 1987): 18–26.

Reveiz, Edgar, ed. *Deuda externa latinoamericana y procesos de ajuste. Experiencias y perspectivas.* Bogotá, Colombia: Colección Debates, Universidad de los Andes, Faculty of Economics, CEDE, No. 5, 30 November 1985.

Rodríguez, José Luis. *La economía internacional. Problemas actuales.* Havana, Cuba: Editora Política, 1987.

Rosales, Osvaldo. *Elementos de una estrategia de desarrollo alternativo.* Doc. DE-52, Santiago, Chile: ILPES, 1983.

———. *Plan Baker, deuda externa latinoamericana y reordenamiento de la economía mundial.* Doc. E1-42, Santiago, Chile: ILPES, 1986.

Saint Gevurs, Ives. "La crise économique et ses effets," *Problèmes d'Amérique Latine*, no. 70 (France, 4th quarter 1984): 86–94.

Salama, Pierre. "Endettement et accentuation de la misère." *Revue Tiers Monde*, no. 99, 25 (France, July–September 1984): 491–507.

———. "Endettement et appauvrissement en Amérique Latine." *Amérique Latine*, no. 18 (France, April–June 1984): 63–69.

————. "Dollarisation et hétérodoxie en Amérique Latine." *Revue Tiers Monde* 28 (France, January–March 1987): 53–78.

Sampedro, José Luis. "Triple nivel, doble estrategia y otro desarrollo." *El Trimestre Económico*, no. 199 (Mexico, July–September 1983): 1655–1675.

Schaff, Adam. *Qué futuro nos aguarda? Las consecuencias sociales de la segunda revolución industrial.* Barcelona: Crítica, 1985.

Schatán, Jacobo. *América Latina, deuda externa y desarrollo. Un enfoque heterodoxo.* Mexico: El Día en Libros, May 1985.

Schvarzer, Jorge. "Deuda externa: un enfoque no ortodoxo desde la perspectiva del deudor." *El Bimestre Político y Económico*, no. 20 (Argentina, March–April 1985): 2–9.

Soto, Hernando de. *El otro sendero: La revolución informal.* Prologue by Mario Vargas Llosa, Diana, 1987.

Stoga, Alan. "The Crisis in Central America: Economic Problems, Prospects and Proposals." *A.E.I. Foreign Policy and Defense Review* 5(1) (USA, July 1984): 13–26.

Syrquin, Moshé. "Growth and Structural Change in Latin America since 1960: A Comparative Analysis." *Economic Development and Cultural Change* 34(3) (USA, April 1986): 433–454.

Tokman, E. Víctor. "Crisis, ajuste económico y costo social," *El Trimestre Económico*, no. 209 (Mexico, January–March 1986): 3–34.

Tomassini, Luciano. "El escenario internacional y la deuda externa de América Latina." *Revista de la CEPAL*, no. 24 (Chile, December 1984): 137–148.

Tseng, Wanda. Article in *Finanzas y Desarrollo* 21(4) (Washington, DC, USA, December 1984).

Ugarteche, Oscar. *El Estado deudor. Economía política de la deuda: Perú–Bolivia 1968–1984.* Lima: Análisis Económico Series no. 10, Institute of Peruvian Studies, IEP Ediciones, 1986.

UNCTAD. "Las tendencias de la economía mundial. Una apreciación general." *Comercio Exterior* 35(12) (Mexico, December 1985): 1131–1140.

United Nations. *La industria en el decenio de 1980: cambios estructurales e interdependencia.* Austria, special biennial issue of the Industrial Development Study, November 1985.

Vaitsos, Constantine V. *Integración Regional Cum/Versus integración guiada por las empresas transnacionales. Autoafirmación colectiva: una estrategia alternativa del desarrollo*, Lecturas No. 49, selection by E. Ortega, Mexico: Fondo de Cultura Económica, 1984, pp. 175–241.

Valle, Alfredo del. "Diseño del futuro: conceptos y medidas," *Revista Teología y Vida* 22 (Peru, Catholic University of Peru, 1982).

White, Eduardo. "Las inversiones extranjeras y la crisis económica en América Latina." *Comercio Exterior* 36(10) (Mexico, October 1986): 855–865.

Wiarda, Howard J. "Central America and the Caribbean: International Dimensions of the Crisis." *A.E.I. Foreign Policy and Defense Review* 4(5–6) (USA, March 1984): 24–37.

————. "The Future of Latin America: Any Cause for Optimism?" *A.E.I. Foreign Policy and Defense Review* 5(3) (USA, April 1985): 28–43.

————. "Misreading Latin America Again." *Foreign Policy* (USA, Winter 1986–1987): 135–153.

Wiesner, Eduardo. "Causas internas y externas de la crisis de la deuda latinoamericana." *Finanzas y Desarrollo* 22(1) (Washington, USA, March 1985): 24–26.

———. "Latin America Debt: Lessons and Pending Issues." *American Economic Review* 75(2) (USA, May 1985): 191.

Wionczek, Miguel S. "Un vistazo a los problemas y perspectivas de la economía." *Comercio Exterior* 36(11) (Mexico, November 1986): 999–1004.

Wood, Robert E. "The Debt Crisis and North–South Relations." *Third World Quarterly* 6(3) (UK, July 1984): 703–716.

Zedillo Ponce de León, Ernesto. "Una síntesis racional de las propuestas heterodoxas sobre el problema de la deuda externa." *El Trimestre Económico*, no. 208, 52(4) (Mexico, October–December 1985): 1165.

2

The state and politics in Latin America

Pablo González Casanova

I. Introduction

1. The national state's crisis

In Latin America[1] the crisis has altered the relations of dependency: a series of state and government policies have been assumed directly by the International Monetary Fund, by the World Bank, and by other agencies of the empire with the agreement of local dominant classes.

In the "letters of intent" and other agreements, Latin American governments have handed several areas of decision-making pertaining to the state over to the International Monetary Fund and to the United States. The transfer of decision-making theory, of decision-making processes, and of the legitimacy and validity of these processes implies the transfer of an important part of power in terms of finances, currency, public and private property, markets, fiscal and tax policies, investment and spending, technology of production, consumption, modernization, "reconversion" and "structural changes"; all of these are redefined by the International Monetary Fund and other imperial agencies, and redefined and adjusted only according to the actual circumstances of each country and each government.

The transfer of governmental and state decisions affects educational, health, and social security policies for the vast majority of the population, particularly when accompanied by public spending cuts. It affects workers' and employees' direct and indirect real wages through devaluation, inflation, and unemployment. It affects policies of support for small and medium-sized enterprises that are not linked to monopoly capital and transnational companies, subsidies, and extensions. It also affects policies of support for middle-class and poor peasants, intensifying their contradictions and weaknesses.

The new policies of financial dependency and transference of the power of the state to the International Monetary Fund (and similar organizations) have increased and linked not only phenomena of dependency but also those of inequality, underdevelopment, and authoritarianism, the latter mostly in relation to labour relations and small producers. To this effect, the market laws of goods and services have been allowed to fluctuate freely, while wages were controlled, and whatever increases were allowed were always kept at a lower level than that of prices. The result has been an increase in workers' exploitation and a decline in workers' share of the territorial product's income.

The new policies, with their growing interference from the International Monetary Fund and other agencies, have stressed the already existing contradictions and disequilibria. They have led the developmental model towards an increased contradiction between the necessity of an industrial development that does not remain "truncated" and the lack of a capital goods industry, between patterns of high consumption and marginalization. They have laid the foundations for permanently devalued and inflationary development, unstable in its balance of payments, with transference and constant drainage of capital, in which international markets close themselves to non-integrated Latin American products, while previously protected national markets remain open. The process of autonomous industrialization is increasingly structurally blocked to substitute imports, and, at the same time, the development of the production of goods for popular consumption is increasingly slowed down. All this occurs with the support and agreement of Latin American states and governments that nevertheless insist on representing sovereign nation-states and on being the organs of their people's will.

Phenomena such as the "deterioration in exchange relations," which were criticized and attacked by these governments, are now being accentuated in the policies adopted by the same governments in order to keep their bargain with the empire. Policies such as control or restriction of foreign investments are now openly criticized – even if they were useful at one time – and are being replaced by growing exemptions and incentives. At the same time, Latin American governments have made the payment of the external debt the core of official and state economic policy. For them, the art of governing consists in keeping their word with the creditors, in making their people accept the creditors' policies, and in presenting the creditors' arguments as their own. This is how, amidst protests and renegotiations, Latin American governments have given the utmost importance to the fulfilment of the norms set by the creditors, beginning with the punctual payment of the debt-tribute. At the same time, they have imposed multiple measures that tend to consolidate a process of "associated transnationalization" in which "national" autonomous plans of development are being abandoned – because they are old and inefficient – in exchange for "maquiladora" policies and assembly workshops linked to the economy of the great metropolitan industrial centres. In this process, the exporting and financial bourgeoisie predominates, be it the local or foreign one, but always the one least interested in the development of an internal market, the one most opposed to legal, educational, and social institutions of the sort that tend to recognize and increase workers' and citizens' rights, skilled work and the highly specialized contributions of university professors and students, as well as politicians.

The process of associated transnationalization implies a radical change in the concept of development and structural reforms. Modernization is conceived of as a transnationalization of the state and society. Implicitly or explicitly, the state abandons the projects of national independence and of economic and social development it entertained during the previous phase. It passes from having conceived of the nation as the base and the objective of the "sovereign" state to yielding to dependent transnationalization as a practice of the "modernizing" and "efficient" state. It goes from having considered "dual society" as a problem, to considering it as a project. Structural reforms, which earlier were understood as the profound transformation of social, economic, and technological relations for its national and sovereign development, and for a politics of justice and social integration, were no longer championed by progressive groups and acquired with the neo-liberals an openly denationalizing and antipopular connotation, hidden in criticism of its rustic nationalism and its authoritarian and corrupt populism. Arguments to this effect are very sophisticated, since they do not abandon the notions of "nationalism" or "democracy," although it is now a nationalism that disarticulates and destroys the structures of the national economy, which are limited and reduced to a part of the *necessary* dual society. The notions of development as growth and redistribution are not abandoned either, but always on the assumption of a social dualism in which, of necessity, one part remains at the margin of development. What is interesting is that the excluded part is glorified as if its existence were the ideal of what is most modern and as if its "reality" were a necessity that must be accepted only in the face of the failure of modern egalitarian myths. The proposal of the "wonderful informal" is the proposal of a dual society and of apartheid as a project of universal organization.

2. The lack of awareness of the national state's crisis

The crisis is one of unexpected scope for the life of the national state, of the political system, and of civil society. Both in facts and in ideologies, it tends to nail the lid on the coffin of the national project that emerged during the nineteenth century and affects its reformulation in the twentieth, a reformulation that attempted to complement the move towards political independence with that towards economic independence, and the move towards electoral participation with that towards economic and social participation. The end of the national state and of the social state turn into the demands and practices of associated transnationalization which, added to the "slimming down" of the nation-state, the privatization of enterprises, the denationalization of basic industries, and the sale of lands and natural resources to pay the debt, put an end to the historical project of politically and socially independent nations, and to economically and socially balanced development. The lack of awareness with respect to this change of historical project is very notable not only among the Latin American bourgeoisie associated with the project, but also among the old nationalist, progressive, social democrat, and democratic forces.

Political organizations and social movements do not in general realize the magnitude of the change in the state, in policies, and in civil society. It is not a lack of understanding of conjunctural and transitory problems but a lack of understanding of a structural problem that corresponds to the historical period that world capitalism is entering. Having defeated nationalist, populist, and revolutionary movements in the 1960s and early 1970s, in the very place where it defeated them, the state, dominated by united blocs of associated bourgeois, tends to establish dependency and "dual society" as a transnational and interregional global structure, and for this purpose uses all the logic of repression, domination, and exploitation in an attempt to "maximize" functions and programmes. To achieve its

57

ends, it uses a three-pronged strategy in which the natural tendencies of the system are accelerated: maximization of utilities, elimination of competition, and control of the actors that rebel against or oppose the process of impoverishment and submission, be they governments, people, nations, or salaried workers.

Transnationalization and the transnational state are not still in the making. These are part of a process in which each crisis or popular alternative dominated by the system would tend to increase dependency, exploitation, and inequality among nations and especially among workers.

There are aggravating circumstances that render high proportions of the world population necessarily useless, marginalized, and condemned to live in extreme poverty in self-destructive situations and situations of collective destruction. This does not eliminate the population in question completely, but serves to control its most negative effects on neighbourhoods, villages, ethnic groups, or entire nations.

Faced with this serious phenomenon, a political and social organized will seems often to be unable to oppose the process and prevent it from going further than the superficial, the spontaneous, and the isolated. Nations – as people – do not react as political and social units with a defensive direction and articulation. At the beginning, they show forms of resistance–adaptation that can be controlled by the state, which is not an unusual phenomenon, since the same sort of behaviour – conformist and passive – had already been exhibited in the early phases of previous crises.

Meanwhile, "adjustment policies" are presented by governments as "scientific" and "technological" policies, meant to eliminate the old prejudices, ideologies, and even "follies" demonstrated by "backward" forces, "ignorant" of reality, "limited" in their knowledge, or contrary to "ethics" and "freedom."

Governments associated with this project of transnationalization present their policies as if they were compatible with sovereignty, development, social justice, and democracy. They are not usually accused of being "traitors" or "puppets of the empire," less still of being simple agents of the bourgeoisie, as was the custom when the old nationalist or revolutionary language was in use. Yet they nevertheless try to present themselves as the heirs of the "fathers of the homeland" and as legitimate "builders" of increasingly sovereign, free, and just nations. Lying becomes their natural way of communicating and thinking. To think is to lie. At the same time, united with the "mass media" and the "centres of excellence," they give encouragement to famous intellectuals of the empire with technocratic argumentation that inhibits alternative thinking and becomes enthusiastic in the face of the new historical step towards actualized colonialism. The phenomena of enrichment, concentration, and transnationalization of capital remain "hidden."

"Policies of adjustment" – applied with this name since 1982 – are today the hallmark of Latin American governments and states. With these policies, none of the objectives the governing class pretend to aim for can be achieved – not the economic, political, or social ones, as has been amply proved by the experience of all the countries involved, starting in 1964, the year in which the first military and financial dictatorship was initiated in Brazil.

In all Latin American and third world countries, the same policies with different names have brought about the same results. The most likely tendency – and the margin of error in this area is almost zero – is that these policies will continue, and that the problems they generate in the state, and with the state, and within civil society will continue to increase too, all of it under the auspices of indebted governments and the IMF, with the support of transnational enterprises and of native large monopoly groups. Yet there is no clear and unified realization of all this, let alone an organized acknowledgement. The only responses that emerge are criticisms, commentaries, and shows of strength, which cannot influence events or alter the process, at least in the immediate future. In any case, doubts, anxiety, and aggression grow and accumulate, while deeper down a nationalist anti-imperialism becomes reformulated as an enormous popular force, with unforeseeable consequences.

Since the economic policies of indebted governments do not really seek to control inflation or to eliminate a deficit in current accounts, or seek sovereignty, or national development, or social justice, or democracy, or government by the people, the political discourse of those who govern is subjected to great logical violence, a violence that tends to hide the techniques of propaganda and alienation of the masses, although this is achieved with growing difficulties. What nevertheless helps them a great deal, and what brings about a sort of generalized confusion, is that the indebted governments and their monetarist demagogy are being criticized by the managerial élite and by the intellectuals of imperialism, who accuse them of not applying sufficient "energy" to their monetarist, neo-liberal, modernizing, efficiency-minded policies, and even their transnationalization poli-

59

cies. They conceal this last observation as they also conceal the fact that a policy of greater "adjustments" in public spending and of new "shocks" in prices, devaluations, and wages would inevitably increase the inequality in income distribution and add to the people's suffering. When the facts become impossible to ignore, however, another strategy consists in affirming that, however "painful" the measures might be, they are *necessary* and there are no other alternatives.

Lying has become the discourse of economic dictatorship, which does not accept any restraint on the process of transnationalization. Neo-liberal rhetoric is the art of persuasion through the use of lies made sacred with "technique" and documented with cinematographic arbitrariness and science fiction. As the deterioration of such a discourse is very likely, its substitute is ready: it consists in reactivating the notions of "national security," "counter-insurgency," and bio-sociology, in its many versions, together with monopoly force, informal economy, and state terrorism. In the meantime, one talks about "restructuring," "modernization," "reactivation," and "democracy" with all the vagueness and imprecision necessary to sell utopian ideas without futures. These utopias, like the intellectual fashions that encourage them, turn out to be false shortly after they appear. The frustrations they give rise to provoke a general climate of discouragement and ingenuousness in the short term, while they provoke long-term reactions of violence and rancour as yet unknown to us – at least from an empirical point of view.

II. Transnationalization

1. Transnationalization of society and the state

The "reactivation" of Latin America and the "restructuring" of the economy, of society, and of the state are seen in the practical and operative terms of an economy of investments of transnational enterprises. The "reactivation" of the economy is *seriously* attempted only at the level of transnational enterprises, or of segments of the associated productive system, not at the level of the nations or nation-states. The nation-state's projects are not *serious*. This *lack of seriousness* is part of transnational domination; it is the ideology of vanquished bourgeoisies. Its phenomenology demands a detailed analysis.

Transnational enterprise in Latin America is more powerful than the nation-state it infiltrates, and with which it associates. If some sectors and areas do develop, they do so predominantly as functions of transnational enterprises. Evidence of this fact is increasingly common.

National governments – in the face of private enterprises – take very secondary decisions when they apply economic policies in their territories and states. Their decisions never succeed in altering the general tendencies of the policies of transnational enterprises' investments. They never succeed in implementing a "national" policy of investment. "Industrial redeployment" and the "new credit flows" take place within a transnational dimension, within a process of world accumulation.

The nation as sovereignty, as majority, is more and more profoundly affected. What is sovereign is not national, nor does it belong to the majority. Transnationalization organizes itself according to its own finalities of accumulation. The "exporter–concentrator" pattern is one of an increasingly dependent and unfair society.

Governments are increasingly weak and, when their leaders look for an alternative policy, they find it difficult to establish a people–government–state association that allows them to challenge contradictions and destabilizations. What is national is not sovereign.

In civil society, the *majority* of the workforce is still unemployed, surviving below minimum standards of living, and experiencing permanent and widespread physical, political, and social insecurity, in terms of nutrition, housing, health, and education. Its capacity to influence or alter these facts is non-existent. The majority is not sovereign, nor is it participatory, nor is it influential. There does not exist any evidence to the contrary.

Some governments offer some resistance, which is promptly integrated within the process of transnationalization and privatization. This occurred with the nationalization of the bank in Mexico in 1982. Some withdraw under domestic and international pressures, as was the case with Argentina's attempt not to pay its external debt at the beginning of Alfonsin's government. Others offer a show of resistance that increasingly reduces their objectives and aspirations, and if they rebel again, as was the case with Peru, their attempts to impose some limits on the shameful submission fail to be clearly articulated in a single front: in the conjuncture, it is not possible to establish a single front for the nation or for the majority.

It is true that it is not possible to ignore the contradictions of the dominant classes and blocs. The functionality of the system lacks dialectics. What is transnational is not just a system, it is a process.

61

Contradictions are more than just a group of broken-down elements. If the empire owns a series of destabilizing and interventionist techniques that it applies in order to impose its economic and hegemonic dictatorship of inefficient allies, of the indolent and rebellious ones, the imperial struggle against the "deviants" among the bourgeoisies and of civil as well as military governments reveals a certain resistance. At a time when Latin American governments and states have lost their economic and financial autonomy and sovereignty to an unprecedented degree, some actions of a political or diplomatic nature acquire a relatively unforeseen autonomy. Occasionally, they are also expressed in the economic area, mostly at the level of opinions.

"Inefficiency," protests, and even outright rebellion by civil and military governing classes are increasingly significant: "inefficiency" in imposing a neocolonial order to fulfil "roll-back" policies (a return to the neocolonialism of the 1950s), the protest and rebellion of subdued governments in some particularly sensitive area for the empire, as when they reject interventionist policies by the United States toward Central America (against Nicaragua), or declare – even intermittently – a moratorium, or threaten – even inconsequently – to suspend the colonial tribute formalized into an external debt, or oppose yet greater cutbacks in social spending or the growing handing over of public enterprises that should become private or denationalized, or when they prevent the Organization of American States (OAS) from becoming an organ of the State Department.

To be aware of and to use these contradictions, however inconsistent they may be, as well as to pay attention to the public and social reforms that magnify the scope for struggle, is part of the most important strategy of strengthening democratic and revolutionary organizations.

2. The neo-liberal offensive and social mediation restructuring

Meanwhile, neo-liberalism, neoclassical economic theory, and monetarism are being used to diminish the "governing" role of the state of dependent nations and its interference in the solution of *national* economic, social, cultural, and technological *problems*, however partial and precarious the state might be in social democrat and popular governments.

Neo-liberalism and the *restructuring or reconversion* of the economy or technology and of society tend to alienate the state's institutions still further from the measures that could be instrumental in resolving social problems, at least for a sector of the *majority*, of a segment of the population. The state loses its capacity to resolve the "national" and "popular" problems of the nation and of the people it claims to represent. But this does not mean that change alone would be sufficient for the class and repressive role of the state to disappear.

The process of restructuring not only tends to increase "extreme poverty," but also does not prepare the state to face it through repression. Rather, it attempts to strengthen the state in the social and political negotiation of a society that is also in the process of being restructured. Civil society is the object of a profound and both natural and induced process of restructuring, through the expansion of the informal sector of the economy, legal and illegal.

In fact, the government of the United States, particularly since the last world war, has adopted measures to counter-attack at the continental level any national or popular reaction against the *expected* consequences of its expansionist policies. Since 1959 it has reinforced and supplemented these measures with a vision and an organization that is not only expansionist in nature but also counter-revolutionary. For this purpose, it has counted on the dominant classes of Latin American countries, especially the groups associated with monopoly capital and transnational enterprises, and on those who depend on them.

To this end, the empire and the dominant classes have at their disposal a rich array of historical and cultural equipment assembled from experiences, structures, and institutions adequate to the task of transnationalization. This cultural equipment includes military, political, and paramilitary (special services) forces; and social movements, from the traditional ones (natives, peasants, workers, university employees) to the most recent ones made up of urban settlers, women, ecologists, religious groups, and various types of minorities. It was not in vain that associated transnationalization and the formation of inter-American institutions began as early as 1948.

The restructuring of the dominant system is nevertheless not limited to traditional forms of repression and negotiation, nor does it correspond only to the institutional or customary style of carrying on politics. It applies microeconomic models of control, which include the restructuring of civil society.

The so-called "informal economy" is the new form that civil society has assumed around the marginalized and the extremely exploited. It is a form that seeks the substitution of a social solution by a private

63

and domestic solution to the social problems at hand. Its importance is evident if one considers that it substitutes political, syndical, and agrarian mediation and the "social security" of the welfare state (however precarious this may be) by the mediations of a market in which the poor are the businessmen.

The informal economy is in the first place an alternative to the overdevelopment, populism, and social democracy that prevailed after the world war until the mid 1970s. It is the mediation sought for by adjustment policies, by policies of lower public spending and of privatization of health, education, and housing services. Secondly, and not less importantly, it is the substitution of unemployed salaried workers by self-employed workers, when full employment is abandoned as a desirable objective (or as an ideology) of economic policy. It is, in the final analysis, a policy of fragmenting the working class.

The market of the poor of the "informal sector" reorients toward "the private solution" a great number of people who would otherwise tend to present a common front. If the middle classes become a poor, small, bourgeoisie, the workers become self-employed.

The mediation of salaried workers is substituted by commercial mediation: marginal businessmen no longer have a government from whom they can demand services; self-employed workers no longer have a boss whom they can confront. For many, the relationship of exploitation disappears, and, for many, political or parapolitical repression becomes unnecessary. The glorifications of the "informal society" in the style of Vargas Llosa are a rationalization of the project of control of the marginalized by way of their transformation into bourgeois, but bourgeois who remain marginalized.

It is true that the dialectics of the "informal sector" can contain some surprises. The immediate and expected effect, however, reformulates the social bases of transnationalization and of a class domination that reduces social spending and redistributes the national product in an increasingly unequal way.

The dialectics of the informal consist also in large groups of individuals, families, communities, and neighbourhoods ceasing to depend on the state, becoming self-sufficient, succeeding in freeing themselves from the marginalized mercantile ideology, from the ideology of underemployment, and eventually constituting autonomous forces, a popular and national alternative. Grass-roots organizations and communities proliferate in the informal world, where some of the most important ideological battles take place. If there is an informal economy, there are also informal politics and an informal struggle for power. The dialectics of the informal open new perspectives. Although these perspectives can be closed, or the system can attempt to close them, informal politics today coincide with break-ups of a historical type, which tend to become larger and to multiply. If their effects seem to reveal an initial conservative phase, they also contain another democratic and revolutionary phase.

3. Transnationalization as denationalization and privatization

Not all these facts are completely new, either at the level of the state or at the level of the society. They correspond to a process that reached its peak during the 1980s, but that has been applied actively since the 1970s, particularly after Kennedy's failed conservative reform known as "Alliance for Progress," the destabilizing policies intended to bring down populist and social democrat governments, and the counter-revolutionary dispositions of "internal warfare." Transnationalization is the culmination of neocolonial counter-revolutionary history, which today attempts to establish an associated and dependent state, eliminating social democrat and populist policies and their negotiations with and concessions to significant sectors of the middle classes, the working classes, and the peasants.

The history of imperialist interventions in Latin America, as well as of military coups, corresponds to a reduction of the nation-state to its dependent character, to its class character, and to its repressive character. But in many cases this history of interventions has been forced to recognize a national and popular power, or a state of well-being, of assistance, of social security that, even today, neocolonialist and neoconservative policies try to eliminate. The latter attack the national character of the state, the national intervention of the state in the economy, and its educational and social intervention. The interventionist process of transnationalization culminates in the denationalization and privatization of goods and services acquired or kept by the state within the project of national reconstruction, of import substitution, of the creation and development of domestic markets, of the assignment of resources used as social investments and expenditures, and of the expansion of collective and individual rights during the populist and social democrat phases of the history of the twentieth century, when the masses imposed these policies.

In transnationalization, privatization, as well as the increase in exploitation and repression, function directly against the nation, the working people, and the citizens. Nevertheless, these three social entities do not confront the problems together. The state associated with the transnational project fights against a society in which the majority of the nation has been discriminated against, stratified, and de-articulated, and finds itself structurally incapable of acting as a united social category. The colonial ethnic factor divides the nation into multiple nations. Social mobilization and stratification divide the working class and the rest of the working people into many levels in which individuals move and have the hope of moving from the poorest strata towards others that offer improved wages and better lifestyles, or from the lowest strata to the middle classes. All this occurs within a spectrum that ranges from subhuman marginalization to a minimal participation in the workers' benefits and goods of survival, which allows them to go through all the forms of overexploitation of labour that have been suffered throughout all the classical regimes: slavery, feudalism, salaried work, up to the groups or nuclei of strategically chosen and well-paid workers.

It is in this manner that, if the state associated to the transnational project becomes openly dependent, oligarchic, classicist, as a defence it maintains and revives the de-articulation of nations into separate subnations and provinces. It also splits the working class into different strata and ethnic groups. It increases linguistic, religious, and ideological divisions. Dominant classes and hegemonic powers utilize whatever differences they find to intensify small communities' rivalries among peasants, tribalism among ethnic groups, confrontations between Catholic and Protestant settlers, factionalism and sectarianism in the ranks of labour unions and popular organizations.

In the past, small and medium manipulations provoked a de-articulation in the very ethnic groups of the conquered and dominated nations and classes. Today, to this de-articulation, which was primarily linked to the history of racism, and later to that of the guild-like privileges of corporatism or to the sectarianism of populism, and later still to the uneven growth process or to the social, cultural, and political mobility and mobilization of the "participants" in development, with considerable increments of the middle sectors and classes, has recently been added the transformation of the "reserve army," which is too large for the present type of accumulation, into a *poor* bourgeoisie. To this phenomenon one must add the process of bourgeoisification of nuclei of highly qualified workers, all this in order to disintegrate as far as possible the dangerous alternative category of the working class, its "centrality."

With the crisis, another structural policy has become stressed, a policy that weakens the working class and seeks to undermine its more advanced and dangerous nuclei. To achieve this, the policy takes advantage of the "competition" crisis in certain industries and of the job-cutting political–economic restructuring. Responding to the "competition" crisis, mines and industries were closed down and a great number of organized workers were fired or laid off. Meanwhile, work was being given to small informal enterprises, or to women or young people who were not organized through a union and who were not likely ever to become organized. They were employed in "maquiladoras," or the formerly unionized workers were employed on a daily basis as temporary or migrant workers.

The state associated to the transnational project, to the oligarchical and class project, not only benefits from the de-articulation of the nation and of the underclasses, it also benefits from the myths of its own power and of deceptive ideologies. What is more, to its restricting power and to the use of violence at decisive moments, it always adds its internal bureaucratic, military, and civil discipline, which aside from coordinating and unifying myths, beliefs, and illusions, coordinates the acts of the state's apparatus. To the restricting power, the state adds the power of institutional discipline, with all the logic of moral awareness and bureaucracies' actions and with all its power of diffusion and internalization by the majorities-masses or the majorities-villagers, either individualized or tribalized.

The illusions of presidents and technocrats, their questionable faith in monetarism with social justice, in national independence, and in modernization, make them use the accumulated logic of frustrated illusions: that of the "Alliance for Progress" of the 1960s for example, or that of "Point IV" of "technical assistance" and "development" with foreign investment of the 1950s, and even that of the founding ideologies of the nineteenth century on "Civilization and Progress," which have their antecedents in the most remote of the enlightened despots of the eighteenth century, or in the deceitfully evangelical ideologies of the first conquerors. The new illusions of the transnational conquest are handled with the desperate rhetoric of those who know that they cannot offer the sky and that on earth they sell false illusions.

The state's transnationalization of its civil and military bureaucracies responds to an institutional project imposed since the creation in 1948 of inter-American civil, social, educative, syndical, and military institutions. The difference in the 1980s is that it finished off the national state and the welfare state hammered into shape through national and social struggles that took off in the irruption of the Latin American masses in the nineteenth century. Transnationalization as denationalization and privatization brings the state back in its "fundamental relation of capitalist domination," stateless and classist, "as institutional complex, centre of political decisions and public administration with numerous economic and social functions,"[2] which favours the bourgeoisie associated with the transnational project.

But this form of expression of the state, this violent demystification of itself, is not just concealed – or tries to hide – in the mediations of the "informal society" and in the limited restructuring of some "heterodox" social policies. It is also found in the attempt to seek the representation of general interests in political systems and in politics, the privileged field of the hegemonic struggle that wants to substitute bread by votes.

In the new project, the historical memory of the dominant classes counts significantly. But the history of the masses and their partial victories counts too, victories snatched away by neo-liberalism, monetarism, and the process of transnationalization.

4. The historic legacy of the state and political mediations

Today's state is the heir of a series of experiences. Among these experiences, one stands out – called the "collective memory" by Halbwachs. It is heir to the traditional oligarchical state, that of landowners and ranchers, planters and overseas businessmen who knew how to use the sword and whip, tone of voice and humiliation, the use of silence and cunning. They came from the oligarchical liberal state, which initiated a capitalist order linked to the world market and imposed private property on the face of communities of villages. This oligarchical state eliminated the barriers to foreign goods, merchandise, and investments. It indebted governments and repaid with wars and territories and it gave guarantees and concessions to key ports, mining enclaves, and plantations.

Today's state remembers the pressures that finished off this other state, the migrations from the countryside to the cities, the growth and thrust of the urban working class (in Buenos Aires, São Paulo, Mexico). It remembers the anarchist and labour struggles, or the outbursts and pressures of the emergent middle class, growing modest but ambitious, bribable and winnable, or the forcefulness of the business bourgeoisie's leadership, linked to incipient industrialization and that demanded help, subsidies, and protection, or the inroads of the uniformed or well-dressed forces of the military and administrative bureaucracy, with their colonel–politicians, their functionaries, their employees, their mediators and available "representatives."

Today's state retains all these challenges to the oligarchical traditional and liberal power that came from alliances and renovations of the same state, until a relatively contradictory project emerged: that of a "welfare state," of a "promoter state." This "new state" developed a strong public sector, which took over the management of infrastructure and became the promoter of the "private sector." As a "populist state," it reformulated alliances and integrated parts of the masses into the political system by playing its "assistance" and "distributing" cards. Later, when the working class was already disciplined, when it was thought that the state had distributed enough, when the arbitration between the rich and the poor who had been integrated, between businessmen and trade unionists, led to their reconciliation to the detriment of the workers, emphasis was put on a "developmentalist" state, on "growing before distributing," on the "utilization of the apparatus and resources for the growth of the productive forces . . . for the take-off on a self-sustaining process."[3]

The dominant classes, the "political class," remember how the "national security state" and the "neo-liberal state" emerged from all these states, with their latest twists of militarism and liberal democracy, and with the same or similar monetarist policies. With all their memories, with all their experience, the dominant classes tried to justify or hide the oligarchical and class character, the predominantly repressive character of the "national security state" through various ideological means, from the conception of an imaginary international or internal war of good "authoritarianism" against "totalitarianism," or "Christianity" against "materialism," or "order" against "subversion," and even of a delayed, proposed trusteeship "democracy" against irresponsible political parties, useless parliaments, seditious freedom of the press and of opinion, demagogic universities, all the way to a vision of a society eaten away by corruption, demanding an energetic cure and a strong government representing real morality and general interests as only the armed forces can represent them, as long as they place themselves at the service of the dominant classes.

The difficulties of hiding repression in governments where state terrorism prevails do not imply that it is forbidden to speak about facts that everybody must know and fear, or that it is an obstacle to continue to hide dependency and transnationalization of national power and economy; even less does it mean hiding the oligarchical

69

character of the domination and exploitation of the people. The issue of "general interest" is expressed in the desire for a return to constitutional government, to electoral political systems, and to civil liberties towards the same dominant class. It is this objective that prevails again today, and it has a long history.

In the last stage of democratic reconversion, the "national security" regimes have begun to give way to civilian governments, a phenomenon that had been foreseen by the Brazilian military long before they were defeated both in the streets and at the ballot box in 1984–1985, a phenomenon that has asserted itself since General Hugo Banzer was obliged to step down in Bolivia in 1979, bringing about a series of coups and counter-coups. This process culminated in Paz Estenssoro's transnationalizing democratic experiment. The tendency of "national security" regimes to give way to civilian government was seen also when Galtieri's government was defeated in the Falklands, and even more in Buenos Aires, where his successor had to call for general elections.[4] The phenomenon became still more emphasized when the Reagan administration transformed the struggle for democracy into its new mediating policy of revolutionary, populist, and social democratic movements.

Of all the forms of concealing the dependency and transnationalization oligarchy and the class character of Latin American states, the myth and the reality of liberal democracy are without doubt the most powerful *in the entire* history of Latin America. Latin American capitalism, which has sustained itself in the accord of the interests and forces of the foreign and national dominant classes, from the primary export economy through the "developmentalist" phase all the way to that of transnationalizing "modernization,"[5] has systematically resorted to democratic, liberal, and oligarchic political mediations in order to hide its narrow class interests and the ties with bourgeois and foreign groups. In the face of the populist or social-democratic state, it now uses simultaneously or successively the "repressive state" and the "welfare state," or the "sinecure state," which channels social demands and discontent to the political field, where the general interest and the rules of the state itself are most emphatically expressed.

The process of transnationalization initiated in the 1960s has placed the state in a repressive and class situation that makes it very vulnerable. The economic crisis of the 1970s and 1980s has increased this weakness. For this reason, the government in Washington and the dominant classes in the United States and Latin America have considered it necessary to revive lost measures and to return to the world of constitutional, legal, democratic, and liberal forms. Regimes of terror introduced since 1964 and even sometimes as early as 1954 – as was the case in Brazil, Guatemala, and many others – have returned to a system that had seemed abandoned: the creation and re-creation of formal life and institutional mediation. This comeback is not taking place in a historical vacuum. In fact, Latin America has one of the richest histories in the formal sector of society, as well as in political economy. This history is not only that of its contradictions but also that of its limitations, which become actualized today and acquire new characteristics.

III. The real power

1. Politics and real power

In Latin America, the dominant classes of the new nations tried to establish laws and constitutions in accordance with their ideas and their discourses on the "sovereign people," "human rights," the election of "representatives," "democratic change of governments," and "balance of powers." On the other hand, they tried to maintain the structures of repressive colonial capitalism and intensified their policies of concession and consensus, although only in very reduced – but significant – ways.

In the field of ideological conceptualization and struggle, Aristotle's notions of how to defend against anarchism and despotism, which inclined toward limited democracy, helped them to develop modern readings of the issue, from Locke to Benjamin Constant. The dominant classes established highly formal democratic systems that placed the sovereign rights of the people, parliaments, judges, parties, and elections under the domination of the new oligarchies.

With the implementation of "representative forms of government," a violent struggle between a conservative alignment of forces and the liberal alignment or bloc began. The first bloc *represented* the landowners, the church, and the army. The second bloc *represented* some members of the same classes, particularly those linked to the world market, and many members of the middle sectors – professionals, employees, "farmers" – who were looking for various types of alliances, some with the more advanced centres of world capitalism, and others with peasant and artisan movements, the former to improve their credit and business situation, the latter to increase their negotiating power or their participation in power with their civil and political rights and those of the people of that time.

"Conservatives" and "liberals" seldom succeeded in imposing the hegemony of the blocs or coalitions they formed, at least until monopoly capital and metropolitan states initiated a new policy that complemented bank loans with direct or indirect investments in industry or primary activities such as mining, petroleum, and plantations.

The "conservatives" sought international support until around 1880, in order to develop their states without the need for drastic transformations in their "fiefs" and customs. Meanwhile, the "liberals" tried to gain access to the international market, and to expand the domestic market by eliminating protectionist policies and sales taxes, and by privatizing public, religious, and communal lands.

If the "conservatives" represented the traditional power of landowners and their contradictions, the majority of the "liberals" represented an equally contradictory movement. This latter expressed the interests of commercial capital, of the middle classes, and of mobilized people. But while the "conservatives" attempted to keep on exercising power, with religious and traditional symbols already in crisis, they were often obliged to add to these symbols the new imperative of democratic forms. The liberals began to fulfil an oligarchic role with the new symbols of "liberalism," "democracy," and "progress" in societies where they achieved hegemony only when they combined their political programme with an association dependent upon the great powers and nascent monopoly capital.

If the "liberals" tended to predominate over the "conservatives," it was because of the support they obtained from hegemonic countries and powers, a contradictory support that led them to the unavoidable duty of *representing* liberalism and democracy as their real project at the same time as they restrained popular demands and established new kinds of agreements for an unequal trade.

Ever since independence, the struggle between conservatives and liberals has meant much more than a simple party or electoral struggle. These struggles implied internal and external warfare, open or covert. When war and violence could be controlled, they gave way to authoritarian regimes whose real power rested on a new type of monopolistic and dependent development, with which the old and the new lords of the land, the large estate owners, the cattle raisers, the mine owners, the industrial plant owners, and the businessmen, associated themselves. Many of them were also high-ranking military men and politicians who served in the highest posts of the repressive and representative systems.

Both constellations of forces exercised real power, with all the economic and military measures at their disposal, while fighting the traditional ideological domination – whether lay or religious – with the modern form of domination: the ideal of a liberal and representative democracy. Liberal democracy was always interpreted by the dominant classes as part of the struggle for power and was regulated as a function of the power they defended or attempted to increase.

2. Popular demands and democratic structures

In the nineteenth century, representative political systems occupied a minimal place in each "real country," but, in addition, they often misrepresented the "formal country" they claimed to represent. Political rights were generally reserved for the male, literate population, middle aged and with guaranteed incomes, employed and in possession of landed properties. Practical politics was the preoccupation and the task of a very small fraction of "formal citizens." Nevertheless, even while oligarchic, paternalistic, bureaucratic, or military politics was formally legalized, the demand of *representing democracy* trained (with a double meaning of the ideal and the cheating) a growing section of the middle class, especially the civil and military public servants and liberal professionals, in their roles as mediators, intermediaries, and heads of sections and factions of the poor with social movements.

The people often rioted and demonstrated, but to little effect and never politically. Although some riots were directed by the lower classes and their organizations, the latter never led political campaigns.

Towards the end of the nineteenth century and the beginning of the twentieth century the emergence of the working class brought about a significant change that coincided with the introduction of a negotiated capitalism in combination with political traditions of repression, concessions, and the new social negotiations. The workers organized themselves under the banner of the anarchists, of revolutionary and parliamentary socialists, and of the populist Labour Party. The oligarchies were obliged to make concessions to parliaments in one case and to populists in another.

In the more advanced Latin American countries, oligarchic and restricted political systems tended to disappear in the first half of the twentieth century: the most important characteristic of the new political systems was the introduction of universal suffrage and a politics of the masses. Both measures gave rise to new imperatives for democratic structures. The change occurred mostly in those countries where the strength of the organized workers' movement was considerable, and where the surplus was sufficiently high to allow concessionary distributions.

On the other hand, in poorer and underdeveloped countries, political systems for the masses were seldom established. In these countries, traditional and new workers could be controlled under repressive regimes, while modern enterprises and agro-industrial enclaves could be run with indebted and servile labour. Countries such as Haiti, Nicaragua, Paraguay, and many more in the Caribbean and Central America did not substantially modify their political systems, if they modified them at all. In these relatively less developed countries, the threat posed by the middle classes and the working sectors to the oligarchic predominance was dealt with by suppressing nascent formal democracy and establishing personal or family dictatorships. They were corrupt, pro-oligarchic, extremely conservative, pro-United States, and highly dependent upon the military and political support of the United States. They were the dictatorships of Maximiliano Hernández Martínez in El Salvador (1931–1944), that of Jorge Ubico in Guatemala (1931–1944), the Somoza dynasty in Nicaragua (1934–1979), the Trujillos in the Dominican Republic (1930–1960), the Duvaliers in Haiti (1957–1985), the dictatorship of Stroessner in Paraguay (1954–1989), and that of Tiburcio Carías Andino in Honduras (1933–1949). In these countries, politics was the practice of violence, and the most significant changes occurred as underground activities that ended in persecution by the police, or even military confrontations. When one of these countries succeeded in achieving a certain ideological and political development, it usually occurred in connection with radical and revolutionary movements. In other words, to oppose was to rebel.

In the twentieth century, new political systems varied greatly in their official and real evolution. Their differences expressed in part the requirements of accumulation in each neocolonial state and in each province of the greater and richer states. They were also determined by political and military struggles, and by the way in which alliances and hegemonic blocs took shape with their arsenals of repression, negotiation, and concession. Within relatively similar class and dependent structures, the leaders and factions that succeeded in controlling the state were particularly influential in the implementation of the political systems. Party politics achieved important victories in Uruguay (1903), Argentina (1916), Costa Rica (1948), Venezuela (1958), and even Colombia (1957). In some of these countries, such as Chile and Uruguay, the communist and socialist parties evolved towards a political system within which they attained a significance similar to the one they reached in some European countries. Populist and nationalist movements and factions became hegemonic in Mexico (1934), Brazil (1930), Argentina (1943), and Bolivia (1952). They were also relatively strong in Peru, Venezuela, Costa Rica, Panama, Puerto Rico, and Cuba.

As some of the political systems began increasingly to resemble European political systems, the structures and the reality lost their more obvious incongruities. This happened in Chile and in Uruguay for long periods and over large areas. The enormous weight of the repressive–oligarchic bourgeoisie seemed to go into hiding. Its dependent and neocolonial condition went into hiding too. It was a time during which very sophisticated and well-documented political illusions appeared. Their apogee occurred after the war and lasted for several decades. They corresponded to the time of effective mediation. While the authoritarian and despotic imposition of the structures as dogmas and beliefs was an exercise in dominant highhandedness by modern tyrannies, in countries where democracy, pluralism, and liberalism succeeded in organizing the political conduct of the citizens and the governing classes, and where the citizens lived the experience of representative governments, political systems seemed to bring together the structure and the reality, the legal constitution and the political one.

The growth of the "formal country," and the expansion and continuity of the "legal country," succeeded in hiding the enormous differences between these countries where, in most regions for long periods of time, it was possible to organize hegemonic power in which negotiation, consensus, and concessions had more solid, extended, and stable bases. In countries such as Uruguay, Chile, and Costa Rica, democratic utopias began to seem the most positive and realistic way, and they succeeded in forming part of the experience and the culture of the majority of the citizens. Politics managed to hide the language of oligarchic, neocolonial power and its capacity for extreme violence.

The change was significant to the extent that it transformed into real categories the liberal, democratic, and social democratic values, and to the extent that it transformed them into political objectives of civilian society, in political philosophies internalized and disseminated by civilian society, despite the very extensive psychological impediments that prevented thinking about their limitations. Freedom, democracy, and tolerance became strategic values to large sectors of the population, and, if people believed in these values without thinking about the need to change the structures of peripheral capital, it later turned out to be impossible to think about an anticolonialist and anticapitalist struggle without thinking about a democratic and a plural struggle.

The advantage of the masses' growing awareness of democratic structures consisted in changing the masses' project into a democratic project. Its weakness consisted in not linking political struggle for democracy with the requirements of a struggle for power.

3. Popular demands and populism

The process of the diffusion of democratic structures and their conversion into the political objectives of the masses was somewhat different in countries where populist and nationalist regimes predominated. In these countries, the new leaders "expropriated" from the oligarchies their authoritarian rhetoric and their traditionally paternalist and repressive logic in order to invest them with popular symbols and strengthen them with concrete measures in terms of social negotiations.

In populist governments, contradictions between form and reality became part of a new rhetoric and of a new logic of power. A certain consensus around the issue of the necessity to violate the forms in order to attain political and social objectives became an essential element in the culture of the leaders and of the masses. The ambiguous discourse of the populist oligarchy altered some of their refined and élitist symbols and adopted popular ones, while they maintained the option of sometimes using the formal language and at other times the "realistic" language of political and social pressures, aiming to obtain concessions and personal or group power, factional power, the power of the union, corporation or sector. Regarding the authoritarian or populist chief or chiefs, their gangs or their followers, their supporters and partisans learned to handle the contradictions of form and reality, in order to conquer and exercise power, or for the exercise of pressure and the logic of negotiation and concession. Loyalty to the "caudillo" or the populist leaders mediatized the loyalty to the people and to the people's organizations.

In those regimes, the leaders and the organizations of the masses used the rhetoric and the new reasoning to fight against the oligarchies and against the great powers. They also used them to betray the masses. "Populist" became a sort of rudimentary expression of negotiated capitalism, negotiation used in a two-pronged type of struggle, contributing to the control of the oligarchies and the control of the masses.

As occurs in the majority of countries dominated by populist regimes, the traditional oligarchy did not lose its main sources of wealth and power, and, as transnational capital continued to increase its strength, the leaders' institutional or personal rhetoric became increasingly incongruous, not to mention their visible conduct. Whereas the exotic or tropical elements of the contradictions between Western structures and local conditions of party politics and elections consisted in the appearance of the unreal European or North American within markedly different conditions, the exotic or tropical elements of the populist contradictions appeared in a nationalist and popular discourse that corresponded to an increasingly transnational and oligarchic politics. The oligarchic politics, increasingly bourgeois and transnationalized, precipitated the crisis of populist democracy and that of nationalist populism.

With the rise of populism a significant change in the handling of forms occurred. The change took place at the same time as populist leaders discovered the logic of national and popular power, and when the masses discovered the logic of pressure as threat and the basis of their own power. If, in the countries where the practice of representative democracy was more developed, there was a loss of conscience in relation to the logic of power, and in these countries democratic institutions tended to become isolated in a merely political arena, in populist countries, on the other hand, the logic of power was overshadowed by the logic of pressure and personal and authoritarian alienation. The forms, as darkening of the real, led in some places to a fight for a powerless democracy and in others to the belief that the people's struggle was reduced to following a "popular" leader or regime. In any case, both movements, the institutional and democratic and the populist and personal, involved a favourable change and a different contribution to the evolution of Latin American political systems: one taught to equalize reality and forms, and the other to see within forms the power of the nation and of the people, or that of its oligarchic and transnational adversaries.

4. The return to democratic structures

The democratic advances that occurred at the beginning of the twentieth century brought about a notable change in systems of domination. The governing class's political conduct had to change, at least in its formal aspects. And when they were not reduced to a ritual of brutal authority, they implied certain concessions. Whatever life formal democracy had, even the most minimal, obliged the oligarchic bourgeoisies to abandon some of their rights, in particular to name openly and willingly the leaders and top office-holders of the state – the governors, the legislators, the judges. In addition, it obliged them to discuss governmental, economic, and cultural policies with real or sham representatives of the organized population and of the legally "recognized" citizens.

On the other hand, some leaders emerged who embezzled the power of the state or bolstered themselves with the help of popular movements – for example, Vargas in Brazil in the 1930s, Velasco Ibarra Junior in Ecuador, Batista in his first period in power in Cuba. These oligarchic–popular leaders were somewhat different from the traditional despots or from the purely oligarchic dictators. Even the most authoritarian sought the active support of their clienteles and even the formal support of a significant part of the population. To achieve this, they were obliged to negotiate with their organizations and leaders, and, even though negotiation implied reproduction and amplification of authoritarianism, this emerged after the recognition of new popular forces. In any case, even if the populist "caudillos" kept behaving in authoritarian and paternalistic ways, they also had to behave as arbiters of social movements and as negotiators of social problems. With them a new style of governing emerged, a style of consensus in which a "popular" non-democratic element was added to the traditional authoritarian systems. And this, with the introduction of social negotiations with whoever felt most "humiliated" and were recognized by their own chiefs or "caudillos", gave rise to an authoritarianism of a popular type, in which traditional political science saw only the authoritarian part, ignoring the popular part. The real aim of these leaders was to feel themselves to be the arbiters of the people and the oligarchy. The fact that they did not surpass this limit necessarily converted them into populist leaders and into actors who unknowingly set the stage for neocolonialism and trans-national penetration.

Neofascist and military governments, which since the 1960s had destroyed democratic–institutional or populist regimes, imple-mented a policy of universal repression, with minimal concessions and without negotiations with representatives of democratic or popu-list groups. Social concessions virtually disappeared for the majority of the population. Negotiations with popular organizations were re-placed by functional negotiations with leaders "nominated" by the police forces, controlled as representatives and controlled in their demands and also in those of the people they represented. This was the case in the military governments in Brazil (1964–1985), Argen-tina (1966–1973 and 1976–1983), Bolivia (1971–1978), and Chile (1973 to date).

The difference between these neofascist regimes and the tradition-al dictatorships is that they govern citizens *deprived* of the rights and concessions previously won by them, and whose experience could not be completely erased, nor would permit a return to traditional forms of government. The neofascist dictators – of the transnational fascist or military regimes – have been obliged to break the imperative of modern society's forms, assuming the supposed role of tutors in a "tutelary democracy," which does not alter reality in any way and in which no one believes anyway. The transnational system's dictators have seen themselves obliged to use a mixture of technocratic rheto-ric and power rhetoric based on the doctrine of "national security" and imposed through crude symbols of terror. At the same time, they have found themselves faced with the necessity of reducing the gen-eral values of "democracy" to the point of negating them as expres-sions of the categories of freedom, sovereignty of the people, social justice, and election of the governing class. Thus they attempted to make their contradictions between reality and forms less obvious by finishing off the forms. In fact, they never pretended to be demo-cratic, nationalist, or populist; they were the tutors of democracy, nation, and people. And they did not even have to resort to the ideol-ogy of traditional tyranny, dressed up with religious symbols, but rather called on a neoconservative, modernizing, transnational ideology of tyranny, which they defended through universal repres-sion and state terrorism. The very priests and bishops who opposed them became victims of this terrorism, as did even the most modern and conciliatory democratic forces, including those that had at one point encouraged Washington to prevent a return to democracy as an attempt to change the interrelationship of forces and increase popular power.

The violence of transnational dictators against priests, citizens, and real peoples has become a violence directed against the religious, lay, democratic, popular, and national structures that altered this reality. It corresponds to a phase of transnationalizaton that is complemented by the return to a governable democracy, trying to impose itself not only through the terror of the dictatorships, but also through a rich history of mass participation in populist or social democratic governments. Today, while returning to democratic structures without corporatism and without social democracy, with much more limited concessions to unions, class sectors, and social movements, one wonders which is going to be more important for the new citizens: the political–ideological experience of the masses in terms of a social and popular politics, or the experience of repression and terror. The history of political systems and of the systems of repression is very significant for them. They are also significant in those countries where they have met age-old obstacles, and where today attempts at openings towards democracy or democratic transition are happening, with growing – massive – participation of citizens who are today considerably more literate, urbanized, and educated.

5. Evolution of political systems and emergent democracy

Considering Latin American political systems retrospectively, one can identify eleven principal types:
  (1) Limited oligarchic democracies, which prevailed in the nineteenth century, with small governing groups organized under a system of personal relations.
  (2) Sham democracies and elections under regimes of neocolonial occupation, which began in the nineteenth century, such as the regime of William Walker in Nicaragua, and which continued in the twentieth century with the presence of the Marines, with electoral fictions such as those of Haiti in 1915, 1922, 1926, and 1930, or that of the Dominican Republic in 1922 and 1926, and the most recent one of Joaquín Balaguer in 1966.
  (3) Democratic systems that combined different forms of traditional oligarchic power with other more bourgeois and institutional forms, such as Argentina in the days of Mitre and Sarmiento, and Chile in the days of Portales.
  (4) Democratic systems that initiated various social democratic poli-

cies with the participation of the middle classes and of organized workers, such as in the Uruguay of Battle and Ordoñez.

(5) Latin American populist systems, which represent various political and social coalitions of organized industrial workers, peasants, the middle classes, and local bourgeoisies under the leadership of "caudillos" and heads of state who advocate a nationalist and social politics while fulfilling the role of mediators and arbiters in group and class conflicts and establishing an integrated system of leaders, gangs, associations, clienteles, and corporative politics, through which they organize the participation of the workers' movement, and that of the peasants and the urban masses. This is the case of Cárdenas in Mexico (1934–1940), Perón in Argentina (1944–1955), and Vargas in Brazil during his second term (1950–1954).

(6) Simulated democratic systems, strictly ritualistic and theatrical, helping military dictatorships (traditional or reformed) to pretend that they are governing according to democratic principles.

(7) Anti-political systems of the post-populist and post-democratic dictators who used "technological knowledge" and "national security" arguments to establish authoritarian regimes based on state terrorism of an experimental basis. These dictators were known as "fascists" or "neofascists" to the extent that they put an end to the earlier democratic or institutional conquests of their people, under the hegemony of transnational capital and that of the associated oligarchic and business forces. Not all authors agree that these dictators should be seen as "fascists" because they are unable to identify the type of mass politics that characterized European fascism: they lack millenarian myths and the minimum surplus to help them. In any event, they seem to be the equivalent of a "fascism of dependence" and correspond to a "military state," which is an important auxiliary to the process of transnationalization. To their contempt and persecution of politicians, they add destruction, persecution, or harassment of party, syndical, and popular organizations. Pinochet in Chile and Videla in Argentina are archetypes of the genre.

(8) In some cases, faced with national and international, popular and even managerial pressures, or due to instructions from the very centre of transnational power, neofascist regimes return to systems of simulated and limitated democracy. The new limited and controlled political systems are more technocratic and military than the traditional ones; the "democratic" struggle is

accepted and is organized as part of internal strife and with techniques of military control, not only in its martial functions but also in the apparently civil ones. This is the case of the elections organized in the early and mid-1980s by the governments of Honduras, El Salvador, and Guatemala. It is a question of technocratic and military systems of sham democracy.

(9) In other cases, when popular and national pressures cannot be controlled by state terrorism, political systems of democratic restoration emerge, through which the government or part of it is left in the hands of civilians, with variations in terms of the amount of political guidance from the military yet without any change in the military hegemony or in that of monopoly and transnational capital. This is the case of Uruguay, Argentina, and Brazil.

(10) There exists, in addition, the political system with a broad base of popular participation, in which the link of the people to the government and to the state is as significant as the election and popular control of *representatives*. This occurs in Cuba with a single party that organizes itself and organizes the state according to a method known as "democratic centralism." This combines the election of leading members of the party and the state – to the National Assembly, to provincial and municipal assemblies – with elections in production centres, in work centres, and in neighbourhoods and localities, the former in the form of syndicates, enterprises, and offices, and the latter in various local organizations. The political system of dismissible representatives operates within a social system in which monopoly capital loses all ability to interfere, and the power of the high bourgeoisie, both managerial and financial, disappears completely. The bulk of accumulation has social and national purposes.

(11) In terms of political systems, the most recent experience emerges from Nicaragua. With a link between the people and the government and even between the people and the equally strong state, and with a significant role for the electoral process, there exists in Nicaragua a system of political and party pluralism. In this country, the political system operates within a mixed economy in which monopoly capital has ceased to be hegemonic. The party struggle takes place under the leadership of a broad popular movement led by the Sandinista National Liberation Front (FSLN), which took power over the state by armed

force. To the electoral struggle for the nomination of representatives to the Presidency and Congress are added internal struggles for the election of representatives in the Front, in production and work centres, and in villages and neighbourhoods.

Both the Cuban and Nicaraguan regimes are part of a Latin American revolution in facts and forms. They correspond to a "revolutionary democracy" that varies in its institutional party struggle, in its political pluralism, and in the political weight reached by the working class within the working community as a whole that hegemonized power. They raise the problem of a political system completely dependent upon the power of the state, and both of them being fundamentally attentive to the necessity of preventing in the first place a hegemonic and interventionist infiltration by the great powers, be it through coups d'état or internal wars, or by foreign intervention. Threatened and hemmed in, they begin to emphasize the need to prevent internal divisions and differences from being used by transnational capital and its associates, or by hegemonic power, its agents, and its mercenaries, so that in any case the internal–international war would be waged against counter-revolutionary forces and with maximum support from the working people, whose participation and link with the government and the state are indispensable to achieve the triumph and the continuity of the rupture of neocolonial and transnational state and society.

The people-state is confronting the economic, ideological, and military might, which, with unbelievable and unyielding aggression, has shown a gruesome inability to negotiate under new terms of postcolonial equality in any economic, political, or social arena whatsoever. In this respect, the principal feature of the new states is a philosophical politics in relation to negotiation that presents some particularly original features, mostly in terms of politics and power. This philosophy consists in negotiating in all areas except those that might weaken the moral, political, diplomatic, social, and military foundations of popular and national power. In fact, behind the new philosophy of negotiation, there lies the preoccupation with not rebuilding neocolonialism or the bases of a new state of minorities. Because of this preoccupation, governments that emerge from victorious armed revolution have to confront the neocolonial blockade and, in the process, are impelled to radicalize their objectives in relation to the social structure and the very social system, all this in order to maintain or increase the popular power they have won through revolutionary warfare. In this sense, the Cuban and Nicaraguan political regimes initiate new types of social and political revolution that profoundly restructure the bases and the institutions of the state. The democratic structures they introduce and the way in which they change the rules of politics and government are closely linked to the political and social transition in which, from an armed popular power, various levels of decolonization and mixed economy are achieved, with a growing role attributed to the working people, not only in the national arena but also in the international one.

The transition to democracy in Latin America was achieved at the time of the Central American revolution and when Cuba accomplished its undeniable success in the economic and social areas, in development, employment, education, health, and housing. Transition to democracy has been achieved after a long history of previous political systems, and with the learned experiences of recent or current political systems – some experiences were of state terrorism, torture, and disappearances, and others were of democratic, popular, and national outlets. The middle classes, in particular students and leaders of the masses, cannot do less than pay attention to the limitations of neoconservative democracy as it struggles against the positive aspects of populism, social democracy, revolutionary democracy, and socialism. In their majority, they do not aspire to a return to the past and tend to predominate over those who criticize them. They don't want to create either another Cuba, or a new Nicaragua.[6] "Nicaraguans say that it is not a question of making another Cuba, but another Nicaragua," Eduardo Galeano noted in a conversation about Che Guevara with Commander Tomás Borge. In Argentina, they want to make another Argentina, in Mexico, another Mexico, and the same in Uruguay or in the Dominican Republic, in Paraguay or in Haiti, another Latin America and another democracy that would be at once formal and popular, national and Latin American. The state – decadent or emergent – faces in this sense a problem that did not exist before: Latin American popular movements want democracy with power. At the very least, this is their tendency.

IV. The struggle for power

1. The struggle for power and the struggle for democracy

Violent changes and legal changes
In the various political systems, power that hides and lies behind its forms appears readily. Power as a reality reveals to the observer certain patterns of physical and symbolic force that are exercised against

representative political systems and against democratic institutions and values. Three phenomena help understand the limits of purely electoral representation and of democracy seen at a purely political level. The first phenomenon has to do with the relation between legal changes of government and violent changes, the second phenomenon concerns electoral processes and the relative freedom of political parties, and the third phenomenon concerns the crisis of political systems when the question arises of changing the social system or its structures.

During the period between 1801 (when Haiti de facto realized its independence from France) and 1975, executive power was taken over 1,763 times in various Latin American countries; 79.1 per cent of these changes were legal, that is, they stayed within legal requirements, while only 19.8 per cent occurred through the use of violence.[7] The proportion remains constant when different subperiods are compared, so that there does not seem to exist a tendency towards improvement in relation to the legal alternative of governing figures or parties. Between 1945 and 1963, however, there is an exception: access to power through violence occurred in 28 per cent of the cases; in all other periods, the proportion is very similar: 1801–1830, 18.8 per cent; 1831–1880, 18.8 per cent; 1881–1944, 18.7 per cent; 1964–1977, 20.2 per cent; 1978–1984, 19.8 per cent.

What is notable is that violent changes of government occur less frequently than legal changes. This is a constant tendency, which poses the question: why does the use of force and violence explain only one-fifth of all accessions to executive power? One possible answer is that dictators stay in power for longer periods than do elected presidents and that on occasion they stay in power not only during their own lifetimes – which tend to be long – but also during the lifetimes of their families. Doctor Francia governed Paraguay for 29 years (from 1811 to 1840); his successors Carlos Antonio and Francisco Solano López governed for 26 years (from 1844 until 1870); Porfirio Díaz governed Mexico for 34 years (1876–1910); Juan Vicente Gómez controlled Venezuela from 1908 until 1935; the Trujillo brothers did the same in the Dominican Republic from 1930 until 1961; the Somoza dynasty controlled Nicaragua from 1934 to 1979; the Duvaliers, father and son, ran Haiti from 1957 until 1985; Alfredo Stroessner governed Paraguay for more then 30 years (from 1954 to 1989). These and many other dictators maintain themselves in power. Once they have reached it, they become re-elected "legally" in such a way that, for each illegal change, there are many legal elections, which in fact are sham re-elections or simple acts of *civic validation*.

The phenomenon, nevertheless, is even more complex. Force and violence frequently contribute to perpetuating a single coalition or class, and not just the same person. Once a military or political group representing a coalition of forces or the hegemony of a class has obtained power through violence, it continues to organize legal elections and succeeds in establishing the equivalent of impersonal, collective, or constitutional power, which can be more or less authoritarian or plural, and which at times can even be liberal and popular. This means that the takeover of the state apparatus is directly linked with force, while the change of government can be achieved according to the legal requirements established by the very same groups, coalitions, or classes that have previously demonstrated their domination of the state or of part of the state apparatus through force.

Once the state has been taken or has been restructured, one legislates on institutions and political systems. Power becomes legitimized and arenas for political struggle are constituted or constructed, making the rules of the game *within* the state. In this way, the very state, party, or group of parties, and the very political system – with restricted or broad elections, by electoral colleges or citizens, indirect or direct – succeed at the same time in continuing and renewing themselves. To give some examples from the period 1930–1975: in Brazil, after the 1964 coup, four elections were held; in Colombia, after the coup of 1957, there were six elections; in Costa Rica, after the "1948 revolution," there were seven elections; in Chile, from the political crisis of 1932 until 1970, eight elections were held; in Mexico, after the assassination of ex-President Álvaro Obregón and the political crisis that led in 1929 to the foundation of the state party, ten elections were held. Observing the general tendency, it can be concluded that the most important effect of state power through force, and often violence, is the principle of continuity and renovation of diverse electoral systems.

The difference between power and politics is clear, as is the difference between a real takeover of power and an electoral triumph within an already established system of power. This difference is so significant that political struggle should never be identified with struggles for power. On the contrary, a clear demarcation between political force in the parties, in parliament, or in the executive and the correlation of forces in relation to state power should be established. When one pays attention to the power of the state it becomes necessary to ponder the strength or weakness of the military, as well as economic and social forces, the role played by public, social, and private enterprises, and that of financial and consumption markets, of means of production organizations and mass communication, and of their links with corporations, the military, and civic groups.

The need to clarify the difference between politics and power is even greater when popular forces contemplate social and economic changes once they have achieved power over the government, either by way of elections or through political struggle. The supremacy of a party or an alliance of parties among the citizens can be sufficiently strong to win elections and under certain circumstances, which are not very common, it can lead to governmental control, as was the case with Chile's Popular Unity. This, however, is never sufficient to govern the state. Any party that wins an election without also obtaining state power will immediately have to face the problem of power. If it rules in tandem with the state, that is to say, if it acts as a state party, or the role of the state is assigned to political parties, the party will face problems that are completely different from the ones that assailed it when it challenged the state itself and the interests of hegemonic classes and coalitions. Political parties can be strong or · weak in the political arena but in the arena of state hegemony they would be tolerated only under previously established restrictions, and under those of the hegemonic classes, unless they succeeded in imposing a new hegemony, a phenomenon that is always outside the rules of electoral change in any political system.

What cannot be chosen
Political systems' limitations are yet more impressive when one considers the legal or illegal situation of the political formations that propose structural changes or changes in the social systems. These formations or political parties are often not eligible. The phenomenon is particularly clear in the case of the communist parties. Their history in the political system is an indicator of the limitations both of the political systems and of the parties. These limitations are seen in their precarious legal position and in the various ways in which governments in Latin America – as opposed to those of Western Europe and even the United States – forbid this type of party under different argumentation, sometimes by legal or institutional procedures, but much more often by arbitrary decision.

As is well known, the sovereign state defines the political and ideological forms to be considered illegal, and can also define the real struggle as illegal. The struggles' limitations are legally defined through decrees or laws that proclaim that certain struggles, such as that between socialism and capitalism, are forbidden. The social reality that lies behind them is officially declared to be subject to legal sanctions. Negotiated and repressive capitalism of dependent countries uses the legal force of the state to recognize or legalize a few struggles and to forbid the majority of the others. As the repressive character of the state and of society increases, illegitimacy and legal or arbitrary persecution of social struggles as political struggles multiply.

The legal or illegal status of Latin American communist parties is a universal and relatively comparable indicator of the formal limitations on elections and political struggles. In the majority of countries, most of the time, one of the real struggles of contemporary history, the struggle between socialism and capitalism, is openly forbidden. The legal option of this struggle is being closed by the state. The problem becomes more significant when alternative structures and alternative social politics, within the same social system, are also forbidden, or when social democratic, socialist, and populist parties that propose moderate or partial changes are rendered illegal.

The risk of alternative parties' illegality affects all regions and threatens to affect all parties. But the communist party is an indicator of this fact. Not only it is more affected by the threat of illegality, but the problem is older and more universal. If we sum up the years between the founding of the respective communist parties and 1980, in 20 Latin American countries we see that communist parties were either illegal or semi-illegal for most of the time. In fact, even in states such as Uruguay where full rights were granted to communist parties for long periods, communists were outlawed and persecuted as soon as the political and social crisis became more acute. In other countries, for long periods communist party activities were declared illegal, as in Chile from 1927 to 1931, from 1949 to 1957, and from 1973 until today. In other countries, such as Mexico, Peru, and even Costa Rica, communist parties have been kept in a semi-legal condition, that is, they have been subjected to various formal and real restrictions on their political activities. And, obviously, there are countries where communists have almost always been considered illegal, such as Paraguay since 1928 (the year of its foundation), El Salvador since 1925 (the year of its foundation), and Nicaragua from 1937 (the year of its foundation) until 1979. But the strongest trend seems to be towards a constantly varying status – periods of legal activity followed by periods of illegality, and vice versa. This is the case in Argentina, where the Communist Party was legal from 1918 to 1929, from 1945 to 1961, from 1963 to 1965, from 1973 to 1975, and from 1983, or in Colombia where it was formally legal from 1930 to 1943 and from 1958 until today.

All these changes from legal status to illegal, their different histories and geography, reveal a general pattern that affects both the political–legal arena and political–legal time because of the possibilities of control it affords the state over opposition social movements, classes, or groups. When state power is threatened and, what is more, when hegemonic classes feel really threatened, they use a combination of various measures: in one case, they see the individual or the "political class" of the opposition as co-optable, in another they consider their elimination through legal sanctions, and in yet others, which are overtly illegal, they use state terrorism, which can be selective, individual, and even collective.

The political system's limits appear to be closely linked to the limits of negotiated capital. The universal phenomenon of negotiation–repression shows a general inclination towards repressive measures in Latin America and in other countries of the third world. In this sense, the history of social reforms through political struggle turns out to be a more limited project than in the metropolitan countries.

The legal limitations of political systems are greater still in normal times. The use of fraud and swindle, bogus ballots, and lack of participation in the electoral process constitute only some signs of a very feeble pluralist struggle. The limited and fragile legality is universally eliminated when the social system itself feels threatened by political parties and movements.

What cannot be changed

Obviously, there are some countries and regions and some stages in political development in which the citizenry succeeds in being an important force in the state. In these cases, the state cannot control the citizenry unless it makes *real* concessions, sometimes for the benefit of the better-organized sectors of the middle classes, of the industrial workers, or even of the better-organized peasants. But even these real democratic concessions, and their forms of expansion, are abruptly and violently destroyed when they become a threat to the hegemonic bloc and its forms of capital accumulation. The overthrow of democratic and popular governments, of social democratic and populist ones, led by civil or military leaders, has a very rich history of men who tried to alter some of the system's structures, relying on the law or on weapons, and who, seeing themselves in serious contradiction with the peoples, or finding their position weakened through internal struggles, were subjected to the whole weight of a power that indicated the limitations of the change according to their interests or their phobias.

In 1909, José Santos Zelaya, leader of a liberal revolution, was overthrown by a conservative movement sponsored by the United States. In 1911, General Eloy Alfaro, President of Ecuador – liberal reformist – was overthrown by a military coup. In 1914, Guillermo Billinghurst, President of Peru, heading a popular government, was overthrown by a coup d'état. In 1924, the Chilean president, Arturo Alesandri, who at the time held a liberal position, was overthrown by the army and the oligarchy. In 1931, El Salvador's president, Arturo Araujo, who had initiated an anti-oligarchy policy, was overthrown by his own vice-president. In the same year in Ecuador, Colonel Luis Larrea Alba, who had socialist tendencies, fell after two months of government. A year later, in 1932, the "Socialist Republic" of Chile, headed by Commodore Grove, lasted 10 days. Seven years later in Bolivia, Major Bush, who had initiated a "socialist military" government in 1935, committed suicide and the oligarchy resumed power. In 1939, in Paraguay, Colonel Rafael Franco was overthrown by a military coup after initiating important socialist and democratic reforms.

In 1945, during his second term of government in Colombia, Alfonso López Pumarejo intensified his liberal policies and was obliged to resign. The following year, in 1946, the populist president of Bolivia, Major Gualberto Villaroel, was assassinated and hung from a street lamp. The traditional parties, the orthodox left, the reactionary sectors, and the army precipitated his fall. In 1948, President Rómulo Gallegos, who headed a social democratic government in Venezuela, was overthrown. In 1954, Getúlio Vargas committed suicide. In his second government he had sought a "social democratic government in the Scandinavian style" and the growing economic independence of Brazil. Also in the same year, "the Guatemalan Revolution" ended (1944–1954) with the resignation of President-Colonel Jacobo Arbenz, brought about by a military invasion from Honduras financed by the CIA. A year later, conservatives, liberals, Catholics, socialists, and communists helped to overthrow the populist government of General Juan Domingo Perón, under the auspices of the great oligarchy of Buenos Aires and of the hegemonic powers. In 1957, in Colombia, Gustavo Rojas Pinilla was overthrown. He had risen to power through a coup d'état supported by moderate conservatives, liberals, and the church. He was overthrown by the same forces, after contradictory populist policies left him without the support of the people and with the hatred of the oligarchy. President for 19 days in Haiti, following an electoral process that had to be interrupted, syndicalist Daniel Fignolé was overthrown by the new dictator Duvalier. In 1958, in Venezuela, Admiral Larrazábal, who presided over the civilian–military junta on the fall of dictator Pérez Jiménez, renounced the presidency of the junta to be the candidate of the Venezuelan Communist Party for the presidency of the republic. Rómulo Betancourt won. He moved to the right.

In 1959, the Cuban revolution triumphed. During the following decades, the fall of populist and nationalist presidents occurred in a predominantly counter-revolutionary atmosphere. In 1961, a progressive civilian–military junta was overthrown by a military coup in Honduras. The years 1963 and 1964 were milestones in the fall of nationalist, labour, or populist governments. In July 1963, President Carlos Arosemena of Ecuador fell victim to a coup d'état. The president had led a centre–left government that proposed to maintain relations with Cuba. In September 1963, the progressive government of Juan Bosch in the Dominican Republic was overthrown, and when, two years later, Colonel Francisco Caamaño Deno hoisted the constitutional flag and armed the people to defend it, the United States invaded. In October 1963, Ramón Villeda Morales was overthrown in Honduras. He had intended to democratize the politics of his country. In Brazil, João Goulart, who had moved to the left, promised to adopt a series of social and nationalist measures and to maintain diplomatic relations with Cuba. He was overthrown after a long process of destabilization on 14 April 1964. In 1966, Arturo Illia was overthrown; this marked the beginning of seven years of military dictatorship. In Bolivia in 1970, General Alfredo Ovando, who unexpectedly attempted to introduce populist–military policies, was overthrown. In 1971, Juan José Torres, the more radical general who succeeded him, was also overthrown and, later, assassinated. The destabilization of his government was tremendous. In 1973, Argentina's peronist president, Héctor Cámpora, resigned from the presidency under pressure from the syndicalist right wing and from all the conservative forces. On 11 September of the same year, Salvador Allende, socialist president of Chile, was assassinated by Augusto

Pinochet, a bloody dictator. In Honduras in 1975, General Oswaldo López Arellano fell one day after the expropriation of 22,000 hectares from the United Fruit Company. He had intended to implement agrarian reform since 1972. He did not originally intend to upset the powerful company. The *Wall Street Journal* accused him of corruption, and a military group that called themselves or thought themselves to be progressive overthrew him. They themselves were also overthrown. On 29 August 1975 in Peru, General Juan Velasco Alvarado, who had nationalized the mining industry, carried out a profound agrarian reform, re-evaluated the indigenous heritage, and was overthrown by a coup sponsored by the right and by the United States. Some months later, in Ecuador, on 11 January 1976, General Guillermo Rodríguez Lara, who had undertaken a moderate nationalist and populist programme, fell victim to the oligarchy and American pressure. In 1978, Melgar Castro, a military man from Honduras who was leading a moderate progressive government, fell victim to a coup. In January 1980 in El Salvador, the government of Colonel Adolfo Majano fell. Since the previous October the Colonel had proposed a policy emphasizing land redistribution and the nationalization of the bank. After a complex game of resignations and growing rightist policies, his successor turned out to be Napoleón Duarte. In 1981, Jaime Roldós, the nationalist and populist president of Ecuador, died in a suspect plane crash. During the same year, General Omar Torrijos, who had headed a nationalist and populist military government – whose principal objective was to regain the Panama Canal's sovereignty – also died in a plane crash. Shortly after, president Arístides Royo (a supporter of Torrijos) was obliged to resign. In September 1982, Antonio Guzmán Fernández, president of the Dominican Republic, committed suicide apparently because of accusations of corruption in his administration. His government was moderately progressive and had succeeded the president of the North American invasion: Joaquín Balaguer.

It is true that the instability of governments does not threaten only reformist, nationalist, populist, labour, or social democratic governments. Nevertheless, they are the principal victims. Emmerich observed that, of 39 coups between 1958 and 1983, 75 per cent (28) resulted in openly anti-populist, anti-democratic, and counter-revolutionary regimes.[8] There is no doubt that reformist governments' contradictions succeeded in turning the implacable forces of the oligarchies and of the United States against them. Sometimes these forces can tolerate reformist governments if they can count on very strong support from the people, the workers, and the middle classes, or if they fence in and control industrial workers through politics, concessions, and negotiations directed by the labour and government leaders themselves, the former through various techniques of conciliation with the bosses, and the latter through other techniques of concession and arbitration that seem to be above both workers and bosses. But if the dominant classes are obliged to recognize the power of these governments and that of the state structures that support them, it gets to a point where the governments themselves change their policies and make increasing concessions to capital in the face of labour, to landowners in the face of peasants, and to foreign monopoly and financial capital in the face of small productive local capital. Such contradictory policies, far from strengthening these governments, weaken them, and if they don't become the counter-revolution's own agents, as did Paz Estenssoro, they suffer sudden attacks of destabilizing policies, which the states and dominant classes have improved considerably and which precede, justify, and facilitate coups d'état and military invasions.

The limitations of political systems are more obvious when they reach their maximum development and when they threaten the social system of neocolonial capitalism. The case of Chile during the Popular Unity government (1970–1973) is the most dramatic and significant experience of this sort. Although it does not seem to be an exclusively Latin American experience or even a neocolonial one, Latin America has demonstrated the limitations of a political system in which the left obtained an electoral victory in the name of a peaceful and legal programme of democratic socialism and in which the elected government was violently overthrown. The Chilean experience was the greatest victory of unarmed democracy in Latin America and also its greatest failure. Some facts are worth remembering because of the way in which they tend to repeat themselves, even in less radical contexts.

As the social system's crisis became more and more acute during the Popular Unity government, as real struggles increased, and as the collapse of the status quo reached crisis point, institutional relations of power and government disintegrated. The political and economic crisis of the system removed the most highly organized groups, the avant-garde and the leaders, from their allotted roles and made it difficult for them to continue to fulfil institutional and formal "functions" without being able to impose and direct new ones, consistent with the popular alternative.

Economic hyper-inflation and monetary instability completely disrupted the structures of institutional government. The break-up of certain traditional mediators left room for new ones. These entered into conflict with the institutional and parliamentary mediators, while conservative, bourgeois, and oligarchic forces revived with old weapons in the midst of social disorder.

Among the middle classes, several long-established organizations, such as guilds and professional organizations, began to fulfil a new role in the oligarchic politics of power. They began to defend their interests in an aggressive way, expressing distrust in the democratic organizations that had controlled class interests in the political life of Chile during the previous 40 years. Democratic institutions were openly questioned, together with the "law" and "political liberties." Reactionary, regressive forces began to act in the name of "order." The elected government, the working-class parties, the trades unions, and the political parties (even conservative parties) became the principal obstacles to a preservation of private interests. At this point everything was done to oust the president, congress, and parliament in order to upset the economy and the monetary system, and also to raise to the maximum pitch the type of confrontation that had began to emerge between on the one hand the organizations of the Popular Unity – unions and parties – and on the other hand the new emergent social actors who tended to control the centres of production and their "territory."

As the dominant classes began to fail in the political control of the system, they moved to open rebellion. After losing the elections for congress in April 1973 to the PU, the dominant classes found themselves unable to defeat Allende's government legally. The dominant classes then gave their growing support to professional associations and to conflict organizations. They also increased confrontations between popular grass-roots organizations and the PU government as much as they could. For this purpose they used the well-known technique of manipulation and destabilization involving the use of *agents provocateurs*. All the natural and "provoked" confrontations led to the 1973 military coup. Then the counter-revolutionary social situation was ripe. The oligarchy, with important sectors of the middle classes and of the army, under the protection of the State Department, were ready for the conquest of a government that had only just won the elections and that had not been able to proclaim its own popular, economic, and military power. The peaceful road to socialism and the most advanced political system in Latin America had come to an end. In fact, the PU government lost its last chance to win state power as soon as it failed to impose a law against the open conspiracy of the governing classes and imperialism. Lacking the power to undertake "systematic change" and even "structural change," democracy's limitations became manifest. The internal divisions of the government, the absence of an avant-garde to take over power and the absence of links with the people's emergent power revealed that the PU controlled the government, but did not have the power in Chile.

2. Formal and informal politics

Elections without power, parties without a favourable correlation of forces, and democratic political systems that do not succeed in imposing the law have persistently shown their extreme inability to solve important structural and social problems.

If political systems are only a part of the state, they are also only a part of society. If universal politicization threatens accumulation and transnationalization, it also obliges the state and the bloc within the state to reduce the space for formal politics. The citizenry react in an informal way in relations with political systems. Lack of participation is one of their responses in the face of meaningless elections and in the face of a party system in which the opposition does not have the slightest possibility of gaining access to the government, not to mention other powers of the state. Lack of participation is an increasing phenomenon – one could say in a functional way – as long as social and cultural development are not accompanied by political development.

The lack of meaning of formal politics balances itself in these cases with informal politics. And if sometimes abstention represents a threat to the state, the state often relies on non-participation not only as an electoral phenomenon but also as an acknowledgement of the absence of political struggle and of political rights. Generalized and chronic abstention becomes tacit acceptance that not all are citizens, and that only the few have the right to choose, to vote, to represent, and to govern. But, in contrast with slave democracies, the citizens' law of these countries can be universal in "form," while, in the informal sector of politics, it does not function *by the deliberate decision of the most marginalized* of the system, who employ apathy, conformism, or rebellion.

The size of politics' informal sector varies from one period to another, and from one country to another. Based on rates of abstention, it is considerable. For example, in the Mexican presidential elections of 1970, almost half of the registered population did not vote. In the elections in Peru in 1980, only 49 per cent voted. In the elections of 1964 in Colombia, half the electorate abstained, and in the 1968 elections two-thirds of the electorate abstained. Something similar occurred in the 1985 elections in El Salvador, in which, out of almost 2.6 million voters, fewer than 1 million voted. Or in the elections in Haiti in 1988, where Leslie Mamigat was elected by 5–10 per cent of the electorate. Aggravating circumstances occur in many more elections, such as the use of armed paramilitary groups to reinforce the official vote or to extract (literally) the votes that the "tutelary chiefs" are unable to obtain through the traditional system of "political clientele." The number of fraudulent votes deposited in the ballot boxes by functionaries and of forced votes given by citizens as "acarreados" lowers the abstention rate artificially in many countries to proportions smaller than a third, when the reality of the "informal" political world produces a much higher proportion.[9]

The vote that appears to be a vote yet is not has a long history. In Mexico it appears in all the elections to the presidency in which the candidate has been designated beforehand and where there is no chance that he won't be elected, a process that has recurred throughout the entire electoral history of Mexico with the sole exception of President Madero (1910). In Argentina, almost all the elections held before the Saénz Peña Law was passed (the law of "universal, secret, and mandatory suffrage," 1912) were ceremonial elections, and those held during the 1930s were ritual or ceremonial too, when the conservatives systematically applied the so-called "patriotic fraud." The electoral rituals under a dictatorship such as that of Stroessner, who sought his eighth re-election in 1988, are obviously bogus and lacking in citizens' suffrage; the electoral unreality derives from the physical act of voting as the facade of a non-existent reality.

This phenomenon is much more sophisticated in Colombia, where between 1954 and 1958 liberals and conservatives alternated in the presidency and shared the other responsibilities on the basis of a so-called "national pact" through which the country elected the candidate within friendly oligarchic groups. In any event, the act of voting corresponds to an act of collective complicity or of timorous conformism in which all hide the absence of reality: the real election is carried out at the margins of formal elections.

In El Salvador's elections it is very difficult to separate military actions from political ones. The army defends the government's votes with its uniformed and undercover paramilitary forces. Obviously, the citizenry uses the same system of armed groups to defend its own votes. But then the struggle for votes becomes a paramilitary, informal struggle, with imprisoned, murdered, and vanished candidates and voters. Eventually, the informal becomes revolutionary. In extreme circumstances, the citizens use elections to rebel, or abstain from using them as an act of rebellion that sometimes precedes or follows a war.

In the democratizing projects of the 1980s, the informal and formal politics acquired new characteristics. Conservative neoliberalism, which is to be found at the base of the project of associated transnational democratization, shows clear limitations for the latter, not only in the political field but also in the social one. In addition, it complements its project of limited democracy with a military project. Transnational democratization is a move against revolutionary, popular democracy. But it is also a move against social democrats and populism.

If monetary policies cannot destroy welfare structures and the "welfare state" in countries where they do not exist because social democratic and populist movements did not succeed – such as in Haiti, the Dominican Republic, Guatemala, and El Salvador – they can nevertheless impoverish them. And if in these countries political movements have no alternative but to adapt to servitude or to fight, the dominant classes unleash all their internal weapons (now reformulated as "low-intensity warfare") in a global, integral, total war: military, police, paramilitary, economic, political, cultural, ideological, advanced technology, psychological terrorism, and even genocide when necessary and possible in the face of world and North American public opinion. In this way, dominant classes counterattack revolutionary democracy's attempts and reduce their own games of controllable democracy to a war instrument, legitimated and disorienting. They complement the process with the restructuring of the state for a military struggle at all levels, from the high posts of command to the "model villages" via "death squadrons." The transnational democratic project combines its electoral and parliamentary structures with "state terrorism." In addition it uses an annoying game for associated governments and subordinate officials who are often criticized by the democratizing crusaders in Washington, the ones defending human rights, the same ones who often send weapons and supplies as "humanitarian help" to fight against their own people. The population's resistance to this type of war is not only military, and sometimes not even armed, more because of the lack of arms than for any ideological reasons.

The population's resistance, its struggle, occurs in the field of informal politics, which is increasingly prolific in the experiences of urban and rural populations, and from indigenous communities; the latter learn to survive in order to fight. They fight with "scattered" cornfields and edible herbs. They learn to cook at night so that the enemy cannot see the smoke from the fire. They teach the children to play without shouting in order not to be discovered. They silence the roosters. They whisper. They express themselves in silence, they cultivate silence. They organize "resistance communes." There, they teach that "a gun is not necessary to fight the army. Tricks serve as well." In their meetings they practise an informal politics of deliberation and of decision-making; also of discipline. They revive their traditions when they confirm that a single power can unite the leaders of each ethnic group: the integration of the leaders more than actual representation through the leaders – although this also exists – is the key of this informal democracy. In order to unite, these people or ethnic groups renounce their linguistic differences – they speak Spanish – and their different ideologies, and they respect equally Protestants and Catholics who are part of this struggle for democracy.[10]

The transnationalizing project of limited democracy pretends to reduce democracy to liberalism. It fights not only against socialism, and not only against social democratic politics contaminated by populism and state politics (the evil). Liberalism disguised as democracy fights against democracy.[11] When dictators fall, freedom of expression, freedom of association, freedom of election, and parliamentary freedom are looked on sympathetically by the population, especially when they are complemented by the practice of human rights previously violated by the police and the paramilitary corps of the "dirty war."

The dialectic of the democratic journey rapidly finds various significant forms. Democratic reconversion does not alter privatizing monetarist politics, and nationalizing politics does not increase social spending by the government, nor does it affect direct income. It does not allow for the judging and the restructuring of police and armed forces that left ample proof of having violated human rights and sown terror. It does not put an end to the fear that dictatorship may return; before, it even used this fear as a permanent form of blackmail to intimidate and bring about conformism. Under these conditions, formal politics and its practices, however far they might extend in these countries, have political, economic, social, and psychological limitations that do not allow for such limited democracies to be able to guarantee a modicum of stability. If informal politics does not develop equally in all countries, it nevertheless tends to become central and even extensive in many countries. Of course a great number of their citizens have known what it is to lose their former individual and social rights, and to fight under terror for a return to democracy. Their informal culture is superior to the past.

The limitations of formal politics in time and space, and its limitations in relation to informal power and force reveal to a growing section of the population not only the necessity of counting on the state's power but also the necessity of getting closer to this power in a struggle whose final objective is to change the system of domination and exchange it for another that can guarantee the depth and continuity of change through the power of the state and of its social bases.

3. The possible and the struggle for power

Many of the measures taken against the national state and the project of development, progress, social justice, and democracy (understood as government of the majority) appear now to be irreversible for the hegemonic classes. If it is improbable or even impossible for the governments of dependent countries to change politics, it is equally improbable and impossible for the governments of hegemonic countries in the capitalist world.

Another, less harmful "exchange relation" might follow the "cancellation of the external debt" – a *highly improbable scenario*. In fact, the *secular* tendency on the one hand, and *world* politics toward the third world and of the third world on the other, confirm *all our experiences* that the trends of industrializing restructuring, with the indicated characteristics, are irreversible and are going to become more accentuated in the capitalist world as a whole. Under these conditions, what seems most probable while the present structure of domination continues is the end of the historical project of the nation-state, of national and popular sovereignty, of balanced and complete development, of social justice, of an increasingly participatory and efficient democracy; and of yet other projects, such as Latin American integration, the union of Latin American states, etc. All these projects, viewed in terms of "common sense" by the dominant classes, or "good sense," or "minimum political sensibility," have ended up or are seen as *illusions* – old and defeated – or as irresponsible and unrealistic *provocations* in the present balance of forces. Taking these projects into the official discourse has only a rhetorical purpose.

The crisis of the national state, of national government, and of the nation appears to be a consequence of an inexorable historical process, apart from partial or deep interventions coming necessarily from a popular base, which would establish a national state and a national government through the hegemonic organization of the working people. Any strategy for a solution to the problems of sovereignty, development, social justice, and democracy presupposes – as Pedro Vusković noted in chapter 1 – a new hegemony. None of the recognized measures is feasible under the present international and internal hegemonic force.

Even if this fact is clear, it is difficult to imagine a return to a social democratic politics such as the one monetarism liquidated; as difficult as it is to imagine a socialist revolution of the classical type, which has so far failed to occur and gives no indication that it might ever occur in Latin America. For one thing, the old alternative, *reform or revolution*, is sliding towards the most varied combinations and permutations of reform or revolution. For another, revolutions tend to accept reform politics with increasing ease, and reformism tends to acquire a revolutionary conscience and position.

What is more, as the working class became disorganized and lost its classical centrality, the class struggle appeared to be systematically diluted by the struggle of the people against the dictator, then against the empire, then against the system. But change in the system generally occurs only through political struggle against the tyrant and through struggle against the empire. In the aware conditions of the present society and world, the struggle for human rights, for social rights, for the force of constitutional rights, and for electoral and parliamentary democracy appears to be a necessary intercession for the struggle for power. If the search for the civil and the constitutional in the face of the military and dictatorial cannot remain there without being condemned to reproduce the social system and the system of domination, it cannot be avoided either. There are possible and necessary battles even in countries where only a mockery of formal democracy has occurred. The struggle for political systems against military systems, and for systems that combine various forms of political and social negotiation instead of predominantly repressive systems, appears to be a constitutional and reform struggle, which in reality must and can be complemented by a struggle for power by the working people.

What is more, the struggle of military men who seek to lead popular movements, and national, *majority* movements, cannot either be reduced to a struggle for the power of the state, conceiving of the state as a "machinery" for repression, representation, and conciliation. Thousands of military men have sacrificed their lives for this project, which seems as incomplete as that which among civilians limits action to the political, the electoral, and the representative. The problem does not just consist in taking over the nation-state machine, for several reasons. First, the United States and other great powers can be found in the rearguard of the present national system of power. Secondly, if a transnational state does not yet exist, there already exists an inter-American system, and the forces and interests displaced by any action of the national majority necessarily turn as much to American support as to the support of the civil and military inter-American system. Thirdly, something exists that is not a transnational state but is the informal power of this state. It is a power bloc at the same time transnational and internal, or associated transnational, the last redoubt of the immense accumulated power of the minorities. Fourthly and lastly, as a counterpart, the necessity still exists of building a state and a majority with a base in a bloc of alternative power, at once democratic and popular.

Politics as the art of the possible for the majorities has a consequence that, with undeniable actual variations, goes from being a political struggle against tyrannies and tyrants to being an anti-imperialist struggle for an emergent democracy that might or might not lead immediately to socialism, but that certainly depends on the working people's power and on social democratic and socialist forces. The art of the possible of the majorities leads in another dimension to taking over the state's power, to the struggle against American interventionism, to the struggle against the inter-American system of dependency, and finally to the struggle against the associated transnational power bloc that heads the large enterprises and businesses of the United States and other countries of the capitalist world, as well as of the large creole capitals.

This long trek, and its revolutionary alternative, which is more democratic and popular than worker and socialist oriented, seems to be possible in part because it is the only option.

4. Interceded and violent struggle

In order to prevent constitutional struggles and struggles for civilian regimes from ending up as means of reproducing the system, we must pay attention to the following:

(1) The struggle and nature of class and bloc intercessions, in which the important point is to change the bloc and the dominant class within the bloc.

(2) The struggle for change in the interrelationship of forces that design and apply a politics of accumulation of forces, a politics of cultural hegemony, a politics of ideological elucidation of the majorities and of their ability to think in political terms.

(3) A new politics in terms of alliances of the majorities, of popular alliances, of nation and nations, in which social movements, political organizations, and military force together allow for the existence and subsistence of a new sociopolitical bloc able to overcome "the conservative social rhetoric" in its various liberal, populist, social democratic, and corporatist versions, as well as abandoning "the fear of people's power" and fulfilling ("because of political idealism") the restructuring objectives of the nation, of sovereignty, of development, of social justice, and of democracy, and all this always within the rationale of the masses, of citizens, of the working people, and of the working class. This alliance presupposes respect for the various levels of awareness and different ideologies in order to enable the more aware and radical and the more ingenuous, moderate, and simple to come together.

The great challenge for mass organizations and their "organic intellectuals" seems to be the problem of not participating in the periodical restructuring of the system, and of achieving a build-up of forces so that this restructuring might end. The challenge consists of constituting themselves into the "power nuclei" of the alternative blocs. These nuclei are different from the classical "avant-garde" because of their necessary variety, simultaneity, dispersion, and integration. They are also different from "popular power" and "dual power" because of their complementary quality and combination of formal and informal politics. In this sense, they are also distinct from the party, which is only political, only electoral. The power nuclei of the alternative blocs emerge within a process of accumulation in which taking over the state's power is mediated by institutional and formal politics. But they adopt both politics – the formal and the informal – and they articulate them instead of confronting them.

The intermediate or partial battles that take place in the liberation arena, or against dictatorships and authoritarian regimes, acquire a crucial importance for popular movements. Through them, two types of phenomenon are unleashed, some of which respond to popular pressure with concessions and reforms (not just with repression), and in others of which repression predominates.

In the first case, political, trades union, peasant, and urban settlers' struggles form part of the history of intercessions that delay the practical establishment of the struggle for power within the guidelines of a predominantly negotiated capital. Negotiated capital tends to divide society and workers through macrosocial processes and political co-option, in which the various types of "mobilization" and "upward social mobility" increase, mostly during the "modernization," "economic growth," "social justice," and "governable democratization" stages. In this case, popular movements and organizations raise the question of the struggle for hegemony first as a struggle for autonomy, but without excluding the unsophisticated ones who do not yet see the class struggle in all its depth. Popular movements and organizations seek a strategy and tactics for the intermediate battle considered as phenomena of negotiation and of political–social confrontation, in which negotiation does not provoke the loss of autonomy in relation to the state or mean that group or individual co-options diminish the strength, unity, articulation, or structure of the people's movements. The problem for mass organizations, or for the new nuclei of democratic and popular power, is that both negotiation and repression reproduce the system of the present dominant bloc without even a pretence of purely formal or governmental concessions, or even economic or social concessions. In reality they do not alter in any way either the structure of economic–military power, or the hegemonic, associated transnational, and national bourgeois predominance.

On the other hand, in countries where the reform of political and social structures or political and social concessions and negotiations are *not* the main response to popular demands and pressures, or where they occupy a very secondary and superficial place in state politics (that is to say, in countries or at times in which repression predominates over social negotiation and concessions), a strategy of intermediate battles and of a build-up of forces confronts a predominantly repressive capitalism. Repressive capitalism has – in general – less capacity to stratify society or the working people with co-option politics. In this type of capitalism, neither modernization nor economic growth leads to upward social mobility. In general, co-option is limited to the repressive apparatus and its special repressive team; these are the ones who are in charge of granting concessions or negotiating within a predominantly repressive politics. In so far as they are "governable modernization" projects, the building of electoral, parliamentary, and union intercessions easily and immediately leads to state repression, and for this reason these forms of intercession are usually reduced to ritual forms imitating a non-existent representative and parliamentary democracy, or an illusory "welfare state." This is an area in which any social security policy tends to be displaced by a policy of charity – limited and also arbitrary. In such cases, colonialist and racist discrimination, with horizontal mobility for temporary and migrant workers as well as for poor refugees fleeing in huge numbers from poverty and insecurity, is the predominant form of social and political control and of social stratification.

The lack of economic and political intercessions in the states that respond with "violent immediacy" and with generalized repression leads popular movements either from starvation to pressure, to repression, and again to starvation, or to political–military insurrectional struggle to take over and transform power. The very system outlaws any opposition or protest, the mark of rebellion, and it accuses rebels of delinquency. It is true that sometimes the pursued person, or "delinquent," becomes a revolutionary and uses methods as violent and illegal as the state itself. There are countries where losing one's weapons is the same as losing one's freedom and one's life and where keeping them is part of a politics of accumulation that goes beyond weapons, to ideology, to the formation of mass politics, and to the culture and structure of emergent power.

One could mistakenly conclude that in these countries and at these times it is easier to make a revolution, and that the revolution is mostly made with weapons. This mistake arises from not realizing that repressive states and governments can organize a lasting structure of terror, and that, even in these countries, rather than a mere struggle for arms, one is dealing mostly with a political, ideological, and cultural struggle, and with creating a will for power that includes *all* the weapons rendered illegal by the tyrant, be they cultural, political, or military.

The problem becomes more complicated still in the real word

where negotiated and repressive (or repressive and negotiated) capitalism combine and occur. In fact, the profiles of each country and their specific variations over time depend on the combinations of the colonialist and racist stratifications with the negotiated and modernizing, corporate, or limited democracy. They depend also on the punctual articulation and extension of the dominant bloc and its bases of support, which also enjoy the benefits of the unequal development of power, and of the guarantees that this participation represents.

V. The dominant bloc

1. The dominant bloc and its evolution

The dominant bloc constitutes the social structure of domination and the use of force, wealth, and surplus. It corresponds to the linking of the various bourgeoisies (national, transnational) among themselves and with the forces of repression, conciliation, arbitration, and negotiation, as well as with co-opted representatives: of workers, peasants, the middle classes, urban settlers, professional associations, or of voters and "citizens." The dominant bloc is the hegemonic structure of the state in the entirety of its social relations. Landowners, bankers, businessmen, politicians, military personnel, professors, journalists, radio announcers, the bourgeoisie in general and the civilian and military bureaucracy, including the trades union, agrarian, and electoral groups, are the socially co-opted movements that make up the dominant bloc.

The bloc's hegemony is the ultimate expression of class hegemony. But the articulation of the bourgeoisie with bureaucracies, leaders, representatives, and ideologists who are mediators or intermediaries for the organized masses, mediatizes class confrontation as an essential characteristic of neocapitalism. This allows for support from the social bases for the dominant bloc, support given electorally or by corporatists, or from the beneficiaries of or "participants" in the fruits of development, who make up a significant proportion of society. The rest of society is left in perpetual political and ideological marginalization, without the structural capacity to articulate the majority of the working class, the people, or the nation, or with enormous obstacles to achieving it given the inter-class structure of the dominant bloc and of the divisions it prescribes between those who participate and those who do not.

At a macroeconomic and macrosocial level, the structure of the dominant bloc manifests itself in the indicators of participation, of surplus and accumulation, or of the marginalization of the latter. Roughly 35 per cent of the participating population[12] receives privileged loans before the rest, although within this 35 per cent the bourgeoisie is the main beneficiary, and within it the monopoly, financial, and transnational bourgeoisie. In a very strict and institutional sense the dominant bloc is characterized by the combination of military men who are landowners or businessmen, and the workers' leaders who are also bourgeois, and by other combinations that hide the most important and the most concealed one between monopoly and speculative capital and marginal and exploited workers.

The dominant bloc is a "government above the government" that confronts or changes the government itself. It is a structure that is above the state institutions and the political systems or regimes, and that combines them with two rationales: that of accumulation and that of power. In its internal composition, the dominant bloc goes from an apex, corresponding to what Dreifuss called "organic élites," to the various bases of social support – "sections" of the middle strata, of industrial workers, of settlers, of villagers and peasants, all of whom allow the dominant bloc to have a politics of the masses. In the middle, it has its systems of repression (military and political), which combine with those of representation (politicians), of concession, marginalization, and participation (paternalist, welfare, corporate, union), of discipline and efficiency (bureaucrats and technocrats), and of hegemony (publicity agents, preachers, teachers, and great intellectuals).

The organic élites are "mediators in the formation of power blocs or moving action fronts, which predispose the dominant class to political struggle. . . . Its relatively autonomous agents are linked in political, ideological and non-mechanical terms – with the class that makes up its social matrix."[13] From an informal class politics of "particular class projects," they provoke their conversion into general demands, into social, national, or simple commonsense demands, proper to formal, international, or internal politics.[14] Outside of the bloc and of its social bases of active support, the marginalized population and the recolonized ethnic groups are found. But the bloc controls them by cutting them off from "participation" and dividing them among themselves, and through procedures that consist not only of intimidation or terror but also of disorganizing their conscience and will, as in religious sects and politics of individual or collective co-option.

The class alliances of the bloc have varied through history. Three combinations can be emphasized: the alliance between local or national bourgeoisies and the imperial bourgeoisie against the working people; the alliance of the local or national, public or private, civilian and military, industrial, financial, commercial, and agrarian bourgeoisies against the imperial bourgeoisie and against the working people; the alliance of the local or national bourgeoisies and the working people against the imperial bourgeoisie.[15] The first combination corresponds in general terms to the oligarchic–liberal state that hegemonized imperialism (1880–1930) and much later to the "national security" state and the neo-liberal state, which developed principally from the 1960s. The second corresponds to multiple nationalist and conservative states and governments. And the third corresponds to populist and social democratic states. The last two combinations have had to be defeated and integrated by the imperial–national bloc. At the same time, the people of the countries where these blocs dominated continue to exercise strong pressure that renders ungovernable – or at least unstable – the representative, participatory, and repressive systems of the majority of Latin American countries. An important historical movement occurred, which in its more general outline corresponds both to a process of imperial expansion and to a crisis of dependency. The process is so contradictory that it made room for the most recent transnational offensive, that of the 1970s and 1980s, which has had some successes and increasingly frequent failures.

2. The present dominant bloc

The politics of power blocs for an associated transnationalization began after the Second World War and became formal from 1948 onward with the creation of the inter-American system. The process always occurred at the level of the organic élites of the empire, in various formal and informal combinations.

In 1940, the US government founded, at the request of Nelson Rockefeller (also its first director), a Bureau of Inter-American Affairs. It was the beginning of a period of great activity in the economic and diplomatic spheres. In 1941, the Inter-American Council for Commerce and Production promoted employers' meetings in favour of "free enterprise" and of "economic development" (170 multinational enterprises) to "free Latin America from Axis influence." In 1942, the Committee for Economic Development began its technical support and its investigations to promote the inter-

American bloc and the associated members of Latin American nations.

In the realm of multilateral diplomacy, a new inter-American politics of associated transnationalization was also taking shape. That which began in 1889–1890 and produced the Panamerican Union (1910) had turned to military interventions using "the Marines" a bit too often and had administered the inter-American system predominantly with North American officials whose headquarters was in Washington. The "national guards" that appeared after American invasions and the Latin American assistants who worked in the Union were not up to dealing with large countries such as Argentina, Brazil, or Mexico. For this reason, it was necessary to orchestrate a concerted infiltration to provide more leeway for the dominant classes and blocs.

At the Panamerican Conference of 1933 in Montevideo, the United States government was obliged formally to accept the non-intervention principle demanded by Latin American governments. From that moment on, a new policy was undertaken, the so-called "Good Neighbor Policy," coinciding with President Franklin D. Roosevelt's "New Deal," which accepted the need to ignite North American expansion – in the political, economic, social, and cultural areas – in association with Latin America's native bourgeoisies, organic élites, and the dominant blocs. This necessity became more urgent as Latin America saw increased middle-class and organized workers' pressure, and as "Keynesian blocs" and "populist" and enlarged social democratic groups were created in the United States and Latin America. The necessity of this association became clearer still as the danger of the Second World War drew near. The experiences of that time, as well as those of the war, consolidated the notion that North American expansion in Latin America had to be associated, as much in informal politics as in the formal.

The Chapultepec Act signed in Mexico in 1945 and Rio de Janeiro in 1947 served to determine the theoretical framework of a new doctrine of non-intervention by Europe or the socialist countries in inter-American affairs and of the dislike of local governments or movements that tried to impose an anti-imperialist nationalism of the right (tainted with fascism or Nazism) or of those who attempted autonomous and sovereign positions, with popular bases and policies (tainted with communism). With these elements, the Organization of American States (OAS) was founded along with other specialized inter-American organs. The OAS formalized the project of associated transnationalization, but its design of imperial domination was clearly revealed a few years later when the United States used all its influence to oblige Latin American governments to support its interventionist policy against the supposedly communist Guatemalan government during the Caracas Conference in 1954. The Panamerican Union had acted in such a way that even the Latin American right accused it of being "a ministry of the colonies," and the same fate seemed to be reserved for the OAS. Although in 1954 Argentina and Mexico abstained from voting against Guatemala, almost all felt that its position as a "junior member" of the imperial enterprise was humiliating and, up to a certain point, threatening. In any case, the process of integration of the pan-American and national associated blocs continued, with their groups of "organic élites" for informal politics, and with specialized structures of the inter-American system for formal politics in the army, for the trades unions, in the agrarian field, for ethnic minorities in education, for the press, radio, and even geography and history.

Meanwhile some alarming events occurred, the first one being the Cuban revolution (1956–1959). Shortly afterwards, the Latin American populist crisis became associated with a "dependency crisis" (Real de Azúa). It was the beginning of new configurations in the democratic and revolutionary forces in terms of alliances, fronts, movements, and coalitions, all of which was particularly threatening to imperial policies. Rockefeller entered the scene again, but this time in a defensive role. With the support of President Kennedy, he founded the Business Group for Latin America in 1961, with 35 "executives" from large enterprises. At the same time, in governmental and private associations, the Latin American Information Committee was created; it was sponsored by 40 enterprises. The Alliance for Progress was initiated, as well as the Peace Corps.

The politics of "conservative modernization" as an alternative to populist anti-imperialism in decline and to threatening revolution included a policy of reorganization of the dominant bloc, with training for armies and police forces for the so-called "internal war." There was an attempt – quickly defeated – to undertake agrarian reform and functional fiscal reforms; there was also a reformulation and stimulation of local managerial organizations and of "research, indoctrination, political action, civic and ideological élites," with the participation of scholars, intellectuals, military people, top clergymen, politicians, and notable villagers, and with eventually permanent visitors who belonged to the pan-American workers' movement

109

(especially from the Inter-American Regional Work Organization), university students, journalists, radio announcers, film makers, community activists, etc., some of them participating in closed groups (top level) and others in open groups and meetings, which improved the availability of adequate information for decision-making.

The project failed in its reformist objectives. Landowners firmly opposed the agrarian reform, while all the high-income groups, including large enterprises, opposed the fiscal reforms. The failure of the hegemonic reorganization subsided into a reorganization of the authoritarian, military, and repressive apparatus. The discontent among the social democratic and populist forces, which had become part of the previous bloc, rendered monopoly and transnational capital's power much more vulnerable. The latter could control the situation only through the use of generalized violence. During these same years American social scientists found themselves in crisis, as did their Latin American counterparts. The crisis reached serious proportions because of the manner in which empirical sociologists became involved in the internal struggle and the fight against the people, and because of the renunciation of members of CEPAL of the economic struggle against international inequality.

The US invasion of the Dominican Republic at the beginning of 1965, realized with the active complicity of various Latin American countries, paradoxically marked the beginning of a certain estrangement. Latin American armies did not accept the State Department's project of creating an Inter-American Peace Force that would include them in an institutional manner. What is more, various governments and currents of a new political and military nationalism broke out in Mexico, Panama, Peru, and Chile.

The problems raised in Latin America were augmented in the 1960s and 1970s by various others having to do with industrial society and with the United States, and with the project of world domination. Towards the end of the 1960s, minorities and students seemed to render North American society ungovernable. During these years, a crisis of the political system occurred, and growing abstention seemed to be leading to a "non-voting democracy." Inflation was rampant, and contributed to excessive social concessions, though its real cause was enormous military spending. In 1970, the United States abandoned the Bretton Woods rules, and the dollar ceased to dominate the international monetary system.

During the great recession of 1973–1975 the political crisis of Watergate began, leading to President Nixon's resignation, while the

United States lost important allied governments in Ethiopia, Iran, and South Yemen. In 1973, the United States could no longer ignore the fact that it had been defeated in Viet Nam. The organic élites and the dominant classes tried to take the offensive again. During the same year, European–North-American–Japanese big business, with more than 500 members, founded the Trilateral Commission – led by, among others, David Rockefeller – which concentrated all its attention on the articulation of a "transnational state." One of the main theorists of the Commission was Zbigniew Brzezinski, who suggested thinking in terms of world perspectives and of interdependency. According to Brzezinski, "the administrators of interdependency" would be the transnational élite made up of international enterprises, graduate public functionaries, and officials. They would have ties that "cross national traditions" in so far as their interests were more functional than national. They would be responsible for "rule making," that is to say, for "the establishment of parameters, rules, and procedures" of globalization. As members of the transnational élite they would be able to ensure that their decisions constituted a coherent whole.

Transnationalization as a counter-attack to the various threats – socialist, populist, or social democratic – was planned in a three-dimensional form: in the politico-cultural systems, in the élite structures, and in the economies. The plan proposed to integrate countries such as Brazil, Mexico, and India during the years 1985–1990.[16] Carter lost in 1980. Democracy continued with "excesses." Expansionist politics suffered new defeats – such as the fall of Somoza and the triumph of the Nicaraguan revolution. Democracy was not sufficiently aggressive. The OAS in its Seventeenth Extraordinary Assembly rejected Carter's plan for a military intervention against the small country; it was "the greatest diplomatic defeat of the United States."[17] The inter-American system was not fulfilling its role. The "democratic" neoconservatives, with a weakened power bloc, were followed by the new Reagan administration (1981). Arrogant in his criticism of communism, populism, nationalism, social democracy, the "welfare state," and the United Nations system, Reagan was at first enthusiastic about the "national security" regimes, an enthusiasm that he later on replaced by another for hegemonic aspirations with impassioned praise for democracy as a liberal and conservative policy.

"Reaganomic" transnationalization appeared as a new project. In fact, it was an attempt to go on the offensive again. It proposed "reconversion" or "restructuring" to weaken and discipline competitive countries and powerful unionism, nations, workers, and the middle classes. It proposed to restructure dominant coalitions, making the military more bourgeois, and the bourgeois more military, and with them the technocrats, scientists, intellectuals, industrialists, publicity agents, and many "symbolic talents."

The project – worldwide – tried to be flexible and pragmatic, and tried to penetrate as domination and transnationalization in finances and banking, in production, in transportation and communications, in mass culture and higher education, in refunctionalizing the political systems and states,[18] and in the international expansion of "the same type of organic élites in other countries."[19] It even proposed to integrate populist blocs after destabilizing them.

In 1988, the neo-conservative project's crisis was evident everywhere. Between "Irangate" and the military, moral, and political defeat of the "contras" in Nicaragua and of associated military intervention in the whole of Central America, the United States had also lost the battle of international, technological, and financial competitiveness. It had lost an important part of its economic base with an external debt of more than $680 billion, and an external and internal debt of $2 million million dollars, twice that of the third world. Its fiscal deficit amounted to $200 billion. To finance its war budget, which reached $300 billion, the United States had been obliged to go into debt and to take over world capitals, to live at the world's expense in a way that disrupted the world capitalist system, and all this at a time when it could not maintain the defence budget of the Atlantic and of Asia.

To the previous crisis was added the US crisis in world political leadership – even among Latin American armies and governments, which had proved during the Falklands conflict of 1982 that the Inter-American Treaty of Reciprocal Assistance was only "an instrument of the United States to harness Latin American military capacity." The open support of the United States – both logistically and diplomatically – was a humiliation deeply felt by the leaders of the area, which weakened the most significant item of the inter-American system: the military. Within its still considerable power, another element was added to the loss of legitimacy of the North American government. It was the decrease in anti-communist phobia, mostly since the rise of Gorbachev. Also, in a more structural way, the crisis of the myth of technological superiority continued, especially with the triumphs of small countries of the periphery in the face of imperial offensives that were almost always based on military technological superiority.

The multiple crisis occurs in one of the most powerful countries of the world, with a state that combines its imperial actions with associated states both in multilateral and in bilateral relations, and that, in the Americas, complements the use of the inter-American system and its various agencies with the activity of power blocs and local organic élites, which are articulated in relatively functional ways.

The weakening of the hegemonic bloc is a fact, as is that of the inter-American system and of the associated blocs of each country. The main source of this weakening is the sustained and general attack on populism and social democracy, and the attempt at replacing these bases with an informal society that evades it as much as the heterogeneous emergent popular movements. The bloc's politics of sinecures has reduced it considerably when one compares it with what it was in the days of populism and social democracy. The last bastion of incipient transnational state power seems to become frustrated because of the crisis of the United States and of the world economy, without having anything to offer in relation to the values of the Modern Age.

3. The popular democratic alternative

Ranged before the above types of structure, the democratic and popular structures can be found in their most varied configurations, such as the growing revival of Latin Americanism as expressed in the demands for the creation of an Organization of Latin American States, of a Latin American Monetary Fund, etc. as a response to the hegemonic crisis of pan-Americanism due to the United States. For the democratic and popular structures, the politics of a build-up of forces, before or after taking over power, resides in the iron determination not to tolerate any disarmament pact that would rebuild the neocolonialist and neocapitalist bloc. Their main tactics consist of forging the process of accumulation of forces with negotiations and concessions that do not in any way diminish the power of the working people within alliances, fronts, and coalitions, while positive policies of ideological formation, organization, and supply, all of which increase emergent power, are being implemented. The harsh dialectic of autonomy, hegemony, and advancement of factions, which in the name of autonomy forbids the organization of hegemony or the development of disarmament negotiations, and which in the name of hegemony harms autonomous organizations, can only be resolved when the autonomous people's organizations impose their unity from the grass roots up.

In countries and periods where negotiated capitalism predominates, struggles for the consolidation of a democratic and popular alternative have a juridical–political legality that is extremely important in accumulation, to the point of *destabilization* and *rupture*. But up to this point, formal and institutional politics is not achieved, and social reforms are highly significant.

In the case of countries and periods in which repressive capital predominates, the democratic and popular alternatives do not enter the formal, institutional arenas. Political systems are mere instruments of international legitimation or of internal legitimation and distraction, and social reforms are all symbolic acts that in no way alter the real structures.

The difference is that on the one hand there are political systems and systems of institutional social negotiation, and on the other hand politics is carried out in secret or by force. In the latter, repression as a form of reproduction of the system does not vanish, but rather combines with individual and social negotiation and with policies of co-option, mobility, and social mobilization. Meanwhile, this repression usually occurs either with uncertain intercessions, or without intercessions, through social negotiation and through political representation and participation.

The problem being emphasized here is that, as in political systems of institutional negotiation, a breaking point seems to occur that leads to a predominantly repressive politics. In the countries and periods in which repressive systems take over proprietorship there seems to come a point at which political, diplomatic, and even military negotiations with new characteristics are imposed. These are new in the sense that popular movements do not agree to lay down their weapons in order to negotiate and they impose the negotiations from autonomous positions of strength.

If the problem is considered by searching for the difference between democratic and popular movements rather than that between negotiating or repressive systems, an emergent history appears in which negotiation and rupture tend to combine and follow one another. Conflicts or confrontation of forces that derive in mediation, arbitration, and mediatization phenomena follow and precede head-on clashes, which lack this type of outcome. In fact, there appear to be "unusual phenomena of negotiation" even in the most acute cases of struggle (as in Central America), while in the cases where negotiation predominates (as in South America and Brazil) there seem to be elements of unavoidable struggle or rupture, even more so if democratic–popular movements insist on their demands for an alternative economic, social, and military politics to that imposed by the dominant bloc. The blackmail of the military coup is thus perpetual.

Struggles for a democratic and popular alternative occur, internally and internationally, at the point when institutions and juridical forms tend to become weaker and to be put aside in the course of the battles initiated to reach a dialogue, a conciliation, or an agreement. The underlying logic in both cases seems to be juridical–political, and bases negotiation on strength, and on establishing their possibilities and limitations at an internal and international level. But force is not used or invoked without a continued invitation to dialogue and peace, to law and conciliation to see if, with the latter tools, in practice and by maintaining the integrity of democratic and popular organizations, the adversaries agree in good faith and succeed thereby in fact in making the necessary concessions to the majority, the citizenry, the ethnic minorities, and the people. The development of this logic can be found in particularly advanced form in Central America with the development of organizations and the awareness of democratic and popular organizations, such as in Nicaragua, El Salvador, and Guatemala. But where the people's struggles lack armed organizations and do not have the expertise and the experience of armed struggle, the logic of struggle and negotiation, of conflict and conciliation, becomes particularly difficult to resolve.

The programme of progressive electoral parties is only a fraction of the people's programme. Parties, fronts, and coalitions make up only a few of the people's organizations. If the programme of the electoral party – with the present correlation of forces and dominant bloc – corresponds to objectives that are in general *electoral* and deceptive, the programme of the people's organizations represents a theoretical and practical problem in which elections, with their protests, criticisms, demands, and minimum objectives, are considered as *a* stage and *a* type of the people's struggle. The people's struggle has in fact a much broader plan in terms of actors, media, and objectives; a plan that is generally but little considered in the theories of electoral parties, and is closer to that of organizations known as "fronts" or "movements," about which there is also little theory and only failed or unfinished experiences, such as Popular Unity in Chile and the Broad Front in Uruguay. In terms of a general avant-garde or coordinating force, or a "commune" able to lead the process in its formal and informal aspects, there do not seem to exist at the moment complete experiences, either proposed in theory or applied in practice. Neither does it seem easy, under these conditions, to organize both the formal struggle of negotiations with the unions, workers, peasants, or settlers, and the electoral struggle for parliamentary, local, provincial, and even national posts, and the informal struggle of organizations with social demands.

But if there isn't a duly noted theory or practice of the party, of the avant-garde, or of the "commune" able to assume the leadership and organization of a front, coalition, or movement that fights in both the formal and informal fields and takes over negotiation, representation, and diplomacy with the same energy that it dedicates to the search for and preservation and accumulation of an autonomous power that renders autonomy a non-negotiable fact, and that seeks a new sovereign hegemony and a new social, economic, political, and cultural system representative of the majorities, neither have the theory and practice of alternative blocs of domination developed a great deal in countries where democratic and popular organizations have obtained, at best, only the re-establishment of a constitutional political regime.

4. Alternative blocs

In general, the history of alternative blocs is that of their destruction or integration into the dominant bloc. Many governments or popular, nationalist, or social democratic regimes could not even generate an emergent alternative bloc and did not succeed in imposing a more or less stable political system supported by all the state apparatus. But the few that have succeeded have frequently seen how, as time goes by, the alternative bloc becomes integrated into the traditional bloc, and how intercession breaks into states of the masses, either social democratic or populist, until they are converted once more into neo-oligarchic and neofascist states with new forms of dependence and also transnational forms.

Countries that succeeded in establishing more lasting alternative dominant blocs within peripheral capitalism itself were Uruguay, Mexico, and Costa Rica. These countries shared two significant characteristics: first, the articulation of an alternative power bloc with social bases in the middle classes and with industrial workers; and, second, negotiation, which from power bases allowed for the association of participants in the old and the new bloc in processes of increasingly favourable accumulation for monopoly, financial, and speculative capital, and favourable to the economy's transnationalization. The limited and manageable opposition of organized workers and the middle layers of this process allowed constitutional life to go on in Mexico and Costa Rica, but it led to a breaking point in Uruguay. Something similar to the Uruguayan experience took place in other countries where it had been possible to impose parliamentary regimes, party democracy (as in Chile), or populist and social democratic regimes (as in Argentina and Brazil). In these countries the demands of the workers and the middle classes were unmanageable. The alternative blocs of power made concessions that increased their contradictions and weakened them. The rupture and fall of alternative blocs and governments terminated the process with de facto regimes.

The only countries that seem to have succeeded in consolidating an alternative dominant bloc of a popular character are Cuba and Nicaragua. Nicaragua has even taken the hegemony of the bloc to the sphere of socialist countries, and this within a system of a mixed economy and political pluralism seeking to make use of all the previous experiences with blocs and classes to establish a revolutionary democracy. The United States has strenuously opposed this, with an ever-decreasing possibility of overcoming it.

In these countries, the dominant bloc focuses mostly on the working people and relies on social democratic, socialist, and working-class movements at an international level. The dominant bloc also depends on other liberation movements in Africa and Asia. The alternative power bloc does not come only from the working class, nor does it come only from political parties. It arises from villages and working people, and from social movements that tend to become political or revolutionary movements.[20]

In the countries where nowadays social movements have stopped the fight against authoritarian governments – civil and constitutional – or for a change of political regime from military and authoritarian governments to civilian and constitutional ones, the history of the alternative dominant bloc is still very uncertain. The only sketch of what could be appears in the organization of the people, who tend to unite political and social movements. The articulation of people's organizations, the one that undertakes its experiences of struggle, either formal or informal, and accumulates force for the political struggle oriented to solving social problems, that is to say, a political struggle for the power of the majorities appears as the embryo of the alternative power bloc.

The existing experiences show that these types of organizations tend to be headed and coordinated by fronts, movements, and coalitions in which the avant-garde and the bases will give greater priority to the democratic struggle than to the socialist one, and to the struggle for national sovereignty before the class struggle, but without neglecting the class struggle, either within the front, or within the country, or at the international level of the region or of the world. The dominant tendency is the struggle for a democracy with power rather than for a socialist democracy, and with various ideologies rather than with just a single one. In this sense, the construction of the new bloc raises extremely novel problems, both in terms of various ideologies and doctrines at the margin of legitimation of decisions by a single doctrinaire and ideological body, and within the logic of "everything for the power of the working people, nothing against the working people," as stipulated and interpreted by the culture of tolerance and ideological pluralism. The struggle seems also to imply a simultaneous defence of formal and informal democracy, as well as of representative and participatory democracy, and of the socialization of production and the means of production, which would not necessarily be "from the state" and which would change private, public, and social property in combinations that would render freedoms effective, in the sense of what a salary represented in the face of slavery, or what self-management represents in the face of the state, and what state property might represent during an as yet unforeseeable time in the face of the great private monopoly.

All these experiences may indicate that none of the possible evolutions or revolutions lead us to believe that the new democratic and popular blocs reproduce the previous experiences of democratization and socialization without important contributions from a particularly new history. Within this history, the struggle for a political culture that uses the previous experiences in order not to fall into corporate neocapitalism or into socialist bureaucracy seems to be a priority. This new culture of society and the state reveals that its crucial task is to express the notions of pluralism, sovereignty, democracy, dialogue, and the power of the masses to great numbers of people, encouraging their determination to struggle for a democracy with power. In the midst of a bewildering crisis, many popular movements tend to portray humanism as a utopia and as a politics of power.

The national, pluralist, and non-aligned project becomes intrinsically a project of "conquest of peace with social justice, democracy and independence." The people's organizations "do not express the ideology or the final specific project of the coalition members." A practical and effective politics depends upon ideological pluralism, mutual respect, and broad dialogue, free of sectarianism, dogmatism, and hegemonism. The organizations form a complex whole whose organic structure implies the functioning of the autonomous, of the "ability to decide for themselves." Within each organization, the constituent members decide their right to carry on their own work, to establish their own relations, to forge their own alliances and their political understandings, as well as to create their own work tools. At the same time the organization of the entire people – plural in its ideology and autonomous in its constituent organizations – is the embryo of a new state and a new society, and it looks to the practice of "consensual agreements" to develop and broaden its politics of alliances. As part of the building of the majority's popular movement, consultation, discussion, and debate are organized.[21] The phenomenon is not a local one, or a provisional one: it is a universal and permanent trend. It appears with varying degrees of organization and clarity throughout Latin America, in parties but mostly in social movements and in the organizations of the people.

Notes

1. We are referring here to the great majority of Latin American countries. We do not of course include Cuba or Nicaragua.
2. Jorge Graciarena, "El Estado periférico y economía capitalista: Transiciones y crisis." In: Pablo González Casanova, ed. *El Estado en América Latina*. Mexico: Siglo XXI–UNU, 1990, p. 40.
3. Ibid., p. 52.
4. Luis Maira, "El Estado de seguridad nacional en América Latina." In: Pablo González Casanova, ed. *El Estado en América Latina*, op. cit., pp. 108–130.
5. Octavio Ianni, "El Estado y la cuestión nacional." In: ibid., pp. 25–39.
6. Eduardo Galeano, in *Pensamiento Propio* [Own thinking], no. 44 (Managua, September–October 1987): 20.
7. Gustavo Ernesto Emmerich, "Ejercicio del poder y carácter de los regímenes políticos en América Latina. 1801–1984." In: Pablo González Casanova, ed. *El Estado en América Latina*, op. cit., pp. 131–160. Note: there is no information on the remaining 1.1%.
8. See Gustavo Emmerich, *Votos y Botas* [Ballots and boots]. Toluca: UAEM, 1985.
9. See Mario Ramírez Rancaño, "Estadísticas básicas sobre América Latina" [Basic statistics of Latin America]. Mexico: UNAM, Centro de Investigaciones Interdisciplinarias en Humanidades, mimeo, n.d., p. 39.
10. M. Lomba, "To Resist as a Response to Violence." *Pensamiento Propio*, no. 45 (October 1986): 13–16.
11. See Alfred Stepan's excellent observations on this phenomenon: *Brasil: los militares y la política*. Buenos Aires: Amorrortu, 1974; *The State and Society. Peru in Comparative Perspective*. Princeton, NJ: Princeton University Press, 1978.
12. Using different indicators, it is possible to say that 65 per cent of the population partici-

pates, if we accept that only 35 per cent live in poverty; see Ramírez Rancaño, "Estadísticas básicas sobre América Latina," op. cit., p. 70.

13. R.A. Dreifuss, *A internacional capitalista. Estratégia e táticas do empresariado transnacional (1918–1986).* Rio de Janeiro: Ed. Espaço e Tempo, 1986, pp. 24–25.
14. Ibid., p. 27.
15. James F. Petras, *Clase, Estado y poder en el Tercer Mundo. Casos de conflicto de clase en América Latina.* Mexico: FCE, 1986, p. 57.
16. Holly Sklar, ed., *Trilateralism: The Trilateral Commission and Elite Planning for World Management.* Montreal: Black Rose Book, 1981, pp. 27–231.
17. See Luis Maira, "The Interamerican System at the Crossroads." *América Latina Internacional*, FLACSO, Santiago, July–September 1984.
18. See Dreifuss, *A internacional capitalista*, p. 112.
19. Ibid., p. 46.
20. Orlando Fals Borda, "The New Awakening of Social Movements." *Brecha*, Montevideo, 8 January 1988.
21. See the communication from the Revolutionary Democratic Front and the Farabundo Martí National Liberation Front (FDR–FMLN) to the people of El Salvador, to the people of Central America, and to international public opinion, El Salvador, Central America, December 1986.

Bibliography

Latin America

Cardoso, Fernando Henrique, *Estado y sociedad en América Latina*. Buenos Aires, Argentina: Nueva Visión, 1972.

Cardoso, Fernando Henrique, and Enzo Faletto. "Estado y procesos políticos en América Latina." *Revista Mexicana de Sociología* 39(2) (Mexico, April–June 1977): 357–387.

De Souza, Hebert José. *O capital transnacional e o Estado*. Petrópolis, Brazil: Vózes, 1985.

Díaz de Arce, Omar. "El proceso de formación de los estados nacionales en América Latina." *Santiago*, no. 37 (Santiago, Cuba, March 1980): 9–80.

Drake, Paul W., and Eduardo Silva, eds. *Elections and Democratization in Latin America*. San Diego, USA: University of San Diego, 1986.

Dreifuss, René Armand. *A international capitalista. Estratégia e táticas do empresariado transnacional (1918–1986)*. Rio de Janeiro, Brazil: Espaço e Tempo, 1986.

Dussel, Enrique, Luis Maira, Miguel Concha, and Theotonio Dos Santos. *Iglesia y Estado en América Latina*. Mexico: CTR, 1979.

Fundación Pablo Iglesias. *Caminos de la democracia en América Latina*. Madrid, Spain: Pablo Iglesias, 1984.

Garreton, Manuel A. *Dictaduras y democratización*. Santiago, Chile: Latin American Faculty of Social Sciences (FLACSO), 1984.

González Casanova, Pablo. "Los clásicos latinoamericanos y la sociología del desarrollo." In: Pablo González Casanova et al. *Sociología del desarrollo. (Una guía para su estudio)*. Mexico: IIS-UNAM, 1970, pp. 7–37.

———, ed. *El Estado en América Latina*. Mexico: Siglo XXI-UNU, 1990 (with articles by Pablo González Casanova, Octavio Ianni, Jorge Graciarena, Marcos

Kaplan, Luis Maira, Gustavo Ernesto Emmerich, Samuel Lichtensztejn, Adolfo Gilly, Jorge Emilio Landinelli and Selva López Chirico, Vania Bambirra, Omar Díaz de Arce, Hugo Zemelman, Cayetano Llobet Tabolara, Julio Cotler, Enrique Ayala M. and Rafael Quintero L., Heinz R. Sonntag, Fernando Rojas H., Guillermo Castro Herrera and Ricaurte Soler, Ricardo Córdova Macías and Raúl Benítez Manaut, Arnaldo Córdova, Haroldo Dilla Alfonso and Alberto Alvarez García, Gérard Pierre-Charles).

Graciarena, Jorge. "Las ciencias sociales, la crítica intelectual y el Estado tecnocrático. Aporte para una discusión del caso latinoamericano." In: Aldo Solari, ed. *Poder y desarrollo. América Latina. Estudios sociológicos en honor a José Medina Echavarría.* Mexico: FCE, 1977.

Ianni, Octavio. *La formación del Estado populista en América Latina.* Mexico: Era, 1975.

Kaplan, Marcos. *Estado y sociedad en América Latina.* Mexico: Oasis, 1984.

Lechner, Norbert, ed. *Estado y política en América Latina.* Mexico: Siglo XXI, 1981.

Marini, Ruy Mauro. "La sociología política." In: Pablo González Casanova, et al. *Sociología del desarrollo (Una guía para su estudio).* Mexico: IIS–UNAM, 1970, pp. 158–188.

O'Donnell, Guillermo. "Reflexiones sobre las tendencias de cambio del Estado burocrático-autoritario." *Revista Mexicana de Sociología* 39(1) (Mexico, January–March 1977): 9–59.

———. "Apuntes para una teoría del Estado." *Revista Mexicana de Sociología* 40(4) (Mexico, October–December 1978): 1157–1199.

Oszlak, Oscar. "The Historical Formation of the State in Latin America: Some Theoretical and Methodological Guidelines for its Study." *Latin American Research Review* 16(2) (Austin, 1981): 3–32.

———. "Estado y políticas estatales en América Latina: Hacia una estrategia de investigación." *Administración y Desarrollo*, no. 19 (Bogotá, December 1981): 1–33.

Petras, James F. *Clase, Estado y poder en el Tercer Mundo. Casos de conflicto de clase en América Latina.* Mexico: FCE, 1986.

Rouquié, Alain. *El Estado militar en América Latina.* Mexico: Siglo XXI, 1984.

Stavenhagen, Rodolfo. "Los movimientos étnicos y el Estado nacional en América Latina." *Desarrollo Indoamericano*, no. 81, year 18 (Barranquilla, 1984): 19–26.

Varas, Augusto. *Estado y fuerzas armadas en América Latina, economía y política de la militarización y el armamentismo.* Santiago, Chile: Latin American Faculty of Social Sciences (FLACSO), 1982.

Zavaleta Mercado, René. *El poder dual. Problemas de la teoría del Estado en América Latina.* Mexico: Siglo XXI, 1974.

———. "Elementos para el análisis del Estado en América Latina." *Tareas*, no. 56 (Panama, February–December 1983).

Central America

Torres Rivas, Edelberto. "Poder nacional y sociedad dependiente: las clases y el Estado en Centroamérica." *Estudios Sociales Centroamericanos* 3(8) (San José, Costa Rica, May–August 1974): 27–63.

———. *Centroamérica: la democracia posible.* San José, Costa Rica: FLACSO–EDUCA, 1987.

Pablo González Casanova

South America – Southern Cone

Cotler, Julio. "State and Regime: Comparative Notes on the Southern Cone and the 'Enclave' Societies." In: D. Collier, ed. *The New Authoritarianism in Latin America*. Princeton, NJ, USA: Princeton University Press, 1979, pp. 225–282.
Tapia Valdés, Jorge. *El terrorismo de Estado. La doctrina de seguridad nacional en el Cono Sur*. Mexico: Nueva Imágen, 1980.

Caribbean

Pierre-Charles, Gérard. *El Caribe Contemporáneo*. Mexico: Siglo XII, 1981.

Argentina

Cantón, Darío. *Elecciones y partidos políticos en la Argentina. Historia, interpretación y balance: 1910–1966*. Buenos Aires, Argentina, and Mexico: Siglo XXI Argentina, 1973.
O'Donnell, Guillermo. *El Estado burocrático autoritario: triunfos, derrotas y crisis, 1966–1973*. Buenos Aires, Argentina: De Belgrano, 1982.
Oszlak, Oscar. *La formación del Estado argentino*. Buenos Aires, Argentina: De Belgrano, 1982.
Rouquié, Alain. *Poder militar y sociedad política en la Argentina*. Buenos Aires, Argentina: Emecé, vol. 1, 1981, vol. 2, 1982.
Sábato, Hilda, and Marcelo Cavarrozzi. *Democracia, orden político y parlamento fuerte*. Buenos Aires, Argentina: Centro Editor, 1984.

Brazil

Alfonso, Carlos A., and Hebert de Souza. *O Estado o e desenvolvimento capitalista no Brasil*. Rio de Janeiro, Brazil: Paz e Terra, 1977.
Cardoso, Fernando Henrique. *O modelo político brasileiro*. São Paulo, Brazil: Ditel, 1972.
———. "Notas sobre Estado e dependencia." *Cuadernos CEBRAP*, no. 11 (São Paulo, 1973): 1–72.
———. "La cuestión del Estado en Brasil." *Revista Mexicana de Sociología* 37(3) (Mexico, July–September 1975): 603–630.
Dreifuss, René Armand. *1964: a conquista do Estado (ação política, poder e golpe de classe)*. Petrópolis, Brazil: Vózes, 1981.
Stepan, Alfred. *Brasil: los militares y la política*. Buenos Aires, Argentina: Amorrortu, 1974.
Weffort, Francisco. *O populismo na política brasileira*. Rio de Janeiro, Brazil: Paz e Terra, 1978.

Chile

Cavarrozzi, Marcelo. "El Estado oligárquico en Chile." *Historia y Sociedad*, no. 19 (Mexico, 1978): 19–48.

Frühling, Hugo, et al. *Estado y fuerzas armadas*. Santiago, Chile: Latin American Faculty of Social Sciences (FLACSO), 1982.

Garcés, Joan. *El Estado y los problemas tácticos en el gobierno de Allende*. Mexico: Siglo XXI, 1974.

Garretón, Manuel A. *Los partidos políticos en la transición y consolidación democrática en Chile*. Santiago, Chile: FLACSO, 1984.

Colombia

CEDE, *El Estado y el desarrollo*. Bogotá, Colombia: Dintel–CEDE, 1981 (Col. *Debates CEDE*, 3).

Colmenares, Germán. *Partidos políticos y clases sociales en Colombia*. Bogotá, Colombia: Comuneros, 1984.

Leal Buitrago, Francisco. *Estado y política en Colombia*. Bogotá, Colombia: Siglo XXI de Colombia, 1984.

Rojas H., Fernando. *El Estado colombiano desde los antecedentes a la dictadura de Rojas Pinilla hasta el gobierno de Betancur. 1948–1983*. Bogotá, Colombia: CINEP, 1984 (Doc. 5).

Costa Rica

Cerdas Cruz, Rodolfo. *La formación del Estado en Costa Rica*. San José, Costa Rica: EDUCA, 1967.

Vega Carballo, José Luis. *Orden y progreso*: la formación del Estado nacional en Costa Rica. San José, Costa Rica: ICAP, 1981.

———. "Costa Rica: coyunturas, clases sociales y Estado en su desarrollo reciente." In: Pablo González Casanova, ed. *América Latina*: historia de medio siglo. Vol. 2, Mexico: Siglo XXI–IIS-UNAM, 1982, pp. 1–37.

Cuba

Dilla Alfonso, Haroldo, and Alberto Alvarez García. "Teoría y práctica de la revolución cubana." In: Pablo González Casanova, ed. *El Estado en América Latina*. Mexico: Siglo XXI–UNU, 1990.

García, Domingo. *La organización estatal en Cuba*. Havana, Cuba: Ciencias Sociales, 1981.

Dominican Republic

Mariñez, Pablo. "Crisis económica y pérdida de hegemonía del partido político en el poder en República Dominica." Paper prepared for the project on State, Civil Society and Crisis in Latin America, PAL–UNU, 1986.

———. "Movimientos sociales y cambio institucional en la República Dominicana (1982–1987)." Paper prepared for the project on Political Processes and Institutional Change in Latin America, PAL–UNU, 1987.

Pablo González Casanova

Ecuador

Ayala M., Enrique, and Rafael Quintero L. "Teorías e ideologías sobre el Estado en
el Ecuador: 1948–1984." In: Pablo González Casanova, ed. *El Estado en América
Latina*. Mexico: Siglo XXI–UNU, 1990.
Dávila Aldas, Francisco R. *Las luchas por la hegemonía y la consoldación política de
la burguesía en el Ecuador (1972–1978)*. Mexico: FCPS, UNAM, 1984 (Estudios
69).

El Salvador

Trujillo, H. "La formación del Estado en El Salvador." *Estudios Sociales Centroamericanos*, no. 28, 10 (San José, Costa Rica, January–April 1981): 117–131.

Guatemala

Aguilera Peralta, G. "Guatemala: el Estado, la lucha de clases y la violencia." *Re-
vista Mexicana de Sociología* 42(2) (Mexico, April–June 1980): 525–558.
———. "Cuestión étnica y Estado militar en Guatemala." *Boletín de Antropología
Americana*, no. 4 (Mexico, December 1981): 139–160.

Haiti

Castor, Suzy. "Democratización y autocracia: la experiencia haitiana, 1975–1985."
Paper prepared for the project on Emergent Democracy in the Caribbean, PAL–
UNU, 1986.
Pierre-Charles, Gérard. *Haití, radiografía de una dictadura*. Mexico: Siglo XXI,
1969.

Honduras

Molina Chocano, Guillermo. "La formación del Estado y el origen minero–mercantil
de la burguesía hondureña." *Estudios Sociales Centroamericanos*, no. 25, 9 (San
José, Costa Rica, January–April 1980): 55–89.
Murga Frassinetti, A. "Estado y burguesía industrial en Honduras." *Revista Mexicana de Sociología* 39(2) (Mexico, April–June 1977): 595–609.

Mexico

Alonso, Jorge, ed. *El Estado mexicano*. Mexico: Nueva Imágen–CIESAS, 1982.
Carpizo, Jorge, *El presidencialismo mexicano*. Mexico: Siglo XXI, 1978.
Fernández Christlieb, Paulina, and Octavio Rodríguez Araujo. *Elecciones y partidos
en México*. Mexico: El Caballito, 1986.
Garrido, Luis Javier. *El partido de la revolución institucionalista. La formación del
nuevo Estado en México*. Mexico: Siglo XXI, 1972.

124

González Casanova, Pablo. *El Estado y los partidos politicos en México.* Mexico: Era, 1981.

———, ed. *Las elecciones en México*: *evolución y perspectivas.* Mexico: Siglo XXI–IIS-UNAM, 1985.

Meyer, Lorenzo. "El Estado mexicano contemporáneo." *Historia Mexicana* 23(4) (Mexico, April–June 1974): 722–752.

Nicaragua

Coraggio, José Luis. *Nicaragua, revolución y democracia.* Mexico: Línea–CRIES, 1985.

Torres-Rivas, Edelberto. "El Estado contra la sociedad: las raíces de la revolución sandinista." *Estudios Sociales Centroamericanos*, no. 27, 9 (San José, Costa Rica, September–December 1980): 79–96.

Vilas, Carlos M. "Las contradicciones de la transición, clases, nación y Estado en Nicaragua." *Estudios Sociales Centroamericanos*, no. 31, 11 (San José, Costa Rica, January–April 1982): 95–114.

Wheelock Román, Jaime. "Vanguardia, hegemonía popular y unidad nacional: tres fundamentos de la victoria y la reconstrucción." *Estudios Sociales Centroamericanos*, no. 27, 9 (San José, Costa Rica, September–December 1980): 13–21.

Panama

Calderón Artieda, C., and E. Méndez Robles. "Formación del 'Estado' panameño." *Estudios Sociales Centroamericanos*, no. 18, 6 (San José, Costa Rica, September–December 1977): 65–74.

Castro Herrera, Guillermo, and Ricaurte Soler. "Panamá: del Estado torrijista a la restauración oligárquica." In: Pablo González Casanova, ed. *El Estado en América Latina.* Mexico: Siglo XXI–UNU, 1990.

Sossa, José A. *Imperialismo, fuerzas armadas y partidos políticos en Panamá.* Panama: Instituto de Estudios Comunitarios, 1977.

Paraguay

Diaz de Arce, Omar. "Teorías e ideologías sobre el Estado en el Paraguay de Alfredo Stroessner." In: Pablo González Casanova, ed. *El Estado en América Latina.* Mexico: Siglo XXI–UNU, 1990.

Lara Castro, Jorge. "Paraguay. Crisis de la dictadura: el límite de la desorganización social." Paper prepared for the project on State, Civil Society and Crisis in Latin America, PAL–UNU, 1986.

———. "Paraguay: la transición incierta." In: José Luis Reyna and Lorenzo Meyer, eds. *Sistemas y partidos políticos en América Latina.* Mexico: Siglo XXI, in press.

Peru

Cotler, Julio. *Democracia e integración nacional.* Lima, Peru: Instituto de Estudios Peruanos, 1980.

———. *Clases, Estado y nación en el Perú*. Mexico: UNAM, 1982.

López J., Sinesio. "El Estado oligárquico en el Perú: un ensayo de interpretación general." *Revista Mexicana de Sociología* 40(3) (Mexico, July–September 1978): 991–1007.

Quijano, Aníbal. *Imperialismo, clases sociales y Estado en el Perú, 1890–1930*. Lima, Peru: Mosca Azul, 1978.

Stepan, Alfred. *The State and Society, Peru in Comparative Perspective*. Princeton, NJ, USA: Princeton University Press, 1978.

Puerto Rico

Bayron Toro, Fernando. *Elecciones y partidos políticos de Puerto Rico*. 3rd edn, revised and enlarged, Mayagüez: Isla, 1984.

González Díaz, Emilio. "El Estado y las clases dominantes en la situación colonial." *Revista Mexicana de Sociología* 40(3) Mexico, July–September 1978): 1141–1152.

Maltos Citrón, Wilfredo. *La política y lo político en Puerto Rico*. Mexico: Era, 1980.

Quinteró Rivera, Angel. "La dominación imperialista del Estado en Puerto Rico y la política obrera." *Revista Mexicana de Sociología* 40(3) (Mexico, July–September 1978): 1110–1130.

Uruguay

Franco, Rolando, "Uruguay: surgimiento, auge y caída del 'welfare state'." *Centro Sociale*, no. 23 (Rome, Italy, Autumn 1976): 65–86.

Minello, Nelson. *Militarización del Estado en América Latina. Un análisis del Uruguay*. Mexico: El Colegio de Mexico, 1976 (*Cuadernos del CES*, 17).

Real de Azúa, Carlos, "Política, poder y partidos en el Uruguay de hoy." In: Luis Benvenuto et al. *Uruguay, hoy*. Buenos Aires, Argentina: Siglo XXI Argentina, 1971.

Venezuela

Gómez Calcaño, Luis. "Estado y clases sociales en Venezuela." In: Juan Enrique Vega, ed. *Teoría y política en América Latina*. Mexico: CIDE, 1983.

Silva Michelena, José Agustín. *Cambio político en Venezuela: crisis de la democracia*. Caracas, Venezuela: Universidad Central de Venezuela, 1970.

Sonntag, Heinz R. "Venezuela: el desarrollo del Estado capitalista y de su concepción teórica." In: Pablo González Casanova, ed. *El Estado en América Latina*. Mexico: Siglo XXI–UNU, 1990.

3

Popular movements

Daniel Camacho

In Huehuetenango, Cunén, Quiché and Zolalá we kidnapped the leaders, the Indians, we raped their women and beat their children; I only beat them, I did not kill, but if I hit them it was because I had to obey orders. . . My job consisted of robbing people, taking them out of their houses, using the protection of the night and our weapons. We were disguised, we were dressed as civilians.

> (Ricardo Fuentes' statement to the newspaper *La Jornada*, Monday, 24 August 1987, p. 22. Fuentes is an ex-member of the Guatemalan ambulatory military police)

Two years ago some leaders and I began to change our opinions, to develop a single idea, a single action, which would allow us to confront and fight the abuse and exploitation we were suffering. It is from then on that the necessity to become one, to create a large organization was born.

> (Alberto Andrago, indigenous peasant from Cotacachí, Ecuador)

I. Popular movements: A single multiple and varied process

The presence of the multiple and varied phenomenon known by the generic name of "social movements" is intense throughout Latin America. Within this category one can include processes as varied as the struggle of the inhabitants of a *barrio* in Caracas trying to prevent the removal of a tree, or the decision of Guatemalan ethnic groups to rise up in arms to defend their millenarian culture, or the convergence of tens of thousands of students on Mexico City to remove existing obstacles to admission and culmination of university studies, or the accusing presence in the Plaza de Mayo (May Square) of Buenos Aires of grandmothers and mothers distressed by the dis-

127

appearances of their sons and grandsons, or the metamorphosis of religious contemplation into social and political practice as a new way of exercising love for one's fellow man in important Christian sectors, or the formation of political organizations that, having tried all other possible means of bringing about transformations within society, as has been the case throughout the turbulent history of El Salvador, finally decided to attempt to bring about this change by force.

Only a brief description of these and many other processes that can be included in this category will make clear the diversity of subjects, historical situation, objectives, forms of organization and leadership, political conceptions, and self-definitions and projects that exist within social movements. What then allows us to consider them as a single phenomenon?

In the first place, its popular character. There are social movements that are not popular but, on the contrary, belong to hegemonic groups such as managerial chambers and associations. Those sectors of society that share conditions of exploitation and domination are "popular."[1] The object of study of this work are the popular movements because within them can be found a utopia of a new society, a point of obvious interest for a reflection on Latin American perspectives.

(In Latin America there exist social movements that lack the character of popular. They are those that bring together influential business and commercial men, landowners, financiers, and industrialists. In general, these movements are not oriented to globally transforming a form of society that benefits them; rather they search only for partial adjustments.)

It is true that popular movements are sometimes reduced to defending specific interests of society's sectors. These interests can be the corresponding sector's own interests, as is the case in the peasant movement, whose principal objective is the specific recovery of land, credit, and ploughing and tilling tools. But they can also refer to assumed interests, as is the case in the religious popular movement, whose motivation is more the defence of general interests than that of the specific interests of its members.

Another common and generally present trait in the diversity of popular movements is the fact that they are to be found at the margins of the state in Latin American civilian society, and often struggling against it.

As expressions of civilian society, social movements act in a clearly distinct dimension of political society. They are not part of the state's apparatus. Nevertheless, they propose state transformations that can be partial or full. The transformations are partial when the movement seeks the adoption or modification of a policy that refers to a concrete point. This is the case of the environmental movement, which attempts to modify policies having to do with nature's exploitation. The transformations are full when the movements unify their struggles, generate a shared project of transformation of society, and constitute themselves in movements representing the entire population. This occurred in Nicaragua in 1979 and is happening today in El Salvador. It also happened in Bolivia in 1952, in Mexico in 1910, in Cuba in 1959, in Granada in 1979, and for some in Peru in 1972. Diverse threads were drawn together into a single movement, a situation that has led it to be called a "Popular Movement" (singular and with capital letters; Pease and Ballón, 1982).

Social movements can work together, in a step following the conditions of political movements, and can even generate a political military movement, such as the Sandinista National Liberation Front (FSLN) in Nicaragua, or the Farabundo Martí National Liberation Front–Revolutionary Democratic Front (FMLN–FDR) in El Salvador. Nevertheless, each one of the social movements that generates this popular movement – transformed into a political or political–military movement – continues to maintain its position as a civilian movement, that is to say, continues to pertain to the environment of civilian society. In the two cases mentioned above, even when the FSLN and the FMLN–FDR were brought about by worker, peasant, student, feminist, or other movements, the latter continued to exist as they were. That is to say, they do not dissolve in the political front; they even generate and feed it. Even in the case of the assumption of power by such a political–military movement, the popular movements remain within the environment of civil society. In Cuba, for example, the student movement constituted one of the generating and sustaining bases of the July 26 Movement.

When the movement came to power, the student movement reconstituted itself and remained in civil society, with coinciding but different objectives from the state's. In the same way, feminist, worker, peasant, and other movements continue to exist and even become stronger. Even when the new state has a popular character, the popular movements continue to fulfil important functions, including that of making sure that in state decision-making processes the interests of the sector they represent are taken into consideration. Of course, the popular movement's functions are not limited to this: they also assume objectives that are proper to civilian society, such as personal self-improvement of its members, and its representation in dialogues or disputes with other actors in civilian society, etc.

Another constant feature, as much in popular movements as in those that, in a broader sense, we have called social movements, is social classes. In today's world, the confrontation between classes acquires complex, varied, and subtle characteristics. Anyone who thinks they see, in today's Latin America, a clear confrontation between bourgeoisie and working class everywhere is as wrong as someone who does not see it anywhere. The bourgeoisie, local as well as international, is in a permanent process of formation, transformation, and diversification. In this process, which has as its objective the search for new and more efficient mechanisms of accumulation, the bourgeoisie runs over, directly or indirectly, whichever social sector happens to oppose it. Facts are apparently far removed from this process. The knocking down of trees in a neighbourhood has to do with how the drive to accumulate imposes itself upon man's relation with nature: if the value of urban land goes up, the presence of trees and green areas obstructs landowners' accumulation. In Latin America, the killing and extermination of indigenous peoples, double workdays for women, restrictions on university matriculation, violation of human rights, inflation, industrial unemployment, and other similar phenomena, are the roots of the struggles of social movements, and are the product of capital accumulation processes among various factions of the bourgeoisie. From that point of view, if one wants to understand social movements, one has to focus directly upon their relation to classes and class struggles.

Another common trait of social movements must now be emphasized: the difference between them and the organizations they themselves generate. In the first place, a movement does not always generate a structure or an organization, and, when it does, it does not fuse with it. The organization is an intercession that may or may not help in the attainment of the movement's objectives. In fact, it has been said of some organizations that they obstruct the movement's objectives. This is true of certain unions accused of acting against the workers' movement. On the other hand, some social movements fluctuate between moments of sophisticated organization and others in which structure almost does not exist, *without* this causing the movement to lose its force.

To sum up, what characterizes social movements in Latin America is their location in civil society, where they constitute a dynamic process (not always structured) in defence of specific interests of sectors of society; social movements are tightly linked with classes and class struggle. When the movements belong to exploited and dominated sectors, they have a popular character and the possibility of generating a single Popular Movement or movement of the whole people, whose objective can be the taking of power. Even in the case of a constituted Popular Movement, with or without a takeover of power, particular popular movements maintain their status as acting upon civil society and, even though they generate and sustain the Popular Movement, they do not dissolve in it, or in the political movement or in the political–military movement.

On the other hand, popular movements represent a new phenomenon in today's Latin America. Their very presence is new; in the past the social protagonists were other forces. In fact, even while the reins of state power and of social control in civil society are held, in the final analysis, by hegemonic groups, it is true that popular movements are opening up more space for themselves, their presence is growing, and their points of view are less ignored. In Argentina, some women, armed only with a great deal of love and courage, and gigantic photos of their vanished sons and grandsons, formed themselves into a determining factor in the fall of one of the most inhumane and perfidious military regimes ever known. Less dramatically, the influence of urban settlers, of women, of the young, and of priests who have chosen the popular option is growing, as is that of ethnic groups and other sectors of society organized into popular movements. This protagonism produces the conditions necessary for a new phenomenon.

The content, the orientations, and the practices of their struggles are new in themselves; as are their at times surprising forms of organization and their new forms of leadership. The new character ascribed here to popular movements has little to do with their antiquity. The ethnic movement is possibly the oldest, since it began with the arrival of the Spanish conquerors. Nevertheless, the phenomenon we are looking at is new according to the above-mentioned criteria. In the same way, movements with traditions and history, such as worker and peasant ones, occasionally present new characteristics in their content, orientations, and forms of struggle.

Nevertheless, the new character attributed to social movements should not lead to confusion. Often the "new " has been emphasized to diminish the class dimension of these movements, when in fact the new forms acquired by social movements are an expression of class struggle. On the other hand, it is appropriate to repeat here what was said above: they are called new because they present new characteristics, even when we are dealing with very ancient movements, some going back to the colonial times, as is the case with municipal or local governmental, regional ethnic, religious or other movements. These characteristics are deduced from the careful observation of the history of various social movements and, more specifically, of popular movements.

According to what was said earlier, an adequate way to look at the reality of these movements in more depth is to consider their battlefields, and their statements and perspectives on the future. This is what will be attempted in the following pages, where we have chosen to look at two types of movement in depth: an ancient but revived one, the indigenous movement, will be analysed in section II, and a newer one, the result of a modern phenomenon called urbanization, the popular urban movement, will be discussed in section III. With the analysis of both we hope to synthesize essential aspects that can be generalized about social movements in Latin America, and about movements that bring together groups clearly located in popular sectors. Later on we will look at another type of phenomenon, that of movements that, despite being identified with popular struggles, consist of individuals from very diverse social classes, even from nonpopular ones. We are referring here to religious popular movements, and in particular one led by a woman, to which we will dedicate section IV. We will briefly discuss the workers' movement in section V. In section VI we will comment on what was mentioned earlier under the name of movements of the whole people. In this way, although we will not deal with all the existing movements, we will achieve a global review of the phenomenon at hand. Finally, section VII will offer a brief methodological conclusion.

II. The original and constantly revived grouping: The indigenous movement

In Latin America, from the beginning of republican life or, coincidentally, from the beginning of capitalism, a contradiction occurred between the form of indigenous social organization, based on joint property (which survives in spite of three centuries of Spanish domination), and the needs of capitalist accumulation, which are to convert the land into a commercial item, to extend the areas of large agricultural exploitation, and to ensure that the flow of free proletarians from the country would increase (Marx, 1965, p. 581). Capitalism's development demands, on the one hand, a free labour force that can be readily hired by nascent capitalist enterprises, and, on the other, the production of a surplus labour force freed from its obligation to the land in order to keep its costs low and to dispose of reserves for its expansion. In addition, capitalism demands the control of growing quantities of land to incorporate them into the system of capitalist exploitation. The capitalist control of the land presupposes that it be subject to free buying and selling, that is to say, that land be incorporated into the market like any other commodity.

To satisfy these requirements, even when the commercial exploitation of many indigenous communities occurs, capitalism tends to expel indigenous populations from communal lands. This permits it on the one hand to put them in a position where they are free to be hired as salaried workers and increase the reserve labour force, and, on the other, to free their lands for entry to the capitalist circuit.

This whole process is known as original capital accumulation. The qualifier "original" comes from the fact that it occurs during the first stage of capitalist development, and that, sometimes, it precedes it. Nevertheless, it does not happen only during this historical stage, but can repeat itself in the following stages. In fact, when, in some isolated and unknown corner, possibilities of economic exploitation that interest capital are discovered, capital comes on the scene with an irresistible force, taking land over and expelling its inhabitants, be they communally organized indigenous populations or peasant owners of individual plots. This phenomenon has occurred and keeps occurring throughout the republican history of Latin America and even now, in this day and age. It is the key to understanding the subjugation of the ethnic indigenous populations, the reasons for their struggles, and the development of the ethnic movement.

A clear example of how the process of original accumulation repeats itself is happening today in Chile where, on 28 March 1979, the decree law 2568 was proclaimed. This privatized land that had until then been communally owned. The justification of the law was that communal ownership was a source of economic and social stagnation. This decree law "not only absorbs Mapuche property into the cultural precepts of accumulation, but also obliterates their ethnic identity by concretely specifying that the small rural estates resulting from the division of the reserves would no longer be considered indigenous land, nor indigenous their owners or the persons who received it" (Vives, 1984, pp. 30–33).

The episodes of expulsion and even manhunting of indigenous communities, which occurred recently in the Amazon of Brazil, by capitalist companies interested in their rich lands are well known. This has occurred in Ecuador too, to occupy petroleum-rich lands. The mollifying work of the Summer Language Institute before the interventions was denounced by indigenous congresses and seminaries. The institute, under the pretext of teaching Spanish, devotes itself to the destruction of indigenous culture.

In short, capitalism's advance represents, for the indigenous population, the theft of their land and the destruction of their culture. The collectivist traits of their culture are being destroyed by the force of capitalism, a force that they find irresistible and that throws them individually into the workforce. At the same time many other processes inherent to the advance of capitalism reinforce this destructive tendency for the cultures of these ethnic groups. It is understandable that the common trait of the various ethnic movements existing in Latin America is the defence of the land and the culture.

Mentioning culture, we introduce an element of the analysis that goes beyond the purely economic. To pinpoint the origin of the indigenous movement just in the original accumulation process would limit us to a narrowly economic view, and, for the same reason, a very poor one from the analytic point of view. There exist many other processes that are more or less closely related, or even not related at all, to the economic process of original accumulation, and that have a direct influence on the discrimination against the indigenous people and on their response in the form of social movements. The analysis of indigenous ethnic movements in Guatemala, Mexico, Ecuador, and Chile will shed some light on these hypotheses.

In the entire area of the Americas subdued by the Spaniards, by the end of the colonial period and with the arrival of independence and neocolonialism, economic and social relations as well as the indigenous culture as it had existed originally had undergone substantial changes. The Spanish conquerors imposed their religion, their customs, and a social organization based on slavery by force. In the face of this, and accompanied by numerous rebellions, the indigenous population resisted the loss of basic aspects of their culture by creating a culture of resistance that still exists today. They introduced, sometimes secretly, syncretism in religion, native motifs in Spanish-style clothing, movements with secret meanings in Spanish-imposed dances, a hierarchy different from the one recognized by the Spaniards, etc. (see Arias, 1985). As a consequence, indigenous culture at the time of independence was not the one the Spaniards had discovered three centuries earlier. Nevertheless, some traits are jealously protected by the indigenous population, and the maintenance of their own identity depends on the protection of these traits. Among them one may emphasize the collective property of the land and the strongly community-oriented social organizations, two elements that are, for the reasons mentioned above, under direct attack from capitalist development's needs.

In El Salvador, for example (Menjívar, 1981, p. 85), the establishment of large *haciendas* by the emergent bourgeoisie meant the plundering of indigenous communal lands owned by the indigenous community. This trend took on gigantic proportions during the last third of the nineteenth century, a time when many indigenous peoples and peasants were forced off their land. Through these kinds of manoeuvres, land and workforces are incorporated into the capitalist sector of the economy. This sector is not able to absorb the entire workforce that is thereby made available, nor is it convenient for capitalist economies to do so because they prefer to keep labour costs at devalued prices. As a result, large numbers of indigenous peasants are left unemployed or in informal and geographically displaced situations. Social pressure of this nature results in thousands of people losing their land and being thrown into poverty. This in turn provokes a fear of class in the sectors of the bourgoisie in formation, and in the already existing oligarchy, which has no alternative but to establish an intensely repressive state that does not seek to reach a consensus or want to negotiate, but merely dominates through sheer force. In general terms, tension, the expulsion of the indigenous population from their land, and the destruction of their culture on the one hand, and the formation of a highly repressive state on the other, the latter generated by the dominant classes' fear, explains to a large degree the uprising and massacre of 30,000 indigenous peasants in 1932 in El Salvador and the civil war that still batters the country today.

The process is similar in Guatemala, where the situation of the indigenous peasants worsened with the liberal reforms of 1871. The entrance of Guatemala into the world market as an agricultural exporter and the process of taking over large portions of land form the basis for the plundering of "the villages of Indians" and of their communal lands, obliging the inhabitants to come down from their large haciendas on the Pacific coast as a cheap workforce (Arias, 1985, p. 68).

The same phenomenon can be identified in Chile where, independence once established, the republican aristocracy needed to control the Mapuches in fixed places of residence, because "while they did not recognize a fixed domicile and acquire property habits (Decree of 7 September 1848), it was impossible to free the land for the benefit of the settlers of the new territory, or to free a workforce for agricultural labour on these lands" (Vives, 1984, p. 26).

In Colombia, "the principal forms of the destruction of the indigenous population" have been the plundering of their land and the imposition of a culture alien to their realities, cut off from their productive and social forms (Suárez, n.d., p. 35).

In addition, as the capitalist production mode increases its reach and changes its form, the indigenous culture suffers corresponding transformations, which acquire characteristics that vary according to time and place. Whereas in Guatemala the binding factor in the struggle of the indigenous population is the ethnic problem, in Mexico it is a community movement (Mejía and Sarmiento, 1987, p. 24). But, within this generalization, what is common to the indigenous movement throughout Latin America is its struggle for land and a culture, the latter having, in addition to its economic importance, an existential meaning of cultural reproduction for the indigenous population. It is not possible to mention here (for lack of space) the numerous battles for land and culture waged on a daily basis by the indigenous population of Latin America. Just as an illustration, we might mention here the persistence of these struggles in Mexico, where, and precisely for the reasons mentioned above, the indigenous movement has identified with the peasant movement (León and Marván, n.d., p. 28).

In Mexico, the declarations and objectives of peasant and indigenous congresses name the land as one of their principal concerns. An important aspect of their representation is the National Coordination Ayala Plan congresses, from which demands for land appear repeatedly as a central point, and especially the Fifth Congress, held in the Tzotzil community of Venustiano Carranza in Chiapas in 1982. Its Declaration of Principles emphasizes the struggle to "recover the poor peasantry's land, to abolish latifundiums, to rescue the natural resources that historically belong to the communities, to organize production and commercialization of the countryside collectively and independently, to rescue, preserve, defend and develop the cultural manifestations of ethnic groups, and to achieve the full recognition of peasant women's rights" (Mejía and Sarmiento, 1987, p. 82). On the whole, the declarations and aims of the majority of indigenous organizations in Mexico share this tone, where, according to Mejía and Sarmiento (pp. 221ff), the indigenous movement's demands, which are primarily of an ethnic, cultural character, do not stop there but rather obey many other motivations. Furthermore, these authors find that the development of ethnic consciousness is driven by the very struggles of the peasant group. This shows, once again, the impossibility of separating land and culture in the indigenous movement.

On the basis of this type of struggle, Mexican indigenous organizations seek an alliance with other popular sectors, and, though horizontally, they establish relations with political parties that are critical of the ruling social system.

Something similar is happening in Chile, where the Mapuches, in spite of the repressive character of the dictatorship, are reviving their struggle to keep their land and communal customs in the face of the law decree 2568 mentioned previously (Vives, 1984, p. 33).

In Ecuador (Chiriboga, n.d., p. 14) at the end of the 1970s, the organization of the indigenous populations was begun in many cases in close alliance with peasant organizations. Together with the recovery of their lands and the struggle against exploitation, which becomes concrete at the moment their products are taken to the market and their labour sold as a cheap commodity, the movement promotes itself through the need to confront the oppression they feel because of their very condition as the indigenous population (Chiriboga, n.d., p. 18). That is to say, one is also dealing with a cultural revival. This is confirmed by the indigenous population's own vision; for them, poverty allows them to remain indigenous. With enough land they could rise to an economic and social lifestyle that would help them to keep their culture (Chiriboga, n.d., p. 19).

In Colombia (Suárez, n.d., p. 23) the ethnic populations were wiped out by imposing on them a type of education alien to their forms of social and productive organization. A foreign language and a foreign religion broke their thought system. But the most profound imposition has been the plundering of their lands, since these are not only the source of their livelihood but also what gives sense to their community. According to the 1980 Number 89 Law and other indigenous rights legislation, the land they occupy belongs to them, but, in practice, this right has been violated by landowners, settlers, and state or private enterprises that exploit natural resources. Today, there exist only a few havens and reserves that correspond in quality and size to the needs of the indigenous population (Suárez, n.d., p. 35).

All that has been said so far has set the scene for the development of an increasingly strong contemporary indigenous movement. In Colombia, the whole of the indigenous movement, allied with the lowest levels of the peasantry, has made the recovery of their land the most influential factor in the unification of their forces (Suárez, n.d., p. 37). In Ecuador, the Cotacachí Federation of Communes is only one example of the advance of the indigenous population's struggle and of the struggle for land and culture (Chiriboga, n.d., p. 18). In Chile, the promulgation of decree law 2568 has triggered the fierce struggle of the Mapuches against a dictatorship that wants to destroy them as a people (Vives, 1984, p. 14). In Mexico, the indigenous population successively confronts local, regional, and national power, seeking the unity of their organizations and fighting battles, which are sometimes bloody, for their land and their culture (Mejía and Sarmiento, 1987, p. 226).

Two very important circumstances appear in the development of ethnic struggles. In the first place, indigenous intellectuals play a role in the activity of the struggles. Individuals promoting literacy in Guatemala and in Ecuador, teachers in Guatemala and Mexico, Mapuche cultural centres in Chile, and unionist cadres in Colombia all stand out as elucidating elements of indigenous struggle and history and often as organizing elements of the struggles.

In the second place, it is inevitable that we come to Mejía and Sarmiento's observation (1987, p. 230) that the struggle of the indigenous populations and the clarity with which they perceive the reasons that the system keeps them in certain conditions do not necessarily occur in direct relation to the degree of penetration and consolidation of the dominant mode of production. On the contrary, in the regions where capital penetration has been slower, or where it has adopted forms that do not necessarily destroy the traditional communitarian relations of production, or, which is the same, where capitalist organization takes advantage of these forms by maintaining them for its own ends, the degree of cohesion and strength of the movement are greater than where the situation is the opposite.

Coincidentally, the complaints of indigenous leaders from Ecuador were mentioned above. According to them, when indigenous populations do not own land, and as a result the young become absorbed in typically formal or informal capitalist occupations, they become less eager to particpate in ethnic struggles. Consequently, it is where some social relations of production proper to the millenarian indigenous society and its own cultural traits have survived that the indigenous population find more possibilities for imposing their right to their own culture.

We might illustrate this fact with the recent history of the ethnic struggle in Guatemala. In Guatemala (Arias, 1985, pp. 62–119), the indigenous population has developed in the course of centuries a sometimes active and sometimes passive resistance to the plundering of their lands, the destruction of their culture, language, and religion, the exploitation of their workforce, the forced migration to take on farming responsibilities, the forced conscription into the army ("fight for the barracks"), and the social prostration that is revealed by the fact that the indigenous sector suffers from more problems than any other sector and has the lowest indices in health, literacy, housing, school attendance, nutrition, per capita income, etc.

The earthquake on 4 February 1976 disrupted the army's lines of communication inside the country, allowing the indigenous population to develop its own autonomous organization in the Quiché. They found new leaders, they established contact between the 22 existing ethnic groups in Guatemala, and they found allies among the poor *ladino* (white) peasants of the south and among student and clerical groups. In this way the movement became stronger, at first with little structure, and extended itself slowly up to the point of forming the Committee of United Peasants (CUC) in April 1978, which succeeded in linking together for the first time all the Guatemalan ethnic groups, and in establishing an alliance with the worker and peasant movements.

The CUC's work, at first clandestine because of previous experiences of repression, then open, provoked a violent response from the army, which on 29 May 1978 occupied the indigenous village of Panzós, killing the population, assembling men, elders, and children, raping and killing women, all in a calculated demonstration of its perversity, complete with the escape of a few individuals to guarantee that their terrified reports of the incident would be known all over the country. The attack on Panzós became the model for the army's later repression of hundreds of villages in order to crush the indigenous "rebellion."

In response, the CUC organized demonstrations and increasingly extensive strikes. With the participation of almost all the ethnic groups and peasant organizations, addresses were given in the groups' own languages and with slogans carefully built around the sensitive issues presented by the basic groups: land, the defence of customs, against the "fight for the barracks," etc. The ecclesiastical communities, among others, became some of the organizing mainstays.

In this process of the constitution of the CUC, the march of the Ixtahuacán miners, who travelled 351 kilometres in search of better working conditions in November 1977, had a great impact. In their march, they crossed the indigenous area of the western high plateau. The organizations developed by indigenous populations and peasants to look after the miners on their journey, to feed them and provide lodgings, as well as to hold meetings in each village, showed the indigenous population its own great potential.

Faced with the vigour of the CUC, the army answered by occupying the area and ruthlessly repressing the indigenous population. An example of their conduct was the incident at the Spanish Embassy where the army burned alive 27 indigenous people who had taken over the building in protest against repression.

In the course of these events, a massive incorporation of the indigenous population into the guerrilla movements took place. The guerrillas' doctrine is based on the Iximché Declaration. This declaration, whose official name is "The Guatemalan Indigenous People before the World," was approved on 14 February 1980, a few days after the Spanish Embassy massacre, by representatives of all the ethnic groups, and ends thus:

May the blood of our indigenous brothers and their example of firm and brave struggle give strength to all the indigenous people to go on and attain a life of justice.

For a society of equality and respect. For our Indian people as such, that they may develop their culture, broken by the criminal intruder. For a just economy in which no one exploits anyone else. For the land, that it be common as was that of our ancestors. For a people free from discrimination, that all repression, torture, abduction, murder, and massacre end. That the "fight for the barracks" come to an end. That we may have the same rights to work, that we no longer be used as touristic objects, for the just distribution and utilization of our wealth as it was in the days of our ancestors, when their life and culture bloomed.

The document concluded with the following phrase from the Popol Vuhl, which later became a slogan: "Rise all of you, call everyone, that no one or any group among us remain behind the other" (in Arias, 1985, pp. 102 and 103). From then on began one of the most dramatic struggles that had ever taken place in Latin America, and one of the most despicable genocides ever known.

Arias notes (1985, p. 104) that it is from then on that, in effect, guerrilla and people became one. The entire population participated in the war and the partisan effort, although only those adequately armed were integrated into permanent units. Others, with less sophisticated weapons, became part of the local irregular forces, self-defence units, etc. The entire indigenous population fed the permanent partisans, provided intelligence, and fulfilled numerous other tasks, all of them indispensable.

The army's answer, advised by the American, Israeli, and Argentine governments, was brutal. Arias (1985, p. 144) describes it in this way:

[the repression] was centred on the high plateau which covers almost the whole of the western part of the country, where the great majority of the indigenous population lives. . . . [The army decided that] it was necessary to act against this population in order to cut off all supplies to the guerrillas and punish the "subversion."

This is how the most ignominious genocide ever carried out in the American continent occurred, that is to say, since the extermination of the North American Indian population during the last century.

The genocide consisted in completely razing villages and all that was produced on the lands belonging to the inhabitants of these villages. This is what is known as the policy of "land clearing." All inhabitants, or the majority of them, particularly pregnant women and children, were murdered, houses were burnt, as well as harvests and grain reserves, the inhabitants' belongings were stolen, any kind of domestic animal was slaughtered, etc. The fleeing population, and those hiding in the mountains, were captured and gathered in strategic villages, which in effect became concentration camps.

The great indigenous guerrilla mobilization was thus contained. Nevertheless, the struggle is definitely not over. In the collective memory of the indigenous society there remains the unforgettable memory of this epopee that succeeded in mobilizing the entire community, uniting it, and affirming its dignity. The indigenous peoples constitute 75 per cent of the population of Guatemala. Many of them are still armed rebels, and in the others hope has not died. They learned to form alliances with poor peasants, workers, students, and priests. For a while, they were the owners of their own society and were only stopped by napalm, widespread assassination, forced migration, arson of their houses and harvests, and the extermination of their women and children. But the indigenous movement in Guatemala is not dead. It is still alive, building new opportunities.

To resume, land and culture are both the simple and the complex demands of the indigenous movement throughout Latin America. The absorption of their members into the capitalist sector of production, the internal strife it has provoked, the prostration and the ignorance to which the indigenous population has been subjected, are all against them. On the positive side, they have a millenarian culture protected by a patient resistance and a project for the future, a utopia, which, according to some tendencies mentioned earlier, seems increasingly possible.

In spite of this encouraging medium-range future, immediate expectations seem to be dissipated by struggles, contradictions, and difficulties, but also by hopes.

As this work hopes to approach a synthesis of the entire phenomenon of social movements in Latin America, it is advisable to contrast the indigenous movement, which is older, although revived, with another movement such as the urban one, which is very contemporary, not just because it is new but also because it responds to a modern phenomenon: the development of the cities today.

III. The city as battlefield: Capital reproduction versus workforce

Another representative social movement in Latin America is the urban popular movement. Capitalist society has its very own characteristics. Within it, the eagerness for profit – the motor of accumulation – plays a very important role with respect to the construction of the urban infrastructure. A garden, a park, a historical relic, have, from the investor's point of view, a very low income yield capacity. For this reason, socially available capital for the construction of buildings, infrastructure, and communications is unevenly distributed between smart neighbourhoods and the commercial centre on the one hand, and the neighbourhoods of the masses on the other. The latter move away to areas increasingly remote from the centre of the city and less cared for by public services.

One of the ways capital guarantees the income yield capacity of its investment in urban infrastructure is by charging very high prices for it. In this way, the low-income sectors are obliged to move away. This was the reason for the struggle of the inhabitants of Fernando de

Mora in Asunción, Paraguay, who, according to Luis A. Galeano's 1986 study, were obliged to abandon their neighbourhood, not by force or expropriation, but because of the high price they had to pay for the installation of a sewage system, the paving of the streets, and hot water.

When the city of Asunción grew, the Fernando de Mora settlement ceased to be peripheral and became part of the very centre of the city, as often occurred in large Latin America metropolises. As a result, the income yield capacity of the area increased considerably. To quote Galeano (1986, p. 235), the Paraguayan press understood the fact perfectly well when it said that "when Fernando de Mora became genuinely urbanized, as a city officially included within the metropolitan urban limits, it also became the beneficiary of the privileges proper to booming large cities, and, at the same time, of its ills: the expulsion of families with limited economic resources from the central areas of the city."

After a very spirited confrontation, in which multiple alliances with other civilian groups were deployed, as well as official threats and the fall of functionaries, the contract with the company building the sewage system was rescinded. Galeano calls this a Pyrrhic victory (p. 244) because the area lost the possibility of obtaining the service as a community and the municipality kept putting pressure on the inhabitants to solve the problem individually through the use of septic tanks, whose prices were as high as those of the company would have been. In short, in spite of the success of the struggle, the inhabitants of Fernando de Mora were sooner or later obliged to move, a situation that would "increase the value" of the area from capital's point of view. This means that the capital invested in the neighbourhood can reproduce itself faster if the present inhabitants abandon the area, allowing for the construction of commercial premises and high-cost apartment buildings. In terms of the displaced inhabitants, this means that they must assume the additional burden of living far away from their work centres, shopping areas, etc. In other words, they must incur a considerable increase in the cost of the reproduction of their own lives.

Often, this extra workload is not limited to these inconveniences, but extends to the very building of a new infrastructure by the displaced inhabitants. Kowarick and Bonduki (1987, p. 45), referring to the city of São Paulo in Brazil, pointed out that "these workers resigned themselves, without considering the sacrifices, to living in distant areas, difficult to reach and practically without any urban facilities, in addition to building themselves dwellings, or contracting a bricklayer to help them during their free time, in the hope of acquiring their own house." After this, the authors cite a comment published in the *Correo Paulistano* (São Paulo Courier; No. 11, August, 1946): "A manual worker acquires a piece of land, he himself digs a well after working hours, buys bricks. . . . In a few Sundays the house is built on the cliffs of Villa Matilde, Villa Esperanza, Villa Guillermina. They are the 'Sunday houses', the ones that tremble in the gusts of wind."

Conclusions similar to those that can be inferred from the previous examples can easily be drawn. In his excellent study on urban popular movements in Mexico, Juan Manuel Ramírez Sáiz (1986) points out a few. On the basis of the analysis of this type of movement throughout Mexico, he concludes that "the objects which give origin to the struggles of the urban popular movements revolve around the issue of the consumption or reproduction of the workforce" (p. 29).

This way of focusing the urban problem leads us to a conclusion with important consequences: the problems endured by the social sectors that have been deprived of the use of the city are the products of the very logic and work needs of the urban development of Latin American cities. It is not a rectifiable marginal subproduct, but an essential and imperative part of capitalist urbanism.

Nevertheless, it is not just a matter of the generation of a reserve industrial army from the unemployed or underemployed sector. It is true that this sector is an important component of the ignored population of the cities, but it does not constitute its totality or even its majority. Ramírez Sáiz (pp. 30 and 31) mentions several studies in Mexico that indicate that, in this type of population, people with stable employment – the unionized and proletarian – predominate. In addition, it was noted that people who lacked stable employment, the lumpenproletariat, were minority groups. Consequently, even if this type of population includes an important sector of unemployed people, who would constitute the industrial reserve army, it none the less is made up of a majority of active workers. That is to say, we are not at all dealing with a type of marginalization.

The problem of housing and habitat is so central that it rapidly transcends the specifically economic sphere and locates itself within the cultural plane. It is for this reason that the urban popular movement acquires such strength. Its struggle grows to the point of embracing almost all aspects of social life. In Mexico, for example, the demands of the urban popular movement not only have to do with the right to housing and the settlement of derelict land, but also include mass urban projects that involve the defence of liberties, the democratization of daily life, and the organization of production cooperatives (Ramírez Sáiz, 1986, p. 15). The urban popular movement in Mexico has succeeded in generating its own original symbols, such as "Superbarrio," a character inspired by Superman, the mythical protagonist of the comic strip. A closer look at Superbarrio will give us a clearer idea of what the Mexican urban popular movement represents. In the first place, he is a contestant in the sport known as "wrestling." The allusion to the spirit of the fight is obvious. His opponent is Catalino Creel, a greedy landlord. But Superbarrio says that his adversaries are also the laws against tenants, and the authoritarianism of officials. He affirms that his strength comes from the union and the organization of all neighbours and that, like Samson, who weakens with the loss of his hair, what weakens Superbarrio is the lack of organization and the despair of neighbourhood residents. For Superbarrio,

the struggle for housing translates itself into a struggle for love. It is necessary to have some privacy to nourish love. Male chauvinism is a cultural phenomenon, learned and transmitted. It can and it must change. The settlers are not just fighting for housing and vouchers [vouchers issued by the government to obtain tortillas below the market price] to buy cheaper tortillas and dairy products.

From the housing problems, this character, who represents the collective feelings of the movement, goes on to the restoration of the rights of women, to the rights to nutrition, democracy, and love (*Excelsior*, 1987; *La Jornada*, 1987; *Doble Jornada*, 1987).

In Brazil (Díaz Coelho, n.d., p. 8), urban movements develop rapidly into a struggle against the high price of basic products. In fact, in 1973, in São Paulo, the mothers' club in the south of the city instigated the great movement against the high cost of living, a movement that had important political consequences.

In Rio, in 1975, the Copacabana's inhabitants embarked on a campaign "for a more humane Rio," denouncing the high levels of pollution, and, in 1976, the Alto Leblon district's inhabitants opposed, although unsuccessfully, the construction of highways, piers, and flyovers within the narrow streets of their neighbourhoods. In 1977, as the first phase of a collective project among all the Rio districts, the Popular Campaign for the Defence of Nature developed, through which the people halted a project to build nine 16-storey buildings in the area known as Copacabana Fort (Díaz Coelho, n.d., p. 11).

In Peru (Tovar, n.d., pp. 83 and 121) the urban movement organized people's kitchens. In Lima there were 625 of them in 1986. The Glass of Milk Programme imposed upon the municipalities by the urban popular movement employed 50,000 women organized in 7,500 committees. In the same city, the inhabitants organized and participated in people's libraries and health teams.

In all these struggles, there is a substratum of great importance – a struggle for dignity. In Peru, according to Teresa Tovar (n.d., p. 75), in the days of Velasco, in the urban movement,

the recognition of certain rights of the citizens went together with an anti-oligarchic discourse and the recovery of the Quechua, and of the national culture which supported the migrant, defended the dignity of the "cholo" [mestizo], and undermined authoritarianism in the face of the "invaders."

In this way, the "invader" became the "settler" and felt defended and recognized as a human being and as an inhabitant of the city and the country, with legitimate opportunities to defend his rights.

We could continue to enumerate more varied and numerous recoveries. Nevertheless, these few serve to make clear the fully comprehensive character, embracing all the dimensions of individual and social life, that the *barrios'* (neighbourhood) struggle represented: housing, clean air, recreation, love, ecology, education, relaxation, democracy, solidarity, and dignity.

In the presence of this rich and diverse community of struggle, the adversary is also varied. In general, what appears on the front line as the visible adversary is the state. Nevertheless, behind this façade, the real enemy is the sectors of society that profit from the status quo. The more immediate adversary is the owners of real estate capital, the clandestine dealers in urban land, and the owners of transport systems (Ramírez Sáiz, 1986, p. 32).

The state sometimes responds with remedial measures, as was the case in Peru in 1986 and 1987 where employment programmes, credit for traders, legal recognition of mothers' clubs, direct help, and other measures were established (Tovar, n.d., p. 93). Even so, the state often retains control of the neighbourhood organizations in order to reduce their ability to act, and even asserts the right to dissolve them, as was attempted in Ecuador during the early 1980s (Unda, n.d., p. 11). On other occasions, the state's response is clear and simple:

repression, as in the already mentioned case of the Fernando de Mora settlement in Asunción, Paraguay, where the state closed the premises of the Association of Veterans of the Chaco War, which had become the centre of the organization of the struggle. Another state response has been to infiltrate the organizations and to co-opt their leaders, as Ramírez Sáiz points out is the case in Mexico (1986, p. 24). A longer-term state response, and a more permanent one, has been the establishment of parallel organizations under state control. This happened in Costa Rica, where the Juntas Progresistas (Progressive Councils) – neighbourhood organizations with branches throughout the country – which had sprung up in great part spontaneously, were engulfed by the government's own Community Development Councils, which had originated from and were financed through the Alliance for Progress.

Through their struggles, urban movements have developed alliances with other sectors. In Mexico, the neighbourhood organizations "in the city almost automatically accompany the independent worker, peasants' and teachers' marches, increasing class consciousness in the process" (Ramírez Sáiz, 1986, p. 15). In fact, under conditions of repression, the neighbourhood associations have served as substitutes for unions. When communication between union members has been repressed in factories, this communication moves to homes, taking advantage of neighbourhood struggles. It was in this way that repression blocked communication in Brazil from 1964 on. In 1978, when the struggle for a return to democracy was going on, with all the difficulties of reorganizing the union movement, it was the neighbourhood movement that eventually achieved the greatest degree of political expression. This occurred in Rio de Janeiro and also in São Paulo, where the struggle against the high cost of living, which, as mentioned earlier, had its roots in a letter from the mothers' clubs, brought, in the midst of a dictatorship, 20,000 people onto the streets, in a demonstration that is remembered as a landmark in the struggle for democracy. In Costa Rica, after the civil war of 1948, when political and syndical organizations of revolutionary inclination were repressed, the manifestation of protest and the beginning of organization took as channels of expression the Progressive Councils.

In general, throughout the recent history of Latin America, the neighbourhood movements have repeatedly shown alliances with the workers' movement, as in Peru between 1975 and 1980 (Tovar, n.d., pp. 72 and 75), and with the women's movement, as occurred in the

147

same country, where public kitchens and "Glass of Milk Committees" became closely integrated with the neighbourhood organizations (Tovar, n.d., p. 112).

In this sense, the announcement of the appearance of "Mrs. Superneighbour" is significant. She, according to her companion "Superbarrio," "has all the power [because] those who are building the neighbourhood movements are the 'Mrs. Superneighbours' and we know that their self-confidence increases constantly" (*Doble Jornada*, 1987, p. 2).

The alliance of the neighbourhood movements with the religious popular movement is also crucial. Among the activists of the latter, we often find priests and other leaders of religious organizations.

As we speak of alliances, it is convenient to mention the relationship between the urban popular movement and political parties. It is clear that the movement's relationship with the present electoral parties, which do not propose major changes in the state, is one of distrust. Nevertheless, some parties, which propose some degree of reform and whose constituency is largely the popular sectors and based upon a discourse meant to express the feelings of the lower classes of the population, attempt to maintain some degree of control over the neighbourhood organizations. In Mexico, "the PRI (Institutional Revolutionary Party), through its multiple apparatuses . . . exercises control and power in this area since the urban movements in Mexico have become an important field of support, negotiation, or possible confrontation for the system" (Ramírez Sáiz, 1986, p. 24). The APRA (American Popular Revolutionary Alliance) in Peru pursues a strong platform meant to reflect the urban popular sector's demands. In fact, the PAIT (Programme of Support through Temporary Income) is directed at the "shanty towns," and this is not the only case.

In many cases, the support of the neighbourhoods' inhabitants for parties of this type, which have a real possibility of access to power, can be defined – according to Unda (n.d., p. 6) – by the adage "Do ut des": give so that I can give. Give me the votes, and I will give you some community building or project. This applies from the candidate for municipal alderman to aspirants to the presidency of the Republic.

In the case of parties that plan a radical change in social relations, in politics as well as in civilian society, the situation is different. This type of party is interested in the popular neighbourhood inhabitant not just for his electoral support but rather as the very base of its activism and as a fundamental determining factor, among others, of its political line. This fact does not eliminate the neighbourhood inhabitant's distrust, which in fact may increase because of the competition between various parties of this type, as was shown in Philip Oxhorn's work (n.d., pp. 15ff), according to which the unification of the neighbourhood organizations of Santiago de Chile was not possible in 1986 because of the contradictions – which turned out to be insoluble – between parties that had real influence in the various neighbourhood organizations. This demonstrates, in our view, not the weakness of the revolutionary parties in the urban popular movement, but their influence and strength, overshadowed, it is true, by the competition between them.

The urban popular movement is not exempt from internal conflicts. It is necessary to mention them to tone down the excessively idyllic picture that might have been gained from what has been said so far. Ramírez Sáiz (1986, p. 24) mentions the problem of political bosses as mediators who dismantle the movement. The phenomenon of reduced influence (Unda, n.d., p. 7), and even its disappearance when it has successfully obtained a specific demand, is also known in Ecuador (Unda, n.d., p. 7). Housing cooperatives may be taken over by the manager and his colleagues, a situation that may lead to the failure to hand over title deeds, the collection of money under whatever pretext, the multiple awarding of a single plot to two or three different occupants, etc. In many cases, these conflicts are reproducing the general exploitation of society, that is to say, they are manifestations of class exploitation; in other instances they are examples of the exploitation of the poor by the poor.

In spite of all this, the urban popular movement has shown and continues to show an increasing tempo in Latin America. Tensions accumulate, conflicts become more acute, and the popular response acquires greater magnitude and depth day by day. On the other hand, in spite of its heterogeneity and diversity, the urban popular movement throughout Latin America reveals, as has been seen in the previous pages, regularities that allow us to consider it as a phenomenon that, in spite of its apparent isolation from country to country, is part of a single cumulative process, obeying the same rules and following a common course.

One must nevertheless be wary of the possibility of overestimating its potential. It seems to be a grave mistake to think that urban popular movements can succeed in being, on their own, the motor of social change. On the contrary, there are specialists in the area who predict their disappearance. Ramírez Sáiz (1986, p. 201) cites Manuel Castells on this. On the other hand, there exists the danger of the co-option of popular organizations by the state and political parties that function within the system. The most important element, however, is the lack of a political project, even a limited or partial one, and the lack of the necessary infrastructure to take over power. It is even highly unlikely that such an organization could establish itself on the basis of these movements. For this reason the exaggeration of those who speak of them as the new motor of history is obvious. What can be hoped for, and this has been proved by the experience of Central America at the beginning of the 1980s, by Chile before 1972, and by Cuba before 1959, is that, from the popular movements in their entirety, a single Popular Movement with a clear project and strategy in the face of power can be established. But here we are already dealing with a different phenomenon: the party, or the political front, or the political–military movement.

Among the other popular movements of importance in Latin America, it is possible to choose a few in order to perceive a certain synthesis of this phenomenon. Having analysed, although briefly, two movements (the indigenous and the urban) that are clearly composed of individuals belonging to popular sectors, the picture would be more complete if we studied another movement, that, in spite of developing its struggles on the side of the people, can be composed of people of various social origins. We are talking about the religious popular movement.

IV. Beyond class: The priests choose the poor

It is said that in 1920 Benedita Cypriano Gomes, called Dica, a peasant girl from Goias, Brazil, suffered from convulsions at the age of 15. These convulsions apparently left her dead for five years, after which she was "resurrected" with miraculous powers. These extraordinary events resulted in the formation of a crowd of followers, many of whom abandoned properties and worldly belongings to live as a community alongside the saint. Many more came on pilgrimages to beg for the saint's favours and those of the saints of her devotion: Saint John, Our Lady of the Immaculate Conception, and the Divine Lord.

According to Zanotta Machado and Selma S. do Amaral, who tell this story in their work on "Religious Movements in Central West Brazil" (1986, pp. 29ff), Santa Dica taught that the earth belonged to

God and for this reason could not be appropriated by man. Consequently, she set up a collective in Villa de Anjos in which work was
communal and the products were distributed according to the needs
of each individual. She became the highest authority in the community, establishing the norms of life: among other things, prohibiting
alcoholic drinks, performing the sacraments of marriage and baptism,
and judging litigations. She preached against private landholding,
against the poor working conditions on private farms, such as the
obligation of working on Saturday, Sunday, and legal holidays, and
against the payment of taxes. She also recruited followers to set up a
city independent from the laws of men. The Church's hierarchy and
the landlords were the first to denounce the movement, whose activists were, for the most part, workers from the neighbouring farms
involved in disputes with their employers.

In 1925, the village of Anjos invaded a neighbouring farm under
the direction of the saint. This provoked the army's intervention at
the instigation of the ecclesiastical hierarchy and local landowners.
The army fired on the civilian population, killing several. Even then
the village refused to give in, and with Santa Dica escaped to the
mountains. Nevertheless, some days later, the saint turned herself
in. She was then judged and sentenced. Later, her jail sentence was
commuted to fixed residence in her native village, where she stayed
until her death in 1970. The repression exercised against her movement in 1925 checked its rebel impetus to the point where, in an
ironic turnround, the government of the state actually won the support of her followers, who, armed and organized in an army led by
the saint herself, participated in the defence of the town of Goias
Velho, the state capital, against the Prestes Column. (During the
1920s, Lieutenant Prestes, an officer in the Brazilian army, led an
insurrection within the army, demanding civil and democratic liberties in Brazil and opposing the oligarchic government. He organized
a "Column" in which rebel active officers participated together with
recruited civilians. The Column crossed the country many times for
several months. The official army was unable to defeat it, but the
Prestes Column did not achieve its goals either, until finally it left the
country. Later on, Lieutenant Prestes became the Secretary General
of the Brazilian Communist Party, and a very important popular
leader.) This irony manifests itself even more dramatically when we
realize that the Prestes Column was fighting for principles that coincided to a large extent with those of Santa Dica's movement: for
collective ownership of the land, against its appropriation, against

151

the exploitation of the farm labour force, for the distribution of produce according to need, and for mandatory work only according to individual ability.

These events, which took place from 1920 onwards, when Santa Dica had her convulsion, quite clearly demonstrate the existence of a sense of social justice born from the religious feelings of the people, and illustrate the role of the religious hierarchy and the state's power in the repression of these feelings. But they also illustrate the ideological weakness of a movement that is not based on thinking that is both theological and scientific.

Qualitatively different was the religious popular movement that grew in Latin America as a result of the Vatican Council II.

The popular religious movement has its martyrs, and this has not weakened it, but rather has given it more strength. One of the most dramatic martyrizations was that of Monseigneur Arturo Romero, Archbishop of San Salvador, who was murdered while celebrating mass on 23 November 1987 by an ultra-right-wing death squad's gunman, under the protection of the army, according to El Salvador's President Napoleón Duarte (*La Nación*, 24 November 1987). The Archbishop's sermons had become the only opportunity in El Salvador publicly to hear a free voice in favour of the poor and public life being objectively discussed without sparing criticism of the left or the right. Crowds met there to hear their shepherd's voice, but in El Salvador objectivity becomes subversive in the eyes of those who arranged for the assassination of the Archbishop.

The popular religious movement does not lack other martyrs. Torture, the cowardly protected marksman, or simple massacre awaited Father Héctor Gallego in Panama in 1971, for having facilitated the economic independence of the extremely poor peasants of Veraguas; Father Rutilio Granada in El Salvador, for having contributed to strengthening the peasant organization in the village of Aguilares; Father Rodolfo Escamilla and Father Rodolfo Aguilar, in Mexico, for helping settlers, poor peasants, and union members in their struggles, which earned them the loss of their respective appointments. The list would be long indeed if we mentioned the other murders, housebreakings, threats, expulsions, illegal procedures, and slanders against priests who have chosen to help the people. What are the bases for such a radical change of attitude of an important sector of the church?

The first argument, seen as prominent by theologians, is the understanding that this process transcends the possibilities of a simple sociological reasoning. There is no doubt that class contradictions are present in this choice in favour of the poor by some members of the clergy. Some theoreticians of Liberation Theology go so far as to use Marxism as a scientific method for analysing society, because they consider that Marxist class theory offers the possibility of explaining the phenomenon of poverty, the object of their preoccupations. Thus the involvement of the clergy in social struggles has a clear class origin; the clergy have chosen the subservient classes. But what is also clear is that the explanation of the popular religious movement does not end there. On the contrary, it would be impossible to understand it if it was not defined, principally, as an ecclesiastic phenomenon, as an interpretation of the world in the light of religious faith. In their enlightening book on "Christians' Participation in the Popular Process of Liberation in Mexico," Concha Malo, González Gari, and Salas (1986, pp. 19 and 20) synthesize what was mentioned above when they say that "in the political choices of Christians and of ecclesiastical communities, an important ecclesiastic, theological, and spiritual revival is at stake, which a simple sociological analysis will never succeed in interpreting." In the same manner, Father Arturo Sosa (1985, p. 22) describes the spiritual experience of direct communication between the priest and the people in this way:

Solidarity with the people, in addition to the collection, the organization, and the distribution of goods, implies also agreeing with their way of being in the world, understanding their lifestyle, participating in their symbols, capturing their vital tone, understanding their myths, knowing their basic concepts – not by mimicry, but with a real solidarity that allows for a historical dialogue. The basis for this point of view is that the poor are not just beings in need; they are also spiritual beings. To throw in our lot with that of the poor of the earth and make ours their just cause involves primarily a cultural dimension. The class dimension is not repudiated, but reasserted, and it becomes integrated within this cultural dimension and is shaped by it. Not the reverse.

The priests reached this profound personal experience after going through various stages in their exploration of commitment. One of the first stages consisted in realizing the repressive role played by the church itself. In the words of Father Sosa (1985, pp. 20 and 21), this realization was arrived at through reaching a breaking point:

From confidence in the re-established order, one goes to the discovery that it is not order, but established violence. One discovers that one is a representative of this "order." It is no longer possible to play such a role: one has

153

been used unwittingly as an agent for the ones above to implant in the minds of the ones below the lie that society is a continuous whole in which, through effort and talent, one can go from below to above without more restraints than that of the law of competition and acquired advantages. These agents (shepherds) go from a sympathetic generosity to the realization that they are living a sinful reality. They must choose: either stay in a situation that creates, maintains, and deepens this social division, or go with those oppressed by it. This option is understood as a conversion.

Nevertheless, the popular religious movement does not just unite priests. On the contrary. Its great strength comes from the support it receives from a broad section of the population. From this point of view, the access to the popular sectors opened up by the popular religious movement is of incalculable value and importance. In the past, some sectors of the people drawn by their growing realizations to join revolutionary parties or movements were faced with the dilemma of having to abandon their religious beliefs, or at least their religious practices, because these parties or movements treated religion as "the opium of the people." This description, used by Marx at a specific historical moment and referring to concrete religious practices in space and time, did not have to be universal and permanent. The choice to help the poor made by important sectors of the Christian community overcomes, for a sector of the church, the specific meaning this expression originally had. With this, a serious problem of loyalty experienced by large sectors of the people was resolved, people who were being exploited and fully aware of the fact, and who refused to engage in the social and political struggle because of the incompatibility between the revolutionary organizations and their own religious beliefs. A great floodgate opened between these two torrents and changed them into a single one, multiplied in strength and size.

On the other hand, it is the popular religious movement that will guarantee the survival of the church in the future Latin American society that will result from the changes of which we are catching a glimpse. Since the Christians are the authors of and the participants in these processes of change, together with other social forces, the new society that is being established will have its own utopia. From this point of view, it is surprising that some sections of the church hierarchy are so blinkered as to try to crush this Christian participation in the construction of the new society.

From the conceptual point of view, it is important to specify that by the term "popular religious movement" we mean exactly what was characterized as "movement" in the introduction of this chapter, that is to say, a dynamic process taking place within society. This movement is sometimes called the "Popular Church" or "Church of the Poor." The popular religious movement has generated a system of thought and theory, Liberation Theology. In addition, it has its organizations, known as Ecclesiastical Communities and also grass-roots Christian communities. Other organizations that have emerged from the movement are the "Word Delegates." In short, the *movement* is called popular religious, popular church or Church of the Poor, the *theory* is known as Liberation Theology, and the *organizations* are the grass-roots ecclesiastical communities, grass-roots Christian communities, and the Word Delegates and the Word Custodians, all of which do not exclude other types and other names of organizations.

The popular religious movement reflects the profound sentiments of worldly justice found at the deepest levels of the people. For oppressed people, religion has often served as a refuge or a focal point of resistance. Syncretism is an example of this: in order to protect and conserve an oppressed culture, it is dressed with the symbols of the oppressor. On many occasions, religious wars also represent the confrontation between the people and their oppressors. In the case of the popular religious movement, personal life experiences are complemented by social hopes. The individual purpose of being at peace with God is complemented by the specific form of achieving it, which consists of being at peace also with men, by helping them to achieve their earthly salvation through social justice – but a social justice that comes from radically transforming the causes of injustice, and not just lessening its superficial manifestations. In short, one is dealing with a different way of seeing religion and of seeing the church. Some have gone so far as to say that we are dealing with two religions (Concha Malo et al., 1986, p. 28); others, like Recife's bishop, Dom Helder Cámara, say that there are two versions of the only Church of Christ (ibid., p. 20).

This conceptual framework is what gives birth to the grass-roots ecclesiastical communities, the organizing base of the popular religious movement. The grass-roots ecclesiastical communities emerge as almost exclusively religious necessities stemming from the scarcity of priests. One of the first immediate antecedents can be found in Honduras at the beginning of the 1960s with the Word Delegates, an institution that, in turn, had its antecedents, after 1959, in the Prayer

Custodians, and before that in the radiophonic schools' monitors, who were believers from villages who served as a unifying force for the Christians who listened to Catholic broadcasts.

As a consequence of the Vatican Council II, some functions previously reserved to priests were entrusted to the faithful within the collective grass-roots ecclesiastical communities in countries such as Brazil, Panama, Guatemala, Argentina, and Peru. In order to mitigate the scarcity of priests, these institutions gave the right to preach to members from the poorest levels of the population. It is not surprising that, as a consequence, the acute material problems suffered by these people came to light.

The grass-roots ecclesiastical communities are composed institutionally of inhabitants of the villages, of those who lack material possessions, of those who lack power and knowledge (Sosa, 1985, p. 8), and of those who unite in a community, which means that it involves all the dimensions of human life in primary and direct relation. People of all ages and occupations and of both sexes participate.

These organizations are ecclesiastical because their *raison d'être* is the church itself. They are a popular way of being a church, a particular form of putting into practice those of Jesus's teachings that do not coincide with the practices of some sectors of the church that have become the allies of the oppressors. But in no circumstances is it another church, nor is it an underground or parallel one. It is, in the words of Dom Helder Cámara, "a necessary spring of the very church of Jesus" (Sosa, 1985, p. 7).

The ecclesiastical communities define themselves as grass roots because their members belong to the poorest section of the countryside and the city. They do not exclude people from higher levels of the population if their intention is to remain at the base without trying to use the movement for their own benefit, and assuming that "they have thrown in their lot with the poor of the earth" (Sosa, 1985, p. 8). These characteristics give the movement its great potential. Being at the base, the communities take care of the whole of human life, the spiritual side as well as the material one, and in both they succeed in outlining the solution to their problems in the most radical ways.

The missionary character of Christian practice, united with the radical nature of the communities and their popular position, has made it possible for the movement to expand with surprising speed. Its community nature allows for face-to-face relations and, if necessary, fragmentation, creating two communities that, in turn, can keep reproducing themselves. This makes room for the establishment of a

156

mechanism of interchange among them, allowing for the interchange of experiences, the accumulation of knowledge, and mutual support. They have held conferences, congresses, meetings, and assemblies at diocesan and national (Brazil, Mexico, Ecuador) and international (Brazil and Mexico) levels (Sosa, 1985, p. 10).

The popular religious movement does not always express itself through grass-roots ecclesiastical communities. It was noted earlier that a movement is not like an organization. Sometimes it takes the form of grass-roots ecclesiastical communities, and at other times it expresses itself in the participation of Christians in unions, parties, cooperatives, political–military movements, or other popular movements. Sometimes it is only a state of mind that spreads among the faithful. It is not exclusive to the Catholic Church. There exists a liberating Protestantism at the national as well as international level, which develops its political practice alongside revolutionary processes (Bastian, in Concha Malo et al., 1986, pp. 302ff). An example of this is the reporting of massacres in Guatemala by the National Council of Churches of the United States. The World Council of Churches supports the revolution in Nicaragua. According to Bastian (p. 303), 15 per cent of the North American population, gathered in 36 Protestant sects, is represented in the Comisión Evangélica de Ayuda al Desarrollo en Nicaragua (Evangelical Commission of Help for Development in Nicaragua), which maintains an active commitment to the Sandinistas. In fact, in Nicaragua, there are many international Protestants who "have thrown in their lot" with the revolution, and many of them have lost their lives in the name of their Christian commitment. In the same way, in almost all the other Latin American countries, there are sections of the Protestant church within the struggle of the people.

On the other hand, other Protestant sects have developed whose interest lies in removing popular sectors from their own struggles and conditioning them to the advantages of the dominant forces. In general, this role is played by the so-called Pentecostal sects, which can be found in almost all Latin American countries. In Brazil, for example, Pentecostal sects are gaining many followers, while Catholics lose them. Zanotta Machado and Selma S. do Amaral (1986, p. 1) say that, according to a demographic census, "in 1940 Protestants represented 2.6% of all Brazilians, in 1970, 5.2%, and in 1980, 6.6%. . . If in 1930, out of all Protestants, a mere 9.5% were Pentecostalists. . . , in 1960, they represented 65% of all Protestants . . . and were in full expansion." This expansion is very interesting

157

if seen as a tendency contrary to that of the popular church, because Pentecostal sects impart to their faithful an attitude totally opposed to any sort of social struggle or recovery. They engulf them in conformism and in values that prevent them from seeing exploitation, and make them accept existing social relations as a sacrifice pleasing in the eyes of God.

In a study of Pentecostal sects in the banana-producing area of Guápiles in Costa Rica, Jaime Valverde (n.d., p. 24) establishes a connection between the sectarian religious affiliation of the workers and their submissive and obedient attitude. He adds that the bourgeoisie who control the banana plantations have developed a policy of using Pentecostal sects in order to keep and secure power in the area. To achieve this, they cultivate good relations with the priests of these churches, they collaborate economically with them in order to strengthen them and transform them into debtors of favours, and put pressure on the workers to join these churches by discriminating against those who do not belong to the sect, a very effective manoeuvre in an area of high unemployment.

From the religious point of view, the success of these sects in drafting and maintaining their members is rooted, according to Zanotta Machado and Selma S. do Amaral (1986, p. 10), in the fact that they focus on and glorify the individual in his particular features through cures and blessings. These authors say that "the basic functions of the cure, linked with the laying on of hands, trances, and exorcisms, allow for a collective catharsis and a particularized and concrete relation of the sacred with the individual." However, the cure is not immediate, and neither are the utopias of the future identified by Pentecostalists as the "new millenium." This only coming once, one goes through the present suffering, which of course, for this very reason, must not be altered.

A similar phenomenon occurs in the Caribbean. For Armando Lampe (n.d., p. 518), the penetration of Pentecostal sects in all the islands of the Caribbean is impressive. The Mahikari movement, coming from Japan, which is not even Christian let alone Pentecostal but which has some similar effects, has prospered in Guadeloupe and Martinique; the Adventist movement has also prospered in Martinique; as has the movement of the Apostle of Infinite Love in Guadeloupe; the Charismatic movement, which is not pentecostal but Catholic and accepted by the church, has taken root in Curaçao; and so on.

For Lampe (n.d., pp. 520ff) these movements are founded on the one hand in a rebellious attitude towards the Catholic Church, which is seen as an instrument of domination, and on the other in the revival of symbols of the Afro-Antillan religions opposed to the culture of the colonialists. All is cleverly manipulated by the new colonizers who, to support their imperialist goals, find a way of placating social criticism and its consequent political practice.

Among the constitutive elements of these sectarian practices the following can be found: the conservation of the body's health (in the case of the Mahikari movement), in contrast with the imposed contempt of one's own body because the colonizer defines it as inferior to that of the white; the belief in the ancestors' spirits, which cease to perturb and instead become protective; the rejection of the Catholic Church, instrument of domination (with the exception of the Charismatic movement); the glorification of the individual; the sense of belonging to a superior culture, an élite, since one's sect has been chosen by God, something that is in sharp contrast to the contempt for the minority in the wider social context; the belief in the utopia of the millenium, which allows for the rejection of the present society without trying to change it, and lessens earthly suffering with the hope of a better world in the future where all one's needs will be satisfied for a thousand years with all the just. This group of beliefs removes the people far away from any political activity. The world is corrupt and only God will be able to change it.

In Costa Rica, Pentecostal sects have grown a great deal too. According to the already mentioned work of Jaime Valverde (n.d., p. 275), the number of sites dedicated to Pentecostal sects rose from 215 in the whole country in 1974 to 1,088 in 1985, that is to say, by more than 500 per cent. Between 1982 and 1985, this number grew 116 per cent. This means, for example, that in the capital city of San José, where there was one Pentecostal church for every 13,116 inhabitants in 1974, there was one for every 3,350 in 1985, an increase that is repeated at almost the same level in the rest of the provinces. This substantial growth has been made possible, in addition to all the spiritual reasons analysed before, by the recourse to important economic resources coming from similar sects in the United States. These external resources are used to finance the first stage of the establishment of one of these churches. Later, when the priests have built up their clientele, they reveal an extraordinary ability to extract money from the believers. The moments of trance serve also to incite

159

the individual to abandon his earthly belongings and to give them to the priest. In addition, the institution of the "tenth part," which is added to the extra produced during the trance, increases the gift still more. Economic success is important to the priest, since his salary is in direct proportion to the income of his church.

This whole picture is important because each conquered soul, for this type of sect, is a potential force that is taken away from social movements and the popular church, because in this area the principal consequence is the separation of these people from the earthly struggle. Based on the facts mentioned earlier, one can conclude that the growth of these sects is as rapid as that of the grass-roots ecclesiastical communities. Another illustrative point is that, at least in Costa Rica, their activity occurs at the same time as that of other sectors in the banana plantations, which have traditionally been the base of the most agitated trade unionism.

The popular church, in contrast, does make a commitment to worldly struggles. It is its way of rendering possible love for one's fellow human. All humanity deserves the best fate in this world, because the body, the human body, is conceived of as the temple of Christ, and Christ too deserves a proper temple. For this reason, the popular religious movement, Liberation Theology, and the popular church constantly steer between the religious field and the political one. They do this in a more permanent way than other movements, such as the popular urban movement, for example, which, once it has achieved its objectives, often becomes weaker. The popular religious movement has more permanent objectives, which have to do with eternal life and for this very reason are difficult to achieve. For this reason, it is a simplification to say that they are a simple product of the crisis (Lampe, n.d., p. 561), because in their genesis and development there exist factors that escape a purely rational concept of the world. The popular religious movement arouses deep feelings in individuals and the collectivities, among them that of glorifying their dignity. Opazo (1985, p. 150) notes:

For a peasant or for a humble manual worker in a marginal neighbourhood, to whom all social recognition has always been denied, the fact of having a place and a group of people with whom to sit down in a circle, express themselves, and be taken seriously, must represent an enormous satisfaction. In this community, they can express their situation and their problems of all sorts, personal as well as family and economic ones. In this same fraternal environment, he receives a religious message as a light that brightens and gives sense to the multiple situations and dimensions of his life.

All this framework explains the commitment of the popular religious movement to the struggles of the unfortunate sectors of the people.

In Central America, for example, the popular religious movement has committed itself sincerely to the struggle of the people. In Nicaragua during the Samoza dictatorship (Opazo, 1985, pp. 187ff) the popular church came out against the hierarchy, which was so far compromised that Anastasio Somoza García was eulogized as "Prince of the Church." The earthquake of 1972 represented a step forward in the development of the popular religious movement. The most evident manifestations were the Word Delegates, organized by the Zelaya Capuchins and the community of Solentiname Island in Nicaragua Lake, led by Father Ernesto Cardenal, who later became Minister of Culture in the Sandinista government. In the principal cities, Christian communities were organized also, and in channelling popular interest developed an increasingly radical opposition to the regime. When repression became stronger as a result of the growing Sandinista struggle, members of Christian communities, priests, and nuns gave protection and assistance to the fighters, opened their churches for the insurrection, and supported the struggle with Biblical messages. A similar process occurred in the countryside. The FSLN (Sandinista National Liberation Front) not only recognized and encouraged the role of Christians in the struggle against the dictatorship but absorbed them into their ranks as militants without any difference whatsoever from the fighters, and subsequently many of them took on high-ranking posts.

The following paragraph, quoted directly form Opazo's work (1985, p. 189) illustrates the situation:

The solidarity [of the Christian communities] with the persecuted increased and, in the concrete conditions in which this solidarity was lived, it involved a political commitment which was assumed as such and explained in the development courses for Word Delegates. For example, in Zelaya, these courses, which brought together as many as 500 Delegates, addressed themes of the following sort: political commitment; What is politics? Where does injustice come from? Where does the right to order others come from? These courses were published and distributed in the communities. In 1975 there were 900 Word Delegates in Zelaya, all coached in religious questions as well as in political thought.

Since the triumph of the revolution, the grass-roots Christian communities have become stronger, and have had to confront the opposi-

161

tion of the hierarchy. Christians continued to rise through the ranks of the FSLN, of the government, and of the army at all levels; Protestants work as volunteers in development projects, Catholic institutions such as the Universidad Centroamericana (Central American University), administered by Jesuits, were involved in the construction of a more just society, in the struggle against aggression, and in the formation of the necessary technical and scientific cadres for the development of a more independent nation.

In El Salvador (Opazo, 1985, pp. 177ff), the church, including the hierarchy, was more prepared to accept the results of the Vatican Council II. The commitment of the bishops and the priests to the popular sector was clear from the end of the 1960s. The church's Development Centres, distributed throughout the country, educated more than 15,000 rural managers. Grass-roots Christian communities were and still are the points of intersection of spiritual problems and material ones. They form the base for the mass demonstrations of peasants and workers in response to repression, to the indiscriminate killing of people in villages, to the expulsion and murder of priests, such as Father Rutilio Grande in the village of Aguilares. The Central American University "José Simeón Cañas," also administered by Jesuits, offered theological support to the liberation project.

Although the church in El Salvador is also divided, since some bishops are the allies of the army and even bless the weapons received by the army from the United States, the majority of the faithful, priests, and bishops reject the regime's repression. Important sectors go even further. The historical account of the lives of the religious martyrs of the popular church in El Savador is as large as is its commitment to the people, and the few lines that can be included here on the topic are totally insufficient to describe the phenomenon. We will mention, following Higinio Alas (1982, pp. 179ff), only the names of Father Ernesto Barrera, chaplain of the workers' union, murdered by 150 members of the police on 28 November 1978, and of Father Octavio Ortiz Luna, chaplain of the youth organizations, murdered by the National Guard on 20 January 1979, when he was with a group of young people, four of whom were also killed.

In Guatemala (Opazo, 1985, pp. 172ff), the institution of the Word Delegates also includes the indigenous population, mostly the young. Priests travel to the limits of the country and through "Catholic action" change traditional practices and link religious and economic activities such as cooperatives, health centres, literacy campaigns, schools, etc. These centres are the focal point of inspiration for the indigenous population, which sees itself valued. The state's response has been repression, sometimes with the help of the hierarchy, which in turn stimulates the radicalization of the indigenous people, who, allied with other sectors, make up and organize the guerrillas.

In Haiti, the Church of the Poor played an important role in the struggle against Duvalier's dictatorship. At a symposium held in December 1982, with the participation of bishops, delegates of seven dioceses, priests, religious as well as lay speakers, the participants called for a "commitment to today's Haiti [characterized by] division, injustice, poverty, hunger, fear, unemployment, lack of land for the peasants, division of the families and insufficiencies in the educational system" (Lampe, n.d., p. 550). Grass-roots communities have developed a great deal, more so in the countryside than in the city, and according to Lampe (n.d., p. 554) the Haitian Church of the Poor constitutes a popular movement and displays its legitimacy within the Haitian church.

In Mexico, Concha Malo et al. (1986, pp. 249ff) show us how the grass-roots ecclesiastical communities have actively participated, becoming involved in the teachers' struggles, and those of the workers, the settlers, and the peasants, a situation that can be explained by the fact that the members of these communities are teachers, workers, settlers, and peasants.

In some areas of Brazil, the grass-roots ecclesiastical communities take the shape of Pastoral Committees for the Land in the countryside (Zanotta Machado and Selma S. do Amaral, 1986). One example is the state of Joias, where the problem of land is crucial. In 1983, the Pastoral Committee for the Land embarked on a campaign for agrarian reform controlled by the workers. Pilgrimages for the land were organized, which included walks, masses, theatre, and music. Everything centred around the issue of the land and the conflicts that had emerged at the time. Around 1,000 workers assembled for the 1984 pilgrimage, and 15,000 in 1984, all coming from the 60 municipalities of the state, in addition to other states' delegations. The participants demanded guarantees for some agents from the Pastoral who had been threatened with death by landlords. The tradition of pilgrimages for the land has been repeated year after year and is about to become a dynamizing centre of the struggle for the land for the Brazilian peasants.

In short, the popular religious movement has offered to the Latin American people, in exchange for many sacrifices, an environment in which they can give a bearing to their struggles, a possibility of reconciling their material needs with their spiritual ones, a way of raising their own often trampled dignity, and a space to establish alliances between various sectors of the people.

Having examined some of the most important popular movements present today in Latin America, it is important to think in what circumstances they could become a stronger, united movement with a common project. In other words, a movement of the entire people. We will dedicate section VI of this paper to this issue.

V. A word on the workers' movement

The role of the working class in the formation of the Popular Movement is a topic that has been raised many times. Often, theoretical or political positions determine an analyst's attitude on the issue. Nevertheless, up to now, the facts suggest that there exists a capacity in the working sectors for outlining objectives and forms of struggle that are much more radical than those found in other social sectors. The conditions under which the working class executes its work are not alien to these facts: the presence of large groups of workers within the same factory, the division of labour, which accustoms them to coordinating their actions with those of the others, the discipline this implies, the fact that it is the manual worker who directly transforms the raw material, their relatively high educational level compared with other sectors, the fact that manual workers work in the most clearly capitalist sector, a situation that provokes a clash between these contradictions and the very foundation of the system, and mostly, the highly visible, crude struggle between workers and capital over the distribution of the fruits of labour.

This proclivity of the working class for radical struggle is far from functioning mechanically and directly. Many circumstances contribute to stimulate or contain it. Among them the traditions of working-class struggle, the characteristics of its leadership, the degree of the workers' consolidation, the social origins of the workers, their antiquity as a class, the repressive bourgeois policy, either demobilizing or reformist, the specific political regime, the specific circumstances of capitalist industrial implementation, etc., all play an important role.

Because there exists an important working class, it does not necessarily follow that it must invariably be the avant-garde of all social movements. In many cases in the recent history of Latin America, the avant-garde has been made up of other movements, such as the student, popular religious, peasant, human rights movements. On the other hand, the diversity of Latin American societies results from the fact that populations are composed of, in addition to the working class, many other varied sectors such as ethnic groups, small rural landowners, peasants without land, day labourers, insecure settlers in urban areas, public functionaries, socially mobile groups such as professors, teachers, and bankers, students with uncertain futures, professionals in the service of the state, etc. In Latin American countries where the establishment of popular movements has reached the highest levels, the political avant-garde has emerged and has sustained itself from this variety of components in the people's make-up.

In spite of this, the working class has not become alienated from the process; on the contrary, it has been present and its presence, in general, implies a more global and radical vision of the struggle. Even in countries like Peru, where the workers' movement was not very big in the mid-twentieth century, the working class had a great influence on the popular struggles of the mid-1970s. Speaking of this issue, Nieto Montesinos (n.d., p. 57) suggests that "the impressive union activity was let loose during the second period of the military regime, when not only were they denied their demands for political participation, but their very social gains were beginning to be cut back."

In Chile, Bolivia, and Brazil, the industrial working class's participation in the struggles for democracy was unquestionable. In Chile, the participation of the miners has been crucial in the confrontation with the dictatorship. The mining industry's leader, Segel, in spite of his affiliation with a centre-right political party, is famous as leader of the copper-mine workers in their fight to protect from the dictatorship the successes the latter wanted to take away from them. Segel is symbolic not on his own but rather because he represents the presence of the working class in the front line of the struggle for democracy.

In Bolivia, the workers' movement, consolidated around the Bolivian Workers' Confederation (COB), was also a determining factor in the fall of the dictatorship that had installed itself in July 1980, and that ended in October 1982 with the victory of the Democratic and Popular Unity government (UDP). The participation of the workers' movement allowed it a determining influence in the new regime, in which at least one of the three tendencies of the COB claimed co-governing rights. Ricardo Calla Ortega says how (n.d., p. 74) a few months after the accession of the UDP to government, one of the

165

COB's federations, the Syndical Federation of Bolivian Miners (FSTMB), demanded the implementation within the Comisión Minera Boliviana (COMIBOL; Bolivian National Mining Authority) of co-management by a workers' majority. Calla points out that this document "in its final paragraphs, declared already that the only remedy for the economic crisis left as an accumulated effect of the dictatorships was the participation of the workers in the processes of economic and political decision-making." The COB's decision, or at least that of a fraction of it, supporting the idea of co-government, led President Hernán Siles to invite it to a discussion on "the feasibility of labour's participation in the government" (Calla Ortega, n.d., p. 80).

In the end, the project of co-government failed, something that could have been foreseen given the hegemony of the bourgeoisie in society and state in Bolivia, and the COB's important internal dissensions. But what is important for this analysis is that the working class was in the avant-garde in the struggle against the dictatorship and in the construction of the new political project, to the point of rendering possible its participation as a social class in civil government. It is possible that this ability to raise the issue of a political project that questions the exclusivity of the bourgeoisie is an attribute proper to the working class. It is not easy to imagine many other popular movements able to go so far. Calla Ortega (n.d., p. 81) poses the problem in this way:

Once again a rich reality for theoretical reflection was manifested: there is a COB, supposedly "syndical," whose workings reflected an unconcealable homology with political organisms. Not only did the COB represent "government's programmes" – an attribute, according to certain ideologues, corresponding only to political parties – but the COB seemed to secure positions that resulted from political calculations theoretically reserved for political parties, and to manage the correspondence of its internal forces. The "syndicate," from what has just been seen, was a real political organ in Bolivia.

In Brazil, within a different framework and with different origins, we also find a working class that goes further than the occasional and specific demand. Ruy Mauro Marini (1985, p. 185) confirms this when he reminds us:

In 1978 the first direct confrontation occurred between the workers' movement and the management sector and the military dictatorship: the car industry strike, which, beginning in San Bernardo, spread later to the other industrial areas of greater São Paulo. This first great strike movement since 1968 revealed a rational, disciplined, and combative working class. The metal workers' strike of May 1978 captured world opinion, increased the petty bourgeoisie's activity and that of the popular sectors, and marked the beginning of a time of disturbance in workers' circles that spread from São Paulo to other industrial centres, particularly those of the southern-central region.

In Latin America, nevertheless, the industrial working class does not constitute the entirety of the proletariat. But its development in other industrial branches extends its range of action to agriculture, the mining industry, services, etc. On the other hand, Marini suggests that the proletariat is constituted by the working class and other social groups. This is his meaning when he says:

In whatever manner, the petty bourgeoisie's reaction in the face of its expulsion from the paradise created by the "economic miracle" has consisted in getting closer to the working class in its forms of organization and its methods of struggle. Its trade unions, particularly the banking, medical, administrative, and professional unions, and particularly within the universities, are today very active, and the strikes they have supported during the last few years stand out in both their number and combativeness. This association strengthens the workers' movement considerably, particularly because it does not just create the possibility of a class alliance, *it creates the possibility of joining effectively, if not all, at least a significant part of the middle classes in the position of services' proletariat. That is to say, salaried service professionals, but with a proletarian conscience.* In fact, only class struggle allows for this sort of permutation, which cannot be given or denied by decree. (Marini, 1985, p. 197; our emphasis)

Marini proposes, both in this text and in lectures that we had the pleasure to hear, that the excessively strict distinction that is often made between working class and proletariat is misleading. For him, the proletariat is much larger than the working class. The members of the proletariat are, in general, those who do not have access to the means of production. These sectors can begin to acquire a proletarian consciousness because classes constitute themselves in the process of class struggle, and are not a direct expression of the mode of production. Consequently, the fact that in Latin America we find extremely varied forms within this proletariat should not provoke either surprise or admiration. In our view, this is a consideration that must be noted in order to solve the perennially discussed subject of social transformation in Latin American society.

167

VI. When the whole people moves

As we delve deeper into the study of social movements, the conviction deepens that each one of them, on its own, lacks the necessary conditions to change the root causes of class domination, which produces situations of inequality against which these movements struggle. If this is the case even for those movements that have a class definition, such as the workers', which, isolated and without alliances, does not have this ability, it is even more true of those movements that are heterogeneous.

The careful observation of popular movements in the recent history of Latin America confirms this hypothesis, because it shows that popular movements have succeeded in achieving their specific goals and have succeeded in changing power relations only when they have generated a political front, party, or movement, that is to say, an avant-garde, able to outline its objectives in general and global terms. There exists an opposite thesis, according to which political parties, and especially the revolutionary ones, have lost prestige and influence among popular movements, which have constituted themselves into a dynamic element, the motor of history. Neither recent history nor concrete research has confirmed this point of view.

Popular movements succeeded in influencing Chile's government between 1970 and 1972 because they themselves created and supported the political movement known as Popular Unity. Outside of this movement, or before it, popular movements could be successful in their struggle for recovery, but not in the basic transformation of the dominant relations of the state and society. Less radically, the same thing has happened in Peru, where popular movements grew with Velasco Alvarado's political movement, acquired a capacity for state reform with Alan García's redefinition of the Alianza Popular Revolucionaria Americana (APRA; American Popular Revolutionary Alliance), and caught a glimpse of a possibility of realizing their project within the United Left.

The clearest examples, however, are Cuba, Nicaragua, Guatemala, and El Savador. In Cuba, the July 26th Movement grew out of an alliance between the student movement and important sectors of the working class. Their long and dramatic struggles did not bring about a global transformation of society until they converged with the political movement that was leading the revolution. In El Salvador, it will only be when workers, peasants, teachers, unions, and student organizations gain the capacity of generating political and military fronts of their own that a fundamental change in society will become possible. Even then the change is held back by the direct participation of the US government through the supply of weapons to the army and the artificial support of the economy. In Guatemala, the indigenous movement began to see a change in the relations of oppression only when it was able to produce its own guerrillas. In this country, in El Salvador, and in Nicaragua, the priests, in keeping with their support for the poor, participate in the political and military organizations as the only feasible route to social justice.

Faced with these realities, and many more that remain unmentioned, history does not provide a single example in which the urban movement alone, or the religious movement on its own, or the workers' movement without alliances succeeded in shifting the bases of domination. With the exception of the ecological movement – and this occurred outside the continent – these movements have not even been able to launch an electoral political party.

Nevertheless, all their transforming possibilities gain strength when they succeed in constituting what Pease and Ballón (1982, p. 23) call a Popular Movement, in the singular and with capital letters. For them, the Popular Movement is a process of the confluence of particular popular movements in a common project to transform society. In this common project, the individual movements' historical memories unite, and they revive a common history, which converges into a utopia. Individual struggles become part of the same struggle, a goal is generated, and the field of action moves towards the political field.

To understand this process in all its dimensions, it is necessary to clarify some points. In the first place, if one discusses a transformation in the relations of domination, it is because there is one sector of society that dominates the others. In Latin America, clearly involved in the process of capitalism's development, this dominant class is none other than the bourgeoisie, the dominant class in the capitalist mode of production. Obviously, other classes, such as the landowning oligarchy, reminiscent of other previous or present modes of production, are also dominant, but secondarily. The bourgeoisie is at once one and multiple. It is one when its general interests are at stake. Some things affect the bourgeoisie as a whole, involving all its factions and sectors. One of these things is the principle of private property. But it is more usual to find great diversity within the bourgeoisie. For example, the transnational bourgeoisie, the owners of large world monopolies, seems to be the most dynamic in Latin

America, and as such is the one that is able to influence in a determining way the course of the other factions. Domestically and internationally, the bourgeoisie distinguishes itself by the activities it controls: finances, industrial concerns, agriculture, and, within the latter, exports of farm products, etc.

This observation on fundamental aspects serves to direct us to another one: a bourgeoisie, or factions or sectors of it, cannot act economically within a society without the existence of a corresponding antagonistic class. In other words, the bourgeoisie could not exist without the proletariat. Not only must the proletariat exist somewhere in Latin America but, wherever it exists, it is the antagonistic class of the bourgeoisie.

Such simple reasoning, which can appear strange at first glance, is justified by the existence of the thesis that denies the proletariat's importance in the class struggle and in the struggles of social movements. For some authors, some of whom have declared themselves Marxist at one time or another, to speak of the central role of the proletariat in social struggles seems an outdated orthodoxy. Nevertheless, what does seem to be accepted is precisely this transforming characteristic that befits the proletariat. In the same way, the assertion, mentioned above, that individual social movements are the "new motors of history" appears to deny, in the establishment of the Popular Movement, the role of the party and, in general, of the avant-garde – as if the recent history of Nicaragua, El Salvador, Guatemala, and before that of Cuba could be written off altogether. Basically, the theses reflect a political position, which is not always explicit, that opposes the revolutionary popular project and prefers, as it has the right to do of course, to pursue reform within the existing regime.

Nevertheless, it is not easy to dismiss the proletariat, the avant-garde, or the popular political project. For this reason it is necessary to dwell for some moments on these issues. When we mentioned, following Pease and Ballón, the confluence of all popular movements into one common action and project, and we gave the name Popular Movement to this process, we were merely raising the issue because the concept of Popular Movement includes, in our opinion, other categories such as social subject, political subject, and historical subject. In other words, the formation of the Popular Movement (in the words of Pease and Ballón) or the movement of the whole people (in the words of González Casanova) is no more nor less than the formation of the social subject of change, or, to be more precise, the social subject of revolution. In addition, the process of creating the Popular Movement, or revolutionary change, implies the establishment and participation of other subjects: the political subject or avant-garde, and the historical subject, which is composed of the revolutionary class.

According to Orlando Núñez (1986, pp. 1–5), the social subject is created with the assistance of all classes and popular forces (that is to say, all the exploited and subjugated ones). This group of classes and forces, some of them formed before the individual popular movements, becomes a social subject when its constituents are victorious in their economic struggles and go on to the political struggle to take over power, a struggle against the exploitative and dominant classes and forces. In Cuba, Nicaragua, and El Salvador, this process has been seen clearly. In all three cases, the specific struggles of the individual movements gave way to increasingly general objectives, that is to say, more widely political ones. Within this process of interrelation, universality develops increasingly at the expense of particularity, to the point of creating a new dynamic entity: the global struggle of the whole people. This is the way in which the social subject of change is formed.

It is important to point out, however, that, as historical facts have demonstrated, this process is inconceivable without a political vehicle able to elaborate a strategy and to lead tactical combats. Depending on the circumstances, this vehicle or avant-garde takes the form of a party, a political movement, or a political front. This is precisely the political subject of change. The relation between political subject and social subject is complex. There are parties that aspire to become political subjects of change, but their relationship with and their leadership abilities over the social classes and forces of the people are so limited and partial that their aspirations are untenable. There are others that make tactical mistakes. In general, popular movements are not sufficiently developed to make it possible even to identify and develop an avant-garde. In the more advanced cases, the political subject or avant-garde has been generated by the popular movements themselves, taking the form of a political front, as in Nicaragua, or an alliance and unity of political military organizations, as in El Salvador and Guatemala, or of a political movement, as in Cuba.

The process of constituting the movement of the whole people does not end there. We have failed to mention the fundamental element, that which imparts to the Popular Movement (or to the movement of the whole people, or social subject) its revolutionary character. The historical subject consists of the social class that has objective reasons to bring about a radical change, that is, to attack the root of the problem. The source of the exploitation and domination of the people is none other than the power of the class or classes that exploit and dominate. It follows that a movement is radical in so far as it has decided to destroy the power of these classes. Objectively, this decision is vested in the class that is antagonistic to the dominant one, the one whose existence and reproduction emerge from the same process, and this is none other than the proletariat. For this reason, in spite of the fact that it is fashionable to deny it, the historical subject of change is still the proletariat, which appears today as the working people.

The category of the proletariat is dynamic and changing. Latin America's proletariat, although similar in essence, is quite different from the proletariat that made the Russian revolution of 1917. To characterize the proletariat one has to begin with the process that gave birth to it. A useful guide is to focus on the creation and reproduction of the bourgeoisie, which is its antagonistic class. In Latin America, the transnational bourgeoisie is perhaps the most dynamic dominant sector. This produces great concentrations of proletarians in the principal Latin American metropolises such as Mexico, São Paulo, Rio, Caracas. On the other hand, as agricultural production becomes increasingly capitalized, it leads to a concentration of the rural proletariat. Although dependent, the local bourgeoisies control parts of industrial, commercial, and agricultural economic activity, over which they establish typically capitalist work relations. This is maybe the most explicit part of this phenomenon. On the other hand, there exist other less direct developments that proletarianize important sectors of society. Concurring in part again with Núñez (1986, p. 6), the following trends can be pointed out: the subordination of Latin American economies to the world market, and at the same time to capitalist production; the existence of an uninterrupted capitalization process since the beginning of the twentieth century; a permanent process of divorcing workers from their means of production; the existence of great numbers of workers who do not have anything else to survive on apart from their ability to work; the subordination, direct or indirect, of increasing numbers of workers of the country to capital and the capitalists; the development of a greater division of labour and of spaces that become increasingly collective in the work centres. All these conditions objectively lead masses of workers into direct conflict with capital and with the state that represents it.

Of course we are omitting here the subjective element, the recognition of one's situation within an exploited class and of one's abilities to fight against exploitation. To understand this, one must make a new distinction between categories that, although similar, do not mean the same thing: proletariat, proletarian, and proletarianization. The proletariat is the productive worker, that is, the worker whose work produces a profit for capitalism. The concept of proletarian nevertheless includes other elements because it is constituted not by the simple adding up of proletariats but rather by a group self-consciousness of their essential role within capitalist society and of their ability to change it. The process of proletarianization includes proletariat and constitutes the proletarian because it not only adheres to but also contributes to the elaboration of its objectives and its political project. It is here that individual popular movements play an important role. In the process of the formation of the movement of the whole people, the individual popular movements adopt and develop the transforming ability of the proletarian. This is what allows for the establishment of a common political project: the appearance of the proletarian as working people.

Within the process of proletarian formation it is important to highlight the fact that, as the capitalist process creates and reproduces the proletariat as a clearly antagonistic class to the bougeoisie, it also generates other social sectors that are both exploited and dominated, and sometimes, in the case of people discriminated against for ethnic reasons, oppressed. Although these groups would not be proletariat in the strict definition of the word, they are antagonistic to the bourgeoisie since their exploitation, domination, and oppression stem from the development of capitalism. For the same reason, their ability to generate or support radical political projects is very great, and their participation in the process of proletarianization is vital.

Observing the process of revolutionary change in Nicaragua, a poor country that has sometimes been said to lack a proletariat, Núñez (1986, p. 6) points out the existence of a process of proletarianization dating back a long time, a process grounded in

the subordination of the Nicaraguan economy to the world market, and hence to the capitalist mode of production; the uninterrupted process of capitalization of the economy since the beginning of this century; the divorce of workers from their means of production; the existence of millions of workers who have nothing else to survive on apart from their own labour, the direct or indirect subordination (real or informal) of all the workers of the country to capital or local or transnational capitalists; the development of more collective work spaces; and the existence of a growing political awareness that led the masses of Nicaragua to fight, before the triumph of the revolution, against a state that symbolized capital, capitalism, and imperialism, and then, after the triumph, against all the expressions of imperialism.

This struggle is in the spirit of proletarian interests, which, as was analysed earlier, coincide with those of all popular classes and sectors.

The same elements of proletarianization can be found in El Salvador. We have already mentioned the characteristics of the process of original accumulation in this country that proletarianized large sections of the population and threw even greater numbers of people into the reserve workforce. The indigenous and rural populations who led the 1932 uprising in El Salvador were proletarians from the great coffee plantations who were already organized within a clearly capitalist scheme.

In Cuba before the revolution, the working class was not only one of the most developed in the continent but also the most proletarianized. Its tradition of struggle is not only undeniable but in addition, because of its heroism, one of the most illustrious in the history of the continent. The political development of the Chilean working class is also clear, as is its central role in the Popular Unity project.

It is to this complex phenomenon that we were referring, while raising the issue of movements of the whole people, when we made the distinction between the social, the political, and the historical subject; that is to say, the group of popular classes and forces, the avant-garde, and the proletariat. It is an old debate, but it does not lose its relevance just because some people would like to bury it, preferring that this type of avant-garde did not exist. In our opinion, without this relation between these three phenomena, individual social movements have a very limited horizon.

VII. Methodological conclusion

We have considered Latin America as a unit. It has been an obvious methodological assumption throughout these pages. We see the development of popular movements in Latin America as a single cumulative process. Although we are of course conscious of the profound differences between countries, and even within regions of the same country, there exist powerful integrating factors. One of the strongest is constituted by the dominant processes. We once heard Darcy Ribeiro say that the real integration of Latin America is accomplished by the transnational companies. In our opinion, these entities and the process of capitalist development that generates them are the most dynamic element of domination, and they have a decisive influence on individual societies, both dominant and dominated. For this reason, there is a link between the ecologists in Venezuela, the May Square mothers in Argentina, and the settlers in the marginal areas of Mexico. All are fighting against the same way of organizing society, one that uses the same logic: that of capital. For this reason, in this paper countries have not been looked at one at a time. On the contrary, the phenomena of study, that is, popular movements, both singly and together, have been seen as a single process, responding to a single causality, and although each movement shows individual features, they all participate in a common future.

Note

1. This concept of "people" has been developed by Pablo González Casanova in *The Hegemony of the People*, San José: EDUCA, 1984; and used in its derivation of popular movement in D. Camacho and R. Menjívar, *Popular Movements in Central America*, San José: EDUCA, 1984; and in D. Camacho, "Social Movements: Some Conceptual Discussions," Investigation reports, No. 54, San José: Social Research Institute, Costa Rica University, 1985.

Bibliography

Alas, Higinio. *El Salvador. Por qué la insurrección?* San José, Costa Rica: Permanent Secretariat of the Commission for the Defense of Human Rights in Central America, 1982.

Arias, Arturo. "El movimiento indígena en Guatemala 1970–1983." In: Daniel Camacho and Rafael Menjívar, *Movimientos populares en Centroamérica*. San José, Costa Rica: Editorial Universitaria Centroamericana (EDUCA), 1985.

Calla Ortega, Ricardo. "La encrucijada de la COB." La Paz, Bolivia, mimeo, n.d.

Camacho, Daniel, and Rafael Menjívar. *Movimientos populares en Centroamérica.* San José, Costa Rica: Editorial Universitaria Centroamericana (EDUCA), 1985.

Castells, Manuel. *Movimientos sociales y urbanos.* 6th edn, Mexico: Siglo XXI Editores, 1980.

Cezar, María do Ceu. "As organizações populares do Recife: trajetória e articulação política (1955–1964)." *Cuadernos de Estudos Sociais* 1(2) (July/December 1985).

Chiriboga, Manuel. "Crisis económica y movimiento campesino e indígena." Mimeo.

Concha Malo, Miguel et al. *La participación de los cristianos en el proceso popular de liberación en México (1968–1983).* Mexico: Siglo XXI Editores, 1986.

175

Díaz Coelho, F. "Identidade e diferenças. O movimento de bairros no Rio de Janeiro." Mimeo.

Doble Jornada. Supplement to the newspaper *La Jornada*, Mexico, 2 August 1987.

Excélsior (newspaper), Mexico, 4 September 1987.

Flores, Graciela, Luisa Paré, and Sergio Sarmiento. "Movimento Campesino y política agraria. 1976–1984. Tendencias actuales y perspectivas." Mimeo.

Galeano, Luis A. "Entre la protesta y la lucha urbana. Dos estudios de casos." In: Domingo Rivarola, ed. *Los movimientos sociales en Paraguay.* Asunción, Paraguay: Centro Paraguayo de Estudios Sociológicos, 1986.

Kowarick, Lucio, and Nabil Bonduki. "São Paulo. Espacio urbano y espacio político: del populismo a la redemocratización." *Estudios Sociales Centroamericanos*, no. 44 (May–August 1987).

Kries, Rafael. "Confiar en sí mismos. Las organizaciones de base en Chile." *Nueva Sociedad*, no. 64 (San José, Costa Rica, Editorial Nueva Sociedad, January–February 1983).

La Jornada (newspaper), Mexico, 6 September 1987.

La Jornada (newspaper), Mexico, 12 June 1987.

La Nación (newspaper), San José, Costa Rica, 24 November 1987.

Lampe, Armando. "Los nuevos movimientos religiosos en el Caribe." Mimeo.

León, S., and L. Marván. "Movimientos sociales en México (1968–1983): Panorama y perspectivas." Mexico, mimeo, n.d.

Marini, Ruy Mauro. "O movimento operario no Brasil." In: *Movimentos Sociais no Brasil. Política e administração*, no. 2, Special edn. Rio de Janeiro, Brazil: FESP, 1985.

Marx, K. *El Capital.* Vol. I, Buenos Aires, Argentina: Editorial Cartago, 1965.

Mejía, M.C., and S. Sarmiento. *La lucha indígena: un reto a la ortodoxia.* Mexico: Siglo XXI Editores, 1987.

Mejía, M.C., and S. Sarmiento. "La lucha indigena en México 1970–1983." Mexico, mimeo.

Menjívar, Rafael. *Acumulación originaria y desarrollo del capitalismo en El Salvador.* San José, Costa Rica: Editorial Universitaria Centroamericana (EDUCA), 1981.

Nieto Montesinos, Jorge. "El sindicalismo obrero industrial." Lima, Peru, mimeo, n.d.

Núñez, Orlando. "Los sujetos de la revolución." Original unpublished, Managua, Nicaragua, September 1986.

Opazo, Andrés. "El movimiento religioso en Centroamérica, 1970–1973." In: Daniel Camacho and Rafael Menjívar. *Movimientos populares en Centroamérica.* San José, Costa Rica: Editorial Universitaria Centroamericana (EDUCA), 1985.

Oxhorn, Philip. "Organizaciones poblacionales, la reconstitución de la sociedad y la interacción élite–base." Santiago, Chile, mimeo.

Pease, H., and E. Ballón. "Límites y posibilidades de los movimientos populares: impacto político." *Diálogo sobre la participación*, no. 2 (Geneva, Switzerland, UNRISD, April 1982).

Ramírez Sáiz, Juan Manuel. *El movimiento urbano popular en México.* Mexico: Siglo XXI Editores, 1986.

Sectas protestantes en Centroamérica. "La santa contrainsurgencia." *El Parcial*, no. 12 (April 1984).

Sosa, Arturo. *Comunidades eclesiales de base en Venezuela*. Caracas, Venezuela: Centro Gumilla, February 1985.

Suárez, Isauro. "Trayectoria y actualidad de las luchas agrarias en Colombia." Mimeo.

Tovar, T. "Barrios, ciudad, democracia y política." Mimeo.

Unda, Mario. " Qué hay de nuevo bajo el sol? Barrios populares y sistema politico en el Ecuador." Quito, Ecuador, mimeo, n.d.

Valverde, Jaime. "Sectarismo religioso y conflicto social en Costa Rica." Mimeo.

Vargas, J. "Movimientos barriales." *Movimientos sociales y participación comunitaria* (Lima, Peru, Nuevos cuadernos CELATS, 1985).

Vives, Cristián. "El pueblo Mapuche: elementos para comprenderlo como movimiento social." Santiago, Chile, mimeo, December 1984.

Zanotta Machado, Lía, and Custodia Selma S. do Amaral. *Movimentos religiosos no centro oeste*. Brasilia, Brazil: Centro Latino de Altos Estudos (CLAE), 1986.

4

Culture and power

Hugo Zemelman

I. Introduction

If we begin with the assertion that Latin American countries face a dual crisis of development (both a crisis of internal inequalities and a crisis of the prevailing system of external economic relations), then we must learn how to recognize such conditions, so that we can adopt an alternative model to the dominant existing one. Otherwise nations face collapse as protagonists of their own future. We hope that we do not have to pronounce Latin America's death sentence.

If it is true that the crisis "has brought to a close, under the banner of pain, a long cycle in Latin American history, it is also called upon to signal the beginning of another under the banner of hope."[1] The historical period we are living in demands that peoples behave as real subjects of history, although, in order to achieve this, they need to reclaim or re-state their identity, which may be possible only by defining their future history within boundaries other than those shaped by the "superimposed values" of the dominating apparatus.

Reclaiming an identity and its possible meaning and direction leads us to scrutinize culture and to understand it "as the ordering factor on the general plane of social life, producing unity, and giving context and meaning to human tasks, making possible the production, reproduction, and transformation of concrete societies."[2] This is why it is necessary to make an analysis of culture,[3] which uncovers

We are indebted to Professor Julia Flores, who supervised the manuscript's critical revision, organized bibliographical references, and added historical references that enriched the text's analysis.

another dimension of society's role needed to reconstruct its history. Penetrating spaces where societies become differentiated and where their identities are established, where the sphere of daily behaviour defines the way societies are developed, entails, in brief, deciphering not only the field of culture but also the political field, where public life and political methods are the result and creation of a culture and where cultural forms are themselves political methods. Thus, the analysis of the culture–politics relation becomes a "heuristic option for diagnosis and evaluation of the alternatives for our societies during the crisis."[4] This option, inasmuch as it synthesizes the creation of identity and meaning, makes it possibile to decipher reality with the aim of understanding history as a political struggle that is undergoing a process of constant construction, and it includes the process of developing alternative project formulations in the light of the crisis in Latin America.

In this work, we have considered culture in its relations with consciousness and will as the basic axis of our analysis. This involves viewing culture as a creation, in other words, as the key to understanding the relationship between past and future, between history and utopia. Consciousness, as a cultural product, synthesizes identity and meaning in social communities, but this consciousness is in turn the creator of culture, for it comprehends the subjects' praxis and historical memory. Consciousness as a cultural product also determines the construction of the future. In this sense, culture is the bearer of a broad mobilizing potential, as the creator and re-creator of the imaginary society, and therefore always open to the possibility of a utopia. Such construction requires will and a project based upon reality. At this point, the relation between culture and politics becomes relevant if we see both aspects as a construction of reality with "directionality," taking social projects as a starting point.

Our outlook is not restricted to proposing a series of general theories on Latin America; we can also reveal genuine problems by viewing culture in the light of its consciousness and will, and the influence of these on power. Power is relevant because it concerns various ways of considering the complex relation between state and civil society, as well as being the battleground of political activity.

If we start from the premise that historical reality is characterized by social projects driven by different social subjects, then the concrete history that has been written and analysed equals the contents of the projects of those particular societies. This implies that historical reality is shaped by power. Thus, we have to understand socio-historical dynamics as the reproduction of projects and actors that constitute the problematic framework where order tends to impose itself and become a unique reality. Therefore, we must see reality as a sequence of "conjunctures" resulting in options. The above leads to two views of the problem of politics: the first sees politics as an operative task directed towards the solution of these options, and the second sees politics as a utopian world, that is to say, as an expression of potential for change contained within the historical horizon that does not necessarily find expression within ideological frameworks.

One problem deriving from this dialectics involves the fact that a utopia for change may still be dependent on the need to enforce power. This opposition might be translated as a major practical political problem, since there is conflict between the will to change and the will to rule. Creative and promoting forces, once transformed in power, lose their capacity to protect themselves within their own political order. This leads us to envisage a growing need to incorporate civil society at the state level, which would mean a reduction in the potential of the new emergent forces, preventing them from uncovering and developing their ability to negotiate, as well as the discouragement of any initiative that might come from civil society.

We are faced with the need to develop a view of history founded on the demand for a "political struggle" instead of on a certain inevitable progression or on a certain subjective voluntarism. This idea, because it corresponds exactly to the assumption that reality is constructed, forces us to rescue the process aspect in terms of concrete analyses and approaches. Utopia and the world of politics stand out as two different ways of looking at reality.

Creative practical policies are not the only expression of utopia, however. Utopia tends to express itself as an often ineffective critique or as a kind of pragmatism. Such is the case of the conservative–authoritarian utopia.

The complexity of society is opposed to the attempts at homogenization that are characteristic of state power. This requires us to solve the problem of diversity at the level of the formulation of national projects. If we fail to consider such complexities, an open conflict may occur between democracy as a value and democracy as a political project. Establishing this complex nature would prevent the various processes from reaching a static position in society.

Lastly, we must analyse the need for power, so that we may confront what we will call "minimal power" and the obstacles of marginalizing culture.

Within this framework, which tends to give rise to alternatives to the industrial–liberal or industrial–authoritarian model, we must consider the idea of progress as resulting from a struggle for the future, without that meaning that we are under the spell of dominant ideology. We must state precisely what we mean by the term "progress" in the economic–cultural context of Latin America.

This chapter is divided into two parts. The first part adopts the viewpoint that Latin American culture comprises a consciousness and will, and that it is necessary to analyse possible options for social construction in Latin America today in terms of power. In the second part, the analysis is oriented towards rescuing the dimension of the construction of the different social projects in a context where severe economic crisis prevails in societies that aspire to the establishment or perfection of democracy.

II. Culture and the consciousness of options

1. Social forces: Dynamics and projects

Possible options for social construction represent situations that shape the relations established between the various projects (or lifestyles) of the different social subjects that are the results as well as the determinants of the context of history. Since reality is the combined result of different interacting social subjects, it makes sense, then, to consider the problem singled out by Durham, "namely that of the function fulfilled by ideas for the preservation of a determined social order."[5] From this standpoint, national culture represents the "sphere of sublimation, and collective learning, which overcomes that which is really given" for each subject, in relation to the particular possibilities that each subject has. It constitutes, therefore, culture's aspect of (anti-state) "civility," which cannot, however, lead us to ignore its opposite. Every culture, because it represents a view of the future, contains also a view of destruction, exploitation, dishonesty. All this relates to the positive and negative aspects of the way power is exercised. As we have stated, behind relations of force, relations of meaning exist; they force us to refer to the reality-constructing projects, bypassing any repetition of historical regularity. In this respect, it is important to recall that the signification of dominant relations tends to be transformed into a reference model from which the models of signification of the other social subjects are defined.

Therefore, culture represents a construction of reality in terms of directionality. This implies that we must include what is particular to each practice and its consequences in the entire project. As a result, facts have to be interpreted as concrete properties of those projects where the strengths and weaknesses of the different subjects manifest themselves in the process of construction or dismantling. That is why the statement is true that cultural facts (and political facts are cultural facts), "whether we like it or not, be they advanced or backward, express aspirations for the future, or an intolerable attachment to an obscure past."[6] "They document a situation and allow us to identify a cultural horizon that is or has been proper to certain social strata."[7]

The basis of our discussion concerns the general theory that culture as a social project, or as a "theoretical dimension of social existence," cannot be mistaken for the configuration that results from the set of state policies. We must distinguish the variety of current and future views that are commonly associated with the emergence of social subjects. The mere national integration of society is a reflection of a society's project that does not respond to the perspectives and necessities of all the coexisting social subjects. A country's reality is shaped by the reality of projects corresponding to their different subjects, even though there is a tendency to view that reality in the light of the dominant project.

However, history does not just tend to be reduced to the content of that project; it also tends to be reduced to the demands of order and control posed by such a project. This observation is important because the content of historical reality, where order is imposed by the dominant project, fulfils the function of defining the legitimate scope of politics. Politics is here understood as a form of operative activity, linked to the solving of problems associated with the maintenance and reproduction of the different social subjects. This understanding moves away from that of politics as a utopia that would break the boundaries of historical reality in terms of order.

This is why political struggle is a consciousness-creating cultural element, inasmuch as it envisages new historical horizons. Culture is a condition of power, and at the same time it is an obstacle to power. No matter what its content may be, "struggle demands mobilization and organization of a great majority of the population, political and moral unity of the different social categories, progressive liquidation of any trace of a way of thinking . . . , and a rejection of rules and social and religious taboos that are not compatible with the rational and national nature of the liberating movement."[8]

A recurrent feature of national liberation movements has been the strengthening of this ability to choose and orientate in an effort to assert an individual identity. Now, when contradictions become more acute, "culture becomes a method of mobilization, and therefore a weapon in the struggle for independence,"[9] as a result of an effort to assert one's own political existence. For this reason it is no surprise that national liberation movements and revolutionary processes are, in general, founded on the recuperation of cultural identity. The fact that independence movements are characterized by an expansion of cultural manifestations, even at the beginning, shows that such movements are preceded by a "cultural renaissance."[10] Recuperation of identity results from relationships between social subjects, who may well become participants in one and the same project, a project that is construed as culture, that is to say, as a horizon of utopian and political possibilities that influence the perception and behaviour of individuals as well as groups. Mobilization is supported by a people's ability to recognize itself as a force with a destiny, which may be self-determined and independent, a people that must overcome all the features of a subordinate culture oppressed by a hegemonic state.

However, the autonomy of dominated sectors depends, to a great extent, on whether or not the interest of the dominated group articulates with the necessity of preserving a cultural or ethnic identity that would be consubstantial to a world-view. If it does, "popular culture, as a whole, becomes a potential ideological weapon for the system's transformation."[11] But this seldom occurs apart from ethnic minorities; what is generally found is a set of ideas that do not even reach the social level of a population's majority, or that are embodied in the political class and from there spread to the rest of society (for instance about the notion of democracy). The problem is that ideas about what has been a tradition or what may be the future are not always consistent with political practice, and so become "broken down into many subcultures."[12] This is what happens when efforts are made to consolidate a national ideology in countries that are heterogeneous in their ethnic, cultural, and economic composition.

This also happens with the adoption of representative democracy in countries that have not truly attained unity. They have reached, at best, the homogenization of the state order, which conceals a great diversity while claiming its own unity. In the case of Peru, it would not be too controversial to question whether ideas on representative democracy will, in that country, become a political culture: "It is a country where such practice is broken down into many subcultures; they have only recently begun their unification, which represents the combination of nationalist populism and representative democracy."[13]

So, whether we view what is needed as a reflection of cultural inertia or as the possible options of social construction, we are faced with the problem of interpreting reality as a consequence of alternatives. This means that we have to solve each option that is historically perceived. Because politics is related to utopian desire, it does not consist solely in the task of taking decisions and choosing operative options, but also requires a cultural creation, such as the permanent constitution of forces. In this cycle of birth and death we must find the social and cultural foundations of the idea that the nation's continuity is a project.

The structuring of reality according to the order demanded by the dominant project is manifested as a constant retrieval of tradition "as a structural component of the political discourse of the dominant class." As an example we can analyse the political class's discourses in Bolivia and Mexico. Although they have a nationalist revolutionary content (despite some differences), they are always present in the state discourse as elements that pretend to "join" classes, groups, and forces. These discourses have been greatly damaged, abused, and rendered useless by a failure to communicate on realistic terms.

Tradition, indeed, fulfils the function of being a true value system that helps to identify subjects in terms of a particular field, such as that of politics. Individuals, as citizens, are therefore surrounded by "landmarks (rather than myths) that come from the past." Such landmarks delimit the political field. They may be either a political figure or any ideological feature that accounts for the continuity of historical development as it may be represented by "the supposed constitutionalism of armed forces or by some definite features of the nation's idiosyncracy."[14]

In contrast to the above is the notion that a nation's history can be reduced to the level of the enveloping ideology that shapes its potentialities in order to determine the direction of its development. This circumstance may eventually lead to the relation with reality being restricted to politics in terms of a task failing to embrace its utopian dimension. In that respect, we can quote the case of Bolivia, where the nationalist praxis and its discourse, in vogue since 1952, have been an obstacle and have in fact prevented the direct exercise of power by those who were, and still are, the subordinate subjects or classes whom the discourse was trying to redeem.

Frequently we find that a historical period adopts the political ideas inherent in new social forces, which are able to meet the demands assailing the prevailing political system, demands that, if unanswered, may even go so far as to question the very legitimacy of the project. The problem consists in whether or not we should permit the development of the other project.

History reveals that financially powerful groups are easily scared by any prospect of broadening the political game; what is questioned is the possibility of a balanced exercise of state if it involves the subordinate interests. This may manifest itself as a conflict between state powers, which affects their efficiency to function. That is what happened at the time of the Popular Unity experience in Chile. The conflict between the executive power and congress paralysed the state. This also happened, in a very different context, in Colombia in the 1930s, during López Pumarejo's term of office. He tried to open up a particular "political game to the new social forces – peasants, workers, employees – that were beginning to make economic and political demands that were repressed during the conservative hegemony." During this period, "Economic powers connected to both parties (liberal and conservative) were scared by the attempt to broaden the democratic horizon. They would not consider state balanced exercise as being possible."[15]

The gap between politics as a task and politics as a utopia can be clearly observed in situations such as the one described above. As a task, politics is legitimate as long as it unfolds within the framework of values adopted by the dominating apparatus, the greatest product of which has been national integration viewed as a prerequisite of the project that reproduces the forces with state control. Utopian politics, on the other hand, can be seen as an expression of the present; the possibility exists of structuring a view of the possible, which in turn represents a view of the present or given situation. In other words, discourse goes no further than speaking about politics; it is not a practice that reinforces the identity and efforts of the subject, either in practical terms or in terms of the consciousness of a historical moment.

We are trying to understand how some social groups face certain options (for instance, the so-called "other, informal economy") that, in so far as they are a real experience, can no longer be understood simply as a "pure anachronism," but rather are "the non-integrated remainder of a utopia that is still in vogue."[16] There might be a case where, in spite of modern capitalism, there are still some forms of consciousness among the groups, as well as the exercise of practices, that may lead us to believe that the scope of politics can be expanded beyond the boundaries defined by a given structure such as a political party.

In popular movements, one political theory after another distorts the political arena, stretching the boundaries in such a way as to make them impossible to recognize, even by the specialist. The intrusion of the struggle in the scope of daily life is neither a tactical camouflage, nor a matter of political ingenuity, but the development of a new society, one that will be broader and less divided.[17]

Incorporating the "remainder" of utopia in the realm of politics as an operative task enhances reality in the perspective of a historical horizon that is not totally structured by social practices. In this sense, it can be said that "changes in culture, including political culture, nowadays are dominated by mass communication."[18] We are referring to "changes in political awareness, in the way politics is regarded, that is to say, in the way one does or does not recognize oneself in politics, in the way the politics of the new generation is being shifted."[19] Utopia, as part of the historical horizon, helps to bring about mobilization, based on the recognition of new dimensions, from which it is possible to begin social construction projects.

Ideology, as a shaper or the possible profile of reality, is, in these situations, subject to the broadest and most varied (in terms of possibilities) demands of the historical movement, for "the discourse struggles to make way for the new." This is what happens when "political" sense is transformed as a result of new emerging subjects.

In order to illustrate the above, we may look at local struggles that give rise, through their claims, to massive movements that go beyond the political field; this corresponds to the classical idea of political struggle by means of parties. Such movements might break up with "explicit claims as well as with the direction towards which party ideologies point." This occurs, in general, within a framework of politics as defined by the demands of a "struggle for the seizure of the state."[20]

The theoretical problem faced is in understanding politics as inherent to power. In addition, or in contrast, politics can be understood as the construction of analytical projects on the operative level of immediate contradictions (since it can be represented by the scope of demands exactly as they are posed in daily life) without relation to one particular problem at state level. This is perhaps the case with various Argentine movements, such as the struggle for human rights, that "span the state environment and go beyond, towards the boundaries of everyday life."[21]

As it has been observed, the "dynamics of social movements, from which political subjects are constituted, implies a series of symbolic manipulations and mechanisms."[22] These mechanisms compel us to probe deeper into their very constitution rather than to see ourselves from a transhistorical perspective, such as at the level of abstraction of the economic reproduction system in general. On the contrary, the posing of future options compels us to reconceptualize reality from the perspective of the constitutional projects. These projects constantly fluctuate between progression and regression, depending on the nature and behaviour of forces in their own effort to assert themselves as subjects. This process will depend on the subjects' development, that is to say, on their conquest of new realities or on their restricting themselves to the boundary of the state sphere. In this respect, we can cite the case of the Bolivian miners and the process of transformation from a traditional subject within the state sphere to their reconstruction as subjects outside that sphere. This has meant abandoning their traditional forms of struggle.[23]

None the less, utopia may, in particular circumstances, respond to the imperative of shortening the historical horizon, in which case the past fulfils the function of a utopia. In a country's history, events may occur that cause a breach in continuity and, therefore, a breach in the contents of the collective memory and the mechanisms of social identification. Thus, the limits of what can be "seen" and stated as "possible" are disrupted. For instance, the image of 9 April in Colombia (also known as the "*bogotazo*") has been transformed into one of the determining elements in the political view of that country's dominant classes. (On 9 April 1948, Jorge Eliecer Gaitán, a presidential candidate representing popular interests and the most likely winner in the elections, was murdered. This incident provoked a popular insurrection in the capital and nationwide that heralded the beginning of the period known as "The Violence": an unmerciful struggle between liberals and conservatives.) Therefore, we should not be surprised that the National Front strongly stressed "the elements of restoration of the liberal order" and "played down any prospects of democratic change."[24] For example, they opened up participation in political power to traditionally excluded groups.

Something else happens when the establishment of a political force itself becomes an obstacle to new developments; the social subject that is constituted pretends in his particular project to reassert his society's continuity in all its complexity – for instance, a pro-coup bourgeoisie that pretends to reform itself by assuming a democratic façade. Readopting tradition after a breakaway situation also implies the restoration of the complex historical configuration that characterized the break from tradition (in this case, democratic tradition). This forms part of a national and international context, so that, if we dispense with that complexity, "false possibilities, options relating to a past that does not exist any more,"[25] may appear. What ideologically is claimed as necessary to retrieve the past is not historically possible any more, unless one is willing to accept that the former historical situation may be repeated.

What we have said above amounts to thinking that history proceeds intermittently, in a way that each one of those moments has the features of collective amnesia. It could be true that history does not unfold in a progressive manner, but it can in no way be admitted that it does not constitute a set of accumulated experiences; even if it is not capable of moving in a particular direction, this does not mean it turns full circle. The past is constantly being reformed in the present, according to the options constructed.

With regard to this idea we can point to two instances as examples of this process. On the one hand, in Argentina efforts to establish a democratic tradition are opposed by the obstacles forced upon them by important military powers. On the other hand, and in contrast, in Uruguay the struggle for democracy centres on a process of restoring the past prior to the military coup; this process has led to a cutting of alternatives and abandonment of new options.[26]

The fundamental problem is that in history we are not dealing with situations that proceed autonomously, with occasional unexpected interruptions. The constitution of each one of history's features is rather the result of a vocation for utopia and the ability to make it feasible. The possibility of acting depends on the historical context in which we are located. It may so happen that the latter is taken for a political system, as well as the opposite, that the political system is placed within a context incorporating other elements that are alien to the system. For instance, if democracy is identified in terms of a context, we do not understand how or why it is vulnerable; we must pay attention to the fact that democracy as a system is inserted in a historical *substratum* that makes of the political system an isolated element within a broad configuration of economic and idiosyncratic elements. Peru and Bolivia are good illustrations of this statement.

In the case of Peru, the elements "limiting the role and value assumed by representative democratic systems"[27] are those responsible for orienting social groups towards the arena of direct confrontation. This has forced industries repeatedly to demolish democracy by means of military intervention. All this shows that the nature of the political system is determined neither by its inner structure nor by its functional logic, but by a reality that prevents, "in democratic periods, citizens from being deprived of rights and opportunities that they should freely enjoy by virtue of written rules, formally granted by such democracies."[28]

Bolivia is, without doubt, the example where the problem of uncertainty between the ideological approach and the historical horizon is most clearly posed. How can we define the viability of a power project that implies a minimum of homogeneity in the cultural, economic, and social fields without paying attention to the reality of a social formation that lacks the unity demanded by the power project. That reality represents, in Zavaleta's words, "the pathetic unity of the diverse," as opposed to the simplified concurrence or unity that is demanded by projects.[29]

2. Society and state: Institutional forms of politics

Historical reality understood as the construction of reality in terms of cultural creation brings us to the discussion of the problem of institutional forms of politics. This is obviously an area we must consider in order to understand how decision-making and its possibilities bring about certain results caused by the actions of varying subjects, such as, on the one hand, social forces, and, on the other hand, nations and ethnic minorities in search of a response to their claims in the short as well as the long term.

The law, as it defines the sphere of politics, forms part of the state level, inasmuch as it is an area of institutional politics, even though its role and content can be differently appreciated by various subjects. For instance, in the case of Peru, it is stated that:

The law is not seen as a mechanism able to counterbalance power, and the instances where its inability can be perceived are not criticized in terms of politics, generally speaking. In this sense, power has its own legitimacy. . . . This idea of law as an intermediate arena in the midst of power confrontation has an inordinate effect on the democratic psychology of this country's populace, where, up to this point, it has been impossible to bring together the force and legitimacy of the majority.[30]

The area of the state is the area of instrumental power. In opposition to this, politics may also generate its own sphere, outside the one established by law. This is the area of power that gives rise to culture and its various projects. This activity of constructing projects not incorporated in the sphere of law may be redirected by it; these are, essentially, efforts intended to enlarge democracy's social base. From the ground of civil society, institutionalization is nourished as a field of instrumental powers in charge of the operative approach to alternatives and their possibilities.

We have previously said that it is in the interstices of society, in very specific areas, where the creation of politics appears integrated into daily life and, in many cases, transcends the state level. This is how significant changes occur that comprehend not only shifts of power but also different ways of coping with such changes. As an example of this role of power in constructing projects, we may cite the efforts of new social movements that are, "unquestionably, the greatest innovation on the political scene, as they pose new demands so far neglected by traditional organisms."[31] Although these movements emerge within traditional structures of expression and power, they act outside of them; they are manifested through different subjects from those embraced by the programmes of political parties, which are not strictly determined by party-like reasoning and practice.

This sort of movement tends to displace politics from the state level, transferring it to daily life. In this sense, such a movement tends towards a reformulation of relations between public and private matters, thus establishing new discourses between political rules and the basic sense of daily life. Within Bogotá's urban area, "objection to the construction project of *Avenida de los Cerros*" is recognized as "a point of departure, which demonstrates the political relevance of *barrio* struggles. Such a project would dislocate a large area of popular neighbourhoods. For the first time a *barrio* claim caused a massive, coordinated movement, and one of the *barrios'* associations became the interlocutor of municipal administration in a large city."[32]

These movements take place in a "review of the political,"[33] which also considers the subjectivity of the protagonists and the meaning of the power struggle. When they acquire an explicitly political nature they challenge the narrow and self-justifying tendencies of certain bureaucratic social struggles, or even of state domain. In other cases, their being critical of authoritarianism and attempts to revitalize society, without stating any deliberately political objectives, "tends to put before the public certain dimensions of life and social organization that had been overshadowed."[34]

Such movements seem to exist in several Latin American countries, even though the contents of their struggles are different. In Chile, for instance, "all movements and trends share a common principle, whether in the conduct of daily behaviour, public life, intellectual elaboration, religious experiences, or the manifestations of art; they challenge authoritarian order, for it is unable to provide sufficient meaning for the construction of real life situations, life-worlds acceptable to society's cultural tradition."[35]

The framework for understanding the meaning and nature of emergent social subjects, as well as the function of regional environments and/or locations in which we can observe the historical memory and will that bring together the new collective subjects, is constituted by the prospects of viable alternatives for the construction of society's projects. These projects are resolved in the tension arising from the conflict with order imposed by power (in terms of a fixing of the historical dynamics in accordance with the reproduction requirements of a particular dominant project) or as new formulations of old projects. In his study of Peru, Lauer points out that, in this way, "some have seen the *andino* tradition surviving in forms of an intense 'assembly' of the marginalized urban sectors. We might, perhaps, be confusing pressing forms of survival with the survival of traditional democratic forms, or the development of other new forms. In any case, this country has been fostering identity by other means, trying to make the inhabitants into citizens, rather than retaining or broadening these democratic practices."[36]

The possible content demanded by utopia or *novum* represents a stage of history that culminates with the idea of a construction of history. This imposes limits on the very possibility of a utopia: vocation for change is replaced by a vocation for government. Truly, the utopian model is now being shaped by the influence of society, that is to say, by its "viability" according to a particular correlation of forces. It so happens that the possibility of disrupting the logics of order contained in utopia is realized in the effort to construct history. Therefore, dreams and hopes are transformed into "politics," in other words, into manageable reality through options whose succession represents a conjunction of all times; past and future come together in the present.

3. The generation of state order: Public and private

All cultural power tends to become instrumental power through mechanisms of legitimation that try to broaden the state sphere. For instance, as long as the limits binding politics to the stability of order are not broken, then electoral participation determines that social forces may assume the same form of expression in state politics as at the level of parties.

Regarding institutionalization as a field of instrumental powers, we must be careful not to confuse law as a demarcation of the field of power with the power of law in its own right. This distinction is important, and it is related to the fact that, in the first situation, cultural logic governs power, whereas in the second we are located within the framework of political logic as formulated by law. All this is related to what we understand as the functioning of democracy.

When law outlines an area of power, democracy constitutes a space for social projects. When, instead, law is an instrumental power capable of counteracting culture-creating powers, democracy becomes identified by a particular social project.[37] In the former situation, democracy surrenders instrumental power to the demands of its own "civilian part," which are manifested in the possibility of manifold projects; in the latter situation, democracy's civilian part is reduced to the content of the dominant project. In the latter case, the project takes over that civilian area, identifying it as its content, so that it is no longer equal to the potential of many projects; on the contrary, it is identified with the order enforced by that particular project. This situation can be illustrated by Chile's case, where "the interaction of civil society is permitted only within the boundaries defined by the military order, taking this situation to "grotesque extremes."[38]

State logic tends to reduce society's set of problems to the parameters of "public order disturbance" and "public order restoration." If politics has to fulfil such functions, it is reduced to the level of state order. In this context, the concept of "public life" assumes its real

192

value, for it appears to be a counterpart of state control and supervision. In addition, it also serves as a mediation between state (or instrumental) power and the creativity of civilian society (power as a cultural creation). This is what constitutes the very core of problems faced by the dialectic between the penetration of civil society dynamics into state structures and the penetration of the state into the civilian area.

The historical process tends to highlight the first trend, namely, the increasing trend towards the penetration of civil society dynamics into state structures. The mechanisms of civil society increasingly form part of a state order. For instance, voting activities are seen as "part of government mechanisms, rather than an act of coexistence."[39]

Is civil society subordinate to political logic in the political culture of Latin America? Is not the argument of homogenization or the unity of the diverse – which is found in Peru as well as in Bolivia – perhaps a reflection of what we are saying?

It is stated that "in Peru there is, or, if we prefer, Peru itself is, a diverse truth in need of articulation."[40] Therefore, there is a risk that in reflecting on the possibility of democracy one may incur a sort of "political and linguistic gathering of a national totality that is not there."[41] For this reason, a dissociation occurs between theoretical thought on representative democracy and the "big mass of electoral manoeuvre," which may be the base for a centralized, homogenizing discourse about a set of values that integrate the national idea with the idea of order. In Bolivia's situation, what happened was a formalization of the political task through rigid organizing structures "whose function was to exercise political control over the masses (whether they are classes or not) at the state level, a political procedure in the party apparatus, especially unions, which limits alternative forms of expression."[42]

A particular feature of political culture is to conform to state logic that wants to homogenize and integrate the heterogeneous sociocultural reality of the Latin American countries, to the extreme where state order becomes the content of the project that society is trying to construct. The reality that power imposes an order is characteristic of political dialectics, thus inhibiting development that is open to the demands that form part of the ever-changing historical conditions, and to the same extent that order determines the sort of power suited to it. This should not be confused with the problem of power being necessary to the project of a social subject, so that it may become a project shared by society.

This is why, in a specific conjuncture, groups may go through a qualitative leap with relation to their organization as subjects, so that what had been only disconnected and "stop-gap" practices and initiatives become components of a large-scale project that fully relocates the group in the framework of a much broader historical horizon transcending the level of piecemeal initiatives. This may be illustrated by what happened in Guatemala as a result of the 1976 earthquake. As a result of that experience, many work practices and action programmes experienced a complete turn around, resulting in a qualitative transformation: "literacy work, Christian communities work, political discussions became true organizing factors with certain perspectives. . . . There was beginning to be an explicit interest in building an effort that would lead to something that could possibly help to change the situation."[43]

We may see groups expanding towards larger historical horizons, or the opposite may occur. The production of projects may be hindered by some mechanisms that, unlike the blocking of alternatives by state authoritarianism, want to impose the content of a particular project as a general horizon, setting a boundary to the options perceived as legitimate, or they may break up the forces that could constitute a threat to state order if they reached some degree of cohesion in the national area.

We may quote, in this respect, what happened in Peru after 1970, when the voting age was decreased from 21 to 18. In the 1980 elections, the expected radicalization did not occur. "A possible reason for this may be the great progress being made at the same time on television in the national territory . . . ; this is relevant in reaffirming the expansion of Peruvian central capitalism." Another reason is that choice in the "government elections" had developed. Indeed, on the one hand municipal elections were added to general elections through "the announcement of elections for traditional governments; on the other, the spread of 'cooperativism' and other forms of association community work (neighbourhood groups, etc.) contributes to the spread of electoral practice on an unheard of scale, and electoral practice is directly linked to the fate of the voting community."[44] Here political practice is extended, whether by integrating social protagonists that lack projects or through its expansion towards other areas that act as a base for the development of social subjects on a local scale.

194

4. Legitimation mechanisms and the exercise of power

The exercise of power contains the capacity to destroy patterns of attitudes, comprehension, and actions that from a particular subject and his project have been transformed into cultural habits. The exercise of power involves all that is wanted and rejected, all that is legitimated and marginalized, all that is possible and impossible to believe and even less to practise, all that is conceived as authentic, and all that is conceived as dangerous and strange, and thus must be destroyed. From this standpoint, to believe in a nation-state means to go beyond the protective boundaries, which are, in turn, the expression of very diverse subjects, cultures, projects, views of the future, and ways of repossessing the past. For this reason, a discussion about the future is meaningless unless it is carried out with regard to the analysis of the method of putting a project into practice, and of the role of respect for these diversities in the exercise of power.

An enlargement of civil society that allows some form of participation by the dominated sectors and the irruption of demands posed to the state order by the society's many diversities (economic, cultural, ethnic, etc.) ends up leading to the restriction of policies again. This is what happened in Colombia, at the end of Belisario Betancourt's term in office when politics was reduced to the level of Congress, so that, "disorder prevailed where a new political order had been attempted, necessitating a return to the old order."[45]

We have to face the fact that the exercise of power reduces the possibilities of the historical horizon that it was claiming to develop as its project. The dialectics of utopian order tend to be resolved in favour of order, since the ideological reduction prevails over the expansion of historical possibilities. This is a manifestation that the logic of political action is a question more of order than of creativity. Therefore, every project has to comply promptly with stabilizing demands, which are one of their main features;[46] this explains the tendency of the historical horizon to be reduced.

This tendency has certain repercussions for social subjects, since the dominant gravitation of the logic of order leads to a lack of articulation of cultural identities that do not adjust to its demands. Similarly, it leads to the socialization of subordinate subjects in the familiar ideological and technological patterns. This helps the nation (with the potential of several projects) to identify with order, or order (which, as we said, is merely the result of the dominant project making use of its ability to reproduce) to be the content of the nation. We may cite as an example the case of the peasant movement in Colombia. This may be considered as being submitted to "the diffusion message of the innovations in the improvement of agricultural techniques, and to religious, (political), and ideological discourse," which, in a wider sense, "will operate to legitimate the adoption of new behavioural patterns required by the 'development-oriented' modernization in the country."[47]

The same could be said about some social subjects, such as the youth movements, which tend to be socialized into the dominant values of mobility and consumerism, which direct them towards certain professional careers vital to the existing order (i.e. engineering, medicine, business administration, etc.), or the workers who are the object of changes in some of their behavioural patterns as a result of technological development. This results in requalification criteria that, in some cases, tend to define their behaviour.

In spite of all order's efforts to homogenize society, we find particular kinds of subject, such as ethnic minorities, that refuse to be integrated within certain system patterns. Because they do not correspond to a modernizing logic, they lose their function in society. In certain cases, these minorities may be marginalized, sometimes even by violent means. As an example we may cite the case of Guatemala, where peasant ethnic minorities have been uprooted, sometimes by force, and ordered out of the towns, allowing their conversion to religious sects totally alien to local customs. In extreme cases, such minorities have been violently exterminated.[48]

5. Maintaining and changing state order

When power is identified with the maintenance of established order, it tends to lose stability, for it is unable to be open-minded about the new historical demands, and it is bound to defend the established political order. This is fundamental to empty authoritarianism; its reason for being is to maintain an order protected against the challenges derived from historical horizons that are being created by social subjects.

The logic of authoritarian political order consists in eliminating all alternatives emanating from social subjects, establishing order itself as the nature of its role. Thus, this sort of political system is oriented towards preventing political interaction from becoming organized, so that it may not succeed in expressing different historical choices. The creation of new possibilities for the development and confrontation of new social subjects is inhibited; this may be expressed through mechanisms that tend to prevent the political struggle from escaping from the institutional arena that is imposed by the system itself. In other words, social dynamics are restricted by a pre-established structure of political subjects.

The clearest example of what we are saying would be the logic of national security that ignores challenges that emerge from the new international outlook on labour and technological changes resulting from the crisis of traditional development models. This way, all internal conflicts tend to be judged from the perspective of world policy, where it is deemed essential not to permit the interference of "alien" powers in the country. This ideological alienation translates as political alienation because it prevents the recognition of changes and growing demands within society.

Authoritarian order requires chaos as an ideological element in order that the common enemy is always present, so as to be able to justify such order disregarding any alternative project. The case of Uruguay may be cited, where the economic reality, increasingly linked to the general crisis of the capitalist system, prevented the maintenance of stability in accordance with traditional values that legitimated political power. In this context, "authoritarianism emerged with its own autonomous discourse, which became an option of order in the light of chaos, but the bipartite structure started to break down, encouraged by unitarian ideas of the left wing."[49] None the less, the pure logic of hanging on to power under the imperative "order versus chaos" is not capable of generating arenas where one can "break in to conquer self-legitimacy. . . transcending the propaganda frameworks of struggle against subversion."[50]

Authoritarian systems are diverted towards the constitution of dominant force capable of expressing different interests, but in such a way as to prevent a political game from tending to "escape from the control of traditional parties, and to develop in other areas."[51] Their limitation lies in the failure to accommodate the development and confrontation of forces.

In view of this one may wonder what the novelty is in the role of the armed forces as state administrators and, at the same time, as political representatives of segments of the bourgeoisie, or of this entire social class. The task of domination is enhanced when power is identified with order, and the political order, in turn, tends to be identified with a social theory, so that the social order resulting from the conjunction of society and political order may be considered as

197

the *only possible one*. This results in the reduction of the entire historical horizon to the limits of an ideology structured around the lack of alternatives to the imposed order. At the level of consciousness, the image is a development of a form of adaptive and pragmatic awareness, accompanied by "the culture of obedience," whose central value is placidity or scepticism. The counterpart of that culture of obedience is the development of a "clandestine culture."

In some Latin American countries (Chile, Argentina, Uruguay), the military control of power tends to go beyond the judging or reordering functions in critical moments in search of an integral organization of public life. Even though its ideological support is still the doctrine of "national security," it also wants to attain a "global reculturing of society."[52]

We can observe, from the facts, how "the military, in times of crisis, progress from being the 'conjunctural arbiters' and come to fulfil a messianic function, based on a high degree of corporate consciousness and of differentiated identity, which expresses their alienation from the rest of society."[53] Such a situation has had serious consequences in Latin American countries where a military regime has been replaced by a democratic and representative civilian government: the appearance of a conjuncture which struggles between oblivion and the assimilation of the past.

If we reject the attempts to recall what has been achieved by power holders in military regimes, we are, at the same time, ignoring the fact that the past has been transformed into an experience of collective memory, beyond the ideological and value agreement or dissent in planning to confront that past. "To look to the future without referring to the past" is to find continuity in history and, therefore, in a people's political culture. Is it perhaps conceivable that people's culture, after years of systematic repression, after all sorts of murder and discrimination, may not reflect this legacy; that it may cynically and naively pretend to return to a previous moment, retrieving the essence of a democratic past that has remained immaculate? This process does not imply the modification of social conditions that help to establish repressive powers; at a deeper level, it means, instead, to leave untouched the authoritarian essence of the dominant classes, which has remained hidden behind a deceptive liberal appearance.

In some countries (Chile, for instance), this deception has found expression in a tolerant attitude towards the proliferation of the organisms of class representation, inasmuch as they help to enlarge the social base of domination. A bourgeoisie, like that of Chile, has come to "perceive that the multiplicity of labour organizations was an opening mechanism, favourable to new alliances."[54] In the light of military experiences, the bourgeois ideologists have not hesitated to admit (until 1973 Chile was considered a typical exponent of the liberal–democratic system) that "constitutions have not been, in their generation, examples of the purest democracy."[55] This perfectly illustrates how the disruption of liberal thought is a reflection of isolated conjunctures within a framework defined by the continuity of authoritarian ideology. Otherwise, how can we comprehend that, from the heart of civilian ideology, and from political abstinence, armies of torture and persecution may arise?

An important aspect of culture that contributes to shaping our way of viewing political reality is the idea one has of political facts, especially state facts. Indeed, any decision on future alternatives is based on our understanding of the continuity or discontinuity of the nature of the political phenomena. That is why, if we depart from a mechanical acceptance of continuity, options will always remain fixed in the past. If we do not profoundly question the armed forces (as a state institution), we are refusing to acknowledge that the imposed political order does not necessarily coincide with the new historical horizon one is trying to follow.

In countries that have only recently adopted a democratic system, it is proposed as necessary "to create the conditions for the foundation of a new pact or national arrangement, and to identify the need for a social pact within a more complex view of conflicts, beyond the pragmatic demands of political struggle."[56] "This implies a transformation of the military culture, overcoming the habit of determining political competence as annihilation of the opponent,"[57] as well as a change in the "militarized" culture for a large part of the civilian population.

The historical horizon moulded by democratic and development experiences of the 1950s and 1960s surpassed even the potentialities of the bourgeoisie. The hegemony strategy that was kept underground ended up damaging its own accumulation and simple fragile structure. It was abandoned to the point of denying the historical possibilities that the bourgeoisie had itself helped to initiate, namely, the strengthening of union movements, the improvement of educational standards, agrarian reform, the establishment of participation mechanisms, the maturing of a new, questioning intelligentsia, etc. However, the historical horizon thus opened tends to be blocked up, according to the logic imposed by the project, which intends to con-

tinue being dominant. Demands for the continuity of political order
dominate its struggle, as they are the only possible characteristic of
both new and old history.

The logic of order dominates over that of development and
change, and is accompanied by a gradual stripping of political power
and its values as a result of its being dissociated from any progress
initiative and being limited to the pure necessity of surviving as an
order. The latter manifests itself at the level of different kinds of
organizations suited to encouraging the construction of history. We
can judge whether or not the organization is suitable either in terms
of the historical horizon where the contradiction between socialism
and capitalism prevails, or according to the more restricted framework of a particular project related to groups, strata, or social forces
with a broader scope. There seems to be doubt that an organization must respond to needs deriving from a *Weltanschauung* and a historical memory, as well as from requirements to respond to future
options. The problem arises when future options, which may mean
a break with the past and, therefore, a discontinuity, have to take
account of the requirements of historical and cultural continuity (demanded by the *Weltanschauung* and the historical memory as a
mechanism of collective identification). However, this discontinuity
may bring about an expansion of the horizon of what the social subject is historically able to perceive. It may, therefore, represent a step
forward in the role of the subject as a social force.

6. Politics and utopia

The construction of reality leads us to the distinction between realism
and potential, which represents another way of differentiating between the task of politics and utopian politics. And so we refer again
to the dialectics between order and its disruption.

The disruption may be a result of the antagonism between various
projects; this constitutes an expression of the history of order, that is
to say, as something relative rather than something absolute. The
absolute character of order will depend on the perception of different
social subjects "as components of the same project."[58] This situation
is best expressed when cultural identity is assumed as a common project by all social subjects; in this case the practices associated with the
project are defined as the only possible reality, while the content of
the common project is mistaken for the historical horizon of possibilities. This occurs when cultural patterns and discursive models are
imposed and all potentialities of reality become synthesized.

An extremely clear example of the above may be found in Mexico, with the transformation of the 1917 Constitution, not only in the Magna Charta but also in the structure that defines the boundaries of all possible realities to be fostered as projects, and that is, as a rule, transformed into an element constituting not only what is permissible but also what is viable. The realization of any possibility is contained within this framework, which represents, on the other hand, the method of recognizing a possible reality.

Another such instance is to be found in the case where the possibility of reality may be a characteristic of the project itself, without considering that it simply represents one option among many others for the construction of reality. It seems appropriate to cite the guerrilla experience in Latin America. Indeed, the idea of a military avant-garde may not be useful in mobilizing the realities of some social subjects, even though it could very well be useful for others. If the struggle's militarist nature is not linked to the sociocultural syndrome and the historical experience, at a transactional and non-violent level, and if it is not linked to the subjects' civic nature, isolation would ensue and, as a result, there would be a lack of action on the part of those subjects. It may also be true, though, that the presence of an activating element may allow us to uncover "what apathy and indolence were concealing of revolutionary potential."[59]

The above may be illustrated in El Salvador's case. Ever since the 1970s, this country has experienced a process of civil war; the guerrillas appear after a succession of obstructions of the demands of traditional organizations. Because of the violence exercised against them (in 1979 and 1980), "apparently there was a diminishing in the popular struggle as a result of repression, but, at the same time, there was a generalization of armed struggle."[60] None the less, the guerrilla leaders themselves admitted that, "in a popular war, the role of the military element is not absolute. It is decisive for a revolutionary movement to know whether it has achieved the necessary military build-up, which, combined with the political elements, may permit a change in the correlation of forces. . . . As we can see, the enemy knows very well that war is determined in terms of who obtains popular support."[61]

The above is in contrast with situations where utopia fails to define viable projects that are linked to some specific social forces.[62] This could be the case with development alternatives that do not clearly acknowledge any subject's identity: we are faced with the problem of the formal survival of democracy and its rediscovery (when it has been lost), where we cannot conclude that there may be experiences proving the establishment of forces that are able to support it, expand it, and reproduce it at a social level. We may observe that, even though an electorate could grow, "the depth of people's rights as citizens, as part of the modernity formed by the democratic text,"[63] has not grown, or, even if these facts have developed, the emergence of a subject with a project capable of being maintained in the face of several alternative projects has so far not been confirmed. Such was the case of Popular Unity in Chile, where, for lack of a subject and a soundly built project (to a great extent this was the result of an atomizing process of political protagonists and dissimilar projects), the objective possibility of the move towards socialism failed to develop as a project. It remained as a utopia without project and subjects with the ability to activate what is.

We may, indeed, discuss the need to create the political and economic conditions indispensable for fully taking advantage of our countries' potentialities, but who is going to create those conditions in such a way as to overcome discouragement by conservative positions, instead of aiding the conquest of a utopia that may profoundly transform reality? How are we going to solve the dilemma that appears in our countries, and reconcile capital legitimacy and accumulation on the threshold of development, as well as the crisis of neo-liberalism? What is there concealed by reality, with the impulse to go up to higher stages? How can we recognize it? Who will be the protagonist of that leap into the new future?

We are at a turning point that demands a new image of the future. It is, therefore, necessary to re-create patterns of self-realization; we are thinking either of social forces or of the nation.

III. History as project construction

1. Culture and national projects

History is a political struggle characterized by the conjunction, forsaking, or imposition of projects pertaining to different social subjects that are working to build the future.

Latin America's history appears to run along an axis that has been fundamental to its development to date; namely the construction of the national project. Political struggles and subjects have developed along this axis in their search for the "optimum republic." This axis is still in vogue now, even though many politicians and intellectuals question its viability. The search for new alternatives for constructing national projects in a specific area, which may combine utopia and political experience, historical memory and consciousness, imagination and will, is urgently needed in order to face the situation described above, because "either we invent or we err," as Simón Rodríguez lucidly used to say.[64]

A project, as an anticipation of historical possibilities perceived by a social subject, synthesizes the elements constituting that subject's existence. That is why projects are constantly modified and their development becomes a dynamic, and sometimes contradictory, process. Inasmuch as a project combines a subject's way of being and acting, it constitutes the nature of its existence and projection into history, as well its potential for the building of a future. Therefore, if the construction of a national project in Latin America continues to be in vogue, the real problem lies in how to construct that national project taking plurality and democracy as a starting point.

The nation-forming process in Latin America assumed a character essentially different from that in Europe. There, the integration of a nation was achieved through a development process that took place over more than a thousand years (which included the transition from a feudal society to a pre-capitalist society, consolidation of languages, and finally the advent of trade, which culminated in the formation of national states, and the consolidation of production relations). In Latin America, this process had a precocious and violent character. Another feature was the destruction of native cultures. All this led to more complicated and weaker forms of national integration. As a result, state construction in Latin America largely preceded the construction of nations.[65]

The first task one has to face is finding an optimum form of organization for the new states. On the one hand, a choice must be made between federalism and centralism, on the other a broad process of creativity and inventiveness takes place. Such was the case with Bolívar's various attempts to propose new systems for the governments of Bolivia and Colombia, characterized by his idea that "only democracy is susceptible to freedom, but the problem is how can we combine power, prosperity, and permanence in it?"[66] This problem is still with us.

Ideologically, the political and intellectual leaders of that time were in favour of popular sovereignty and ideas of democracy based on the Enlightenment philosophy, or American representative democracy. However, their belief in the need for a strong government, and in the idea that the people are not educated towards a self-governing state,[67] slowly gave way to the development of the concept of national unity, understood as a reconciliation of several oligarchic interests, leaving out the popular classes. The restricted character of democracy evolved in most cases towards presidentialism or dictatorship. Such restriction prevented the political integration of nationalities. Ever since, "theoretical adherence to the principle of representative democracy, and its derogation in practice, appears to be one of the fundamental features of Latin American political order."[68]

The nineteenth century in Latin America is characterized by struggles for an establishment of projects; even though they were coeval, their characteristics were different. While on the one hand liberals and conservatives fought to impose their projects, searching for an order that had not naturally arisen from independence, on the other, outside these struggles, other movements, expressing ethnic or caste struggles, were the means to manifest the restlessness of great population masses, marginalized from power.[69] In a great many Latin American countries, liberal projects were imposed upon conservative ones that were striving to maintain traditional pre-capitalist production within an economy that was beginning to be ever more infiltrated by foreign capital.

The advent of capitalism and imperialism at the end of the nineteenth century caused a disturbance of national sentiment in Latin American countries. This first became noticeable in the construction of cultural projects that replaced the local ones; dominant classes tending towards cosmopolitanism, for instance (French-like customs and manners, etc.), were mostly responsible for that. Secondly, the disturbance of national sentiment showed itself in internal consolidation as urban centres became isolated from the countryside (where the relations of pre-capitalist production coincided with export-oriented economies), so restricting the possibilities for autonomous domestic development. In this context, positivist philosophy seemed to prevail under the slogan "order and progress"; it ended up by justifying despotism and dictatorships throughout the continent.

The task of ordering civil society from the top is carried out through a centralizing state, as well as through the creation of national armies to repress popular movements. Nevertheless, an unorganized civil society, unsettled in its political alternatives, and the appearance of imperialism (which greatly contributed to changing the political and social structure) allowed, at the beginning of the 1920s, the development of alternative projects of a national character, whose roots lay in popular culture or which at least contributed to retrieve such roots. A new consciousness started to develop among the middle classes and petty bourgeoisie, as well as among the working classes from popular, national, and revolutionary positions.

From then on, national projects politically adopted the policies of labour parties (anarchist and socialist) and liberal parties, even though they were also manifested as popular movements with agrarian claims. At the outset of the twentieth century, the appearance of alternative projects was expressed through armed mass movements, popular and revolutionary.[70] These movements proposed a return to their own roots. Problems began to be approached from different angles; the Indian question ceased to be a moral or ethnic one, and came to be viewed as a social and economic problem whose centre lay in the nature of ownership;[71] "an empire of reason and feeling develops, educating our peoples in the cult of the future."[72] The nation, with a new concept of ownership,[73] was to be developed on the basis "not of a restoration, but of the future integration of America in its historic past."[74]

In order to achieve this, "it is not enough simply to develop an intelligence, we must also develop a will."[75] The twentieth century has introduced several processes in Latin America: firstly, the national expression of classes, which gave birth to revolutionary nationalism and became a contradictory phenomenon (that has so far not been sufficiently studied); and, secondly, increased awareness among the popular classes of the viability of their future projects, which benefited the experiences of the great mass movements of this century. The construction of Latin America's national project compels us to search for our own and "to develop an awareness of how values may acquire new categories."[76] In order to attain this, it is fundamental that subjects as well as peoples are dedicated to the task of reconstructing the possible. Such construction implies the creation of utopias; the generation of will and consciousness, which are developed from the unknown, may shape that utopian world and help it materialize in the future.

2. The past as a project

As we attempt to define a feasible future, we encounter the fact that projects are oriented by an effort of restoration; we are faced with the force of a country's cultural continuity. The future tends to represent an attempt to return to the past. Since the chosen option may be represented by returning to a longed-for situation rather than by an image of the future as a new birth, utopia does not necessarily acknowledge that its roots may be in a time to come, renewed and free of past confusions. It is important to know whether the options that create history are embedded in the past or in the future. In this sense a false future may arise from oblivion, in other words, from historical discontinuity, while the true future is located in the retrieval of the past based on the construction of options that may not simply be a repetition of worn out solutions.

Longing for the past has been a typical feature of the thought and behaviour of the dominant classes. From the beginning of this century we can observe a nostalgia for traditional beliefs in the superiority of the old aristocratic values that were already in decline. Aristocratic ideology, which despises the bourgeoisie, leads to the glorification of not only traditional values but also "families and men belonging to those groups on which natural superiority was bestowed." In this vein, Gilberto Freyre speaks of the "quasi-mystic *Aryanism* of those who, like Oliveira Vianna, base the superiority of the old Brazilian aristocracy on racial prejudice." In his book *Evolution of the Brazilian People*, he states that large land estates, typical of the agrarian social structure, differentiate the aristocracy from property tenants and slaves. "The lords, their family, their relatives. . . almost all of them, wholly belonging to the Aryan race,"[77] they are all members of the aristocracy. Regarding Mexico, Bulnes, without being so blatantly racist, condemned socially climbing groups as "corrupt parties," which meant to criticize the possibility of rising to power by means of suffrage. "The exercise of democracy. . . seemed a degrading exhibition to those who felt possessed, not only of the means of production but also of dignity at an almost sublime level." They could not possibly accept democracy, for it was incompatible with their aristocratic ideology; they would never accept "the mediation of bourgeois groups, so as to keep control of them in normal situations." This seignorial crisis strengthens the feelings towards a past that it tried to retrieve with profound nostalgia. Such sentiments found expression in the literary works of the members of traditional families;[78] they attempted to resurrect the values that prevailed in pre-capitalist society.[79] This is what the poet López Velarde called "intimate reactionary sadness." It is a nostalgia that acknowledges the antecedent of the famous distinction between civilization and barbarism; it recognizes this duality, but inverts its origin.

The ideological expression of such thought is typical of many intel-

lectuals, such as José Enrique Rodó, who is outstanding for his eloquence in his work *Ariel*. In it, "a lively feeling of the élite" is not
only justified. Transferred to the sphere of politics, "it promoted
scepticism before incipient democracies."[80] This aided the development of aristocratic despotism, which would be adopted by individuals and groups participating in a rapid process of upward mobility, and would contribute to spreading the aristocratic spirit, which
was already dominating Latin American countries, even from the
second half of the nineteenth century.

The rise of middle sectors

The struggle against liberalism may be considered as an antecedent to
the profoundly anti-democratic thought of dominant groups, whether
or not it was of aristocratic origin and style. The liberal state, and
modern civilization as a whole, were condemned with the church's
consent. That oligarchy considered itself to be "the unshakeable
foundation of the social and political edifice," which could be condemned only by "anarchists and upstarts."[81]

At the beginning of the twentieth century, the development of the
social struggle was what definitely caused the displacement of this
way of thinking and its corresponding state form. Indeed, the oligarchic state crisis opened the way for processes of economic modernization that led to an unrestrained process of social mobility, which, as
we shall see, gave rise to different ideas on society and power.

Internal contradictions within the dominant and hegemonic group
began to arise. This group was harassed by economic and political
demands from the rising middle and popular classes; such demands
became effective through the gradual spreading of universal suffrage.
A sector was generated that maintained the liberal–bourgeois tradition, along with another that was devoted to promoting "changes
from within the system, such as guarantees allowing an internal
course of action that would be forbidden to anyone with the intention
of bringing about changes from outside the system."[82] This new sector was represented by such projects adopted by the social democrat
and Christian democrat parties. There is no denying that this internal
polarization of the aristocratic dominant group is but a consequence
of the irruption of middle sectors, which, from the 1920s, reappeared
time and again. In this context, one cannot ignore such facts as those
presented by Haya de la Torre, Getúlio Vargas, Marmaduke Grove,
Jorge E. Gaitán, Juan Domingo Perón, and Víctor Paz Estenssoro.

This ideological expression assumed very real political forms, as

207

has been demonstrated in our time. In 1948 in Colombia, and in 1945 in Argentina, oligarchies "were completely insensitive to the problems they were creating for the future, binding themselves to solving problems from the past."[83] This was evidently a result of their inability to define a future project, and it was also an indicator of their attachment to a certain tradition that compelled them to "re-evaluate their remote origins."[84] This need was cast forth with the idea of "re-evaluating the colonial period in order to search within it for the first existence of a national soul." This is the Hispanic tradition, which became "one pole of popular thought," for it stated that the foundation of Latin America's nationality can be found in the colonial world.[85]

None the less, the position of the bourgeoisie as having the greatest disposition for change has always been a bias towards the bourgeois classes, rather than being truly prepared for a transformation. In cases where the political game has gone beyond the boundaries of intra-bourgeoisie struggles, the bourgeoisie has not hesitated to sacrifice all liberal and democratic values, going so far as to yield to political situations where "opposition parties were persecuted, minorities were looked down upon, civil rights were trampled on, and basic human rights were ignored by true police-states."[86] The lesson to be learnt here is that the main obstacle for bourgeois liberalism lies in the danger that it may lead democracy to a system that endangers the bourgeoisie's social and political project. In this case, political dynamics end up transforming democracy into a representation project that may become alternative, instead of continuing to be identified with one social and political project alone. This has forced democracy to adjust the dominating mechanisms every time it has decided to allow political participation.

Domination adjustments and options
Since World War I, the liberal bourgeoisie has had to adjust the mechanisms of power so as to ensure a more stable and effective control over the possible development of alternatives as a consequence of the rise of new social and political protagonists. Formulas may vary, from attempts at isolating the one and only political front to an argument between groups over the delegation of power. The 1929–1930 crisis refined these processes. Such was the case with Trujillo in the Dominican Republic, Somoza in Nicaragua, Ubico in Guatemala, Machado in Cuba; this was also the case of politicians who, without

being openly repressive and militaristic like the former, held a strong conservative viewpoint, such as Uriburu in Argentina and Leguía in Peru. The problem lies in how to transform the middle and popular sectors, which began to emerge in the 1920s and 1930s as undeniable instruments, in order to reinforce the dominant system and thus prevent them from being a channel for disruptive political options. Popular sectors were particularly "prone to directing their tremendous power to favour anyone who would seduce them;"[87] the same thing had happened before with middle sectors, which had, at first, simply followed "some aristocratic or oligarchic sector."

In the context of alliances and the political game derived from these new forces entering the political arena, aristocratic groups "still remember the patriarchal organization – an expression of the *hacienda* – and its orientation towards a clientele state."[88] Even after many years of exercising liberal democracy, large popular sectors have updated the paternalist idea. Corporatism and communitarianism, finding their political and ideological representation in Christian democrat parties, are an expression of this. However, the critical situation resulting from an instability caused by the new forces could not be resolved within the narrow framework of central ideologies that, owing to their own ambiguities, could not guarantee stable political control. Such was the case of the radical regimes (1948–1952) and the Christian democrat rule (1964–1970) in Chile.

Old nineteenth-century slogans of "order and progress," which Brazil has even engraved on its banner, or Julio Roca's "peace and management" in Argentina continued to express the orientation of those who tried to lessen political activity in order to ensure capital profit. "Politics must fit within rigid frameworks that will prevent any disruption of public peace." The predominance of the logic of order and its identification with a particular social project urged a restriction on the limits of political participation that would be representative of society's alternative projects. The effort to exclude these forces, middle classes, and popular sectors from public life became the pattern to follow, in spite of the fluctuations determined by the need for political alliances, which always appeared as power instruments but never as possibilities for the generation of political options that differed from the dominant ideology. In order to achieve this, they had at their disposal all sorts of means, from electoral fraud, or the imposition of legal restrictions, to what Vallenilla Lanz called "democratic Caesarism."

In many Latin American countries, "the *caudillo* [leader] has been the only force of social survival;"[89] during the 1970s and 1980s it became the institutional figure of the armed forces. It represents an authoritarian form of exercising power that became even more necessary when, at the beginning of the 1980s, it had to face an economic and financial crisis. The crisis was dealt with through neo-liberal strategies, thought of as economic strategies inherent to democracy. This is even more relevant when the problem of new forces is not constrained by having to share power within a larger alliance system, but when such forces endanger the preservation of Western Christian cultural values, as the proposal for a society inspired by socialism might seem to traditional forces. This is why liberal democracy has to be identified in terms of "Western" and "Christian" values. Therefore, any attempt to transform the liberal economy, which is based on the free interaction of private ownership in order to achieve the goals of social justice, begins to be seen as an attack on those values. Furthermore, power must not only fulfil the function of preserving order; in addition, it must retain its ideological and cultural identity. This identity is often thought of as being closely associated with the Hispanic tradition. Such is the case of Vasconcelos in his *Breve historia de México* (Brief History of Mexico), as well as his statement on the "Spanish vs Saxon" conflict included in his *Raza cósmica* (Cosmic Race). This proposal ends up by being mixed up with Catholicism, and even with the fundamentalist form of it.

Retrieval of the colonial Hispanic past adds up to the search for the national spirit, whose very existence the positions of revolutionary thought are challenging. None the less, that spirit is not just determined by the historical past; it also recognizes a telluric root, as supported by the Bolivian Jaime Mendoza in his statement that "when we speak of the Indian, we are implicitly speaking of the earth;" we may also quote the idea that "culture is but the expression of a fragile force." We find this idea of the past and the earth expressed by several authors, such as Euclides de Cunha, Graça Aranha in Brazil, and, of course, Vasconcelos in Mexico, not forgetting Samuel Ramos and Leopoldo Zea.

These concepts convey what is innate in a nation, what is different, and what is native, and they are now being manifested in military development that has become the main instrument in the fight against leftist feeling, which is accused of being anti-national and of favouring alien trends and ideas.

The authoritarian tradition and the present crisis
The exposition on democracy contained in Rodó's *Ariel* may be helpful in recognizing the basic components firstly of the aristocratic
oligarchy and secondly of the bourgeoisie.

Any equality of conditions in societies' order, as well as any homogeneity in
nature, are comprised of an unstable balance. Conquered equality may represent only a starting point for society, once democracy has accomplished
the negative task of erasing unjust advantage. There is still a positive task to
be performed. Democracy's positive task, and its glory, consists in provoking the revelation and control of true human superiorities by means of effective incentives.

These words seem to anticipate by several decades what has been
asserted in neo-liberal notions; namely that development is the result
of the active behaviour of people who want to take the risk of transforming ideas into monopolies and, in turn, of transforming monopolies into industry. This is an authoritarian and anti-democratic
tradition of bourgeois thought, strengthened in the present crisis.
Circumstantially, bourgeois thought does not just have financial and
economic significance; it mainly assumes political significance, for it
constitutes a reflection of, as well as an ideological response to, the
East–West conflict. This situation has worsened proportionally to
new American expansionary policies inspired by neo-liberalism.

In this context, it is necessary to examine the different aspects of
Latin America's increasing rightism. We shall analyse the most
relevant points necessary for understanding the relation between
culture and power.

THE BLOCKING OF SUBVERSION. There is absolutely no doubt that in
Latin American society as a whole there is a tendency towards the
right. The imposition of neo-liberal policies and the reduction of the
state's role as the main agent for development are some of the symptoms of these rightist tendencies. We must also mention the state's
tendency to lose legitimacy in its monopolizing force. In Central
America, the rightist trend manifests itself more obviously and bru-
tally. Since the end of the 1970s, the advancement of progressive
political forces has entailed a ruthless struggle intended to retain the
state's privileges. In addition, there exist polarizing dynamics caused
by pressures resulting from America's geo-political strategy in that
part of the continent.

The defence of privilege by the dominant group creates an internal contradiction. Indeed, right-wing politics, because it basically claims to defend a social order, is sometimes interpreted as a need to foster political measures intended to undermine the social basis of progressive and revolutionary forces; this may very possibly help to divide them as well.

Such is the case in El Salvador, where the "modernization" measures of Christian democracy (attempts to formulate minimum benefits for the masses and improvements in the state's system of resource exploitation) have led to the appearance of a coalition of forces centred around the Partido Alianza Republicana Nacionalista (Arena; Nationalist Republican Alliance Party). The ultra-conservative ideologies of this body help to support "a project of oligarchic restoration," without hesitating to envisage genocide against the Frente Farabundo Martí para la Liberación Nacional (FMLN; Farabundo Martí National Liberation Front), following the Guatemalan model. In Guatemala, the "scorched earth policy was successful, and some think the present government has in 'its hands' the possibility of institutionalizing a new regime" without having to appeal to foreign military assistance, which means that "a return to normality and stability is closer."[90]

It is important to highlight that, in Central America, projects of political construction, which depend on excluding progressive forces, find expression in Christian democrat parties oriented towards the constitution of political systems that may remain stable and maintain control on behalf of oligarchic groups allied to the military. The relevance of Christian democracy as a revival of the traditional dominating system derives from its representing an opening to other social sectors that have remained excluded from the strictly oligarchic bloc. One instrument of this opening is corporatism, which can never be in conflict with the armed forces because they are, on the contrary, visualized as a real power in society. This is, in turn, a result of the political dynamic (as in El Salvador and Guatemala) being dominated by counter-insurgency requirements. The problem is, therefore, that in the present conjuncture of Latin America, beyond the Central American sphere, an alliance is being attempted between Christian democrat oriented movements and the armed forces in order to upset the alliance between the military and the oligarchy, starting with a clear recognition of their right of guardianship (including veto) over the actions of civil government. Such is, indeed, the case in Guatemala and Honduras, Argentina and Brazil; they are the closest examples of what could happen in Chile should a civilian government be imposed.

Apart from attributing a police-like and repressive character to regimes under military influence, the military presence is important in the political field because of the rift that occurs in the ideological and cultural patterns of the civilian population when the conduct of politics according to a purely military logic becomes a tangible reality. As we have seen in Argentina, torture, extermination, and kidnapping have actually taken place, and could happen again. "The threat has become omnipresent to the point that the maturation of society depends on its ability to assume that wounding reality"[91] even though that would imply the questioning of a country's self-image (and this is where cultural continuity is broken). This is, no doubt, why Chileans have difficulty in putting up with society's militarization when the behaviour patterns of a civilian culture still remain (even after 14 years of a military regime).

THE MILITARIZATION OF POLITICS. In order to maintain a stable order, political discourse has an ever greater correspondence with military demands. Some extreme cases of a fairly generalized situation exist in El Salvador and Guatemala on the one hand, and in Colombia on the other. In Chile and Paraguay the political order is confused with order enforced by a military logic that identifies, in turn, with the particular content of a social project. This creates a polarizing situation that makes it difficult for projects with a centrist character to be viable, especially when the polarization created by the politics of militarization is deepened by the sharpening of the East–West conflict. This conflict allows, in turn, the reinforcement of the process of political militarization.

The above finds a clear manifestation in Central America, "where political forces must adapt their discourse and proposals to the existing warlike correlation. . . . For this reason, it would be incorrect to think that there may be centrist political forces that would be an alternative to the 'extremes' (right and left)."[92]

From a broader viewpoint, the right-wing tendency of Central American culture and politics "is closely related to the power culture imposed by the Reagan administration from 1981."

Neo-conservative thought subordinates every option to the elements of geopolitical power, so regressing to the worst moments of the Cold War that arose immediately after World War II. However, it is also relevant to refer to polarization, promoted by the Americans in light of the conflict with the socialist world. This, too, is a response to the need of old and new oligarchies to protect their threatened domination. The conservative spirit is much stronger than the empire's modernizing discourse.[93]

This process is clearly demonstrated by the resistance to reform in El Salvador and Guatemala. The expanding wave of rightism embraces countries that, as in the case of Costa Rica, have maintained a tradition of subordinating military power to civilian power for almost half a century. Now, violating two basic principles of its 1948 liberal revolution, Costa Rica has begun to encourage the creation of military forces. Between 1977 and 1985, its regular military and paramilitary forces increased by 396 per cent.

The logic of the external enemy hints at a definition of the arena in which the political game might take place, that is to say, what is permissible and what goes against the national interest. In order to do that, a force is required that may be ideologically identified with that option and, at the same time, may be capable of complying with the old slogans of order, peace and progress, which, although dating back to the end of the nineteenth century, have been revived by present dictatorships, such as the Chilean one, or in civilian regimes with an extreme right orientation.[94]

The case of Argentina may be cited to illustrate this fact if we accept that "in the last 30 years the state has been in charge of formulating and imposing the idea of an internal threat, and a state of internal war that is always present." This functions to adapt the dynamics of civil society to meet the demands of an order, guarded by the praetorian guards, whose ideological expression is a doctrine of national security. This doctrine "perceives society as the source and refuge of the enemy, hidden in everyone's conscience, that must be mercilessly annihilated."[95] All this implies the obligation to break off with forms of political representation that contribute to shape a region of public relations among forces that may eventually be the agents of heterogeneous social projects. The real risk would be that such forms would conflict with the established order in the medium or long historical term. From this standpoint, bodies of state power will be ever more autonomous from the rest of the state that is apparently controlled by civilians.

POLITICAL ORDER, CULTURAL TRANSNATIONALIZATION, AND THE ECONOMIC CRISIS. Proof that rigid order is unable to withstand even the smallest challenges is demonstrated by the fact that, in an increasing number of countries, strikes are considered to be disruptive challenges. Therefore, a union movement must limit itself to immediate economic claims, while politicians, in turn, must limit their actions "to the inorganic and discontinuous electoral and parliamentary consensus"; this means that "institutionalized democracy, which is programmed to take these political frameworks as a starting point, supposes the existence of social forces with no political definition and political organisms with no social mass organic force".[96]

Nevertheless, even worse situations might arise, without going as far as civil war, such as the impossibility of accepting even that political activity is restricted to the inorganic and discontinuous electoral and parliamentary consensus. An example of this occurred during the elections of March 1986 in Colombia, when the electoral contest was plagued by intimidation and murder threats. It is structurally impossible to open up the political arena to projects that might constitute the embryo of an alternative to the established order, for example the Unión Patriótica (Patriotic Union).[97] The above is founded in an international context characterized by increasing economic and technological interdependence as well as the possibility of making contact through instant electronic communication. This determines that the transnationalization of social and cultural life (a process with which political decision-making cannot be unfamiliar) is situated within the conflict between capitalism and socialism. That the very existence of the nation-state faces a dilemma of survival is a fact of our times. That is why the recurrence of nationalization in the political discourse is a fundamental requirement of development and of the preservation of peace.

No situation can better illustrate what we are saying than the present conflict in Central America, where polarization, deriving from the economic and political relations that characterize international relations, is added to the social dynamics inherent in the national society along with its inequalities and injustices. At the international level, the conflict between the two antagonistic fields has ended up becoming an approach to understanding what national societies are. It is no exaggeration to say that the transnationalization of a country's national life forms the basis of a loss of its decision-making ability. This is equivalent to its becoming politically, socially, and culturally right wing.

Today's right wings are basically cosmopolitan. However, we are not dealing exclusively with aspects of transnationalization. It is also important to look for other angles in the effort to rediscover possibilities for a national discourse. The weight carried by the empire's metropolis has to be counterbalanced. The images produced and transmitted from its centres spread behavioural expectations that are socially not very creative in third world countries in general. In some Latin American countries, there is the danger of suffering from social amnesia; the behaviour of some social groups, especially among the young population, is distinguished by consumerism and individualism. "Cynical attitudes in the face of the social reality, conservative political positions and immoderate greed are not discarded."[98]

This tendency to the right is not unfamiliar in the economic crisis. For instance, in Costa Rica, "the economic crisis experienced at the end of the 1970s demolished the myth of the state as a benefactor." This led to a right turn during the 1980s.[99] An explanation of this would be that economic crisis precipitates the rise of political power blocs that are more closely linked to monopolistic and transnational capital. This means that these political sectors are much more dependent on foreign economic and political centres, and they are, therefore, more sensitive to the political tendencies of those countries, in particular the United States. On the other hand, the rightward process creates so many *faits accomplis* in its manifestations as a strategy that they are unlikely to be overcome by an alternative economic project that fails to get to the roots of the problem. This is what redemocratization processes teach us.

Alfonsín's administration in Argentina, with its social democratic programme, has not been able to offer a national development project, binding itself to be the militaristic and oligarchic heir; during this period, "the grand bourgeoisie has not succeeded in establishing its hegemony over Argentine society as a whole."[100] It has been unable to offer a development model of productive forces or an internal market. On the contrary, Argentina is reaffirming its integration in the world economy as a body of resources rather than as an investment market of financial profit. This structural crisis compels the state to a feedback of terrorist mechanisms in the state as well as in civilian society, that is to say, to authoritarian policies of order.

Another example of a feedback of conservatism as a consequence of the economic crisis can be observed in the Dominican Republic, where the effects of the crisis, "far from questioning order, seem to have strengthened the conservative option even further."[101] For this reason, Balaguer's victory represents the "explicit vindication of rightist authoritarianism by large middle and popular sectors." This situation is not incompatible with a consumerist attitude according to "fashionable patterns of developed capitalist countries, especially the

United States," owing to its openness to the outside world. Therefore, the function of "bourgeois hegemonic consolidation" – fulfilling the consumerist dream – cannot be forgotten.

But the revival of conservative thought is linked to its neo-liberal strategies for development, which pose a long-term problem: democracy. The current adjustment of exporting monopolistic bourgeois projects tends to end up eliminating liberal democracy, for it endangers its project. The mechanism underlying such danger is that democracy gives rise to the political interaction between projects that may, in time, become contradictory to their interests. Chile's experience of Popular Unity (1970–1973) is the most eloquent as well as the most tragic proof of what we are saying. None the less, the neo-conservative project may have more subtle mechanisms at its disposal, and achieve the same strategic goals, without going to the extremes of Chile.[102] Such goals may, indeed, be reached by transforming the state into an instrument that functions only for neo-liberal style development projects. Some instances of this are: the 1980 Constitution in Chile; the strategic disruption of industry; the autonomy of the central banks, with complete control over monetary funds, regardless of the executive power; changes in economic legislation, such as that on mining and oil concessions; privatization of social security; legislation on the fishing trade and housing to facilitate equal capital participation; land concessions granted to timber and oil companies; and even the legalizing of trade in dollars, as in the case of Febres Cordero in Ecuador or the one-sided reform of clause 24 in the Cartagena Agreement, which has been happening for many years in order to facilitate the penetration of foreign capital.

What is at stake, deep-down, is the neutralizing, or rather the nullifying, of the whole juridical apparatus, institutionally and juridically, to prevent any reform of the present neo-liberal conservative strategy. The aim is to create every possible obstacle to any policy aimed at interrupting the process (which has already begun) favouring the predominance of large transnational capital in order to make dualism into a development strategy. In other words, the issue is to create societies with a modern sector, highly concentrating all economic, political, and cultural benefits, and enjoying the protection of the armed forces against the rest of society, which will have become a marginalized mass.

This will be possible if the popular sectors are in a weak position in the face of the conservative offensive. In order to prevent this, the popular forces must accomplish the huge task of finding new areas for

217

mobilization and organization, with a directing ability that, without losing the broad perspective of speeding up the pace of historical transition towards more just forms of social organization, does not become disconnected from the present, where men live history with all the strength and weakness necessary to transform that experience into a future project.

Almost all styles of popular struggle go through a period of great transformations because of the tensions caused by unemployment and increasing poverty, and they often lack a clear political perspective. This has somehow not prevented some intellectuals – in countries subjected to marginalization, police harassment, or state terrorism – from concluding that the left has lost vigour as a school of thought and the strength to construct an alternative. On the contrary, the main challenge of our time is the battle to gain ideological autonomy for the exploited classes when they do not have it, and to reinforce it when they have some historical experience of it. These classes might be exploited, but they are not submissive, which illustrates the problem of their political direction – the problem of a party that would be able to join the battle and retain a sufficient degree of realism to respond to the daily exigencies of a struggle inspired by a future vision. This implies a clear-headed awareness, so as not to fall into the trap of historical horizons and not to be subjected to the political horizon imposed by dominant sectors. Political groups must fight untiringly for independence in a political sense, that is to say, in a cultural sense.

Unfortunately, this is exactly what does not happen with popular sectors in many countries. Instead, we see those forces unable to become hegemonic classes with the necessary impetus to support, encourage, and defend a political project that may break away from the horizon imposed as the only historically viable one.

3. Revolutionary thought

Revolutionary movements in Latin America: The opening and closing of historical horizons

It is impossible to ignore the fact that the frame of reference of ideological discussion directed towards change in society is the great problem of our time, namely, the struggle between socialism and capitalism. From this standpoint the problem is which are the most significant subjects to launch the struggle, and which are the most profound and accurate ideological notions.

In the 1920s and 1930s, the absence of a theoretical creativity "able to develop political programs and strategies as a response to specific political conditions"[103] led to great formulations of Marxist inspiration that were but the adaptation of ideologies developed in Europe. The theoretical realm is open to new interpretative creations of history and utopias, such as in the work of Haya de la Torre and Lombardo Toledano. Well into the 1930s, the dogmatism of communist parties led them to abandon their revolutionary programmes and to adopt policies that met the demands of a democracy under construction, replacing the dominant oligarchic models, at least until the big crisis. We can recall the case of the Chilean Communist Party, which, because of its own political and ideological orthodoxy, could not understand the meaning of emergent popular movements (such as the Socialist Party, founded in 1933), branding them as "petit bourgeois organizations trying to adapt to the radicalization of the masses, and using Trotskyist ideology to fight forcefully against the formulation of a proletariat class party."[104] This orthodoxy, sensitive to the changes in international political relations resulting from the fight against fascism in Europe, prevented the support in 1936 of the left-wing plan centred on, and conducted by, a figure like Marmaduke Grove, whose aim in 1930 was to join the Frente Popular (Popular Front), an alliance whose axis was the middle and petty bourgeoisie.

Communist criticism, despite being sectarian, reflects a serious background in Latin American popular and revolutionary movements. Indeed, we must candidly recognize the dangers presented to the leadership of revolutionary movements when they have been controlled by intellectuals of petty bourgeois origin. Less than 10 years after the above incidents, we find the experience of the Bolivian nationalist reformist revolution, which massively incorporated workers, peasants, and the majority of the popular urban sectors "under a nationalist anti-imperialist program headed by the petit-bourgeoisie."[105] We need to remember the tremendous involution of the Movimiento Nacionalista Revolucionario (MNR; Revolutionary Nationalist Movement), which was the political protagonist of that movement, and whose main leaders acted in circumstances that had been presented as an irreversible process. It had, perhaps, been forgotten that, during the first half of the 1940s, the failure of the Lombardian project and its subordination to a project clearly organized around sectors of the bourgeoisie had already been confirmed. It was not until the 1960s, with the Cuban Revolution, that we again see movements seeking support in the popular sector, as in the case of what has been called "Guevarism and Castroism," which, beginning with the Cuban experience, outlined strategies for peasant struggle in alliance with urban sectors, such as students and petty bourgeois groups.

A great discussion started on the problem of the conditions for revolutionary processes. The economicist approach began to be questioned in revolutionary formulations, such as the one stating that the *sine qua non* for the process is given by the development of productive forces, or the questioning of the working class as a main protagonist of revolutions. From the 1960s on, the "foquista" notion openly questioned whether or not a country has to go through a stage of dynamic capitalist development in order to enter the stage of socialist revolution. This notion found theoretical expression in the theory of dependency.

Indeed, up to the end of the 1950s, the proletariat "is not capable of imposing its own global policy" within the people's fronts; in other words, it is not capable of "imposing policies of restraint on the bourgeoisie's interests and its hegemonic aims." Popular movements prior to that date tended to "a recognition of the hegemony of dominant classes." Dominant classes, in an effort to stabilize their domination, established sporadic alliances with middle and popular sectors, which, for this very reason, became instrumental allies. This recognition of hegemony "could be implicit, but it lies at the very root of the project and its boundaries, in the state as an arbiter, in national reformists, in authoritarian and conciliatory ideology as well as in participationist and democratizing ideology."[106] In some countries this coincides with suffrage and the spreading of union organization, but is always combined with repressive measures, such as anti-communist laws.

In fact, during the 1950s and 1960s, we can observe a certain broadening of democracy, taking it beyond a purely political instrument intended to foster social projects. It instead begins to develop as a means of opening the way for a project. The highest expression of this is found in populist movements; even though they do not represent a clear, consistent, and viable alternative, they pave the way for the social and political participation of other forces that are opposed to the power bloc. These forces, as they grow and complicate the political game, entail questioning democracy itself as a system of heterogeneous social forces. Populism being neither an alternative to the oligarchic and bourgeois dominant project, nor capable of establishing stable mechanisms for the reproduction and balancing of power, ended up, in the 1950s and early 1960s, preparing the ground for the militarism of the 1970s. Militarism became the instrument of the restoration of the traditional bloc damaged during the developmentalist and democratic period.

The 1970s are known for the effort to consolidate domination in a new way, through coercive regimes not based on hegemony. That effort is contained within two revolutionary experiences: that of Chile (1910–1973) and the victory of the Sandinista revolution in July 1979. Armed forces appear "as an embryo for reconstructing the state as a class instrument."[107] There is an attempt to transform them structurally, giving greater coherence to the relation between political power and class interest. This, in turn, leads to a reconstruction of the relation between civil and political society in the light of the needs posed by political state order, in other words, in the light of centralized power demands without democratic parliamentary mediation, which only weakened it. According to this logic, civil society must be subordinated to the demands of a stable and guaranteed order. Armed forces are, therefore, transformed "into the civil and political embryo of a new society where the mechanisms of civil society (particularly those of legitimization) are subordinated to the restrictions of political order, so that their development does not lead to their detachment from the demands of that order."[108]

The Chilean and Sandinista revolutionary experiences provide important lessons about the problem of constructing hegemonic direction. Theoretically, the main problem could be enunciated as follows: the tempo of structural transformation must be subordinated to the constituting tempo of organic political direction. If this is not mature enough, the revolutionary force's objective possibilities of imposing its project diminish, but it is also true that the struggle may generate suitable directing structures. The Chilean and Sandinista experiences offer different lessons in this respect. The Popular Unity experience demonstrates a breakdown between the tempo imposed on the project and the constitution of organic direction because the struggle did not succeed in generating an adequate structure of political direction, that is to say, an organic unitarian expression, instead of a simple confrontation between conflicting or openly antagonistic directions. This was the discrepancy between Popular Unity and the Movement of the Revolutionary Left (Movimiento de Izquierda Revolucionaria, MIR), or between the Socialist and Communist parties. The cost of this breakdown between the process's tempo of change

221

and the construction of adequate political direction was that "the bourgeoisie was able to recover its directing ability and ideological cohesion (which had been lost in the late 1960s and early 1970s owing to the confrontation between traditional political rightism and Christian democracy) much faster than power could be consolidated in popular movements."[109] In Cuba, the opposite occurred: despite the various organizations that existed within the guerrilla movement, a revolutionary power rapidly emerged.

Chile illustrates an inability to create the power required by the struggle's conditions. The structure of direction adequate for the electoral conjuncture (a type of struggle culminating in the presidential elections of September 1970), namely the existence of several parties and their corresponding spheres of influence, was not only in order to go further into the process, but also in order to exercise and manipulate the distribution of power through elections. On the contrary, the achievements of the electoral struggle posed the need for new power forms, and either this was not understood or it could not be confronted. The Chilean left was not able to break with the ideological and cultural horizon within which it had been unfolding for several decades.

Nicaraguan experience demonstrates the way to construct a directing structure that is able not only deliberately to maintain itself within the framework of a revolutionary outlook but also to have a clear sense of the immediate reality. Its ability to integrate forces and tendencies that were previously contradictory in a rapid, organic, and collective operative direction, as well as its clarity in constructing a mass political apparatus, are an expression of the fact that the process of change has to correspond to the parallel construction possibilities of a directing political structure. The Frente Sandinista para la Liberación Nacional (FSLN; Sandinista National Liberation Front) succeeded because "it did not reduce the revolution problem to the notion of an exploited class. . . . From the beginning, it put forward the nation, and the dialectics of class and people with a clear awareness of their various struggles."[110]

What we can generalize about from the Nicaraguan experience is "the need for hegemonic politics." This does not mean that its forms of organization and political practices have to be imitated. However, what is definitely propounded is the need to find the most suitable political direction when our people's struggle, particularly due to the economic crisis and American neo-conservativism, is carried out simultaneously at the level of foreign economic oppression, against cultural neocolonialism, and against authoritarian political forms that ever more rigidly maintain an "order that ensures capital's progress."

The Chilean experience is an example of how ideology may fulfil the function of closing a historical horizon instead of opening one. That is to say, it links the idea of history and its struggles to ideologies that, as in the case of Marxism, result in "limiting rather than guiding the imagination of future revolutionary leaders. For this reason one must be constantly alert so as to make sure that theory does not become a dogma."[111]

In order to prevent that from happening, one must keep an open mind about the theorizing on accumulated experiences that may enrich revolutionary theoretical thought.[112] Great theoretical gaps can be observed in the need for an adequate theory about the Cuban transition, Nicaragua's insurrection, El Salvador's political–military struggle,[113] the frustrated experience of Chile's Popular Unity, as well as Argentina's, Uruguay's, and Brazil's insurrections, and today's Peruvian guerrilla movements. We speak of theorizing in the sense of becoming aware of the protagonists capable of transforming the imposed order, and, at the same time, of parting from the logic of immutability and inexorability used by capitalism to impose itself.

Therefore, the battle to construct counter-hegemony consists of the formulation of social projects perceived as viable, and then the ability to change in relation to daily life. This means developing a new determination and understanding for a distinct practice. This is what has been happening in Nicaragua in the midst of armed struggle against American aggression. Indeed, such an experience proves that democracy is constructed from daily practice, from the microsocial world, in the mechanisms for creating and exercising power, be it participation, joint government, joint management, or self-management systems; accessible power should have the potential to radiate out to social life as a whole.

The difficulties of left-wing movements in constructing hegemony are reflected in their relation to democracy, conceived as a viable formula of social justice with freedom. Democracy's political and cultural aspects have been underestimated, with what concerns only basic needs being one-sidedly highlighted. This is a result of imperialistic harassment that has forced the favouring of a reductionist class outlook that implies "an idea of proletariat dictatorship" as a "party's vertical leadership in the name of class, excluding the need for slowly achieving a hegemonic base as part of the general consensus."[114]

For the same reason, it is important to develop a leftist theory that might overcome the ignorance of political democracy. But achieving this requires solving the problem, on the one hand, of fostering political interplay, but, on the other, of recognizing that the only arena of political interplay is the one that corresponds with the basic guidelines of the revolutionary project.

Civil society's potentiality and the reduction of the struggle to the political state sphere

As we have outlined, ever since the Central American experience, the struggle against the bourgeoisie and the group of conservative forces is not just a dispute in the sphere of general principles (this is perhaps what the Chilean left wing forgot); rather it is mainly a dispute in the sphere of daily practice. This is why the divorce between politics and people's concrete problems must disappear. In this respect, we should consider that left-wing movements have, historically, tended to give pre-eminence to political society, largely because its thought is based on a logic of power that certainly ends up identifying with the state form of power. For this reason, the effort of constructing the new society's project is confined to the state. The state is the great architect of a new hegemony, leaving aside, as a secondary question, the fact that power is the result of a hegemony that is being constituted every day, at every level of social life.

This implies that "civil society" should be incorporated into the political struggle for power, but in a context defined by culture, idiosyncracy, customs, the past, and people's experience and sociology, that is to say, in a complex and rich context with a diverse dynamism. This complexity expresses the presence of many forces of a different nature; therefore, the pluralism of the revolutionary project consists in its ability to become a reflection of this social multifariousness. It is, therefore, right to state that if the struggle on the political state front concerns the destruction of the reactionary state power, the struggle displayed by civil society aims at "the creation and strengthening of an alternative and revolutionary power."[115] The reason for this is that the effervescence that might be generated in civil society against the trend of the homogenizing order in political or state society can create the conditions for developing a form of theoretical and critical class thinking that seeks to recognize the value of contents that are not evident but are potentially hidden in it. The problem lies in how to differentiate between change-inspiring forces, and forces that are a manifestation of the micro-social dynamics with a multifarious nature (economic, social, ideological, cultural), a nature that complies with the project's construction. In this sense, no project can be reduced to practices inherent in political society, but civil society's roots must be rediscovered. When we speak of projects, we are considering democracy as one of them.

The great challenge is to understand that representative democracy might cease to be bourgeois democracy's patrimony; it should rather form part of the manner of making politics in socialist societies, "if its historical authoritarian tendency is to be overcome."[116] From the viewpoint of the alternating power exercise, we are facing "the most difficult challenge for revolutionary socialist society, namely the development of a pluralistic system involving parties that compete for power" but do not break away from the boundaries of the revolutionary project. All this depends on the premise that plurality exists within the framework of values that are favourable to the "fundamental questions universally accepted by the people." However, it so happens that, in all revolutionary transformation processes, the ideological inertia of the masses is identified; this might stimulate the re-creation of values that are not congruent with the new society's project demands. The ensuing dilemma is over accepting pluralism and the limits of tolerance for attitudes, positions, or even non-revolutionary parties.

None the less, plurality might also be understood not as being circumscribed by power competence but rather as an interplay of pressures, on the part of society, to orient the construction of revolutionary projects. This must be capable of channelling expectations and demands that do not constitute a clear programme of social interests accompanied by a desire for power, but are an expression of cultural, ethnic, religious, linguistic, or state interests. In other words, they are part of civil society's conflicts, which may generate pressures for the social order that is being constructed even though they may lack a true alternative project. This means (as is shown by the Sandinista experience) that revolutionary struggle must be taken "to all levels of civil society (schools, universities, churches, art and culture centers, labor unions, mass-media, etc.), to wherever there may be an opening to ideologically exercise mass revolutionary behavior."[117]

A distinction must be made between struggling *from* civil society, in an effort directed towards the national level of power, and struggling *in* civil society, the situation in which the political-state forms of revolutionary struggle find themselves, for the battles lack, at this point, a strategy allowing them "to accumulate forces for the movement as a whole."[118] Because of social, cultural, and ideological heterogeneity, it is harder to arrive at the formation of a true collective will when the latter option is chosen. But the problem of relations between party and social movement, or between parties and fronts (understood as a party of parties), will have to be discussed within the context of the great ideological and cultural complexity of civil society.

Indeed, political parties must be careful not to forget that "class" does not just develop at a political level; it is rooted in the diverse reality that is the setting for the heterogeneous dynamics constituted by history – a history that is being shaped by human beings who are, at the same time, members and activators of human groups.

Revolutionary construction and plurality

Discussing old and new subjects is a way of entering the debate about the relationship established between social dynamics and the possibility of constructing the social and political capability of carrying out a social project. As we have pointed out, not all group forms that characterize civil society are capable of forging social projects, or, even less, of struggling to find alternatives to the dominant conservative neo-bourgeois project. Today's struggle is not just concerned with new development strategies or new forms of state organization. It is a struggle to transform values and ideology, so that "capitalism may be internally undermined by socialist values and ideas."[119] This value transformation is part of the struggle for the conquest of power, but is never a simple result of having won it. The ideological struggle for a profound change in our societies is mixed with the effort to construct a hegemonic counter-culture.

The political and ideological offensive of the new right wing brings revolutionary movements face to face with a historical commitment to assume the highest political efficiency. How does what we have said about pluralism affect this situation? A hegemonic counter-culture requires a counter-power that is an authentic expression of the cultural creation of those constituting the revolutionary movement, instead of being a simple instrument, since bourgeois hegemony depends on the "penetration of values and ideas in civil society's fields"[120] rather than the control of political state institutions. In this context, how can we solve the question of an ideological counter-offensive in relation to plurality? Nicaragua's response is that all pluralism must be thought of as mediated by "unity around revolutionary principles and strategy," so that pluralism does not mean transforming the avant-garde into a "coordination or eclectic synthesis of different positions."[121] This brings to the centre of the debate a social movement for change that is able to articulate, in a convergent process, the plurality of organizations that pretend to become its direction and where the people may be being expressed.[122]

Therefore, plurality may be understood in terms of the possibility of several projects, or as the alternatives for constructing the same project. The first meaning implies a heterogeneous idea about the direction of the revolutionary process. In this sense, owing to the inertia of masses, the weight of bourgeois values will determine that the alternating political interplay in power is basically oriented towards preserving the established order. Similarly, when democracy is defined from that standpoint, it is necessarily confused with a closed project of society, or one excluding any other constructive alternative.

If we instead understand plurality as the various ways of constructing a project, we are not starting from a consideration of values of inertia; the heart of the problem lies in the construction of a direction. Thus, construction is not merely an instrument, but a counter-culture or new hegemony.

Two contradictory approaches are presented within this outlook. On the one hand, breaking away from the past occurs at the moment of winning power; therefore, the construction of society's projects is resolved simply in the exercise of power reduced to an instrumental state form (supposing the subject that exercises it is already constituted, which is not the case). The other view suggests that power is constructed during the process of exercising power; politics therefore has to be understood as a cultural creation (supposing the subject or subjects have to be constructed as points of support for the project's realization). In this case, plurality consists of the fact that the social project has to be large enough to express the multiplicity of interests and organizations that are part of the nation's sociocultural dynamics.[123]

This is why the project betokens, on the one hand, a central direction, even though its modes of historical realization might be diverse and multiple, and in any case identifiable with order only as imposed by instrumental state logic. But, on the other hand, within the project's politics of construction, it must be recognized that the same political and ideological guidelines are not valid for all sectors and all social forces. This is what has happened whenever the guidelines used to mobilize the working class have been applied to middle sectors. In this sense, it could be stated that one of the great limitations of Leninism is to have *transformed* labour *psychology* into a global form of strategy. This limitation was aggravated when the experience of the 1980s taught us that the most dynamic political sector has not always been the working class, but larger and more heterogeneous groups that are "defined by their sociocultural identity rather than by their economic structure," such as: settlers, the unemployed, students, professionals, state employees, housewives and women in general, artists, university people, etc.

In the discussion to recover all the concrete richness of reality, which breaks away from reductionist and globalizing ideological patterns, Christian-inspired thought represents a real contribution. If anything characterizes the discourse of liberation theology, it is the rescuing of a liberating practice from "its tiniest, most diffuse, quasi-spontaneous forms, among believers of the city and the rural popular classes";[124] it tries to rediscover the holy message of the Scriptures in the reality of the oppressed, with a view to constructing their own subjects of liberation. Christians also bring in a dynamic organization that outstrips those that strictly follow the political party. What their discourse reflects is civilian society in its manifold forms of expression and representation – neighbourhoods, communities, parishes, namely, the places where workers reproduce.

None the less, the above states that the construction of power happens simultaneously with the constitution of social subjects, which are not a purely conjunctural and micro-spatial expression of the dynamic inherent in civil society, but are capable, on the contrary, of becoming participating subjects in the realization of global change projects. It is necessary to go beyond the micro-social plane, contributing, from this plane of reality, to give a direction to social processes within the framework of national society; this is a condition for social change, for, without "massive population participation, and with a total economic, political, and social crisis, similar to Nicaragua's,"[125] it is not possible to think of transforming popular forces in Latin America.

We must, however, always depart from the daily, confusing, multifarious reality that assumes historical realization in each man's existence. What we have stated so far poses a challenge to the theoretical way of thinking in which (sometimes abstract and formal) reality is often left out of the discussion. A full theoretical and ideological elaboration must be encouraged under the imperative of a constant and consistent self-critique. As to the avoided debate, it leads to the posing of false dilemmas as a response to a predominance of dogmatic reasoning, trapped by theoretical manipulations that have nothing to do with the complexity of historical processes, rather than to the demands of reality.

With these statements, we approach the problem of the relationship between ideology and popular awareness. One of the main obstacles for revolutionary movements has in fact been the masses' lack of awareness. The masses are thus driven away not so much from ultimate political and social objectives as from methods of struggle.

The masses' separation is due to a lack of correspondence between the ideology of active avant-garde centres and the latter's dominant consciousness. For this reason, it is important to have a profound understanding of popular consciousness; in this sense, understanding Christian values is of the utmost importance. Marxism has not yet become the generalized form of popular consciousness.[126]

We are now at a point in history when Christianity, as it defends the struggle of the oppressed, contributes ideologically to strengthening the domain of progressive forces, thereby becoming an anti-bourgeois ideology. No doubt, what we must be concerned about is the ambiguity of Christian praxis. Nor must we ignore the fact that within Christianity "there are theologians who posit the ambiguity of evangelical messages," asking questions about "where the discourse of universal Christian love will be efficiently realized." What is most relevant, though, is the Christian transformation of an intimate value into a mass ideological force through formulations of liberation theology.

This transformation has led conservative American ideologists to denounce this particular Christian trend, and even the church at large, as a subversive force. In a 1980 document written by the Santa Fé Committee (Ronald Reagan's presidential campaign advisers), entitled "New Inter-American Politics for the 1980s," starting from the premise that the American continent is under attack, "penetrated by Soviet power," opposition of liberation theology is defined as one of the strategic objectives of North American foreign policy. To that end, the Institute on Religion and Democracy (IRD) was founded in Washington. "Marxist–Leninist forces have used the Church as a political weapon against private property and productive capitalism, infiltrating the religious community with ideas that are less Christian than Communist."[127]

One question that remains unanswered is which social project corresponds to the outlook of Christian values. Historically, answers vary from the Spanish Falange model to guerrilla movements of Christian origin, such as the Bolivian MIR and the Argentine "montoneros," going through Christian democrat experiences that are quite akin to the social democrat option. In any case, the main problem lies in finding the strategy that is most congruent with Christian values, because it is quite different to pose the value problem considering man as an individual still not alone, rather than as a subject of a collective endeavour that promotes in-depth social changes. We are dealing with man as strategy's soldier, and not as proof of a wounding reality.

The dilemma lies in developing a value realm that gives content to a utopia of historical construction rather than to the realization of man as a person. Does this mean that the highest hierarchical system of socio-historical values may lead to the subordination of man's realization, in all his potentialities, to a utopia that is supposed to become reality? Does Christianity, in turn, reinstate man's project? Is Christianity the personal experience of the human in society and the consciousness of Marxist man in history? All this is incarnated in the socialism–bureaucracy equation. If we are to solve the problem so that both terms may be fully integrated, which one determines the other? What happens to democracy when utopian society is still a project struggling to construct itself, rather than a living present, and when revolutionary transformations have not yet consolidated their position over minority and privileged interests?[128]

4. The Latin American crisis: Legitimacy or accumulation?

Neo-Keynesian proposals to promote, through the state, an active policy that attempts to avoid recessionary cycles and high unemployment by means of the efficient management of monetary and fiscal policies correspond to the idea accepted in Latin America during the 1950s and 1960s that inflation is a necessary evil inherent in the capitalist market system when it operates close to full employment. By applying a policy centred on "effective demand administration," industrial economies reached satisfactory economic growth levels and moderate inflation rates in the two decades following World War II.[129] In the 1970s, when that policy became ineffective, and it became inflationist to stimulate production (the GNP of industrialized countries dropped to 3.1 per cent a year and inflation reached critical levels in some countries), a whole spectrum of new phenomena was generated, such as "stagflation," which is economic stagnation with inflation. The way opened to new influences deriving from neoclassical theory, centred on the idea that society's well-being improves only when some individual has increased their usefulness without decreasing that of others; hence, a redistributive policy would not allow for an improvement in society's well-being.[130]

Opposing the dominant Keynesian concepts, the supply-side economists claimed that it is not possible to affect real demand through a policy of income and expenditure – "taking money away from some to give it to others" – and that any state intervention policy ends up reducing the incentive to produce and encouraging inefficiency and unemployment. "All programs to promote equality and fight poverty undermine production, from which real demand derives." On the other hand, this conception considers that most state expenditures are unproductive and wasteful of the population's resources; in addition, the negative effect of government regulations "on production and trade to protect the environment, health and public security" weakens prices and makes technological change and innovation impossible to afford, leading inevitably to a tendency towards decreasing productivity.[131]

The philosophy of the new economic approach is expressed in the idea that "the crucial source of creativity and initiative in any economic system is the individual investor. Economy does not bloom spontaneously, or due to government influence. Their development is a response to the creativity of individuals willing to take risks to transform ideas into monopolies." In contrast with the notions of the classics, perfect competition must no longer exist, because future demand exists only in producers' minds.[132] This idea shapes the ideological framework of the current American administration, led by the supply-side economist school, whose ideas are also reflected in the International Monetary Fund's formulations.

The meeting point of the IMF and the supply-side economists consists in the fact that both single out the need to reduce demand by reducing public sector expenditure and in the conviction that the market should foster consumption growth, "eliminating the public sector's distorting action." Such a policy has been systematically applied in Latin America in order to deal with external deficits, that is to say, to reduce demand through public expenditure and market and foreign trade liberalization.[133] Thus, some structural factors that explain external imbalance as due to other reasons, such as a drop in export prices, are left out of the analysis. The solution is always the same: monetary contraction in a free market and free enterprise system. What is objectively achieved is the creation of room for the expansion of transnational monopolies, the bearers of technological innovation.

The need for an expanded notion of private property and a critique of excessive interventionism on the part of the state, which has now degenerated into a Leviathan, constitute the basic ideology of the "Monetarist Manifesto," which today dominates international economic relations. This manifesto defines ever more rigidly the growth patterns for third world countries, because of the pressure exercised by multilateral financial institutions and by the governments of industrialized countries. It is stated:

If poverty and misery persist, despite the general increase of national output and the political efforts for redistribution, that is due to our society being capitalist. Conversely, the real reason for this being so is that our society has never been truly capitalist, because what capitalism is accused of is not derived from its nature, or from its supposed laws, but from the fact that the state, trespassing the natural boundaries for its actions, prevents the efficient functioning of adjustment mechanisms which are linked to the competition game.[134]

This has consequences not only at the level of economic growth, because the essential idea is that "free market capitalism alone leads to democracy" while the state's participation in the economy leads to totalitarianism. Such is Friedrich von Hayek's[135] theory, the main exponent of which is Milton Friedman.[136]

As Friedman states: "there are only two ways of coordinating the economic cooperation of millions of people: one is central direction, which implies the use of force (that is the modern totalitarian state's and the army's technique); the other is individuals' voluntary cooperation (that is the market's technique)." Hence, the state should be limited, because its function is to "protect our freedom . . . , induce compliance with private contracts, and foster competitive markets."[137] The market fulfils the function of eliminating control of economic activity by political authority, and therefore eliminating the source of repressive power. Under the banner of political freedom, the creation of the room required for international big capital reproduction is justified. This is possible thanks to the failure of Latin American national bourgeoisies to promote their own development, due in part to their inability to transform the unequal relations of exchange that have been imposed as the context in which national economies function; this is a result of the world economy being controlled by transnational capital.

The previous statements break into Latin America as a global and generalized neoconservative strategy emerges, interrupting a long tradition of conservative thought that has reaffirmed the development projects of a national society, whose most prominent antecedent is the considerations of the Comisión Económica para América Latina (CEPAL; Economic Commission for Latin America) about the lack of equilibrium faced by these societies.

The economic and political counter-reform concealed in the present monetarist programme upsets a long period of social and political achievements that were the result of the great mobilizations of the 1940s and 1960s. It de-articulates the state as a subject and dismantles social welfare programmes such as the effort to prevent unemployment, correct inequitable income distribution, and provide health benefits and housing and education for the great national majorities. This approach to development implies that political authoritarianism goes hand in hand with market functioning. The free market promoted by neo-liberalism, as demonstrated by the extreme case of Chile, requires the creation of a police state, the repression of public liberties, the elimination of political exchange, limiting freedom of speech, abolishing the right to strike, freezing wages, etc. All this goes along with the de-articulation of the state as a launching platform for equal development, culminating in a true privatization of the state, such that it becomes an "authoritarian instrument for repressing and controlling groups marginalized by the market. Market law is the law of the strongest, and therefore it brings forth martial law, and market fascism."[138] This is what Samuelson calls "fascist capitalism," which is characterized by generals and admirals seizing power, sweeping away their leftist predecessors.

The neoconservative plan thrives during economic crisis. During the last 15 years, the countries of Latin America have experienced a development whose main feature has been external imbalance, which eventually became a brake on the growth process. This problem was accentuated in the 1970s as deficits grew; deficits rose on average 23.3 per cent a year, going from $3,411 million in 1970 to $27,740 million in 1980. This means that the total increase was 813 per cent.[139] Something similar occurred with the rise in exports. In 1975, exports fell drastically, being concomitant with the scale of imports, which do not stop "owing to the intensity of import-substituting industrialization, which is the dominant strategy in that area."[140] No doubt, a determining element in external imbalances has been payments (in the form of profits and interest) to foreign capital. However, the most interesting aspect of this situation is that it has allowed the parasitic nature of a bourgeoisie lacking dynamism to be exposed, a bourgeoisie that has become the main agent of a plundering economy.[141] Precisely this situation has been the basis for the establishment of authoritarian regimes that, following neo-monetarism, have tried to liquidate all previous experience. Characterized by populist and development-oriented politics, this experience considered industry as the dynamic sector of accumulation, and thus demanded support for "the growth of a strongly protected internal market."[142] With or without military regimes, now that democracies have arisen from defeat, the economic policies they apply have not altered, and we are still using parameters of growth that are designed for the protection and reproduction needs of big transnational capital.

From a strictly economic standpoint, the justification of this new orientation, expressed in foreign trade liberalization and the encouragement of foreign investment and the import of foreign goods, posits development policies that will certainly have a detrimental effect on society. Experience has shown that CEPAL's model, oriented towards import substitution to improve or counteract impaired exchange terms, though it has helped industrialization, has not favoured the creation of an efficient, well-integrated productive structure capable of absorbing essential technological innovations. This was partly due to the fact that it relied on an excessively protectionist structure that was both non-discriminating and lasted too long,[143] creating a captive market that led to high prices and costs and restrained manufactured exports. Perhaps it is more significant still that the model developed by CEPAL was not able to solve the problem of foreign dependence either. This problem continues to manifest itself "through investment links and external debt, while exports are still concentrated on primary products."[144]

From this standpoint, developmentalist thought "could not create a theoretical alternative",[145] being, therefore, interrupted as a school of thought, because it could not integrate "an economic theory of management of the great macroeconomic aggregates into a coherent system, either towards short-term desirable objectives, or towards long-term priority ones."[146] This led to a theoretical void in Latin America, inasmuch as the development problem requires an approach capable of relating micro to macro aspects. This was true in the case of dependence theory, born in the 1970s, which did not construct a foundation upon which to develop a policy of effective reconstruction.

This void, along with the inferior position of national bourgeoisies, has spurred the development of new monetarist theories that advocate, as we have seen, the death of the state and a return to the free market. In spite of this failure, we must stress the significance this effort had for intellectual independence, which continues to be a permanent challenge, and the search for development alternatives. This must be achieved without abandoning the broad perspective of historical change, and without neglecting microeconomic phenomena closely related to the demands of change-fostering policies, so that concern for changes that may solve long- and medium-term problems does not lead us to forget the short-term transition.

The construction of a theory of putting projects into practice poses two main challenges: on the one hand, the development of a historical utopia as a motivating force to go with ideological programmatic proposals; and on the other hand, paying careful attention to transition as we develop tactical and strategic efforts to construct a reality according to the guidelines pointed to by the ideological programmatic proposals. In this sense, it is symptomatic that rightist discourse has found greater congruence and viability in constructing alternative proposals compared with the social democratic positions, illustrated primarily in the cases of Peru and Argentina as well as, at times, in revolutionary discourse itself, as in the guerrilla experiences. On a level more closely related to the exercise of power, the same is illustrated by the experience of Popular Unity in Chile. It is important to stress this because, in the Latin American crisis situation of 1988, historical challenges re-emerged as ever-more polarized options in increasingly difficult formulations.

We have observed the re-emergence of a neoconservative discourse that coincides with a critical conjuncture of developmental models (corresponding to a great theoretical and ideological void). This discourse proposes a return to previous stages of social development. But are rightist forces really looking to the past? How can we characterize the ideological profile of a theory able fully to understand the conservative trends in neo-liberalism? What is the story concealed behind current options for developmental policies? The present period of indecision reflects a break with dominant groups' former history; or perhaps we should say, despite some groups having displaced others, is power generating an act of legitimation in emerging groups – a power similar to that which characterized social distinction in older dominant groups?

In terms of facts, this means there is neither a new future nor a project to construct it that does not look to a past that remains indelible, immutable, and, therefore, ahistorical. Where, then, can we find the truth of the subject and its projects?

5. Crisis, political will, and post-modernism

The need for imagination and criticism
There is no denying that greater complexity in political analysis is encountered as we increase our ability to react to our circumstances, and that this complexity emerges equally as a product of a society that has gradually become a much more dynamic space where new stages appear from which ever-increasing dynamism may be attained. Some social arenas may be generated without passing through the state political domain. This brings us back to the old problem of whether the state grows at the expense of society, or whether society recovers territory formerly held by the state, or whether what is happening is a "recomposition of the classical distinction between the public and the private, the state and the societal spheres."[147] What is unquestionable is that we are facing a crisis in state order that some might see as an expansion of the social; for us, it consists primarily in the notion that society is manifested as the result of social subjects arising and developing in times and spaces that are distinct from the political order.

Historical reality and arenas where processes of change might be initiated become a vast horizon, in so far as they are not circumscribed by a space defined by the state as an apparatus whose control might precipitate those processes. The main risk in reducing what pertains to politics to the state sphere lies in confusing it with simple technologies of power, for the aim of politics is to delimit power's actions in terms of a historical utopia. Hence, power, beyond being an instrument of politics, is a cultural creation that begins with its own exercise; politics is a vision of options that, once translated into practice, may become viable social constructions. What determines power as a cultural creation is, indeed, the transformation of options into practices, for it means a determination of the possible as the object of practices that lie within a framework of options susceptible to recognition by the subject from his utopia that is striving to become a project.

Because of this, power cannot consist of a simple calculating rationality; it also consists of the simultaneous constitution of forces that will transform options into viable practices. This implies "participation of collective subjects constituted by individuals."[148] For this reason, power becomes historical consciousness: it is the appropriation of possible reality. The crux of discussion is the recognition of dynamic nuclei from which reality might be appropriated. Since this appropriation constitutes a construction of social subjects, it is accomplished through projects that are not exclusively generated in the state sphere.

In relation to this, the question posed has to do with total domination as an obstacle to any possibility of visualizing and fighting for options. It is said that in any society there are "gaps or interstices" where domination does not penetrate. This is Deleuze's famous distinction between a "despot's codified centre, and the nomad's ubiquitous periphery," the latter resisting the despot's codification. The discussion refers to the very hazy problem of whether society's functional logic prevails or not. This logic centres on a demand for order and the homogenization of diversity: this is what we call state logic. If we position ourselves in the context of logic's unquestionable predominance, we discover very serious obstacles to the awakening and channelling of civil society's dynamics. Fear, apathy, and an immobility resulting from these two, and generating in its turn new fears and apathies, definitely lead to the imposition of an ideology of survival characterized by so-called psycho-cultural "security territories." These are forms of democracy lying outside the field of recognized possible relations, so that individuals, as they reach their limits, may feel protected, and their actions will not represent a threat to state order. The most pathetic manifestation of this phenomenon is not so much fear as the absence of demands; that is, the predominance of the most basic needs.

The predominance of the logic of state homogenization has a long tradition in Latin America. Indeed, culminating in the independence process, efforts were centred on the project of nation-state creation. Sovereignty always assumed a state connotation, for it was – and continues to be – confused with strong governments capable of confronting forces that dissipate the "national." Thus, what pertains to the state ends up becoming a political arena, and therefore an actors' arena. The actor *par excellence* is thus born: the political party.

No matter what we have said so far, we must beware of confusing real subjects with the ways in which they express themselves. Real subjects are generated and arise from all social spheres (gaps or interstices), assuming either mass or class forms; they might adopt social, cultural, religious, trade union, or political organic expression; they might be stable when projected over a long period of time, or appear in conjunctural moments. Mixing up both planes can lead to the mistaken belief that history is reduced to daily experience, merely because daily experience is also history. Underlying the discussion on rescuing the social from the statal, we find the imperative of incorporating the micro-social into the macro-social if we want to understand social processes as products of different types of social subjects.

But rescuing the social from the statal also leads one to deny the existence of a privileged social subject, and this does not help in the construction of alternative global projects. As stated before, we must attempt a "politicization of what is social, and a socialization of what is political, but from the bottom up, neither from the state, nor falling into the populist temptation."[149] This does not mean, however, that historical processes are erratic; they are merely rich and complex. The challenge lies in giving a course to history. In order to do that, a fundamental force is required, but this does not mean that this force need be a sort of entelechy constituted by a complex weft of dimensions (economic, cultural, psychological, etc.) that make of the force itself a field of forces operating in other layers of time and space.

The rescue of the civil (social or micro) does not reflect a new intellectual effort. It is rather a symptom of the hegemonic domination crisis associated with a crisis in the Latin American bourgeoisie's accumulation strategy that is, in addition, concomitant with the increasing complexity of the historical conception. In particular, it has left behind the mechanistic and fatalist idea of transition from one form of society to a superior one. Aspects of social reality that had previously evaded analysis are being increasingly incorporated into the study of history as a process of political creation, partly through "people's small but relevant daily themes." In fact, they have always been present, because any truly imaginative political task cannot think, let alone act, purely on the level of great historical transformational projects.

It is necessary to incorporate the moving, imprecise, and multifaceted field of historical happening. However, we must point out that dogmatic thought, or the non-creative use of potentially powerful categories, has turned its back on these realities through which the historical processes operate.

Interpretation without the will for change

Efforts towards an interpretation of reality in which the state is neither the dominant subject nor reality's exclusive sphere imply incorporating the heterogeneous forces that inhabit reality's different spheres into theories of their dynamics. It is particularly important to rescue types of actors inherent in certain realities. In this respect, we should acknowledge the importance of the peasant community, a prior condition for popular organizations, and whose role might be conclusive for redemocratizing processes when they consist of effective popular participation; such is the case in several Latin American countries, Peru being a prominent example.

But these social subjects tend to be ignored in ideological approaches oriented toward rescuing and highlighting individualism, such as in De Soto's neo-liberal attempts, that consider the informal sector as "a result of individualism"[150] alone, without taking into account the communitarian element and the value of popular organization. Economic crisis has been useful as a catalyst for the emergence of collective heterogeneous subjects (social movements), although they are not always capable of representing social projects that offer themselves as alternatives to the dominant one.

If we think, for instance, of the informal sector as a reserve for the formation of new social subjects, we must be aware of its limitations. Of course, it constitutes an extremely heterogeneous population, for it includes a variety of occupational categories, not all of them having experience in collective and organized forms of social struggle. In addition, what may prevent their maturing as subjects with a potential for autonomy is the fact that they are a dispersed labour force and therefore subjected to tension given their lack of legal protection and employment stability.[151] One must be careful when conducting analyses of civil society; one problem is recognizing the richness of its dynamisms and potentialities, while a very different one is transforming each one of its segments or sectors into subjects capable of supporting development alternatives. This is why we must go beyond simple descriptions of civil society's movements, social explosion, or politicization and recognize the embryos of social wills that may launch transformative processes, instead of limiting ourselves to giving accounts of the multiple forms through which social creativity is expressed.

Forms and values of struggle

Authors with recent histories of leftist inspiration tend to maintain that "strategy and instrumental efficiency end up determining ideals, wishes, and prophesies, instead of the latter determining strategic decisions," for "the experience of means not being suitable would end up by establishing what is desired."[152] The premise that supports this reasoning is that the possible legitimates options and adequate methods by which to struggle for them; this conceals the fallacy that something is possible only if the means to achieve it exist. What happens, in that case, to means construction? Viability is never a given, for it also has to be constructed, that is to say, one must know how to discover what is historically possible. To achieve this we must break the historical horizons we are locked into.

In this sense, the forces of change not only are expressions of a moment of the historical processes but also involve the breaching of the imposed limits keeping us within the boundaries of one idea about what is possible or impossible. The search for the possible consists not of an adjustment of ideals towards the possible but of the way of making viable what is defined in terms of political goals. To think otherwise means that the adjustment implicitly constitutes the forsaking of ultimate ideas, at least in the case in which they express the need for a profound transformation of reality. This being so, since revolutionary principles imply "a distance between desire and reality as an element defining its own identity," the very adjustment itself might "be interpreted as an indication of the obsolescence or superfluity of socialist ideals in modern contexts."[153] For this reason, the search for the possible translates (if one aspires to maintain a view of history that is not defeatist) into the constitution of subjects capable of fostering alternative projects, according to utopia's demands. If it were not so, political struggle would be reduced to an instrumental logic with no utopia to subordinate it, namely, a tactical game, with no prospects for advancement, that would be exhausted in a merely conjunctural struggle.

On the contrary, political struggle is a part of the logic of options that finds a viable path to utopia, which is *not* the same as the "adjustment of ideals" to the instruments' efficiency. These are also constructed. To maintain the opposite means to confuse political struggle with the reduction of tensions and frustrations, that is to say, with psychological compulsion.[154] This is, perhaps, what happens to those who purport to encourage profound transformative policies as long as they do not affect their privacy as individuals. In such cases, the demand for peace and tranquillity will certainly prevail. However, there is no denying that the "adjustment process" is part of the effort to find suitable means to bring utopia closer to historical materiality. In this process, fears, contradictions, maladjustments, and tensions must be overcome, and within the framework of the tasks dictated by utopia. The most important of these "means" is promoting the constitution, orientation, and organization of social subjects able to support and reproduce revolutionary projects.

Therefore, political action cannot be circumscribed within restricted time horizons. It is a problem not of chronological time but of history. In other words, it is not just a problem of tactical efficiency but one of creating potentialities capable of transforming the historical horizon, because political action is measured not by its tangible effects in a predictable term but rather by its ability to potentiate and maintain the socially constructed force that may then undergo variations. These variations are the concrete forms history assumes as it is constructed. We do not share, therefore, Koalkowsky's opinion that beyond a few years a radical uncertainty prevails, and the category of possibilities begins dissolving. If this were so, there would be no more politics than what might be sketched with the existing instruments; that is to say, the politics of the future (which is the essence of politics) is nothing but a remoulding of a consolidated present. This is what is hidden in the Latin American intellectual discourse inspired by post-modernism.

In Latin America, we find politics to be purely the interplay of instrumental powers, politics as simple power technology, with no other goal than to accommodate itself to the empire of a conservative utopia. Hence, processes such as those in Central America, where the struggle for utopia is a struggle for the present, and the present is the embryo that will fertilize utopia in the longer historical view, are extremely hopeful. Struggles in those countries are lessons not only on how an ideal is constructed, but on the ethics of commitment, which go beyond the limits of predictable days, or of the tangible results or emotional maladjustments caused by conjunctural failures. We must learn that protest and criticism are not sufficient. We must be capable of proposing, supporting, and reproducing projects, so that, if something has to be destroyed today, it may represent the exit to a new and better future.

A sensation of immobility
Today, a significant part of Latin American intellectual life is experiencing a crisis that, for the moment, has not moved out to the masses of the world. Criticism of dogmatic thought, especially that

with Marxist tendencies, has led to the rejection of ways of understanding history that, despite having some tendency to schematism, fulfil a liberating function. A profound difficulty in transforming the theoretical consciousness into historical consciousness can be observed. But what is noticed is a loss of historical sensibility, understood as a reality that is constructed; this cannot possibly be confused with the postulation of models, because, although utopia is an activating force for the present reality's potentialities, it is not rule. In the latter sense, it can, indeed, be concluded that "proposals for a future assume a high degree of provisionality and experimentation."[155] There is a crisis of the idea of the ineluctability of progress, for one must "be open beyond the boundaries imposed by progress's metaphysics." Today's crisis does not allow us "to foretell a transit to the desired place, in a determinist fashion, but often the opposite."[156] We have no certainty about what path history will follow.

Today's neo-conservative experiences and renewed crisis give evidence of "the many times and spaces that have not been thought of."[157] What seemed resolved in the 1950s and 1960s and, therefore, historically obsolete, has come back with renewed vigour to impose itself and win adherents, often from various social origins. The achievements of popular struggles that were seen as immutable and irreversible, such as labour and social security victories, freedom of speech, and the right to organization, not to speak of political democracy, show their frailty today. We now face a dramatic transformation of the parameters of ideological analysis.

Indeed, the power idea extended to the social sphere, the difference between instrumental power and power as cultural creation, the form of articulation between the public and private spheres, the idea of the political not simply as power technology but as an activation of the social that gives it a directionality and reincorporates utopia as an ideological force capable of stimulating reality's potentialities, the replacement of the idea of progress by the idea of construction, which from the actuality of each day may project itself into history's time, and the replacing of teleological and dogmatic reasoning by the search for viable options, all compel us to work towards a new political imagination that breaks with everything that has been regarded as unchallengeable so far, so that we may discover the new challenges posed by history, with all their surprises and mysteries. But we must do it without abandoning the prospects for reading a reality that urges the existence of the force essential for constructing it. Without complying with this, anything we might think will only be a reduction of politics to an intellectual exercise that will not transcend to the historical real.

6. Democracy as utopia and as politics

Democracy's main problem from our standpoint is to know whether it constitutes a project or an arena where many projects can develop and, therefore, a way of regulating the struggle between them. In many Latin American countries there is a pretence of encouraging and consolidating democratic systems that function as sets of rules that construct a political order. We wonder which order is being constructed, to which project the order constructed through democracy responds? Is democratic order closest to a consensus? What stability and direction might this consensus have? It is legitimate to assert that the debate on democracy cannot be confined to classical political institutions; it has to include sectors and social forces defending opposed, even antagonistic, positions. Does this confrontation take place within the democratic order itself? Is not this conflict, hazily circumscribed, perhaps what prevents democracy from responding to the "need for certainty," which cannot possibly be resolved when the political system initiates the game but does not know when and where to end it? Is it possible to consolidate the democratic system by stopping the political game, which implies excluding forces branded as anti-democratic according to that particular order's needs? Would that not be equal to stating that every democracy has to protect its own dynamics, leading, as a consequence, to the so-called authoritarian democracy that military regimes have feigned, and continue to feign, and argue is democracy's natural extension?

Uncertainty not resolved by democracy is perhaps the expression of the main contradiction between accumulation and legitimacy when the latter prevents the former from growing and progressing. Does this mean democracy is always the political order of a certain project, it being impossible to speak of an order capable of reconciling antagonistic projects? Does this statement place us before democracy in an instrumental position? We can speak of democracy as being instrumental or not only when it is linked to the nature of the economic and social project, democracy being a vehicle of it, for its instrumentality depends on the project having or lacking an excluding character. Indeed, what significance can the appeals to ideological plurality and the alternation of the exercise of power have if the economic and social project implies social, political, and cultural marginalization and inequality? Can a socially and economically egalitarian project become anti-pluralistic? What is at stake is whether an egalitarian project of social justice can recognize different forms of expression or that pluralism can guarantee, within a political order corresponding to the project, that its dynamics might be channelled through participation and activating mechanisms into real moments of decision. Is it possible in the present context of sharply polarized, if not openly de-articulated, Latin American societies to speak of an inclusive collective order, of a pluralism of social subjects? If democracy is the arena of many conflicting projects, it necessarily fulfils an arbitrating role between those interests. However, recent history has proved that dominant groups, whether of older aristocratic or recent bourgeois origin, are not willing to submit their interests to any arbitrating relation.

In Latin America, we can observe the transformation of the democratic state into an instrument of the classist-inspired economic strategies of exclusion; such is the case with neo-liberal strategies. Hence, for the popular movement, achieving democracy goes hand in hand with defeating the classes associated with those strategies, revitalizing the processes that constitute forces capable of promoting and supporting alternative projects. Yet one must not lose sight of the fact that democratic construction starts with the struggle to conquer it, for its eventual exercise will have to be congruent with those initial practices.

Now, what happens to the ideal of democracy as an expression of a negotiated consensus between forces?

Ideological plurality is not necessarily compatible with plurality of power; if it occurs, what is the reality that is constructed? How are reversible elements articulated with irreversible ones in different processes of social transformation sought for by different competing proposals, whether they originate in revolutionary or conservative projects? Can perhaps conservative and revolutionary trends alternate in the course of history? Do the demands of consensus consist precisely in that, or is it a process of blunting the edges of particular projects so as to allow for an ideologically, politically, and socially harmonized advance between different conflicting forces, an advance that may be the basis for effective regulation among them? This logic is neither the logic of change nor the logic of a politics designed to respond to the inequality and growing polarization of Latin American societies. The question raised has to do with the obvious objective character of democracy, beyond ideological and programmatic definitions. One way of approaching this analysis is to determine how it is being appropriated (or constructed) in discourses of power. In other words, we must determine how power understands and legitimates itself. Nothing is more useful, in this regard, than studying the stances of the Latin American political leadership, though we will emphasize positions that take as a premise the creation and maintenance of a uniting consensus. We have already touched on the positions of revolutionary and conservative thought.

Democracy in the discourse of power: The present dilemma
Today, the discourse of democracy faces the following dilemma: is it possible to introduce and consolidate democratic forms in a context characterized by a crisis of economic growth patterns and the breakdown of the hegemony of the dominant classes?

The questioning of representative forms is ever more pressing, even within the framework of political systems characterized by great stability. Cracks can be observed, revealing conflicts within systems, even though their consequences cannot be predicted. It is interesting to see the release of inner conflicts, even though it is not possible to create short-term alternatives, either because the bourgeoisie's interests are represented by the consensus project (this could be Colombia's case), or because attempting this, rather than representing an alternative, threatens state power. This dynamic tries to replace one project with another, even if the one being replaced represents the bourgeoisie's interests; this may be explained by intra-bourgeois conflicts, seen in Mexico after bank nationalization in 1982.

This dilemma forces us to question whether there exist forces that can initiate another change. The subordination of the left to populist or "principled" positions has become widely generalized. In none of these cases has the popular movement been able to question the economic and social order forcibly imposed by neo-liberal strategy with enough vigour so as to be able to reverse those tendencies. If we think of populism, we might understand it as a consequence of the predominance of petty bourgeois leadership, or, more specifically, as a need imposed by competition between different political forces. That is the case in the Dominican Republic, where democracy "has turned out to be fatal for revolutionary ideas." In the 1978 elections, "the populist party could count on the support of several leftist organizations," the left remaining in a precarious position, partly because it lacked any prospects of its own.[158]

The leftist movement has been paralysed by its fear of a return to authoritarianism, unaware that this fear originates in the ideology of chaotic order used by dominant classes to cling to power. When that fear is overcome and the leftist movement in general is no longer trapped in the urge to act "efficiently" imposed by political interplay, such as the recourse to populism, it tends to revert to "principled" or openly dogmatic positions. At this point, political realism becomes a function of the degree to which, reality being every bit as much a construction (without falling back on early twentieth-century discussions on revolution or reform), the left finds an immediate answer to the problem posed by the viability of revolutionary politics; that is to say, the left might maintain the autonomy of the popular movement by large movements or subordinate the popular project to democratic consensus movements without losing historical perspective. At the root of any of these possibilities is the notion that political direction (be it to avoid short-term reformist tendencies, "principlism," or ultra-leftism) should be able to unite the daily claims of different sectors in one programmatic body of strategic political thought. None the less, Latin America's prevailing discourse on prospects for change today favours a consensus strategy. For this reason, we deem it timely to finish this analysis by looking at the nature of the politics of consensus or balance of forces identified with democracy, so as to fix its limits as well as its potential for finding new paths toward economic and social development. No sources are more representative than those who are politically responsible in Latin American countries.

Characterization of the discourse of democracy: Project or political space?

What are the limits of democracy's ability to accept alternative economic and social projects? What does its plurality truly consist of? Historical experience has proved (the Popular Unity experience is one of the most convincing proofs) that anti-democratic trends can develop within democracy; this occurs when classes directly affected by transformations abandon democratic methods. Hence, in the battle for greater social justice and equality, one must think of mechanisms that can defend democracy from such trends, for "the bourgeois social order's defensive mechanisms" are not sufficient.

Popular Unity represents an extreme case where democracy's inability to become an arena for alternative projects became clearly evident. It assumed instead the character of a "shell" for certain social projects, even though, at times, it also assumed the character of an arena for a political struggle subjected to rules. President Alan

García, in his inaugural speech in Peru on 28 July 1985, asserted that democracy "has to be pedagogic, capable of convoking, persuasive, and exemplary," and he added that democracy "has to call back its stray children," but according to that established "by law and using state popular force." This same speech, however, recognized that "those who see the end of their privileged position often support their unjust defence by subverting the economic order. In that case, state order will know how to deal with them, applying legal discipline firmly and effectively."[159]

But the political–democratic arena may also be conceived of as the component of a project that will be executed by future governments. In the case of Mexico, the Frente Democrático Nacional (National Democratic Front), as part of its electoral platform, is critical of the government for a politics that works directly against historical struggles and revolutionary achievements. At bottom, this criticism refers to the fact that the historical arena constituted by the principles of the Mexican Revolution, and consecrated in the Constitution, has lost its value through policies of privatization and concessions to foreign interests. This criticism is in part a response to the Partido Revolucionario Institucional (PRI; Institutional Revolutionary Party) considering itself to be shaped "by an alliance of classes and historical currents," so that if the attempt at economic power concentration were ever to succeed in "subduing or levelling the vital plurality of sectors and militants, the Mexican Revolution would end up as a rhetorical resource, hardly useful as a mask for any sort of government, or any variety of 'entreguismo' [policy conceding the exploitation of basic resources to foreign companies."[160]

In both cases, we can detect an effort to create a project in an arena where others might converge, as long as they do not break that historical space's limits, and so that the use of state force can be avoided (as in the case of Peru) or, conversely, that this space could be reduced to a particular project to the detriment of other possibilities (as in the case of Mexico).

For Alan García, the state is the arena of a plural project, identified with the majority, which, "without fear, I call revolutionary, identified with those who suffer from misery," and in whose name he states that "democracy must be authority and energy, cannot permit subversion and, even less, death."[161] The state is meant to be the order for such a project.

For the National Democratic Front, the state's sphere, as the result of a combination of forces, must no longer be a vertical apparatus, and must become a consensual political society within a framework defined by the historical project of the Mexican Revolution. Hence, it is critical for the Mexican state when it says it has become a project that imposes an order excluding alternative orders. This makes it imperative that the arena be recovered for a revolutionary project that could reverse the course of the new economic strategies intended to re-integrate Mexico into the world economy. Hence, the PRI faces a dilemma in reconciling the national character of a project that reflects "the consciousness of what we are and what we want to be" with the demands of a strategy oriented towards modernization of the economy, making it "more dynamic in the international market." Here we can clearly see the variations in the concept of the political arena and its relation to the concept of project. For the PRI, order, represented by state juridical and political organization, is identified as the only viable project for the modernizing project, and therefore by nature exclusive. For the National Democratic Front, state juridical and political order is merely the arena for projects that are distinct from that of modernization.

A more liberal expression of democracy's problematic as a project or as an arena can be found in Alfonsín and Carlos Andrés Pérez's ideas. Alfonsín,[162] for instance, suggests that "a project based on a participatory society and an ethics of solidarity" (which are two fundamental pillars of democracy for him) might coincide, "while there might be divergent means of implementing them." If democratic procedure is the one that brings us closest "to the ideal of a rational consensus," resulting from the free acceptance of the same rules regulating its behaviour, the question becomes: "How can such a procedure be implemented, for that is precisely where divergence begins?" According to this system of thought, democracy is a set of principles (we could also say this is utopia) whose practical realization would translate into different operative forms or projects. Pursuing this logic, "it would no longer be possible to contrast the socialist ideal and the democratic ideal, inasmuch as an overall conception of democracy cannot leave out of its formulation and practice such a decisive sphere for the individual's self-realization as that of productive labour."

Democracy, as the construction of an open arena for political creativity, demands participation, which in turn implies having to overcome apathy so as to create the psychological and cultural dynamism indispensable for the attainment of a consensus in political and social relations.

If we follow the path of promoting political apathy and restricting participation, as the so-called "new right" intends, we would run the risk of losing what makes the democratic system valuable. We would hamper the processes of reflection and deliberation necessary for the achievement of a general consensus.

Is democracy necessarily defined by the majority? Democracy is a mechanism for solving the problem of the conflict between freedom and justice whose main feature lies in the confluence of all the political and social sectors that have different notions about each of these terms. Therefore, a solution by means of particular policies is but the expression of the relation established between different forces defending their own opinions. Consequently, the majority is still a solution to the problem and one that may undergo changes according to the course followed by social dynamics. That is why the search for consensus cannot be mixed up with majorities. The search for consensus reflects an arena of possible public relations where the arena is not identified with the project of a particular force. The majority, on the other hand, represents the actual content that the search for consensus finds at a specific historical moment.

Alfonsín reiterates this problematic when he affirms that "the will to share democratically may be expressed by a confluence encompassing practically all political and social sectors in the country, and it is indispensable as a source of clear rules so that all may live together in our fatherland." At the same time, it is necessary to have the will to make (in the economic, cultural, social, and institutional spheres) "the changes necessary to sustain that living together. . . in a different sort of convergence, perhaps of a lesser scope, for it will have as an axis a programmatic base that, of course, cannot possibly be shared by all." Hence, executive power in democracy requires "a plural adviser," including alternatives for elaborating structurally transformative projects.

The idea of space prevails over that of project, for democracy demands a pact that commits all sectors to live together despite their differences; and these differences will be expressed in particular projects. From this standpoint, we might rescue Alfonsín's statement that "democracy is never attained because it is not a crystallized system, but a cooperative and participative methodology that must be constantly expanded and adapted according to social and economic changes."[163] It represents a dynamic ideal, which compels us to mount an uninterrupted search for "new institutional mechanisms and new spheres into which social life may penetrate."

Democracy and participation

Creating a democratic arena in which different projects may coexist implies a constant incorporation of demands pertinent to civil society through different participating mechanisms. This participatory space must be autonomous, so that it can effectively avoid simple manipulation and assume the character of an effective route to political decision-making centres.

In this sense, it is suggested that democracy, if considered not only as an arena but also as a project, is realized when autonomy from the exterior is urged in order to free "the ability to construct our destiny in a juster society." The main goal of this society can be understood "beyond the economic dimension, in terms of revealing and bringing out all of man's potentials, in his dual situation as individual and part of the social whole."[164] We are dealing here with a utopian conception of man's self-realization that, politically, demands the full incorporation of society's potentialities, potentialities that often take on a subversive character in relation to the order established by the state. Equality, brandished as a banner by the bourgeoisie, has ended up by breaking up the bourgeoisie's domination. It is appropriate to wonder whether society's potentialities are being incorporated through participation, or if their incorporation is intended to be a way of shoring up the political order's legitimacy.

Any alternative project aims "to redefine bourgeois liberties in the light of new conditions and objectives," particularly in relation to their exercise. Indeed, it is thus that the value of liberty is transformed into a component of a class or social sector's specific project. Hence, demands for certain rights are not demands for a certain value, properly speaking, but demands for access to that value, and particularly the exercise of that value. We are all free, but not all of us can be equally free. The difference between a value and its exercise is the difference between an arena of democratic possibilities and the realization of those possibilities, which involves a particular form of exercise that implies its demotion and the consequent exclusion of those who have no right to the value, according to a different manner of exercising it. Because of this, any process of social change from within democracy poses the challenge of creating "many and new forms of communication and influence over people in power, in order gradually to establish a relationship that may allow the state to gather the opinions and initiatives of the masses, directly and through a party system."[165]

Democratic participation demands cultural changes. "Democratization is a cultural phenomenon. It demands a new concept of authority, and a regeneration of social relations beginning with the family and school, maturity in language and civil behaviour, tolerance and respect for the rights of others, and leadership legitimacy."[166] Understanding options as relative, and never as historical truths, overcoming sectarianism, enriching public relations, respecting others, are all aspects of democratic culture. However, this is not, and has not always been, the case. Democratic experiences find their greatest obstacle in the authoritarian tradition.

Constructing democracy today is and must be, to a great extent, a self-educational and self-assertive task, an effort to neutralize not only openly authoritarian groups or organizations, but also authoritarian tendencies operating unnoticed in every one of us and in the country's collective mentality.[167]

Incorporating into daily culture a consciousness of human rights and the will to preserve them is the result of a political–cultural struggle against apathy, individualism, and lack of social responsibility and civic conscience, which is, in turn, the result of a form of living together and social construction that we understand as public life.

Participation also implies understanding the state as a flexible apparatus that does not reduce or harden its own logic of bureaucratic control, but spreads to different spheres of social life, which may gradually assume decision functions. However, any state reform that implies democratic participation is a constant questioning of power itself, leaving open the arena for developing and deepening popular culture and its potential for creating new historical horizons, social and cultural organization, and, therefore, the possibility of group and personal affirmation.

Such possibilities exist in representative democracy, though they are constantly curtailed by state power. "Preserving representative democracy . . . entails adopting procedures that strengthen the role of political and social organizations functioning as mediators between civil society and the state."[168] If they do not actually assume the function of decision-making apparatuses, they contribute to "the inevitable tendency to mediation and bureaucratic embeddedness." Therefore, it is correct to think of democracy as a permanent process of change leading to articulation between the particular and the public.

The unsolved problem posed by the perfection of participatory channels is how to correct the state's tendency to become "an oversized, overbureaucratized, inefficient, and obsolete machinery,"[169] which implies facing power's tendency to concentrate. Power might have a democratic origin, but because of its control dynamic it tends to resist change; for this reason, it ends up, sooner or later, transforming its exercise into a non-democratic process. This is particularly true in polarized societies that have not found a political and social point of balance. It is different when the power bloc does not have inner conflicts within the same class. We need only think of liberal and social democratic democracies, as in the United States, the United Kingdom, or Scandinavia.

The dilemma can be summarized in the contradiction between the opening up of participatory channels and the resulting adjustment in political institutions, which, however, does not mean a loss of power understood as the instrumental ability to launch a project. We can cite, in this respect, what Mexico's "PRI's Basic Electoral Platform"[170] says when it points out that "in the coming years we will continue to face the democratic challenge: to widen political participation and step up the pace of the perfection of our institutions, and their adjustment to the ever more diverse and plural character of our society." This was restated later by the presidential candidate when he established decentralization as part of the effort to "acknowledge diversity while avoiding apparent contradictions between Mexicans as they share their needs and expectations."[171]

In this sense, we cannot forget that democracy has undergone, in many cases (in Chile for instance), an evolution from an exclusive system of the conservative classes working to solve disagreements between fractions and groups to a system open to other social and political forces, which, as they exceed the spaces accorded to them, begin using the system as a vehicle for their demands and interests. This means that the system becomes unstable, leading to the rapid loss of the hegemony, and later the control, of conservative groups. Thus, democracy finds its crucial limit when the majority status of bourgeois or centre–right ideological groups passes to a majority with an opposed ideological leaning, be it popular or leftist.

Hegemony, majority, and public life
A political system focused on the constitution of a majority is the essence of democracy. But that is not sufficient if we consider that this majority is dynamic and introduces transformations in democracy's social content and consequently in its ideological content. This raises a question about the objective possibility of a democracy with a capitalist development project becoming a democracy with a socialist project without deviating towards authoritarianism. Or does the solution

lie, perhaps, in the structuring of a negotiating state as the arbiter of plural dialogue? Would this not mean that history's development culminates in arenas that recover diversity, constituting the odd and intricate profile of a new society? Indeed, what happens to relations of exploitation and submission? Does society's development cease in moments of balance between the different forces that construct history? Do they nullify one another? Do they combine to the point of merging, or does it rather mean that a force with the greatest capacity for co-option and ability to forge instrumental alliances in its own interests will prevail?

In relation to the problem of the majorities, despite what we have said before, some more immediate themes can be presented that are prominent in the formulations of democracy's power discourse. First, there is the organizational form democracy may assume; this theme is discussed in chapter 2 above on the state. Here, we will refer only to the problem of the ideological and cultural distortion undergone by organization in its representational function – a distortion even to the point of lessening its value. In Mexico, criticism of the PRI that it has become a "redoubt of growing authoritarianism bringing the grass roots into line and controlling them rather than being the agent of their claims and aspirations," implies a loss of content in organizational forms, and therefore a loss of hegemony. The reduction in democratic participation aids the imposition of a "policy of exploitation and inequality," which might, in the long run, lead to "a state ever more deserted by the people, and that may, in turn, lead to a nation without a state, finally entailing the total loss of the state."[172]

In order to avoid finding ourselves employing development strategies founded on dualism, that is to say, on marginalizing the very majority that ought to be the pillar of democracy, it is indispensable that political organizations be revitalized with real content, granting them representation and hegemony. Democracy is not compatible with economic strategies oriented toward wealth concentration, for these imply the construction of an unrepresentative institutional edifice lacking the real participation of the majority's forces. To prevent this we need political forces that constitute political organizations loyal to "majority interest . . . , but which may also be nimble and competitive, free from the burdens generated by the exercise of patrimonialistic power and the authoritarian manipulation of society."[173] As President Alan García has declared, in order to achieve the goal of distributing wealth and preserving the value of freedom and popular participation, "Peruvians must unite in the sole front of those who can fight against imperialistic threats."[174]

The constitution of a majority as a force cannot be separated from its content as a project, for its supporting basis is of a programmatic nature. At the same time, the very concept of majority implies the presence of and respect for a social and ideological plurality. The majority's demands are vigorous demands because it is a question not of a simple political coexistence but of a social construction. As Alfonsín has pointed out, "this country [Argentina] needs a new collective capacity for cooperation and participation, ready to review old tasks, unjust structures and obsolete behaviour."[175] He adds that, despite the fact that "a programmatic convergence implies the coincidence of the aspirations and objectives of society's revitalizing forces," this does not mean an appeal to "a monochrome ideological conglomerate," for the idea is not to construct absolute monopolies that "replace the creative dynamics of loyal competition between ideas and parties."[176]

How can we make plurality and political efficiency compatible? Or does political efficiency consist in alternatives arising out of that majority, but without breaking the political continuity needed for the process to consolidate?

But breaking off is sometimes unavoidable. For instance, the return to democracy after a dictatorial interregnum does not necessarily mean a return or a restoration of democracy, but rather means a true construction. It does not consist of an institutional change or its stabilization; it forces "a profound reconsideration of cultural contents,"[177] a change in a mentality trapped within its authoritarian features. Authoritarianism creates passivity because it feeds on it. It is the logic of risk imposed through intimidation and fear that compels one to retreat into oneself and ignore what pertains to others, turning the materialization of the collective into a threshold beyond which lie unknown dangers: public life becomes undesirable.

Encouraging antagonisms to flourish, public life eliminates fear, thus generating confidence through the actions it stimulates. Confidence attracts will; will, in turn, encourages struggle and the inspiration to break the blockades and open up the historical horizon. Public space, even with its fears, is becoming livable, comfortable; it is ever more the natural sphere of our lives. As a result, culture is being reformulated, and the habits and perceptions of our relation to reality are changing, leading to an overcoming of scepticism and apathy, the two foundations of authoritarianism. These conditions are essential to the initiation and maintenance of democratic construction.

A nation needs a consciousness. Paraphrasing what Alan García has said about Peru, without a consciousness one can serve only external interests, so that all one can do during each economic cycle is to submit to the oscillations of the international system. To deprive peoples of this consciousness is part of the strategy of low-intensity war and low-profile diplomacy. Causing maladjustments in their identity, they attempt to make people forget their history and geography.

Peru, down the centuries, having been part of an organized agrarian empire, forgot its mountainous geography. It forgot its native cultures and began to be oriented towards the consumption of foreign products, appropriate to plains that did not exist there. Thus it acquired a false self-image.[178]

Public life not only allows for the strengthening of a national consciousness, it also means confrontation between citizens. It represents a setting of open faces and the dropping of masks, where the future can be designed through debate and participation. It is the nation being nurtured on personal and daily life. It is a plaza, not a refuge. It is struggle, not disguise.

Public life is the arena where conflicting forces are recognized; for this reason democracy, which is based on the notion of majorities, cannot do without public life because that is precisely where the forces that are the makers of history are born and transformed, and where they disappear. In public life, the subjects are recognized as the parts of a historical whole. There, the nation is revealed as a heterogeneous and dynamic subject. The nation, thus constituted, consists of the ability to take advantage of and transform a reality it recognizes as its own because, if it lacks consciousness, it will not have the will to construct its own destiny.

Notes

1. Pedro Vusković, "Pesadumbres y esperanzas en la América Latina de los 80." *Latinoamérica: Hora Cero*, no. 1, year 1, Mexico, July 1987.
2. Guillermo Bonfil, "La querella por la cultura," *Nexos*, no. 100, Mexico, April 1986.
3. Subsequent references to national monographs concern studies in each country on the subject of "power and culture." Documents come from the Latin American Perspectives (PAL) project. Some of these works are included in Hugo Zemelman, ed. *Cultura y política en América Latina*. Tokyo: United Nations University, Mexico: Siglo XXI, 1990.
4. Rosario León, monograph on Bolivia.
5. See E. Durham, "Cultura e ideologia." In: *La teoría y el análisis de la cultura*, Mexico: COMECSO, SEP–Guadalajara University, 1987, pp. 1–45. We can cite, in this respect, the case of Uruguayan and Chilean societies, where the ideas of peace, order, legality, and democracy were traditionally the central axes in these communities' discourse and

political development; as these concepts lose their correspondence to economic order in crisis, they begin to be called into question, and the result, in turn, becomes a questioning of the established social order. This clearly shows how, in each society, a value code and a symbolic structure are constituted; when they lose correspondence or become contradictory, it leads to criticism and nonconformity with a certain established order.

6. Alberto Cirese, "Cultura hegemónica y culturas subalternas." In: *La teoría y el análisis de la cultura*, op. cit., p. 307.

7. Ibid., p. 316.

8. Amílcar Cabral, "La cultura: fundamento del movimiento de liberación," *Tercer Mundo*, no. 1, Mexico, April–May 1975, pp. 4–5.

9. Ibid., p. 75.

10. We may cite, as an example, the case of Guatemala, where reaffirmation of ethnic identity at the end of the 1960s led to a process of struggle for the cultural autonomy of dominated sectors, which later became the central factor in an organized political movement that aspired to power, even by violent means. Data from A. Arias's monograph on Guatemala.

11. A. Arias, monograph on Guatemala.

12. M. Lauer, monograph on Peru.

13. Ibid.

14. See Fernando Butazzoni's monograph on Uruguay, and Néstor García Canclini's work on Argentina. Both of them refer to "founding myths" that exist in some Latin American countries that base their utopia on repeated attempts to "found" society again, preventing any other kind of opening to state and political class.

15. J. Martín-Barbero and Margarita Garrido, monograph on Colombia.

16. Ibid.

17. Ibid.

18. Ibid.

19. Ibid.

20. Ibid.

21. See García Canclini, monograph on Argentina.

22. See Durham, "Cultura e ideologia," op. cit., p. 152.

23. León, monograph on Bolivia.

24. Martín-Barbero and Margarita Garrido, monograph on Colombia.

25. Butazzoni, monograph on Uruguay.

26. In this respect, see the works of Butazzoni on Uruguay and García Canclini on Argentina.

27. Lauer, monograph on Peru.

28. Ibid.

29. Cf. René Zavaleta Mercado, "Las masas en noviembre." In: *Bolivia, hoy*. Mexico: Siglo XXI, 1983, p. 18.

30. Lauer, monograph on Peru.

31. García Canclini, monograph on Argentina.

32. Martín-Barbero and M. Garrido, monograph on Colombia.

33. García Canclini, op. cit.

34. Ibid.

35. José Joaquín Brunner, monograph on Chile.

36. Lauer, monograph on Peru.

37. In this respect, Mexico and Cuba are good examples. In Mexico, the party in power since 1929 has gone so far in identifying with the government that it is impossible to distinguish the two institutions or their projects because the two of them take the 1917 Constitution as their basis. Nevertheless, democratic institutions do not assume a real content; it is merely formal. In Cuba's case, we see a clear example of reducing reality to a project that does not leave any room for alternative options, thus removing the possibility of new political developments outside the established project.

38. Brunner, monograph on Chile.
39. Lauer, monograph on Peru.
40. Ibid.
41. Ibid.
42. León, monograph on Bolivia.
43. Arias, monograph on Guatemala.
44. Lauer, monograph on Peru.
45. Martín-Barbero and M. Garrido, monograph on Colombia.
46. That is the case of political reforms of formal expansion of the political arena with a view to opening up a participatory space, without diverging from the course of the formal order, or from the system. See the case of Mexico, and the so-called 1976 political reform, in the monograph on Mexico by Jorge Alonso *et al.*
47. Martín-Barbero and M. Garrido, monograph on Colombia.
48. See Arias, monograph on Guatemala.
49. Butazzoni, monograph on Uruguay.
50. Ibid.
51. Martín-Barbero and M. Garrido, monograph on Colombia.
52. García Canclini, monograph on Argentina.
53. Ibid.
54. Hugo Zemelman, "El partido como sujeto social." In: *Estado, poder y lucha política.* Mexico: Villicaña, 1986, p. 111.
55. Brunner, monograph on Chile.
56. García Canclini, monograph on Argentina.
57. Ibid.
58. Julio Ortega, "Cultura nacional y revolución." *Cambio*, no. 7, Mexico, Extemporáneos, April–June 1977, p. 45.
59. Martín-Barbero and M. Garrido, monograph on Colombia.
60. Joaquín Villalobos (a member of the FMLN's command), "El estado actual de la guerra y sus perspectivas." *Revista de Estudios Centroamericanos*, no. 449, El Salvador, Universidad Centroamericana "José Simeón Cañas", March 1986.
61. Ibid., p. 78.
62. Bolivia's mining proletariat is a good illustration of this: from being a central and traditional subject of a movement, it disintegrates as a traditional subject, in the search for new means of expression.
63. Lauer, monograph on Peru.
64. Simón Rodríguez, educator and philosopher of the Hispanoamerican Enlightenment, was a teacher of Simón Bolívar.
65. As the wars of independence came to an end, a process of economic reordering started in Latin America; it was accompanied by ideological renewal. Nevertheless, this period of history was marked by violence. If the middle classes (Creoles, the educated, etc.) removed from power by the Spanish government began an independence movement, imposing their project and leading their struggle, they were soon overtaken by popular classes that amalgamated into large movements, and also introduced their own projects, making the leaders incorporate those demands into their own project. An example of this is Hidalgo and Morelos' decrees that restored land and abolished taxes.
    At the end of struggle, and once independence had been achieved, the Creoles realized that, though they had reached their goals, this did not imply a change in real society's structure. Middle-class projects looked toward enlightenment, freedom, and abundance, but they became aware of oppression, ignorance, and misery: how, then, could they carry out the project of a nation? The first efforts at a national and social articulation, at state formation, occurred within the framework of pre-capitalist relations and were expressed through different classes' projects. On the one hand, popular projects proposed agrarian claims, tax abolition, etc., and through independence wars involved the peasantry and

some ethnic groups in an incipient national sentiment. On the other hand, the middle classes' project concerned state organization, health and public education, and national assertion. It is important to single out the role played by "caudillos" at that time in the articulation of a nation and state ideal.

66. Simón Bolívar, "Discurso de Angostura," 1819, states ideas previously expressed in the "Carta de Jamaica," 1815.

67. For that time's thinkers, the national project was focused on the need to educate people, postulating as a condition for political emancipation mental and spiritual emancipation and the repudiation of the colonial legacy. For this generation, which included Echeverría, Sarmiento, Alberdi, Bello, Mora, Bilbao, Lastarria, and José de la Luz Caballero, the moulding of a new man was necessary, and they turned their eyes to Europe as a model of modernity. Contradictions were expressed as a struggle between "civilization" and "barbarism" (Sarmiento), between "progress and regression," between "*esprit de corps*" (church and army) and "public spirit" (Mora) and politics as "an instrument at the service of education" (Alberdi).

68. Tulio Halperín-Donghi, *Historia de América Latina*. Buenos Aires: Alianza Editorial, 1975, p. 178.

69. See the cases of Bolivia, Mexico, Peru, and Colombia, among others.

70. Such are the cases of the Mexican Revolution (1910–1917), movements and struggles for independence in Cuba, and armed struggles against foreign intervention in Venezuela and Nicaragua.

71. José Carlos Mariátegui, *7 Estudios de interpretación de la realidad Peruana*. Lima: Ed. Amauta, 1969; and Manuel González Pradera, *Horas de lucha*. Caracas: Ed. Ayacucho, 1976.

72. José Enrique Rodó, *Ariel*. Buenos Aires: Ed. Espasa-Calpe, 1948.

73. Andrés Molina Enríquez, *Los grandes problemas nacionales*. Mexico: A. Carranza, 1909.

74. José Martí, *Nuestra América*. Havana: Ed. Crítica, Centro de Estudios Martianos, Casa de las Américas, 1991.

75. José Vasconcelos, *Ulises criollo*. Mexico: Ed. Jus, 1958.

76. Ernesto Guevara, *La formación del hombre nuevo en Cuba*. Montevideo: Marcha, 1965.

77. José Luis Romero, *El pensamiento político de la derecha latinoamericana*. Buenos Aires: Paidós, 1970, p. 115.

78. See, for instance, Ricardo Güiraldes, Benito Lynch, and Enrique Larra in Argentina, and Carlos Reyles and Javier de Vianes in Uruguay.

79. José Luis Romero, *El pensamiento político*, op. cit., p. 118.

80. Ibid., p. 122.

81. Ibid., pp. 132–133.

82. Ibid., pp. 146–147.

83. Ibid.

84. A different tradition attempts to defend the Indian tradition, as the Mexican Revolution had already done, especially in countries such as Peru and Bolivia. In the latter, Franz Tamayo, Jaime Mendoza, and the magazine *Kollasuyo* can be singled out. In Peru, we have Luis Valcárcel, Ciro Alegría, and José Ma. Arguedas.

85. José Luis Romero, *El pensamiento político*, op. cit, pp. 168–169.

86. Ibid., pp. 153–154.

87. Ibid., p. 51.

88. This is currently the case with the Colombian state, which seems paradigmatic to us as a reflection of the clientele where the old political class finds support.

89. José Luis Romero, *El pensamiento político*, op. cit., p. 141.

90. Raúl Benítez and Ricardo Córdova, "América Central: el neoconservadurismo emergente." In: Agustín Cueva et al., *Tiempos conservadores: América Latina en la derechización de Occidente*. Quito: El Conejo, 1986, p. 140.

91. Luis Rubio, "Argentina: la promesa incumplida." In: Agustín Cueva et al., op. cit., p. 153.

92. Benítez and Córdova, "América Central," op. cit., p. 132.
93. Ibid., p. 144.
94. For Chile's case, see H. Zemelman, "Chile: El régimen militar, la burguesía y el Estado (panorama de problemas y situaciones, 1974–1987)." In: Pablo González Casanova, ed. *El Estado en América Latina.* Mexico: Siglo XXI–UNU, 1990, pp. 291–332.
95. See Luis Rubio, "Argentina," op. cit., p. 154.
96. Ibid., pp. 173–174.
97. In 1985 and 1986 about 1,000 leaders at every level of Colombia's Patriotic Union were assassinated.
98. Magdalena Galindo, "Causas y límites de la derechización en México." In: Agustín Cueva et al., op. cit., p. 119.
99. Benítez and Córdova, "América Central," op. cit., p. 144.
100. Magdalena Galindo, "Causas y limites," op. cit., pp. 126–138.
101. Roberto Cássa, "Reedificaciones políticas en la República Dominicana." In: Agustín Cueva et al., op. cit., p. 217.
102. It is likely that the bourgeoisie had finally learned that it is not necessary for their interests to have recourse to brutality, as in the Chilean model, and the same for the United States.
103. Orlando Núñez and Roger Burbach, *Democracy and Revolution in the Americas.* Managua: Vanguardia, 1986, p. 65.
104. Report of the South American Bureau of the Communist International quoted by H. Zemelman, "El movimiento popular chileno y el sistema de alianzas en la década de los 30." In: *Estado, poder y lucha política.* Mexico: Villicaña, 1986, p. 120, and in *América Latina en los años treinta,* ed. Pablo González Casanova, Mexico: UNAM, 1977, p. 438.
105. Núñez and Burbach, *Democracy and Revolution,* op. cit., p. 69.
106. Pablo González Casanova, *La hegemonía del pueblo y la lucha centroamericana.* Costa Rica: EDUCA, 1984, pp. 63–69.
107. Ibid., p. 69.
108. Hugo Zemelman, "Democracia y militarismo." In: *Estado, poder y lucha política,* op. cit., p. 46.
109. Ibid., p. 66.
110. González Casanova, *La hegemonía del pueblo,* op. cit., p. 78.
111. Núñez and Burbach, *Democracy and Revolution,* op. cit., p. 94.
112. Clodomiro Almeyda has posited this in his book *Sociologismo e ideologismo en la teoría revolucionaria* (Mexico: FCE, 1976) where he says:
   [political expression in recent years] has led us to confirm, within a Marxist left linked to theoretical work, the coexistence of two sorts of approaches to the social problematic that contradict each other; their parallel actuality creates a sort of intellectual schizophrenia that is damaging, unfruitful, and paralysing. On the one hand, some stick to certain interpretative schemes of reality, elaborated according to Marxist categories, that are only schemes and, therefore, only abstract approximations and simplified views of a more complex reality that needs to be enriched with new determinations to take account of actual situations that are, ultimately, those we are interested in. Opposing them, there are others who, leaving aside their formal and "principled" adherence to Marxism, are oriented in political practice, as well as in theory, by purely empirical considerations according to the immediacy of experience, forgetting that the phenomenal and data world conceals and veils a deeper reality that transcends them, articulates them, and explains them. In reality, we can see only what is manifested.
113. In this respect it is worth mentioning Commander Joaquín Villalobos' contributions. "El Estado actual de la guerra y sus perspectivas," *Revista de Estudios Centroamericanos,* no. 449, El Salvador, Universidad Centroamericana "José Simeón Cañas," March 1987.
114. Núñez and Burbach, *Democracy and Revolution,* op. cit., pp. 106–107.
115. Ibid., p. 229.
116. Ibid., p. 140.
117. Ibid., p. 229.

118. Ibid., p. 233.
119. Ibid., p. 243.
120. Ibid., p. 235.
121. Ibid., p. 125.
122. In the case of Chile, to contrast it with the Sandinista experience, it was not possible to structure a mass movement independent from political organizations and therefore able to exercise autonomous pressure on the parties so as to force them to break with their clientelist power logic; this translated into a political atomizing of the popular social forces (Hugo Zemelman, "Ideología y viabilidad histórica." In: *Estado, poder y lucha política*, op. cit., pp. 65–106).
123. For instance, in Nicaragua they have had the clear-sightedness (so far) to continue, after taking power, in a struggle for mass support, without being reduced to the "vertical imposition of state policies, but responding to the needs and interest of the masses. . . [In addition, the United States aggression] has not eliminated activities producing pleasure, such as sports, music festivals, or parties after combat or work" (see Núñez and Burbach, *Democracy and Revolution*, op. cit., p. 168.
124. Miguel Concha, *Teología de la liberación*, Chihuahua, Mexico: Meca, 1988, p. 1.
125. González Casanova, *La hegemonía del pueblo*, op. cit., p. 57.
126. Hugo Zemelman, "Interrogantes acerca de cristianismos y revolución." In: *Estado, poder y lucha política*, op. cit., pp. 215–225.
127. Concha, *Teología de la liberación*, op. cit., pp. 17–19.
128. Zemelman, "Interrogantes," op. cit., p. 221.
129. "For the U.S., Canada, and the Federal German Republic during the years 1960–1973, it was close to 3% yearly; in England, France, and Italy it was 4.7%, Japan 6.1%; all this was accompanied by high economic growth rates of 4% in the US, 9.4% in Japan and the Pacific, and 4.7% in Europe; unemployment, in turn, never surpassed 5% of the economically active population" (René Villareal, *Monetarist Counterrevolution: Theory, politics, economy, and ideology of neoliberalism*, Mexico: Oceano, 1983, p. 69).
130. The central point of growth in neoclassical theory is that "market capitalism tends to be a situation of permanent imbalance," with the modification that "the concept of short-term balance extends to the long term" (ibid., p. 73).
131. Ibid., p. 113.
132. Ibid., p. 115.
133. Ibid., p. 216.
134. Ibid., p. 471, quoting Henri Lepage.
135. Frederic von Hayek, *Camino de servidumbre*, 1940.
136. For example, Milton Friedman and Rose Friedman, *Free to Choose*. New York: Harcourt Brace Jovanovich, 1980.
137. Villareal, *Monetarist Counterrevolution*, op. cit., p. 468.
138. Ibid., p. 480.
139. Ibid., p. 146.
140. Ibid., p. 151.
141. Ibid., p. 155.
142. Ibid.
143. Ibid., p. 175.
144. Ibid., p. 177.
145. Ibid., p. 179.
146. Ibid.
147. Benjamín Arditti, "Expansividad de lo social, recodificación de lo político," paper read at the Identity, Modernism and Post-Modernism seminar, 20th anniversary of CIACSO, Buenos Aires, Argentina, 14–16 October 1987, p. 19.
148. Henry Pease, "La posibilidad democrática en América Latina," paper read at the 20th anniversary of CIACSO, Buenos Aires, 1987, p. 11.

149. Ibid.
150. Ibid., p. 10.
151. We have carried out a more detailed discussion on the subject of new social subjects and their ability to elaborate a project in a paper for the Fundación Dag Hammarksjöld: see "La alternativa como política de transición histórica" in the chapter, "La economía informal, ¿base de una alternativa viable?", pp. 41–64, Santiago de Chile: CEPAUR, 1985.
152. Ángel Flisfisch, "Los ideales de la izquierda: la racionalidad del cambio," paper read at the 20th anniversary of CIACSO, Buenos Aires, October 1987, p. 45.
153. Ibid., p. 33.
154. Ibid., p. 16.
155. Arditti, "Expansividad de lo social," op. cit., p. 4.
156. Pease, "La posibilidad democrática," op. cit., p. 8.
157. Ibid., p. 10.
158. Cássa, "Reedificaciones políticas," op. cit., p. 219.
159. Alan García, "Discurso de asunción del mando presidencial," Lima, mimeo, July 1985, p. 3.
160. Porfirio Muñoz Ledo, quoted in Jorge Lazo de la Vega, *La corriente democrática*, Mexico: Posada, 1987, pp. 257–272.
161. Alan García, "Discurso de asunción del mando presidencial," op. cit., p. 7.
162. Raúl Alfonsín, speech at the Eugenio Blanco Foundation, 12 November 1985.
163. Ibid.
164. Carlos Andrés Pérez, lecture at El Colegio de México, Mexico, 1987.
165. Clodomiro Almeyda, "La democracia en el período de transición del capitalismo al socialismo." In: *Pensando a Chile*, Mexico: Universidad de Guadalajara, 1987, p. 51.
166. Cuauhtémoc Cárdenas, interview in *Por esto* magazine, Mexico, 14 October 1987.
167. Raúl Alfonsín, speech at the Eugenio Blanco Foundation, op. cit.
168. Carlos Andrés Pérez, lecture at El Colegio de Mexico, op. cit.
169. Raúl Alfonsín, speech at the Eugenio Blanco Foundation, op. cit.
170. Approved at the National Convention of the Institutional Revolutionary Party, November 1987.
171. Carlos Salinas de Gortari, Campaign Thesis, Mexico, CEN, PRI, 1987.
172. Cuauhtémoc Cárdenas, interview in *Por esto*, op. cit.
173. Porfirio Muñoz Ledo, "El PRI y la renovación política del país," paper read at a round table organized by the consultative council of the IEPES, Tepic, Nayarit, 21 October 1986.
174. Alan García, "Unidos todos los peruanos," speech on the day of fraternity of the APRA movement, Trujillo, 22 February 1986.
175. Raúl Alfonsín, text of the *Document on programmatic convergence*, 2 October 1985.
176. Ibid.
177. Raúl Alfonsín, speech at the Eugenio Blanco Foundation, op. cit.
178. Alan García, "Al rescate de la historia," speech at the Biennial Conference of the FAO, Rome, 11 November 1985.

Bibliography

Monographs on "Culture and Politics in Latin America" (PAL–UNU–Siglo XXI)

Alonso, Jorge, Manuel Rodríguez Lapuente, and Jaime Sánchez Susarrey. "La cultura política y el poder en México."
Arancibia Córdova, Juan. "Honduras: historia, política y poder."

261

Arias, Arturo. "La cultura, la política y el poder en Guatemala."
Béjar, Rafael Guido. "La cultura política en Nicaragua."
———. "El Salvador, Aspectos sociopolíticos del poder y la cultura."
Brunner, José Joaquín. "Chile: entre la cultura autoritaria y la cultura democrática."
Butazzoni, Fernando. "Una visión cultural del Uruguay de los ochenta."
Casimir, Jean. "Cultura y poder en el Caribe."
Cassá, Roberto, and Otto Fernández. "Cultura y política en República Dominicana: la formación de la identidad histórica."
Castro H., Guillermo. "Cultura, política y poder en Panamá: los años ochenta."
Chacón, Alfredo. "La cultura como política en Venezuela hoy."
García Canclini, Néstor. "La dinámica del estancamiento: cultura militar y poder civil en la Argentina."
Lauer, Mirko. "Cultura política y democracia representativa en Perú."
León, Rosario. "La cultura política del nacionalismo revolucionario y la cultura como política en Bolivia."
López Segrera, Francisco. "La cultura, la política y el poder en Cuba (1959–1986)."
Martín-Barbero, J., and Margarita Garrido. "Notas sobre cultura política y discursos sociales en Colombia."
Ribeiro, Darcy. "Cultura y enajenación."
Roitman, Marcos. "Política y mitos políticos en Costa Rica."
Segovia, Jerónimo. "Cultura campesina y poder político en Paraguay."
Silvia, Ch., Erika. "Ecuador: el dilema de la identidad nacional."

Selected references on culture and power in Latin America

Agosti, Héctor. *Sociología y cultura*. Mexico: Cartago, 1981.
Aguilar Camín, Héctor, et al. *En torno a la cultura nacional*. Mexico: SEP–INI, 1976.
Bate, Felipe. *Cultura, clase y cuestión nacional*. Mexico: Juan Pablos, 1985.
Bayón, Damián (narrator). *América Latina en sus artes*. Mexico: Siglo XXI–UNESCO, 1980 (series: América Latina en su Cultura).
Bonfil Batalla, Guillermo, et al. *Pluralismo cultural, cultura popular y cultura nacional*. Mexico: Museo de las culturas populares, SEP, 1981.
Cabral, Amílcar. "La cultura nacional y la liberación." In: Hilda Varela, ed. *Cultura y resistencia cultura. Una lectura política*. Mexico: SEP–El Caballito, 1985.
Carrillo Flores, Antonio. *El nacionalismo en los países latinoamericanos en la posguerra*. Mexico: El Colegio de México, 1945.
Casimir, Jean. *La cultura oprimida*. Mexico: Nueva Imágen, 1981.
Castaño, L. "El desarrollo de los medios de información en América Latina y crisis de la libertad de expresión." *Revista Mexicana de Ciencias Políticas y Sociales*, no. 8 (Mexico, April–June 1962): 291–306.
Cirese, Mario Alberto. *Ensayos sobre las culturas subalternas*. Mexico: CISINAH, 1979 (Cuadernos de la Casa Chata).
Colombres, Adolfo, ed. *La cultura popular*. Mexico: Premiá, 1982.
Cueva, Agustín, et al. *Tiempos conservadores: América Latina en la derechización de Occidente*. Quito: El Conejo, 1986.
De Ípola, Emilio. *Sociedad, ideología, comunicación y cultura*. Mexico: Nueva Imágen, 1979.

Fanon, Franz. "Sobre la cultura nacional." In: *Los condenados de la tierra*. Mexico: FCE, 1973.

Fernández Moreno, César, ed. *América Latina en su literatura*. Mexico: Siglo XXI–UNESCO (series: América Latina en su Cultura).

Franco, Jean. *Historia de la literatura hispanoamericana*. Mexico: Ariel, 1986.

———. *La cultura moderna en América Latina*. Mexico: Grijalbo, 1986.

García Canclini, Néstor. *Las culturas populares en el capitalismo*. Mexico: Nueva Imágen, 1982.

Gilly, Adolfo. "La acre resistencia a la opresión (cultura nacional, identidad de clase y cultura popular)." *Cuadernos Políticos*, no. 30 (Mexico, October–December 1981).

González Casanova, Pablo. "Cultura nacional y cultura universal." *La semana de Bellas Artes*, no. 104 (Mexico, SEP, 28 October 1981).

———, ed. *Cultura y creación intelectual en América Latina*. Mexico: Siglo XXI–UNU, 1984.

Henríquez Ureña, Pedro. *Historia de la cultura en América hispánica*. 3rd edn, Mexico–Buenos Aires: FCE, 1955.

Landi, Oscar. "Cultura y contracultura en la transición a la democracia." *Nueva sociedad*, no. 73 (Caracas, July–August 1984).

———. "Sobre lenguajes, identidades y ciudadanías políticas." In: Norbert Lechner et al. *Estado y política en América Latina*. Mexico: Siglo XXI, 1981.

Mattelart, Armand. *La cultura como empresa multinacional*. Mexico: Era, 1974.

Monsiváis, Carlos. "Cultura nacional y culturas populares." *Cuadernos Políticos*, no. 30 (Mexico, October–December 1981).

Najenson, José Luis. *Cultura nacional y cultura subalterna*. Mexico: UAEM, 1979.

Report on the First National Encounter, "Sociedad y Culturas Populares," Mexico: UAM–Xochimilco, 5–9 July 1982.

Ribeiro, Darcy. *El proceso civilizatorio*: *de la revolución agrícola a la termonuclear*. Buenos Aires: Centro Editor de América Latina, 1971.

Soler, Ricaurte. *Idea y cuestión nacional latinoamericanas*: *de la Independencia a la emergencia del imperialismo*. Mexico: Siglo XXI, 1980.

UNESCO. *Los medios de información en América Latina. Factor de desarrollo económico y social*. Paris: UNESCO, 1961.

Various authors. *La teoría y el análisis de la cultura*. Mexico: Comecso–SEP, 1987.

Villegas, Abelardo. *Cultura y política en Latinoamérica*. Mexico: Extemporáneos, 1978.

Williams, René de Visme. *Culture and Policy*: *The United States and the Hispanic world*. Knoxville, Tenn., USA: University of Tennessee Press, 1949.

Zavaleta, René. "Clase y conocimiento." *Historia y sociedad*, no. 7 (Mexico, March 1975).

Zemelman, Hugo. *Historia y política en el conocimiento*. Mexico: UNAM, FCPS, 1983.

5

Struggles and conflicts

Eduardo Ruiz Contardo, Raúl Benítez Manaut, and
Ricardo Córdova Macías

I. Introduction

Latin America has been integrated into the world system much more
quickly than have other areas, owing to the speeded-up process of
decolonization that took place in the nineteenth century. On the
other hand, colonialist power rotation, and its projection onto Latin
America, has contributed to the achievement of political autonomy
alongside linkage in economic terms, giving rise to situations of acute
dependence and the subordination of young countries' economic
structures to the international system, which has rapidly acquired an
imperialistic form. During the nineteenth century, England was on
the rise; in the twentieth, it was overtaken by North America.
Almost from the beginning of the history of the United States as a
nation, Latin America has been a sort of "backyard" as a result of the
so-called Monroe Doctrine, formulated in 1823. Given its geographical location within the United States' closest area of influence, America's hegemonic projection has had a great influence on Latin America's power and international negotiation spheres.

The historical configuration of Latin American nation-states was
turbulent and conflictual from the first years of independence. The
struggle between liberals and conservatives was the axis of nineteenth-century politics. In some countries it still determines politics;
such is the case in Colombia, this conflict being the main reason for
the serious problem this country faces now, a struggle between those
who want democracy and those who are trying to reproduce an exclusive oligarchic domination in the twentieth century. In addition, we

have the aspirations of a set of social groups and political forces, with their hopes and ideals, the struggle for socialism among them.

The 1980s were definitely lost years for Latin America. At the same time, they were years of evaluating and discussing the continent's possible course and perspectives. The worst economic crisis has shaken brutal military dictatorships as well as countries with democratic governments. The crisis has unified the different countries with great rapidity. Problems become common challenges. The best examples are, no doubt, debt in the economic field and the struggle for democracy in the political. Conflicts, in turn, merge and integrate: the political conflict over democracy cannot be solved if countries do not have the capacity to provide minimum welfare conditions to their citizens, particularly the least favoured. The same happens in the battle to better the terms for debt payment, or the battle not to pay it, an idea being pushed by many political forces representing popular interests. Debt is a political conflict between debtors and creditors, and it is at the same time an internal political conflict between those who deny the possibility of breaking the chains of the international financial system, fearing to see the interests of dominant sectors allied to big capital affected, and those actually affected by stabilization, adjustment, trade liberalization, wage control, and other policies, namely, popular majorities. There is a decisive consideration in the conflict over debt: indefinite renegotiation, which is, in fact, the conservative solution to the problem and the approach adopted by most governments, is a source of permanent conflict in political terms. This is due to the peoples' increasing ability to resist. Debt prevents growth, compromises new democracies' legitimacy, and wears out social structure. This explains the strength of political forces that did not previously enjoy wide popular support. We can mention, as examples, the Alianza Popular Revolucionaria Americana (APRA; American Popular Revolutionary Alliance) in Peru (the central point in Alan García's presidential campaign in 1985 was a radical redefinition of debt payment conditions), the Frente Democrático Nacional (National Democratic Front) in Mexico, the rising popularity of leftist and social democratic political forces in Brazil (all of them proposing a redefinition of the debt's payment terms), Rodrigo Borja's electoral victory in Ecuador, and Carlos Andrés Pérez's in Venezuela; these appear and reappear in the political panorama of their countries, because of, among other reasons, their opposition to existing international economic relations.

Another dimension of the conflict is located in the struggles for

265

national liberation and democracy in many countries. This element unquestionably gives a new dimension to the possibility of realizing popular aspirations. In Central American countries with a military and dictatorial tradition, such as Nicaragua, El Salvador, and Guatemala, people's revolutionary organizations fracture imperialistic hegemony and strengthen the reality of non-alignment. These struggles for national liberation are, at the same time, struggles for constructing a state that may truly satisfy popular interests; they are new dimensions in the battle for democracy. Central American conflict, extended by attempts at oligarchic, military, and imperialistic resistance, is, no doubt, the most notable tension point – though it is not the only one – in Latin America. In Colombia – where the oldest guerrilla war in the region continues to be waged – political, military, and social conflicts over liberation and democracy are very acute. Haiti, with ups and downs in its popular struggle to overcome the vices and inheritances of Duvalier's dictatorship, is another country where the conflict over democracy reaches extraordinary dimensions. Not less important are the attempts at consolidating democracy in the face of constant military strife in Argentina, Brazil, and Uruguay. The political struggle that unified the Chilean people against the dictator Pinochet, and the restoration of political life, as well as the considerable rise in the number of battles in Mexico to make a formally democratic government respect what the Mexican people won in the 1910–1920 revolution, also tend to unify the region's other struggles for democracy and liberation.

This underlines the radical change undergone by political struggle in Latin America. Democracy is a universal value and is an instrument defined by most Latin American political organizations – of the right, centre, and left – as the way to have access to power. Thus, a new relation between democracy and power is developing. One struggles for power in democracy; democracy defends itself. Power is lost or gained. This element gives a new dimension to democracy. Democratic openings, democratic shams, democracy's defence, and the struggle for democracy coexist in the same national space. The struggle for different conceptions of democracy is also carried on militarily, as is the case in Nicaragua (with popular defence against an imperialistic–counter-revolutionary war), in El Salvador, and in Guatemala with powerful revolutionary movements. In this context, struggles and conflicts of a different sort – though no less important – such as those at the corporate level, in turn, concern democracy. They strengthen or weaken it, combining struggles for democracy with struggles for the popular and the national, or struggles against the popular and against sovereignty, for example, military interventions that establish "democratic" regimes. Examples of this are the political regimes in the Dominican Republic after the 1965 intervention, in Grenada after that of 1983, and in Guatemala and El Salvador with the revived, formally democratic system that was designed to counter insurgence in the 1980s.

Defending democracy in Latin America becomes the main goal of popular political struggles. "Civil society" is revalued in every country, though the emphasis put on the problem depends on the national situation. In Mexico, respect for voting is fought over, while in Colombia, Guatemala, and El Salvador it is human rights; in Argentina, Uruguay, and Brazil, the struggle is against the military to prevent them from staging coups, and to see that justice is done for military criminals; the struggle is against dictators in Paraguay and Chile, and against open foreign intervention in Panama and Nicaragua. Democracy is not only elections and civil governments; it is also popular mobilization, and even insurgence in extremely conflictual situations.

Despite these differences in conflict levels and conflict particularities in different countries, it is important to emphasize that in global terms there is a hegemonic conflict going on with the United States. The United States wants to control the democratization processes in South America so that moderate governments emerge in the political field, and so that the thoroughly unequal structure controlled by big national and transnational capital may not be touched. In Central America, sophisticated interventionist doctrines of "communist restraint" have been applied, such as the so-called "low-intensity war," which has been a failure from every point of view, the persistent attempt to overthrow the Sandinista government, as well as the effort to make El Salvador's government annihilate the guerrilla forces of the Frente Farabundo Martí para la Liberación Nacional (Farabundo Martí National Liberation Front) and neutralize the powerful popular movement. It has also failed in its plot with the chief of Panama's Defence Forces (Fuerzas de Defensa) to attempt to change the text of the 1977 Canal Treaties, one of the most important achievements in the Latin American struggle for sovereignty and decolonization. In the Caribbean, the intervention in Grenada in October 1983 is, without doubt, the most telling instance of the imperialistic ability to deal with its splintering hegemony under absurdly unequal conditions, even from the standpoint of the most paranoid national security ideology, in what was a true "David versus Goliath" battle. Cuba's

267

presence makes the limits to imperialistic military power absolutely evident in that area. Latin America confronts a great power asymmetry in relation to North American imperialism in a hegemonic conflict.

In this paper we present an analysis of Latin American conflicts and struggles at two different levels: regional and national. At the regional level, our reference point is the struggles for democracy, because they permeate political struggle in every country. We also mention the most notable inter-state conflicts, their causes and expected outcome, as well as analyse the times when these conflicts were accompanied by military clashes. Central American conflict is analysed because it was unquestionably the most relevant problem of the 1980s in the continent, stressing the efforts for peace. Drug trafficking is also taken into account because of the dimensions this phenomenon has attained, and the potential for conflict between narcotic production and commercialization – at both the domestic level in each country and the regional level.

At the national level, the main political conflicts in 20 Latin American countries are studied. The central thread of this analysis is a diagnosis of the political system and the main conflicts, from the standpoint of the struggle for democracy or for a larger democratic sphere. Efforts to consolidate democracy out of military systems and the remarkable activity, of a new type, of social forces that formerly did not participate in political struggle or whose political weight was not focused on it, are mentioned as a new and important paradigm. Sections are divided according to the type of political regime, its stability, and the presence of structures where the popular component stands out. The case of El Salvador is also analysed as a country experiencing a revolutionary crisis.

II. Democratic struggles are the struggles of the present

It has been stated that the crisis of dominating authoritarian forms historically responds to the needs of capitalist development in so far as, at certain stages, a formally egalitarian society allows a more open market of labour-merchandise. However, historians of democracy in advanced capitalist countries assert that this statement is far from corresponding to real experience, which has implied more sacrifice and higher costs for the masses.

Any democratic conquest has entailed force, movements, repression, etc., in the snatching of bits and pieces of freedom away from "power." Generally, it would seem that the rise of a democratic ideology is a condition for people's realization of the subjected and exploited groups; this is not so for dominant sectors, which are, rather, the creators of a power culture. From observation, it can be anticipated that, for Latin American dominant groups, democracy turns out to be a way of exercising domination of a strictly "instrumental" character. To this end, it is convenient to pass over – conceptually and practically – democracy's definitions and contents, and particularly its projection, to which important groups of social scientists willingly submit.

No matter what sense we give to the idea of democracy, it refers, explicitly or implicitly, to the majorities' presence on the different planes of a society's life; it means that the presence of the social system's base is to a certain extent considered in national management. When a democratic ideology popularly arises, it is not exhausted in a finalist sense; it maintains the sense of being a political mechanism for the realization of ideals. Thus, it permanently acquires a relation to the idea of sovereignty, and, ultimately, a relation to the idea of liberation for important sectors.

Any analysis of this problem must not forget that democracy is a political category with a special connotation, and, as such, it represents the possibility of broader forms of social articulation. This is how it is associated with greater spaces that may allow a free dynamics to articulate huge social groups both among themselves and with the political system. Struggle for democracy implies a struggle for arenas that will allow a constant reproduction of civil society. In this sense, the existence of greater or lesser arenas for realizing different forms of social articulation in its highest dimension brings with it the social connotation given to the national.

Starting from interest differentiation and its corresponding representative forms – especially when they are expressed in a contradictory way – different readings of what must be possible in democracy emerge. This is why democracy is essentially conflictual, and has a greater or lesser solving ability according to the extent of hegemonic domination. Indeed, different behaviours resulting from different interpretations give content to system repression, negotiation, representation, participation, and mediation categories. In fact, it would seem that two complex factors are found in the genesis of the variations: (a) the use made of the economic surplus and what it means in terms of values and symbols in everyday life; (b) the dimensions and qualities of the groups participating in decision-making articulations.

269

In the case of countries undergoing the restoration of democracy, it seems to be methodologically important to assume a democracy–dictatorship–democracy cycle. At first sight, three hypothetical analytical paths are proposed: (1) the failure of the dominant attempt substantially and steadily to modify the conditions of capitalist development by liquidating or neutralizing the economic and power bases of popular movements; in other words, the failure of a modernizing bourgeoisie's consolidating project, attempted in optimum economic and political conditions, to construct a new state that would institutionalize and legitimate those conquests; (2) the basic persistence of popular sectors defending their rights to political and economic participation, and their relation to the defence of sovereignty; and (3) the contraction of the dominant groups' autonomy in defining popular projects, which restricted their spheres and alliances for exercising power democratically.

In a certain sense, important traditional groups try to retrieve a democratic history that re-establishes state institutions with no major innovations or reforms, but changes have occurred that make those institutions incongruent with the expectations of grass-roots political sectors. They pretend to rescue a state reduced in its economic and social functions while struggling to hold off more pressing popular expectations; the value of civil society is recovered before the state, but the validity and practice of a speculating individualism as the "modern" essential social personality is maintained. These incongruities call forth more rigid political control mechanisms because democratic formality does in fact permit a "liberation" from increasingly powerful conflicts. Among the incongruities that stress conflicts is the pretence of establishing democracy while essentially maintaining an economic model that is authoritarian in its concentrating and excluding trends in the economic sphere, and this is also projected onto the political sphere.

Democracy and military or civilian authoritarianism are two alternative, recurrent stages in the maintenance of "governability." From the dominant standpoint, "governability" permanently requires taking steps in order to recuperate the dominant bloc based on necessary internal restructuring and changes in the positions of some political and social sectors. Democratic governability implies a greater or lesser openness according to the specific "conflict." Somehow, dominant projects always imply a so-called "provisional" confrontation that has to be legitimized, often during "transition" stages towards new and more adequate "forms."

The search for governability within the framework of formal democracy reproduces the intrinsic contradiction of the dominant sectors. On the one hand, dependency and weakness are perpetuated, hindering the expansion of the ruling alliance. On the other hand, legitimizing arrangements are maintained along with restrictive values such as technocratism and apoliticism within the framework of maximum economic "freedom," the sacralization of order and the rejection of social mobility as well as of egalitarianism, a contempt for the masses, the underestimation of the popular, the totalitarian compulsion to identify the history of the national state and government as proving the assertion that "power incarnates truth." In fact, the possibilities and actual scope for representing popular interests are reduced so that the juridical–political structure may act as a mediator in the formulation of national policies.

In the case of countries undergoing the restoration of democracy, it is important to undertake a detailed study of the configurations of pro- and anti-coup alliances in successive systems, as well as look at the reasons for different behaviours. These alliance systems are: (1) alliances that tend to isolate the popular movement; (2) alliances that, at the point of struggle for democracy, turn out at first sight to be very large, with popular interests combining with bourgeois frustrations; and (3) alliances within the new democratic exercise, where the popular movement is again isolated and its opportunities for expansion are impaired. In bourgeois forms of manipulation through alliances (alliance system (1)), a contradiction arises between the possibility of democratic deepening and democratic "governability." From the economic standpoint, this contradiction is manifested in the privileged stability of economic interests superficially beyond the need for reactivating production, a steady demand for economic sacrifices from the population, the preservation of patterns of accumulation, and obedient service to illegitimate foreign debts.

Theoretically, relations between economic factors and their political effects are clear. However, a factual demonstration is required to examine the limits of Latin American capitalism and its thorough incompatibility with political claims apparently supported by the bourgeoisie. The factors that condition the capitalist model lead to profit rates that are incompatible with any redistribution attempt, and they generate a level of concentration that prevents growth internally. Under such conditions, are the necessary structural changes possible, given capitalism's functioning parameters? Is democratic stability possible without structural changes?

In the area we are dealing with, the history of the relationship between the bourgeoisie and democracy has been contradictory. On the one hand, this class pretends to modernize social and political relations in times of industrialization, imagining that these relations develop social and political mechanisms that affect "free" accumulation. On the other hand, at the very heart of the social composition of the authoritarian domination relation, private interests may be "expressed" but not "represented." Large bourgeois factions and their allies require a more participatory democratic plan for their domination, but, in a democratic opening allowing popular representation, the democratic system becomes dangerous to them and their project loses sense.

Differences concerning concepts as significant as sovereignty become extreme; so do others that give an account of a practically irreconcilable degree of ideological and cultural division in national societies. On one side, we have transnationalizing, denationalizing social fragmentation. On the other, we find a popular, integrating sense of the national and its democratic social relations.

There is also a difference when it comes to democratic contents, which gives rise to important contradictory dimensions. On the one hand, the idea of democracy emerges as an ideological and theoretical support for the liberal trend on which free ownership, private accumulation, and the free labour market, that is, the system of inequality entailed by capitalism, all depend. On the other hand, it is understood that democratic values represent the validity, even though only formal, of egalitarian and participatory values. Both dimensions are necessary for capitalist reproduction, though their simultaneity is contradictory; the second one completes a theoretical link that ends up being antagonistic.

It would seem that the operating force of limited democracy depends on an unstable balance enclosed within agreement, coexistence, and conciliation. If imbalance occurs in the course of the masses' search for egalitarianism and participation, which is linked to democratic deepening and hence to national liberation and socialism, they become unmanageable for bourgeois interests. If imbalance results from stressing the competitive features of current capitalism, on whose accumulating levels our countries depend because of their variable capital (wage) costs, it causes a combination typical of Latin American bourgeois democracies: authoritarian and repressive neo-liberalism.

III. Struggles for democracy and popular behaviour

A global outlook on conflicts and struggles in today's Latin America, and on their relation to the democratic phenomenon, must keep in mind some nuances that characterize the universe under study in order to avoid sweeping generalizations that may distort a faithful understanding. In order to concretize, four factors must be considered: (1) the sort of social actors that intervene in struggles for democracy; (2) the political situation of each country in the present conjuncture; (3) what each actor is actually pursuing in their democratic search; (4) the kind of struggle they implement to attain their goals.

In democratic struggles in the popular field, three types of actors can generally be identified: political organizations, corporate organizations, and social movements. Political actors are organizations whose main aim is to acquire and exercise power, or at least to participate in it, so as to reproduce the system's socio-political structures or to encourage the creation of alternative structures. Corporate organizations are those whose essential goal is the search for and defence of economic benefit for their members. Their main expression is trades unions and peasant groups. Social movements show a greater heterogeneity. They might have a communal, regional, ecological, ethnic, youth character, etc.; and their action often transcends immediate needs satisfaction.

What is the social delineation of each of these actors? Within the heterogeneous mass of "the popular" – which includes all those who, one way or another, are exploited or oppressed by the system – political organizations can be classified, in a very simplistic manner, into those that represent worker and popular sectors and those that homogenize middle sectors. As with practically all Latin American political organizations, both of these types really represent more than one class, and we are referring here only to the bulk of each social sector. Usually, the organizations' leadership, the "guiding" middle sectors, tend to assume a bourgeois orientation.

The social delineation of the corporate is more limited and specific. It is a kind of organization principally linked to the working class. Labour unions and poor segments of the middle sectors (teachers, public employees, etc.) make up its essential components.

Social movements tend to be heterogeneous. The "marginalized," the young, women, Indians, and the residents of lesser developed

273

areas find expression in these movements. If they are defined at all, it is by the precariousness of their participants' social and economic situation (in their popular segment, for there are also bourgeois and middle-class social movements).

These social actors move in a world of marked differences. Analysis of different Latin American countries reveals a variously greater or lesser imprint of democratic elements in their political regimes. Some enjoy democratic stability; others entered into a democratizing process only a short time ago; a third group are those that, struggling for democracy, have to fight a dictatorship. In the cases of Cuba and Nicaragua, the effort is centred on constructing and stabilizing democratic popular hegemony. In the case of El Salvador, there was a civil war where struggle for democracy acquired an ever-greater intensity and scope.

Naturally, this context determines the actual content of democratic struggles. It can also be shown that there are three levels within democracy that are being fought for. The first one – which is the base for the second one – is formal democracy. It refers to a juridical–political structure of a representative character, and broad electoral participation. The next level is "social" democracy. It is the organization and expression of arenas opened up within a formal and real democracy. Even though this is a goal of nearly all political organizations, it is particularly relevant for corporate organizations and social movements. The corporate democratic goal is to enlarge organizing capacity and therefore negotiation. It tries very hard to exert influence on the state's economy and social policies. Social movements also struggle at this level, but with a different emphasis. In so far as they are intermittent organizations with specific objectives, they function at the level of "expression" rather than broadening the organizational level. In order to be satisfied, their demands have to be listened to. Rather than knowing and having influence on the state's general economic policy, they want the state to be the one to recognize – and satisfy – their specific economic needs. The third level is that of "popular" democracy, which is the objective of political organizations bent on constructing an alternative popular hegemony. This level appears as a consequence of and simultaneously as a negation of limited formal democracy.

The fourth aspect to be considered, the type of struggle, is more concrete, and therefore it does not sustain prior classification. Before starting the analysis on how the social agents fight for democracy in a particular context, it is pertinent to single out some aspects that in a greater or lesser degree appear in every country of the region:

(a) A serious economic crisis, with its most obvious manifestations:
(i) the negative evolution, for Latin America, of foreign trade exchange terms; (ii) the enormous external debt.

(b) An economic policy designed by the IMF and applied by Latin American governments – with the exception of Cuba and Nicaragua – whose ultimate aim is to comply with financial obligations to international creditors. This policy obviously entails a loss of sovereignty and a move away from the national on the part of those states.

(c) The increasing economic, social, and cultural distance between the different segments of the population. If homogeneity was never a feature of Latin America, differences are now greater than ever, even in the least heterogeneous countries like Argentina and Uruguay. The accelerated income polarization in the 1980s has been a very important factor, producing many conflicts and political struggles.

In the Caribbean zone, the analysis has not been made in an individual–national fashion, but that does not reduce the possibility of acquiring a global view on Latin America. We have included in our study the most important countries: Cuba, the Dominican Republic, and Haiti. In the Caribbean (insular as well as continental), political struggles have, in some cases, a high decolonizing element both in French territories – Guadaloupe, Martinique, and French Guayana – and in those with consolidating democracies emerging from recent independence processes whose model is the British parliamentary system – Jamaica, Belize, Guayana, Trinidad and Tobago, Grenada, Dominica, Barbados – or struggles with an openly populist and nationalist character that have sometimes been hindered by disguised or direct interventions by the United States – Jamaica and Grenada. A case deserving particular study is Puerto Rico. Conflicts and struggles occur between those who support integration with the United States as another state of the American Union, those who prefer the present status as an Associated Free State, and those who struggle for the island's independence.

IV. A national panorama of conflicts and political struggles

1. Countries with stable political regimes

Five Latin American countries have stable political regimes: Mexico, Venezuela, Costa Rica, the Dominican Republic, and Colombia.

None the less, each case of political stability has particular features and differing degrees of conflict. The case of Colombia is outstanding because there is a virtual civil war going on in that country. In Costa Rica and Venezuela can be found a lesser degree of political conflict. In all five countries, conflict situations have increased along with the economic crisis; the debt problem becomes paramount and its payment enormously restricts the state's mediating ability. However, the strength of the state structure, its basis in civil society, and the development of the political system have cushioned the political conflicts.

Mexico

The stability of the Mexican state and political system depends on a combination of hegemony and authoritarianism. From the 1910 armed revolution – which was the most thorough anti-oligarchic popular revolution in Latin America in the first half of the twentieth century – the "class coalition state" was born. This state has ruled the country hegemonically, reinforced through fundamental popular corporate organizations – peasant, worker, and middle class – and by means of generating a broadly accepted national state ideology, very advanced labour legislation, a broad social security and educational system, etc. At the same time, political relations have acquired a strong degree of authoritarian centralization, hiding behind a crowd of institutional and juridical structures and procedures typical of Western civilizations.

In 1982 the most severe economic crisis since the 1930s was unleashed. President Miguel de la Madrid's government (1982–1988) faced the crisis with a neo-liberal International Monetary Fund-oriented strategy that made payment of the large external debt (more than $100 billion) its main goal. State intervention in the economy was reduced; state management of the bureaucracy was diminished ("rationalized"); modernization ("reconversion") of industrial plants was encouraged in order to make them internationally "competitive"; foreign capital was given facilities (many "maquiladora" plants have been installed); above all, real salaries were reduced. The living standards of middle and popular sectors experienced a serious fall from the beginning of the crisis, with more than a 40 per cent drop in the purchasing power of salaries.

The social effects of the economic crisis have cracked the hegemony of the 50-year-old state power, the Partido Revolucionario Institucional (PRI; Institutional Revolutionary Party). The Acción

National party (PAN; National Action Party), which is ideologically akin to the American neoconservative trend, gathered support from segments of middle and popular systems. Other strata of those sectors – students, teachers, and intellectuals – aligned themselves with popular organizations that gathered around the nationalist and progressive coalition around the Frente Democrático Nacional (FDN; National Democratic Front), which is comprised of political parties situated to the left of the PRI and of numerous social organizations. The central issue of the struggle carried on by the PAN, as well as the FDN and the rest of the political opposition, is the demand for effective suffrage and an end to electoral fraud.

The PRI's hegemony has been diminished, but it has not yet disappeared. Popular sectors – workers, peasants, the "marginalized" – are increasingly sceptical about the official party. They demand, as an essential, respect for organizations independent from the state and its party. The electoral growth of the opposition has been remarkable in recent years, and a qualitative change in the political system, one reaffirming legislative power, is foreseeable. Mexican democracy's future – whether it will deepen or remain limited – depends, to a considerable extent, on the electoral success achieved by different sectors or the political opposition.

The basic corporate organizations of workers and peasants (the Confederación de Trabajadores de México, CTM, and the Confederación Nacional Campesina, CMC) are closely related to the state through the PRI. The stability of this relationship is derived from a network of mediations and commitments between state and corporate organizations. The new economic policy applied in the 1980s split that pact, making evident the growing corporate conflict. Even official union leaders (known as "*charros*") have posited the need for the introduction of substantial changes in economic policy. From 1982, the number of strikes has increased and independent union organizations have been strengthened. Among them, we might mention the teachers and peasants. The struggle for the right to independent organization is an essential contribution to democratization that is happening within unions and confederations.

In the 1980s, numerous social movements appeared that are a challenge to the state because their demands prove to be hard to satisfy because of, among other reasons, prevailing economic limitations and because they reinforce opposition. Peasant and housing movements are impressive in Mexico City – especially since the 1985 earthquakes – as are environmentalist and student movements

277

fighting against the élitist project of "rationalizing" university education. Among "marginalized" youth, new forms of organization are also appearing (sometimes they have a delinquent manifestation, as in the so-called "*bandas*"). This set of movements has a very high democratizing potential.

Despite manifestations of the rising political crisis, the soundness of the Mexican system is remarkable. Troubled by a tremendous economic crisis that seems only to get worse, with a government policy that is dismantling most social welfare institutions, and experiencing a considerable reduction of its hegemonic capacity, it still shows some mediating abilities that have succeeded in preventing the present situation from leading to a social breakdown. However, after the July 1988 elections for president, deputies, and senators – the elections were branded as rigged by the right as well as the left opposition – the system has faced the challenge of restoring the lost consensus in the short term, accepting its deterioration, which benefits the opposition, whether in the form of PAN (neoconservative) or FDN ("cardenista", which has become the Partido de la Revolución Democrático (PRD; Democratic Revolutionary Party), or accepting the support of one or the other of these parties so as not to paralyse the political legitimation function traditionally carried out by the Chamber of Deputies.

Popular independent – political and corporate – organizations are still weak. In a confrontation where the situation is polarized, the popular element would be very unlikely to succeed. In the present circumstances, political crisis and authoritarian advancement would be closely connected. The popular movement urgently needs to develop its level of organization and increase its political force. Only thus will it be able to achieve its demands through pressure on the state and neutralize the danger of an authoritarian backlash; only then would it be able to react to crisis.

Owing to the accelerated participation and politicization process undergone by Mexican civil society between 1987 and 1988, Mexico found itself with an unstable balance between the three main political forces. At the centre of the political spectrum is the PRI, with state control and all its apparatuses; to the left is the PRD as a political–electoral counterbalance, and to the right the PAN. As a result of the 1988 political process, which was undoubtedly the most important since the 1930s, Mexican society has focused the struggle on deepening electoral democracy, where electoral respect is the axis of political struggle.

Though there are three political forces, the projects of the nation are basically two: the neo-liberal conservative one driven by the PAN and the PRI's dominant sectors, and the popular–nationalist one, headed by political forces grouped around the FDN–PRD and the PRI's progressive sectors. The course Mexico will follow depends on the confrontation between these projects and its outcome.

Venezuela

Venezuela has one of the most stable political regimes in Latin America. Its political reality is characterized by the high income from oil production. The state is the main manager of the economy and, since the overthrow of dictator Pérez Jiménez in 1958, the state acts as investor, employer, and redistributor. Political parties are recognized as agents of state tasks on which social demands are focused. In Venezuela, the popular is mediated by the action of the prevailing political parties: the social democratic Acción Democrática (Democratic Action) and COPEL, which is basically Christian democratic. These parties' struggle is purely electoral. It occurs within a formal democratic framework, not in pursuit of it.

In the 1980s the main tension-producing factor in the political arena was the drop in oil prices on the world market. This reduced the state's mediating ability in relation to popular and middle sectors. Protests arose from the corporate sector in reaction to a lowering of the majorities' standard of living. In addition, a corporate struggle continues over the maintenance of the traditional weight and influence in state decision-making. Social movements are isolated and still weak. The struggle for independent organizing is the central point for them. This struggle bestows a social character on political conflicts as democracy deepens. There have also been campaigns in the public employee sector for wage increases and social movements demanding state action on public services. Similarly, environmentalist movements have appeared; in the student sector there have been protests that, in 1986 and 1987, led to violent clashes with the police. Lately, a tendency towards increased conflict has been observed resulting from IMF monetarist measures, which entailed the elimination of fuel and public transport subsidies, price freeing, and increases in the cost of public services as well as higher interest and exchange rates. Venezuela has the highest per capita income in the subregion, but it displays one of the greatest degrees of relative inequality. According to official data, 8–12 per cent of the population hold 70–75 per cent of national income, while 70 per cent of the population have only 10–15 per cent of the income. In 1984 it was estimated that 60 per cent of the population were living in conditions of "critical poverty." Nearly two-thirds of the inhabitants of Caracas live in marginal neighbourhoods. Meanwhile the banks declared that 1988 was a bumper year for profits.

On the other hand, political negotiation has gradually acquired an élitist and bureaucratic quality that effectively takes political representation away from the organized masses. Discontent has expressed itself through new forms of political participation that seriously question the political system. Spontaneous urban uprisings were critical junctures after Carlos Andrés Pérez took office in early 1989. These were motivated by the application of economic measures recommended by the IMF, which directly affected the standard of living of the majority.

Costa Rica

The traditional and sound hegemonic structure of the Costa Rican state, based on a stable political regime in which negotiation and consensus have predominated since the 1948 liberal revolution, has been hit by a profound economic crisis since the early 1980s. This country's situation has become more vulnerable given its geographical location between Nicaragua and Panama, two of the most conflictual countries in Latin America. In the last two elections (1982 and 1986) the Liberación Nacional (National Liberation – social democratic) and the Unidad Social Cristiana (Social Christian Unity – neo-liberal right) parties polled more than 90 per cent of the total votes. These parties have hegemonic control over the popular sectors and have wide support from the middle and high sectors. The right-wing tendency of some middle layers is well expressed by these two parties, which have themselves swung right (especially Liberación Nacional), mainly motivated by the Central American crisis and the government's alignment with the United States against Nicaragua. None the less, the population's democratic mission persists, and political struggle operates within a culture strongly rooted in respect for the vote. Leftist organizations lack political force and are divided.

Among corporate actors, discontent has increased because of the effect of the economic crisis on the state's redistribution capacity. Political struggles concentrate on localized confrontations, employing land seizure, road blocks by disgruntled communities, sit-downs in public squares, hunger strikes, etc. So far, the state has succeeded in negotiating these conflicts. However, the deterioration of fundamental institutions of redistribution, such as social security and public education, encouragement to producers, and other pillars of government action, are all sources of possible future political conflicts. If the economic crisis worsens, and the government does not succeed in articulating its mediating mechanisms in the corporate–popular sectors, a radicalism unknown since the 1948 liberal revolution may appear.

A conflictual element has been the support given by President Monge (1982–1986) to the United States in the military aggression against Nicaragua. There is much domestic opposition to this involvement in a regional conflict, and the struggle is concentrated on neutrality and peace. Similarly, there is opposition to the formation of state security and police bodies. These demands had been taken up by President Arias in his efforts to reach a peace agreement in Central America; this led to the so-called "Arias peace plan," issued on 15 February 1987, which was the foundation of the Esquipulas II agreement. Contradictions in this country's government and its constant realignments reveal the present weakness of organized popular forces.

The Dominican Republic

In the Dominican Republic, Juan Bosch's administration was the first democratic government in the twentieth century after dictator Trujillo's death in 1961. Bosch was elected in December 1962, and was overthrown after seven months in office by a military coup in September 1963. A triumvirate ruled until April 1965, when it in turn was overthrown by a civilian–military movement that intended to reinstate ex-president Bosch. This movement was known as "constitutionalist." This led to the intervention of the United States on 28 April 1965, under the pretext that the movement was led by communists. Between May 1965 and 1966, the Dominican Republic underwent a great political–military convulsion, in the midst of which elections were held, still under North American occupation. Conservative candidate Joaquín Balaguer won. This was "democracy" imposed by a foreign power. Balaguer remained in office from 1966 to 1978. During this time social and political protests were severely repressed. In the early years (1966–1974) he even used paramilitary groups to curb opposition. Balaguer combined repressive policies with a modernization project for the country whose central feature was agrarian reform. He thus tried to gain popular support. Oligarchic resistance, mainly of great landholders and cattle dealers, together with the effects of economic crisis – the drop in sugar prices and rise in oil prices in world markets – hampered Balaguer's aim of enlarging his social support bases, and opened the way to the social democratic option. The Partido Revolucionario Dominicano (PRD; Dominican Revolutionary Party) ruled from 1978 to 1986.

State corporate structures being undeveloped, struggles and political conflicts are expressed through social movements. Several methods of protest are used: labour lockouts, strikes, seizure of facilities, peasant land occupations, neighbourhood lockouts, etc. In April 1984, there was social uprising on a national scale. Leftist parties and unions joined this protest. There was great mobilization against wage limitation measures imposed by the International Monetary Fund; more than 100 people died. In the Dominican Republic the state lacks mediating institutions in relation to the population like those of Mexico, Venezuela, and Costa Rica; this fact alone means any political conflict must be expressed as an open challenge to the state, giving the democratic system a special brand of authoritarianism. What is popular and democratic is mainly concentrated in social movements, which gain force and autonomy from the state and political parties. Those movements' strength is accompanied by a great weakness: the inability to link the social to the political, coinciding with a lack of awareness about the causes of the situation and little or no power or will. A clear example was the uprising of April 1984. As in other Latin American countries, the Catholic Church plays an important role in these movements.

In the Dominican Republic there is a crisis of hegemony because the state and political parties do not have the ability to satisfy the increasing social demands. Since 1966, we can observe a political cycle in which the conservative right headed by Joaquín Balaguer and the PRD contend for power. The PRD government crisis, which was partly a result of the international economic crisis and partly due to corruption, helped the right to win the 1986 elections, bringing Balaguer back for yet another term.

Colombia

Political conflict in Colombia is extremely varied and intense. Official violence and inequality of distribution have generalized a situation of violence: rightist, leftist, drug traffic-related, and common law offenders.

Colombia had the largest guerrilla movements in Latin America, and they have neither been defeated nor had access to power. In the 1980s, violence and conflicts were widespread throughout the country. Rural guerrillas, mainly grouped in the Fuerzas Armadas Revolucionarias de Colombia (FARC; Revolutionary Armed Forces of Colombia), the Ejército Popular de Liberación (ELN; Popular Army of National Liberation); and the Movimiento 19 de Abril (M-19; the 19th of April Movement), grew in political and military capacity during the 1970s and 1980s. One guerrilla organization, M-19, has had the ability to develop armed struggle in urban areas. The rise of guerrilla warfare forced President Belisario Betancourt (1982–1986) to seek a peace pact and to recognize the guerrillas as a political force representing an important sector of the population.

Efforts to maintain domestic peace were interrupted in November 1985 when M-19 occupied the Palace of Justice in Bogotá, and the army, refusing to negotiate with the insurgents, bombed and set fire to the building, killing more than 100 people, most of them innocent civilians. This event determined the success – within the state – of the most aggressive counter-insurgency project, to the detriment of political negotiation.

One form of violence favoured by the dominant sectors and the armed forces is political assassination carried out by "death squads." Colombia boasts one of the highest rates of human rights violations in Latin America. More than 1,000 popular leaders have been killed by such squads (most of them between 1985 and 1988) – mainly leaders of the Unión Patriótica (Patriotic Union), a political assembly of one of the guerrilla groups that dealt with the government and whose members wanted to take advantage of an amnesty to take part in the electoral struggle.

A doctrine of national security was constitutionally legalized in 1974. The population being under an almost permanent state of siege, Colombia is, no doubt, one of the Latin American countries where civil society's militarization is greatest. Landowners, industrialists, settlers, etc., participate in society in an armed way. This country has the highest rates of delinquency and daily violence.

In recent years there has been a remarkable rise in the number of popular protest movements: peasants constantly seize land, urban settlers campaign for better housing and basic urban services, students and housewives struggle in an atmosphere of daily violence. Because of the gravity of human rights violations several groups have lately arisen to struggle "for life." The "National civic lockout" called by the Central Única de Trabajadores (Workers' Confederation) in October 1988 had as its main demand "the right to life." It was branded as subversive by the government.

The ever-increasing presence of drug traffickers adds to the picture. Colombia is divided, geographically as well as in terms of political and military power, into government, guerrilla organizations, and drug traffickers. Drug trafficking has become one of the most important activities in the economic field. Being illegal, the true extent of its resources is unknown. According to pro-government journalistic sources, in 1988 alone, the state acquired $5 billion from the seizure of foreign currency in the central bank by means of a tax amnesty. That was the source of GNP growth of 4.4 per cent for that year. Income from cocaine sales and exports greatly exceeds that from coffee.

Drug trafficking gives rise to far-reaching conflicts and struggles, playing an important role in the corruption of politicians, soldiers, and judges. It employs a great number of marginalized urban popular elements and peasants – being one of the bases of informal community – and it generates a new relation between politics and power: "narcopolitics." The only way of reversing this situation will involve a radical change in the traditional structures of the dominant oligarchy.

All the above-mentioned elements – guerrillas with enormous political and military capacity, serious human rights violations, drug traffickers with great economic and political power, and a political system that does not satisfy popular demands – make Colombia one of the most conflictual countries in Latin America.

2. Countries undergoing the restoration of democracy

Ten Latin American countries are in a process of democratic restoration: Argentina, Bolivia, Brazil, Ecuador, Guatemala, Honduras, Panama, Paraguay, Peru, and Uruguay. They are experiencing the transition from military governments to democratic regimes based on liberal democracy's fashionable postulates. Some of them previously had long, stable democracies that were overthrown by coups d'état, such as Uruguay. In others, such as Guatemala, Honduras, Paraguay, and Bolivia, militarism and dictatorship have been the historical norm. In Ecuador, Panama, and Peru, in spite of military governments, the regimes have not had, comparatively speaking, a highly repressive content in terms of the typical methods of exercising power. In some countries, repression reached dimensions formerly unknown, Argentina and Guatemala being the most dramatic cases. However, the common denominator today is that, in all of them, political forces are searching for a stable democratic regime capable of consolidating political and social institutions and bringing the state closer to civil society, and meanwhile restraining the political ambitions of the armed forces. In most of these countries, democratic restoration is mainly channelled through reintroduced electoral processes and transition through organizational meetings which, in turn, draw up the new constitutional texts.

Argentina

Democracy in Argentina, as an aspiration, was always a central part of political culture. The restoration of democracy after the military regimes adopted the form of a negotiated return to a constitutional organization and direction of society. But the economic and social support of the present political structure is weaker than formerly.

Democracy has come after a "dirty war": the selective assassination by ultra-right-wing armed forces and paramilitary groups of popular leaders and people connected with any opposition activity of a popular kind. Dictatorship took political participation away from the middle sectors without giving them anything in return, and neither did it guarantee their security. When the armed conflict had ended, the military's need for self-justification led them constantly to re-create the enemy; they looked for it in the middle social strata. In addition, with their neo-liberal policies, they demolished salaried workers' standard of living. The middle sectors supported the democratizing process and their votes led to the success of a centrist alternative.

The military coup of March 1976 inflicted a defeat upon the entire spectrum of popular sectors, their representative structures, and their projects. The powerful economic interests that cause external debt, that feed on it, placed themselves in the centre of things; financial activity was more valued as unemployment increased and salaries and production diminished. The consolidation of these interests was interrupted in 1982 by the Falkland Islands disaster brought on by the military, their supposed allies.

The political actors in the democratic restructuring process are the same as before, but with a different emphasis. The old parties, including the "*justicialismo*" (Peronist), all pretend to be parties of "order" (bourgeois order, of course): the Church, powerful economic groups, and the armed forces. The armed forces lost power in the

285

midst of a general rejection after the bellicose adventure of the Malvinas Islands. Unfortunately, they soon recovered their ability to harass and threaten democracy. Peronism and the Unión Cívica Radical (Radical Civic Union) hegemonize democratic aspirations. From the standpoint of economic groups, the essential task of the political parties is to facilitate the development of conditions that would permit their forms of accumulation and profit. For them, democracy is valid in so far as it permits them to make a profit.

For corporate sectors, particularly workers' unions, democracy's arrival marks the moment when they can reunify their forces. They try in vain to modify an economic policy that is no great departure from that of the dictatorship. Confrontations grew. The defeat of the Partido Radical (Radical Party) in the parliamentary elections in September 1987, as well as the successful general strike in November of that same year, were the people's response to the government. The economic interests want to consolidate their positions and provoke a confrontation between workers and government. The eight industrial chambers have come up with a stabilization plan that includes a privatization plan for public enterprises, the dismantling of state controls and an indefinite wage freeze, lowering public expenditure on education, social security reform, raising the retirement age, de-monopolizing telecommunications and air transport, the sale of 50 per cent of the oil fields of Yacimientos Petrolíferos Fiscales, external debt capitalization, and economic deregulation. In fact, the aim has been to maintain or decrease the redistribution levels of the dictatorship. This has been called "wild capitalism," and is supported by the alliance between the country's major creditors, the most powerful internal economic groups, "liberal" army chiefs, and a great number of liberal and "*justicialistas*" politicians.

The weakness of the political system does not allow for a mediating mechanism for the interests of the majority in order to stop the powerful economic groups. President Raúl Alfonsín claimed to have accomplished democratic recovery, tolerating the policies of economic vested interests, and turning his back on the most basic needs of popular sectors; yet even this did not prevent the World Bank from cancelling credits to Argentina. After his first year in office, Alfonsín totally lacked the authority to dictate economic policy, a factor that made the crisis much more acute.

In such circumstances, the opposition candidate Carlos Saúl Menem won more than 47 per cent of the votes on a very basic and conservative platform, appealing to Catholic religious fervour and feudalism. Menem intends to reinstate the old Peronist plan of reconciling capital and labour; in order to do that, he is counting on his connections in the chambers of commerce and on the power of the most conservative unionism linked to productive cutting-edge industries. On the other hand, he has initiated good relations with insubordinate military men (*"carapintadas"*) and with the most reactionary sector of the Church. Despite their recent frustrated democratic experience, the great working mass places renewed confidence in him.

Argentina, one of the richest countries in its region, has produced the most devastating comparative pauperization of its labour force, which is one of the worst paid in the world ($30–40 a month). Impoverished masses break into supermarkets, in search of a minimal subsistence, projecting their longings for justice and autonomy onto the traditional forces of an essentially conservative opposition: radicals or Peronists.

Brazil
In a comparative analysis of Argentina, Uruguay, and Brazil, we find that in Brazil the democratization process occurred in a more controlled manner. Given the relative success of the project begun by the military, mainly in economic terms, the military did not leave power only as a result of social pressure. In the face of growing popular opposition, conspicuous since the metal-workers' great strikes in São Paulo in the late 1960s and early 1980s, they started a negotiated retreat from the country's principal political forces.

Indeed, despite the obvious collapse of the economic "miracle," which soon became evident in high inflation, increasing unemployment, and the largest external debt in the third world, the power bloc did not lose its ability to manoeuvre in domestic politics. A considerable fraction of the bourgeoisie and its representatives attained for themselves the direction of the redemocratizing process; even among the military there was a strong trend in favour of such a process. General Gobery de Couto e Silva, a man who symbolized two decades of dictatorship, was, significantly, both the theoretical author of the 1964 coup d'état and the ideological mentor of the original redemocratization. It was wiser to have a controlled transition that would allow the military to shift the responsibility for the crisis onto the whole nation rather than remain stubbornly in office and make the armed forces a target for popular discontent.

In 1985, the political veteran Tancredo Neves was elected president by an indirect parliamentary vote after complex negotiations that implied, among other things, that the vice-presidency fell to the conservative José Sarney. Neves died shortly before taking office, leaving Sarney as the nation's leader.

Sarney's administration has been characterized by three essential features. First, an erratic economic policy has tended to overcome the crisis. That policy has led him from the famous Cruzado Plan – in vogue during most of 1986, being a "heterodox" attempt at controlling inflation through price and wage freezes – to the 1987 Bresser Plan, which is closer to the International Monetary Fund's "orthodox" policy, and finally, at the beginning of 1989, to the Verano Plan, which is a desperate effort to control an inflation rate of almost 1,000 per cent. As to the handling of the external debt, President Sarney has wavered between a fleeting attempt to declare a unilateral moratorium to submissive agreement with creditors' demands.

Secondly, inasmuch as his prestige and popular support have receded (from late 1986 on, approximately), Sarney has decided to lean on the most conservative political groups, especially the military. These sectors, in fact, imposed a five-year mandate in his favour when, after his third year in office, the popular outcry already was "diretas já," which expressed the demand for the election of a new president by universal suffrage.

Thirdly, despite the continued use of shows of force (armoured cars in response to big strikes, bloody repression, as in Volta Redonda's case, tolerating large estate landowners' "white guards," frequent spreading of rumours of "possible" coups d'état), Sarney's government has had to respect a series of democratic advances ranging from regular elections for the various national and regional governmental positions to the expression, through various means, of the different social movements continually springing up around the country.

The trends and nuances of the Brazilian political spectrum are otherwise very broad, and their correlation of forces extremely unstable. There are at least 20 political groupings of national significance. On the right, properly speaking, are Partido Frente Liberal (PFL; Liberal Front Party) and the Partido Democrático Social (PDS; Social Democratic Party). The left is basically represented by the Partido de los Trabajadores (PT; Workers' Party) and Comunista del Brazil (PC do B; Brazilian Communists). In between is a wide range of social democratic parties such as the Partido Movimento Democratico Brasileiro (PMDB; Brazilian Democratic Movement Party) and the recently formed Partido da Socialdemocracia Brasileira (PSB; Brazilian Social Democracy Party). In addition, there is the heavy weight of a leftist populist current, represented by the Partido Democratico Trabalhista (PDT; Workers' Democratic Party) and its well-known leader Leonel Brizola.

In November 1986 the Brazilian political spectrum seemed universally dominated by the social democratic PMDB, which won in every state in Brazil except Sergipe. By November 1988, however, the correlation of forces was totally altered. The Partido de los Trabajadores, which in 1986 polled 6 per cent of votes at the national level and only 10 per cent in São Paulo, in 1988 gained control of that city's prefecture (São Paulo is the second most populated city in Latin America, after Mexico City). The PT also became the country's second political force, close behind a seriously weakened PMDB, whose remaining constituency lay in the least developed areas. In 1988, Brizola's PDT had significant victories in cities like Rio de Janeiro (the second most populated city in Brazil), making its leader a viable candidate for the 1989 presidential election. One paradox of the kaleidoscopic Brazilian political spectrum is the advance of the PT, with the resulting viability of the candidacy of Luis Ignacio da Silva (the well-known union leader nick-named "Lula") for president. This caused Brizola to move from being on the extreme left of the political picture to becoming an accepted figure, even for the military – a sort of "lesser evil" for some rightist sectors.

In 1988 the left was greatly encouraged. Another important event that year was the promulgation of a constitution characterized by strong conservatism in economic matters (resolute defence of private ownership, not even a hint of agrarian reform, etc.) and considerable achievements in social matters and democratic liberties (broad right to strike, advances in women's rights, etc.). This involves an apparent contradiction that does not seem to be exclusive to Brazil; it is instead a rather typical feature of present Latin American transitions.

The largest Latin American country has a promising as well as worrying future. Popular expectations are advancing steadily, manifested in direct electoral action intended to defend their democratic positions and purchasing power. On the one hand, the relatively embryonic leftist organic structure is still far from displaying the programmatic consistency necessary to advance a popular power strategy beyond local achievements. On the other hand, popular processes reveal this democracy's inability to absorb the occasional sharpening of class conflicts and their political repercussions. Therefore, a larger confrontation with a right that is strongly linked to military forces is foreseeable, and this right would not hesitate to snatch away the opportunities granted to popular forces by democracy.

Bolivia

From 1952, when the people destroyed the oligarchic state, Bolivian state history has been a chronicle of the failure to construct a national power with hegemonic structures. The only achievement was to make democracy a more than ever conjunctural phenomenon. Bolivia is the country with the most coups d'état in Latin American history. In spite of militarism, democracy in Bolivia is the result of a permanent popular–unionist struggle, mainly of mine-workers. This explains the right's frequent recourse to the military to establish its political projects.

After General Hugo Bánzer's (1971–1978) dictatorial government was overthrown, a long period of political crisis ensued. In four years (1978–1982) a series of governments followed – two of them devised by Congress and six de facto – while the economic crisis rapidly worsened. Among the crisis's accelerating factors was the fall of tin prices in world markets. In 1982, as a result of popular pressure, the armed forces placed Hernán Siles Sauzo in power, in recognition of his 1980 electoral victory. Siles's administration is the story of a centre–left government's inability to deal coherently with the political and economic crisis. Popular pressure demanded a solution to popular problems. The state showed great weakness and ineptitude, and the situation became unmanageable. The economic crisis reached catastrophic levels, with 20,000 per cent yearly inflation and an increasingly pauperized standard of living for the popular masses.

Víctor Paz Estenssoro, leader of the Movimiento Nacional Revolucionario (MNR; National Revolutionary Movement), which had rightist tendencies, won the 1985 elections, with support from the Acción Democrática Nacional (ADN; National Democratic Action), headed by Bánzer. Paz tried to reduce the social reach of the state to a minimum, to negotiate the external debt without confronting international finance centres, to reduce tax expenditure, and to limit wage increases even more. From a strictly neo-liberal standpoint, this project succeeded, but its social and political costs were extremely high (unemployment was massive and the so-called "informal" sector of the economy was strengthened), provoking the resistance of important popular sectors. The regime reverted to martial law twice and militarily occupied labour centres and imprisoned union and political leaders.

The corporate bloc, headed by the powerful Central Obrera Boliviana (COB; Bolivian Workers' Confederation) has assumed a defensive position in Bolivia. The economic and political conjuncture favours the government rather than the COB, because the mineworkers' capacity to pressure the government has been weakened as a result of the tin crisis. In addition, the government can count on some popular support. The growth of the "informal" sector has partially atomized the popular sectors, the population surviving thanks to independent forms such as the cultivation, processing, and sale of coca leaves, an industry that has now become an important factor in the economy's stability and recovery. At the same time, traffic in contraband has intensified. The profits from coca trafficking and contraband goods are higher than the income from the economy's formal sector.

Bolivian miners – and their union organizations – are the hardest-hit victims of their country's reintegration in the new international capital order. Tin, once a basic raw material for transnational industries, is now of marginal importance since its replacement by other products. The government's response to proletarian wage claims is to close mines. The popular masses' excessive corporatism, which was once their strength, depended on a capitalist logic of production. Popular struggle has become diversified as peasant and Indian struggles become relevant (many of them claim the right to the traditional production of coca leaves). All of them coincide in anti-state protest, to which repression is the only response.

"Narcopolitics" has meant an important conflict, given the great economic and political power accumulated by drug traffickers. One example suffices to show the extent of this problem: the production of coca leaves grew from 6,000 tons in 1970 to 152,000 tons in 1986. This has led to great violence. In addition, it meant growing pressure on Bolivia by the United States, culminating in North American military intervention. In mid-1985 the State Department announced the withholding of aid granted by Congress, making it conditional on a guarantee that Bolivia had taken forcible action against drug trafficking. In 1986, in a spirit of accommodation, the Paz government authorized North American military forces to land and take action against coca plantations and processing labs.

In terms of Bolivian popular political actors, one may say that, thanks to their struggle's consistency and heroism, they have sometimes accumulated a lot of power, but they have never found a way to expand it as a hegemonic element in the social whole. The syndi-

291

calists have outlived their own politics, and, in doing so, have lost any long-term prospects. As long as a popular project with hegemonic (national) ability is not constructed, its weakness or strength will depend on fluctuations of capitalist development on an international scale.

Ecuador

Ecuador belongs to the group of Andean countries with a pronounced oligarchic economic and social structure. Modernizing attempts occurred first in Bolivia (1952) and later in Peru (1968); in Peru, reform processes began partially to modernize structures. Only Ecuador kept the old structures until the early 1970s.

In February 1972, a coup d'état put General Guillermo Rodríguez Lara in power. Based on a nationalist reformist ideal similar to that of his Peruvian colleague Velazco Alvarado, Rodríguez Lara tried to modernize the country through an agrarian reform that was, however, less thorough than the Peruvian one. He fostered national industrial development, starting from an incipient base. He strengthened the state economy sector, and he pursued a nationalistic policy concerning the oil resources discovered in the late 1970s, which later allowed Ecuador to attain quite high growth rates, particularly in big cities and among their high and middle-income strata, sectors that were considerably enlarged.

The process of return to democracy culminated in 1979. This process was urged on by popular movements, as well as by large sections of the bourgeoisie. None the less, power did not end up in their hands; it went, instead, to Jaime Roldós Aguilera, a candidate of popular origin strongly influenced by the social democratic current already getting up steam in Latin America.

Keeping the third world-oriented foreign policy introduced by Rodríguez Lara's regime, Roldós attempted a redistribution in domestic affairs. His plans were thwarted in May 1981 when he died in a plane accident that was never clearly explained. The same happened to Vice-President Oswaldo Hurtado (1981–1984), who tried to stabilize Ecuadorean democracy, but without a clear project for economic development. The "mini-war" with Peru in 1981 (while Roldós was still alive), the economic crisis devastating Latin America from 1982, and drought and floods in Ecuador between 1983 and 1984, all made Hurtado's managerial performance appear not at all successful to the population. They turned to the Ecuadorean "new right" candidate, León Febres Cordero. Between 1984 and 1988, Ecuador had an extremely authoritarian government that did not respect parliament's decisions or the Statute of Judiciary Power, and created a climate of insecurity and fear among the citizens, at levels unknown even during the military regimes of the previous decade. In addition, Febres Cordero's economic policy was an experiment in pure and harsh economic neo-liberalism, applied under theoretically democratic conditions, which nevertheless ended up a complete failure, even in terms of the growth of the gross national product. At the end of his term in office, Ecuador sank into one of the worst crises in its history.

During his term, Febres had to face strong opposition from popular sectors. What finally undermined his regime was the military uprising of Air Force General Frank Vargas Pazzos in March 1986, who denounced the government's high-handedness and immoral economic practices, and demanded a return to real democratic coexistence. Vargas Pazzos was imprisoned and received an amnesty from the National Congress. The President's subsequent revolt against Congress meant the law had to be applied in unusual ways: Vargas Pazzos was not liberated until Taura's air force commandos kidnapped the President. Thus, in January 1987, they forced him to comply with the parliamentary decision.

The 1988 presidential elections revealed, in the first place, the exhaustion of the Ecuadorean "new right," whose candidate won fewer votes than expected. Secondly, the elections revealed populism's persistence; in the figure of Abdalá Bucaram, it got enough support to compete in the second round. Thirdly, these elections brought social democrat Rodrigo Borja Cevallos to power (he took office in August that same year), evidence of the growing strength of this ideological trend.

Having put an end to Febres Cordero's authoritarianism, and having restored a climate of democratic coexistence, there is still another great challenge for Doctor Borja in Ecuador: to see whether he is capable of overcoming the present economic crisis through an economic alternative clearly distinguishable from the neo-liberal one and the International Monetary Fund's formulas. Up to now, nothing seems to indicate that Ecuadorean social democracy may have, in this field, more imagination or power than other Latin American countries. This limitation could produce problems in a context where the social climate could deteriorate rapidly.

Indeed, an Ecuadorean majority expressed its disagreement with the newly established government economic policy, thus giving another turn to that area's revolving door of implementing centrism as a solution to authoritarian problems. Those centrist schemes, though, tend to exhaust themselves rapidly because they merely perpetuate transnationalizing neo-liberal economic formulas, which concentrate and marginalize the majority of the population.

Guatemala

Guatemala is one of the Latin American countries where the hegemonic crisis is gravest. The Guatemalan state structure clearly reflects this country's socio-economic reality. It is a system based on the intensive exploitation of manpower – with inadequate technology – on very large landed estates. (Manpower basically means Indian peasants, who comprise most of the population.)

In Guatemala we see an overlapping of two main types of conflict: the economic social problem and a long-running civil war. The former, a product of sharp social polarization, involves as political actors a dominant class made up of a landowning sector accustomed to possessing everything and not yielding anything and an entrepreneurial sector strongly influenced by the other. Both of them come together in a conservative and racist ideology that sees the Indian peasant as a tool rather than as a human being. The popular sectors, for their part, are made up of Indian peasants, poor "*ladinos*" (mestizos), the urban proletariat, pauperized middle classes, and other sectors such as students and employees. The second conflict is armed warfare. Ever since the 1960s different leftist groups have staged armed uprisings against the various military and civilian governments that have arisen since the 1954 counter-revolutionary coup. Between 1977 and 1981 the popular revolutionary project gained momentum and the regime was weakened and isolated. A large popular mobilization derived from urban unionist action, peasant, Indian, and Christian organizations, and increasingly active guerrilla movements.

In 1982 this situation changed as the result of diverse factors. The armed forces carried out counter-offensive actions that disrupted guerrilla fronts and diminished insurgent activity. This activity's main weapon is genocide against the civil population, which, between 1980 and 1984 alone, left some 75,000 people dead and 1 million displaced refugees, living within as well as outside the country. At the same time, the military wants to return government to civilians so as to rebuild mediating political domination and consensus.

Within the dominant bloc there are multiple contradictions. In March 1982, General Efraín Ríos Montt carried out a coup, and was "dismissed" a year later by General Oscar Mejía Víctores, who was responsible for encouraging the last phase of the offensive against the guerrillas. The political opening then promoted consisted of creating an arena for political parties to settle and organized, and was intended to become the Asamblea Nacional Constituyente (Constituent National Assembly) by the time of the presidential elections of December 1985. This process culminated in Christian Democrat Vinicio Cerezo's winning and taking office in January 1986.

In 1984 and 1985, the absence of noticeable corruption and the armed forces' relative lack of interest in politics allowed the parties to recover their role as social mediators. The constitution, as well as the government, emerged with a legitimacy that previous military governments entirely lacked. This passage from military to civil government initiated discussion on a transition to democracy, though only in very particular circumstances – with armed conflict and military tutelage over the political process.

Coup attempts have been numerous ever since Cerezo's ascension – such as the one of May 1988. These are generally understood as means of putting pressure on the government to prevent it from encouraging any initiatives that might affect the military institution. Primarily, the armed forces reject any possibility of dialogue with the insurgents. The guerrilla forces, for their part, joined in the Unidad Revolucionaria Nacional Guatemalteca (URNG; Guatemalan National Revolutionary Unity). They experienced severe hardships between 1981 and 1984, and have proved to be extremely resilient, maintaining constant military action in some of the country's regions.

The future of political conflict in Guatemala will depend on the economy's ceasing to favour oligarchic élites and favouring instead the popular sectors, as well as on the acknowledgement of the legitimate demands of the political forces removed from power in 1954. Otherwise, domestic peace will remain quite distant from Guatemala.

Honduras

Compared with the other Central American countries – except Costa Rica – Honduras seems to be the country with the least internal political conflict. The newly apparent conflicts derive mainly from the regional crisis, and are due to the United States' role in the military strategy against the Nicaraguan government and the FMLN's appearance in El Salvador.

Honduras is one of the Latin American countries where state institutions and the functional bases of the economy are weakest. They have been subordinated to the United States in the economic, the political, and the military spheres for the whole of the twentieth century. The Honduran economy revolves around the United Fruit transnational company. In spite of that, there have not been such extremely repressive regimes as in neighbouring countries. Democratic structures being precarious, they have to put up with tutelage from the armed forces. The military has been greatly influenced by the United States, principally in the post-war period. Since 1954, when a military cooperation pact was signed with the United States, the government has been a territorial rearguard for Central American counter-revolutionary military forces, starting with Guatemala. It is now in a position to threaten Nicaragua. Since 1983, about 2,000 American soldiers have been established in Honduras on a semi-permanent basis.

In order to prevent Honduras from having a political crisis similar to that in Nicaragua, El Salvador, or Guatemala, the United States has promoted a transition to a democratic regime since the late 1970s. In November 1981, elections were held. Power was disputed by the main political parties, the Liberals and the Nationals. Liberal candidate Roberto Sauzo Córdova won, and he remained in office from January 1982 to January 1986. In 1986 he was succeeded by José Azcona Hoyo, also of the Liberal Party, who continued to support Nicaraguan counter-revolution and maintained the United States presence.

In the 1980s, new conflicts emerged. A guerrilla movement arose whose short existence lasted from 1981 to 1983. Conflicts appeared with the southern population, mainly coffee growers whose lands had been greatly affected by Nicaragua's counter-revolution. Even coffee harvesting had decreased for this reason. Many social protest movements have appeared – union, peasant, and student. Many of them demand that the United States army and counter-revolutionaries get out, as well as wanting neutrality in relation to the regional conflict. Struggle for respect for human rights has developed noticeably, especially since 1981–1982, a period that saw a remarkable increase in violations.

Conflicts and struggles in Honduras depend, to a great extent, on how the regional crisis affects internal conditions, which basically means the presence of counter-revolutionaries and the support given to them by the United States. Another element to be reckoned with is the serious economic situation of the majority of the population; Honduras has the highest poverty rate in Central America.

Panama

The Hay–Buneau–Varilla Treaty signed in November 1903 – ceding the Panama Canal's control and domination to the American government permanently (the Canal was built right *after* signing) and also ceding the adjacent area, and, in addition, granting the United States the right to intervene in Panama's internal politics (though this clause was abolished in 1936) – is the reason for a profound anti-imperialist, nationalist sentiment among the Panamanian people.

In 1968, the National Guard (today the Defence Forces), led by a group of nationalist officials, took power and initiated a new kind of relationship with the United States and a novel relation between the state and civil society, particularly with the popular sectors. From 1969 on, Omar Torrijos became the country's highest official. In domestic affairs he tried to install mechanisms to allow the population to participate more in decision-making. The Asamblea Nacional de Representantes de Corregimientos (National Assembly of Town Council Representatives) was a legislative organ created for that purpose. It had a broader and more popular character than typical Latin American liberal democracies. It was intended to structure a state moulded by nationalism and populism, with the military as a pillar of the new political structures. The Partido Revolucionario Democrático (PRD; Revolutionary Democratic Party) was formed at the same time, and for the same purpose – it wanted the political leadership of this process. Foreign policy, from the 1970s on, focused on rescuing the Panama Canal and dismantling the American military complex, which was mainly located on Southern Command. As stipulated in the Torrijos–Carter treaties, signed in 1977, Panama would recover the Canal and the adjacent area at the turn of the century.

Torrijos's death in 1981, and the start of the economic crisis, disrupted the plan. In 1981, Panama entered a profound political crisis, indicated in part by the instability of the presidential institution. Since then, six presidents have held office: Arístides Royo, Ricardo de la Espriella, Jorge Illueca, Ardito Barletta, Eric del Valle, and Manuel Solís Palma. Similarly, the economy's precariousness – because of great dependence on foreign aid, very weak industries, the absence of national wealth, and the overdevelopment of finance capital and trade – makes Panama a very vulnerable country.

With the Reagan administration, in 1981, the United States government made efforts to revise the treaties so as to maintain an American presence in Panama beyond the year 2000. At the same time, a very important sector of Panama's bourgeoisie feels closely linked to the United States, seeing the departure of Southern Command and the Canal's reversion to Panama as threats to its interests. Hence the very intense political conflict that broke out in mid-1987. At that time, this sector, organized around the "Civil Crusade," pushed to overthrow the chief of the Defence Forces, Manuel A. Noriega, so as to eliminate the government's populist orientation and militarist nationalism.

The Panamanian government faces a serious legitimacy crisis. It is unable to satisfy popular demands because of the external debt, capital flight, the partial dismantling of the Centro Financiero Internacional (International Finance Centre), and its lack of resources, owing to the United States' refusal to pay Panama its share of the Canal transit toll as specified in the Torrijos–Carter treaties. In January and February 1988, the United States applied the most extraordinary pressure – unsuccessfully – to overthrow Noriega, provoking some of the tensest moments in the political conflict. The situation was kept under control by the Defence Forces and the government. The conflict became still worse during the elections of 7 May 1989, when the whole Pandora's box of American pressure was unleashed, the United States government clearly stating its intention of intervening to ensure that Panama had a government in line with American strategic interests. The United States supported the Alianza Democrática de Oposición Civilista (ADOC; Democratic Alliance of Civil Opposition) against the Coalición de Liberación Nacional (Colina; National Liberation Coalition), headed by the "*oficialista*" PRD.

The Panamanian conflict has demonstrated once again that American interventionist policy in Latin America continues. It has counted on the complicity (in some cases) and the weakness (in others) of most Latin American governments, and the Panamanian case was no exception.

Paraguay
In Paraguay's history, the coup d'état has been used repeatedly by political leaders of the traditional parties, the Partido Colorado (Red Party) and the Partido Liberal (Liberal Party), as means to power. In 1954, a faction of the Red Party, in opposition to another government faction, appealed to General Alfredo Stroessner for a change in the country's political leadership. Being firmly established in power, Stroessner displaced the civilians of the Red Party. The period between 1954 and 1960 may be described as the formative moment for a

dictatorial regime personified by Stroessner. The Red Party became the government party. The regime concentrated political power by severely repressing the leaders of the opposition parties: the Liberal Party, the Partido Revolucionario Febrerista (Febrerist Revolutionary Party), and the Partido Comunista (Communist Party). At the same time, a repressive policy was also imposed on society in general. In 1959, labour strike movements and student demonstrations against the regime were badly weakened.

Stroessner owes his grip on power to his ability to readjust the dominant bloc when changes in economic and social structures demand. In order to understand such longevity, we must understand two essential elements: a partial neutralizing of social conflicts through agrarian policy, and strategic subordination to Brazil. The first, beginning in the 1960s, was a policy of distributing parcels of land to landless peasants, which did not affect the large landed estate structure because it used instead depopulated lands owned by the state. This reform increased the number of small landowners, thus diminishing social tensions in regions of greatest demographic density. The second element was the building of the Itaipú dam in co-operation with Brazil during the 1960s. This huge building project produced many changes: it noticeably increased foreign capital investment (it cost US$14 billion), and it generated previously unknown industrial and financial development. These changes manifested themselves in the social structure with the appearance of new bourgeois sectors, an enlarged middle layer, and the expansion of salaried labour – all outstanding structural transformations. The modification of the social structure in conjunction with economic growth meant the consolidation of the system's supporting base. Thus, new dominant sectors – industry and finance – were incorporated into the power bloc, which was dominated by a civil–military political bureacracy, while the middle layers and the salaried sector strengthened the bases for dictatorial control. In 1980 the end of the dam project gave ample proof of the limits of the economic boom's political usefulness. Therefore, as the dam came to an end, and economic crisis and political conflict revealed themselves as deeply interwoven trends, so ended the dictatorship.

External and internal pressure and power bloc conflicts culminated in the military coup of 2 and 3 February 1989 led by General Andrés Rodríguez, who had for a long time been the dictator's right-hand man. General Rodríguez promptly convened presidential and parliamentary elections. The voting was held on 11 May, in the midst of allegations of fraud. Nevertheless, Rodríguez managed to get support from a majority hoping for a democratic initiative that would bring new political and social dynamism to the country.

The Partido Liberal Radical Auténtico (Authentic Liberal Radical Party), activists of the Febrerist Revolutionary Party, the Partido Demócrata Cristiano (Christian Democratic Party), and the Movimiento Popular Colorado (Popular Red Movement), all members of the Acuerdo Nacional (National Accord), together with some factions of the *"oficialista"* Red Party and representatives of social movements, all find common cause in the need to replace dictatorial power with a representative democratic regime. The contradiction between authoritarianism and democracy is still visible on the horizon of Paraguay's political future. The authoritarian solution to this problem will depend on the ability of the political leadership of the current power bloc to rearticulate the control and political marginalization of the majorities, and to do that it may hand over power to a reliable member of the political bureaucracy. On the other hand, the way to democratic transition will be secured only by the political leaders developing organizations and the ability to construct an alternative project.

Peru

In today's Peru there is a triple crisis: economic, social, and political. This country suffers from the worst effects of the general Latin American crisis. Since 1985, when Alan García, leader of the Peruvian Alianza Popular Revolucionaria Americana (APRA; American Popular Revolutionary Alliance) took office, the economy clearly showed recession, extremely high inflation, an external debt of more than $14 billion, whose payment took the nation's total exports, and enormous capital flight.

Under such conditions, García designed his "Aprista revolution," refusing to adopt the neo-liberal policy advised by the IMF. He announced that the government would use only 10 per cent of exports to pay external debt interest. García's economic programme sought the rationalization and growth of the Peruvian economy, enlarging the domestic market (incrementing real wages and encouraging temporary employment programmes), transferring resources to lower-income sectors, fixing minimum prices for some agricultural products, and freezing prices. In July 1987, García, consistent with his position, nationalized the finance system.

The Peruvian political setting was completely reformulated after the 1968 coup, which placed in power a military–reformist project, based, at first, on an accelerated modernization of the country (the so called "Inca Plan") whose pillar was the nationalizing of some strategic industries and agrarian reform. In 1976, General Bermúdez came to power. Impelled by the country's rising political mobilization, he convened a Constituent Assembly in 1978. In 1980, rightist candidate Fernando Balaúnde Terry won the presidential elections. Today, the political spectrum is shaped on the right by Acción Popular (AP; Popular Action) and the Partido Popular Cristiano (PPC; Popular Christian Party), in the centre by the APRA, and on the left we find the Izquierda Unida (IU; United Left), a coalition formed by seven political groups that plan a struggle within the legal constitutional framework. On the extreme left are the Túpac Amaru group (which wages an armed struggle, mainly in the cities) and Sendero Luminoso (Shining Path; skilled in highly developed rural guerrilla warfare, especially in the most poverty-stricken areas), whose actions are sometimes branded as terrorist because they often affect a large number of innocent victims.

A considerable source of political conflict lies in the virtual civil war that confronts the armed forces, particularly against the Sendero Luminoso. This group was born at the end of the 1970s in the Andean region. Peasants, pauperized from time immemorial, survive in isolated communities. It is a region separated from the rest of the country in many ways: they speak a different language and have different customs, and justice is practised differently. Based on an "Inca" authoritarianism, Sendero Luminoso dogmatically applies Maoist principles of "protracted people's war," trying to besiege the cities from the countryside. It has achieved considerable success in organizing in rural areas, using the province of Ayacucho as a centre of operations. It considers that Peru is a semi-feudal and semi-colonial nation, that warfare must be brought from the countryside to the cities, and that the country is now in a revolutionary situation. Its military actions began in 1980; these actions have a voluntarist, authoritarian character, and often try to sow terror, responding to a historical background of paternalism and messianism. As a result, the Izquierda Unida has been badly damaged, not having any ground left to develop its organization. Because of the counter-insurgency war being waged by the armed forces, arenas for political action are closed, and politics is partly militarized, though not as much as in Colombia, Guatemala, or El Salvador. In 1984, 13 provinces were declared emergency zones by the government.

Popular support for García had been quite high despite the population's susceptibility to the economic crisis; they question the APRA's ability to respond to popular interests, as opposed to using the people as a means of access to political power. The Aprista programme would be consolidated only if it could give way to a democratic organization of the popular. This would strengthen its support bases, which is essential to face the fragile political balance between Izquierda Unida, APRA, and the political right, which is increasingly radical and strong in its opposition to the regime. All of them are beleaguered by Sendero Luminoso and Túpac Amaru on the one hand, and military forces waging a counter-insurgency war on the other. As in Colombia and Bolivia, narcopolitics also has its place in the conflict's spectrum, owing to the ever-increasing power of the traffickers and the growing profits derived from coca planting, processing, and trading.

Stability and consolidation of the democratic political system depend on what the government does to restore the economy and to benefit the majority of the population, the plural society and the cultural identities of the different groups that make up contemporary Peru. If this is not achieved, it can be expected that the military conflict between guerrilla organizations and the armed forces will intensify, allowing the right to recapture political power.

Uruguay

In Uruguay, democracy became a constituent part of the national identity. The Uruguayan state, which up to the 1960s had the greatest hegemonic structure of all the subcontinent's countries, managed to instil in the citizenry electoral democratic values as a natural form of political participation; rejection of military authoritarianism became a cultural tradition. Yet dictatorship established itself after the 1973 coup upset all national traditional values, in particular the popular ones.

The population's rejection of the regime was expressed in the most diverse ways, even taking advantage of forms imposed by the military government. Thus, the regime was toppled in the 1980 plebiscite that had hoped to legalize dictatorship.

Transition from the military regime to a representative democratic one is a process that began with that plebiscite. It was institutionalized between the November 1984 elections and March 1985, when Julio María Sanguinetti took office as president. It arose out of a pact with the military based on the agreement known as the "Naval Club

Negotiations" of August 1984. Popular mobilization and protest, widespread between 1980 and 1984, was a decisive element in these negotiations, which led to the military's retreat from the government apparatus.

During the transition, the traditional political parties, Colorado (Red) and Nacional (National), which were clearly bourgeois, though with factions opposing the military regime (but not opposing its economic policy), enjoyed a revival. The return to action of political parties was tolerated by the dictatorship and legalized by internal elections in 1982. The Frente Amplio (Broad Front), a centre–left coalition, also had a recovery, as did the Central Sindical Única (Unique Trade Union Confederation), which found semi-legal functioning mechanisms in 1983. The left has gone as far as leading and organizing the rejection of the dictatorship and resistance to its neo-liberal economic policy.

These three political forces have tried to encourage a stable representative democracy, but they differ in the social contents they attribute to it. From the time of the Concertación Nacional Programática (National Programmatic Agreement), from October 1984 to February 1985 on, any agreements signed with a future government plan in mind had to gain the support of all sectors belonging to the working class, the progressive middle strata, and social movements. These groups wanted to modify the anti-popular economic orientation and put an end to the military's conducting of the civilian judicial system.

Differences in this transition broke out as soon as the Colorado government came to power in the person of President Sanguinetti. The government violated the agreements of the Concertación Nacional Programática, keeping the economic orientation unchanged and granting amnesty to military and police human rights violators. Parliamentary opposition was left in the hands of the Frente Amplio and a few leaders of the Partido Nacional.

In the new democratic stage, the greatest resistance to government policies and the greatest conflicts have originated in the corporate sectors – mainly the trade unions. The situation is such that, in the confrontation, the government speaks of a "union dictatorship," which weakens the labour struggle's prestige, in a governmental attempt to draw a parallel between military authoritarianism and the working class as "enemies of democracy."

Despite the levels of conflict, one of the factors that makes the return to democracy in Uruguay sounder is that all the political forces see democratic representative structures as the most suitable for the "national way of being," though they have been, in fact, the historical forms of the bourgeoisie's political legitimization. They also respect them as part of their rights and culture, and as part of the style of their majority struggle.

3. Countries with dictatorial regimes

At the end of the 1980s only two countries had military and dictatorial governmental structures: Chile and Haiti. We have seen how democracy in Latin America exhibits – or conceals – many authoritarian traits; in these two countries, authoritarian forces, having recourse to generalized repression, prevail as the main implements of maintaining social order. These countries differ in their history, and in the ways military and dictatorial power is exercised. They have different levels of economic development, of civil society's organization, and of democracy's presence in their political culture. Haiti is one of the most backward countries in the continent; Chile has an average development rate. The types of conflict are also dissimilar because of the different political development of the social bases and of institutions.

Chile

Chilean political history is outstanding for its extreme clarity. Chilean national state structuring happened earlier and was less chaotic than in neighbouring countries. The party system, as in many European countries, expressed the interests of all the main sectors of society.

Also crystal-clear was the collapse of the bourgeois political hegemony during the alternative popular project that came to power in 1970. The right's reaction was clearly tragic. There has never in Latin America been such a systematic attempt to eliminate any popular or revolutionary elements as there was in Chile after September 1973. Extermination has been the goal; crime is the method. The regime established by Augusto Pinochet's dictatorship de-articulated and eliminated the state's social functions. Failing to achieve hegemony, it resorted to an extreme authoritarianism in order to crush the popular movement and impose the neo-liberal policy recommended by the empire.

Since 1982, the neo-liberal model has been in crisis, and the state has intervened in the economy in order to prevent a greater disaster. Though the state's role grows, the basics of the model are maintained. It is the beginning of a new political stage. "Underground," the parties have begun recovering their role as essential agents of social sectors. There are many nuances: a military–civil ultra-right that has Pinochet as a central point; and a more pragmatic right that intends to save the regime by sacrificing dictatorship – this sector's interests coincide with the recent orientation of American politics towards Chile; at the centre, the leadership of the Partido Demó-crata Cristiano (Christian Democratic Party) is open to the right and closed to the popular; and a left formed by the parties grouped around the Unidad Popular (Popular Unity), which discusses plans and links alliances capable of provoking mass mobilization, such as that of 1986.

Christian Democracy, as the basic axis of the centre, manages somehow to hold on to some predominance in the political scene. It tries to arbitrate, presenting the democracy/dictatorship dichotomy as the main conflict. According to this, the solution would be to restructure formal democracy and respect for individual rights. However, respect for political–popular organizational arenas is left out of their formulations. The centre claims to mediate the Chilean political spectrum, without admitting that the social structure has changed profoundly since the military coup. The new social polarization has generated new forms of resistance and popular struggle. Multiple social movements have been added to traditional corporate political organizations, such movements having in Chile a predominately community expression. These movements do not figure in the negotiating claims of the centrist political forces. For the right, they exist only as an object of repression.

The Chilean left had to face two new problems. The challenge is both to link the different forms of the popular, which – with different levels of consciousness – entails different conflict mechanisms, and thus, consequently, also to seek the unification of all these trends in a political project that makes the popular the foundation of a new type of democracy.

No doubt, the most significant political moment during the highly conflictual dictatorial regime was the referendum of 5 October 1988. Because the anti-dictatorship forces won, the referendum opened the door to democratic recovery. The conflicts resulting from this process will certainly be intense, because the power struggle between the centre, right, and left is greatly reminiscent of the correlation of forces in Chile in the 1960s and during the Popular Unity government led by Salvador Allende. The political interregnum has begun.

When the crisis will occur cannot be precisely known. However, a long period of conflicts can be expected. The extreme right has military support as it gears itself up in an inflexibly anti-popular posture. The people, for their part, are recovering organization and strength, making economic claims, and posing the question of the possibility of a highly concentrated economic model.

What is remarkable is the effort of all forces opposing the regime to become unified, from Christian Democracy to the Communist Party, represented by presidential candidate Patricio Alwin. Their goals converge on democratic recovery, which, though limited, is an important step toward the isolation of the dictatorship and the reinstatement of democracy in the 1990s.

Haiti

Until 1956 Haitian politics was negotiated between the élites. They employed state formalities and military forces (democratic governments frequently interrupted by military coups) established by the United States during its long occupation of the country (1915–1934). This led to a big political crisis. The armed forces solved this by means of rather questionable elections in which François Duvalier was the winner.

Haiti's socio-economic structure exhibits incredible inequality. The dominant sectors are formed by large landed estate-holders in the countryside and big traders in the cities. The dominated live in the misery of semi-feudal servitude or in unemployment. Duvalier built, based on this system, an extensive interwoven structure of violence and control, extending even to Haitian daily life. Armed forces not being enough, his dictatorship was founded also on the Tontons Macoutes, a huge network of paramilitary agents always at the ready for crime and torture.

During the long dictatorial period there several attempts to overthrow the regime, some by bourgeois sectors and others by revolutionary groups. All of them failed, resulting in the strengthening and consolidation of the regime. After Duvalier's death in April 1971, his son Jean Claude inherited power without any major resistance. American support, relative economic prosperity, and the absence of political alternatives created by the dictatorial monopoly of power were found useful by him. In the following years the urban economy was slightly modernized. Using foreign capital, some assembly industries were established, but in the countryside agriculture remained in crisis: land exhaustion, drought, population growth, and land being held by new units of production using modern methods all made for a critical situation. All of this combined in such a way that the old pre-capitalist methods prevailing in the fields did not allow the survival of even the peasantry. Thousands of peasants migrated to the cities and abroad, mainly to the Dominican Republic and the United States (the Boat People). This situation was compounded by the world economic crisis of the 1970s. In Haiti, unemployment reached more than 50 per cent, and the poverty levels of the majority are among the highest in Latin America.

Within this context, a continued and varied popular mobilization developed, partly organized and conducted by members of the Catholic Church at the end of 1985 and the beginning of 1986. Fearing the radicalism of mobilization, Washington cut off support for the dictator. He went into exile in France in February 1986. He was replaced by a National Council of Government (CNG) in which members of the armed forces were predominant, and which enjoyed the full support of the Reagan administration.

The two years of CNG rule (February 1986–February 1988) saw constant conflict between the popular and oligarchic sectors. Each party put forward a plan antagonistic to the other as a solution to the crisis. The popular sector demanded, although in a fragmentary manner, the construction of a democratic regime in which human rights would be respected, fair elections, and the guaranteed right to freedom of organization and freedom of speech. The oligarchic sector, bent on shutting off any possibility of political participation by the majority, sought mechanisms to establish an authoritarian regime, a "democratic" élitist regime. The political conflict picked up momentum, but found itself caught on the immutability of the traditional economic and social structure.

The essential facts of this confrontation are as follows. Duvalier's repressive political organization was dismantled as soon as he left the scene; increasing social mobilization also contributed to this. A very progressive constitution was approved, which secured, among other rights, the autonomy of the body in charge of the electoral process, in order to prevent prominent members of the dictatorship from interfering. The right reacted by reorganizing the alliance between the armed forces and the oligarchy. The first elections, held in November 1987, were nullified by bloodshed. In order to legitimize neo-Duvalierism, the CNG held new elections on 17 January 1988. The democratic opposition did not participate, and Leslie Manigat, a

Christian Democrat and rightist candidate, won in spite of massive abstentions at the polls. Manigat was overthrown by a coup in mid-1988.

Between Duvalier's fall and Manigat's election, five important points can be identified where civil society, mainly the popular sectors, expressed its rejection of the provisional government. The first occurred between February and March of 1986, accompanied by widespread street protests and strikes. The second was in May and June of 1986, when Duvalierists were urged to abandon the government by street demonstrations. The third crucial moment was in October of the same year, when the election for the 41 members of the Constituent Assembly provoked a 95 per cent rate of abstention. The fourth, as proof of popular discontent, occurred in 1987 with a series of national lockouts called by the Democratic Front to protest against the CNG's repressive measures against union organizations and the Independent Electoral Council. The fifth was the rejection of the electoral process by popular majorities, who do not consider elections to be a way of solving popular demands, because, as in the polls, elections take place in the midst of generalized terror. On 29 November 1987, ex-Tontons Macoutes gangs went to the polls and assassinated voters. The elections were cancelled and put off until January 1988.

Since the fall of Duvalier's regime, the popular sector has declared itself with the vehemence of fury restrained for decades. Popular anger exploded in many social mobilizations: peasant struggles for land recovery and against taxes and misery, regional movements against economic and administrative centralism, movements in poor neighbourhoods in Port-au-Prince and other cities demanding services, and numerous demonstrations demanding Duvalierists' punishment. When many conflicts accumulate over the years into a political crisis situation, social mobilizations manifest themselves also in an "accumulated" manner.

In contrast to the social movements' vitality, corporate and police actors were inchoate. The long Duvalier dictatorship had monopolized every level of organization. Not even the oligarchic political organizations showed any consistency. The dominant sectors were gathered around the institutional actors with the highest organizational level: the armed forces. As the Tontons Macoutes were rapidly breaking up, the army was in charge of maintaining social and political order.

The serious conflict of hegemony and political domination in Haiti is internalized in the only institution that has succeeded in maintaining some inner coherence: the armed forces. In 1988 they carried out the coup against Manigat; they established themselves in power and started an internal fight leading to the so-called "sergeant movement." This movement broke with the principal structures inherited from Duvalierism. It is characterized as a military reformist movement, similar to that of El Salvador's "military youth." Thus, existing polarizing and political conflict is transferred from civilian society to the military, making the country's struggle yet more complex. This movement, however, did not achieve its political purpose, and General Prosper Avril took over power.

4. Countries with popular hegemonic power

A variety of aspects distinguish the revolutionary processes of Cuba and Nicaragua; only the essential feature allows us to present them together: popular power as a hegemonic element of state power. In both cases interesting processes have unfolded that tend to stress the majorities' democratic political activity in decision-making mechanisms.

In Cuba and Nicaragua, sharp political conflicts ending in the collapse of military dictatorships – Fulgencio Batista's in 1959, and Anastasio Somoza's in 1979 – have as a common feature a total crisis of the state leading to popular armed revolution. In both cases, government regimes were constructed with a hegemonic popular component. In addition, the economy radically changed orientation, trying to satisfy the needs of the majority of the population. The basic difference between the two countries lies in ideology and the goals pursued by the state. Since 1961, Cuba has defined itself as communist; in Nicaragua, the Sandinista government is plural, and does not contemplate socialism as an economic and socio-political regime, at least not in the short and middle term.

Cuba
The conflicts and struggles in Cuba since the revolution's victory present a totally different picture from the rest of Latin America. These conflicts are located at two levels, the internal and the external, and they are closely linked.

Internally, constructing socialism – which is known as the transition – based on unifying a great number of civil society's demands but mainly those of the working majorities, became the main objective of

309

unions, peasants, students, the military organizations, etc. This process began in April 1961 at the time of the battle in Playa Girón against US-supported invading forces. The battle started as a revolution whose orientation was declared to be socialist. Unification of this set of political forces was consolidated in 1965 with the founding of the Communist Party of Cuba (PCC), which has become the most important political institution in the country.

Externally, the first crucial moments appeared not only in April 1961, with the Bay of Pigs invasion, but also in October 1962 when the majority of the population supported Fidel Castro's government in the famous "missile crisis." The political, commercial, and military isolation of the island put Cuba in a very difficult geopolitical position. Conflict with the United States, defined as a "permanent cold war," determines and explains an important part of the Cuban attitude towards the outside world. This conflict has obviously had strong repercussions internally. It has, sometimes, produced inner conflicts of great magnitude. One of them was the counter-revolutionary war waged in the Sierra del Escambray at the beginning of the 1970s. After 1966, the counter-revolutionaries had been totally defeated. Another conflict resulted from Cuban migration to the United States, which produced divisions within thousands of families. Between 1959 and 1962, 200,000 Cubans migrated; 1962–1965, 300,000; 1965–1973, 240,000; 1973–1977, 20,000; and 1977–1980, 140,000. Between April and September of 1980, the Mariel became an open harbour for voluntary migration. This eased the conflict.

Cuba's isolation from many countries has been expressed in the total absence of any form of relations. During the 1960s Cuba supported many revolutionary groups in Latin America. During the 1970s and 1980s Cuba normalized diplomatic and trade relations with many countries, and strengthened those it already had with the socialist bloc. From 1973 to 1974, Cuba was linked to Angola's government, and from 1975 it contributed considerably in defending Angola from South African aggression while the United States gave support to the counter-revolutionaries. At the end of 1987 and the beginning of 1988, military engagements increased, and the military situation became more clearly defined. It is estimated that there were up to 50,000 Cuban troops in Angola. The agreement for their evacuation was signed in December 1988. These facts identify Cuba as an important protagonist in the international system. Between 1977 and 1980 the first steps were taken to normalize relations with the United States. On 1 September 1977, an office was set up for American interests in Havana; similarly, an office opened in Washington to deal with Cuban interests there. Ronald Reagan's taking office as president in January 1981 paralysed the nascent process.

At the political level, there is a conflict in Cuba between bureaucratic, technocratic, and authority-centralizing trends and revolutionary postulates about consolidating popular participative democracy.

Institutionalizing revolution, as in many countries, dates from the beginning of the revolution and enormous economic isolation. In the 1960s the first "rectification" process, known as the "struggle against voluntarism," began. Later, another "rectification" was the "struggle against idealism," which tried "to correct deficiencies in economic planning mechanisms." The *economic calculation* model was imposed, applying it to the whole group of socialist countries. In 1972, Cuba entered Comecon, which strengthened mercantile relations and centralism. By the 1980s, there was an attempt to reverse the consequences of having applied profit as a motor for the economy, and a struggle to "rectify mistakes and negative tendencies" that had arisen after 1984. From 1986 on, this line became a determinant of political practice and economy. Amid all these rectifications, the Cuban economy has the fastest growth rate in Latin America, and it has achieved more than any other country in lessening social inequalities. This is one of the reasons for the low level of political conflict.

In the socio-political field, conflicts and struggles in Cuba are regulated by institutions created in the 1960s and 1970s. State–society relations are mainly conducted through consensus and negotiation. From the 1970s an alternative political structure began to develop. This structure is unique to countries where the transition to socialism is happening, where the popular acquires an exceptional dimension. This structure is known as *poder popular* (Popular Power). It is constituted by the Asamblea Nacional del Poder Popular (National Assembly of Popular Power), which is constitutionally considered to be the seat of supreme power, for it fulfils legislative functions and has the authority to appoint the Council of State and the Council of Ministers. In addition, there are provincial and municipal assemblies of Popular Power.

Popular Power attempts to counteract the bureaucratic tendencies of the political and economic system, and in this the people are responsible for participating in their democracy. The Cuban political regime's structures are based on the Communist Party, the Council of Ministers, the Council of State, Popular Power, and the armed

311

forces. Counterbalancing mechanisms appear between those structures where political balance prevails, producing a high degree of consensus and hegemony within civil society. This is evident, because conflicts are not against the state and the system; they happen within it, and they help to define its orientation. The degree of consensus was confirmed in 1980 by a referendum: more than 90 per cent of the population approved of the socialist regime. We could single out other such examples.

In the future, it can be expected that Cuban political conflicts will continue to express themselves in this opposition between "rectifiers" and "bureaucrats," and will be mainly expressed inside the system. Another element that may possibly be conflictual in the near future is power rotation, as the time to replace Fidel Castro's leadership draws nearer.

In international affairs, Cuba's diplomatic relations with other countries will continue to normalize. Relations with the United States being tense, there have been only partial successes in the effort to normalize the conflict resulting from Cuban migration. In the Central American conflict, Cuba has supported most of the peace proposals, basically supporting the Nicaraguan government.

A new factor that will influence the course of Cuban politics is the redefinition of the Comecon as a result of the rapid changes of government (in some European countries, even the socio-economic system is questioned) in the socialist bloc countries. As cooperation agreements between the Soviet Union and Cuba had not been modified since *perestroika* in 1985, a remarkable change in Cuban relations with those countries was apparent. Cubans say Soviet-style reforms are not necessary because there was never Stalinism on the island, and revolution was the result of a great mobilization of most social sectors, unlike the countries where socialism was imposed through reform at the end of World War II as the forces of the Soviet Union passed through those territories on the way to defeat Germany. This difference gives Cuban socialism a legitimacy that socialist European governments never had. One of the most important moments for Cuba will be the defining of the country's course of action (and of the current socio-economic and political system) at the Fourth Communist Party Conference at the end of 1991. Among other things, even theoretical problems on the transition to socialism in the third world will be discussed because of the challenges faced by changing Western European countries and the Soviet Union.

Nicaragua

Since the victory of the Sandinista revolution in July 1979, Nicaragua has begun the construction of a new society. This process is happening in the midst of many conflicts, the military aggression and economic siege promoted by the United States being central among them.

The war of aggression, which for Nicaragua is a war of sovereignty and defence of independence, forced an alteration in the primitive economic strategy of the Sandinista regime, which originally favoured large public investment projects in order to encourage, in particular, all agro-export sectors and to lay down a solid economic infrastructure.

Warfare, the negative evolution of the international market, and internal needs compelled Nicaraguans to adopt an even more conjunctural strategy, giving priority to defence, internal market supply, and traditional types of production, especially in the agrarian sector. The need to promote agricultural production for exports as a source of currency remains an important challenge.

The war that raged between 1980 and 1988 meant great human and economic losses for Nicaragua. The economic damage is estimated at more than US$1 billion (equivalent to three years of exports), and there are estimated to have been more than 30,000 victims. Between 1985 and 1987, more than half of the government's budget went on defence. Counter-revolutionary groups operated basically from Honduran and Costa Rican territory. Aggression has passed through three stages. The first one, between 1980 and 1982, was characterized by the transition from dispersed and disorganized gangs formed by ex-members of the National Guard into a real army. The second stage, from 1983 to 1987, saw the ever-increasing "covert" and open participation of the United States; counter-revolutionaries created several battle-fronts in Nicaragua's interior. The third stage coincided with a slow-down in the tempo of aggression, a split in the counter-revolutionary forces, their strategic defeat, and the processes of peace and amnesty, encouraged in Nicaragua in 1987 and 1988, when the Esquipulas II Agreement was signed, its greatest achievement being the Treaty of Sapoá, signed in March 1988.

From the beginning of the revolution, agrarian problems have been the main focus of programmes for change. Cooperative and state enterprise formation was greatly encouraged; large and medium-sized landowners were also given support and integrated into government production plans, while land distribution to the poor peasantry went on at a slower pace. This generated much conflict and tension in the countryside. Production cooperatives then became a pivotal point of Sandinista organization and expansion; they also became a target for counter-revolutionary groups. After 1984, agrarian politics changed. Land distribution was speeded up and even adjusted when necessary to peasant needs and aspirations. Prices, services, and salaries also changed, which in turn accelerated the disintegration of the counter-revolution.

Another important political conflict has been the ethnic regional problem, particularly on the Atlantic Coast which is peopled by an ethnic minority known as the *"miskitos."* During the revolution's early years, the Sandinista government tried to introduce in this area the same social and economic development programmes designed for the rest of the country. The government encountered resistance from the *miskitos*. The United States sought to take advantage of the general discontent to establish a base for a military attack against the regime. The Sandinista government understood the specific problematic of social organization, as well as the socio-cultural dimension of the Indian population; it promoted political amnesty for Indian rebels. At the same time, it pushed for an Atlantic Coast autonomous regime at the constitutional level. Recognizing the polyethnic character of the Nicaraguan people, its legislation on Indian matters has been the most progressive in Latin America.

The solutions found by the revolutionary leaders, and the popular base for all the problems and conflicts arising in everyday Nicaraguan life, consolidated the revolutionary process and stressed its democratic and popular orientation.

Sandinista candidate Daniel Ortega won the presidential elections of November 1984. Legalized at the polls, the revolution's legitimacy, first won by the Sandinistas in the battles of 1978 and 1979, was consolidated. Constituent Assembly representatives were also elected at that time, and in 1986 this body approved the new constitution, and accordingly became the Legislative Assembly.

Since the victory of the 1979 revolution, internal political and social conflicts have been principally solved by consensus and political negotiation. The negotiating spirit was transferred to the military and international conflict from the time of the signing of the Esquipulas II Agreement in August 1987, when Nicaragua agreed to direct dialogue with the counter-revolution. This effort produced the signing of the Sapoá treaties on 23 March 1988: a 60-day total ceasefire was agreed upon.

There is no doubt that the future of Nicaraguan political conflicts will depend on compliance with peace agreements; this will allow for what is now a military conflict to become a political one. Similarly, the serious situation of the country's economy is another potential source of political conflict. The Sandinista government faces the urgent need to improve the population's standard of living. Unfortunately, the infrastructure in Nicaragua was partially destroyed by civil war (particularly in 1978 and 1979) and defensive war (between 1982 and 1988), plus the additional destruction caused by hurricane Joan (end of 1988), which caused damage estimated at US$800 million.

The "low-intensity wars" in the Nicaragua–United States conflict may be considered as an attempt to strengthen rightist political opposition in order to create a situation similar to that found in Panama. At the same time, the United States will undoubtedly try to continue the trade and financial siege so as to make Nicaragua one of the Sandinista National Liberation Front's weak spots; the right will certainly take advantage of this situation at the elections, possibly those of 25 February 1990.

5. Countries undergoing revolutionary crises

During the last few decades, some Latin American countries have been through a revolutionary crisis. At the end of the 1950s it was Cuba, at the end of the 1970s it was Nicaragua, and in the 1980s it was El Salvador. Other nations experienced a boom in popular organization, but did not reach the stage of a revolutionary crisis. Such is the case of the Dominican Republic in 1965, of Chile between 1970 and 1973, and of Guatemala between 1980 and 1983. In those countries, the United States' intervention, along with military initiatives to halt popular organization – even using terror and genocide – held back or aborted any tendencies toward a revolutionary situation.

In El Salvador, most observers have defined the situation as revolutionary. There is a dispute over economic, political, military, and territorial power between the popular and oligarchic poles. Other authors have called this situation an "organic crisis," because of the degree of decay in the dominant bloc in the organization and mobilization of the subaltern sectors.

As a consequence of a development process characterized by high income concentration (the oligarchy was formed by 14 families at the

315

beginning of this century), due to the predominance of foreign capital, and by a political regime devoid of democratic mechanisms (the landholding, coffee-growing oligarchy and the military top brass share power), El Salvador has arrived at a serious political crisis that was widespread during the 1970s. Between 1970 and 1979, popular organizations appeared at every level – union, peasant, student, teacher, as well as progressive clerical organizations. There was a time when even in the army a progressive–nationalist trend could be detected, a segment aware of the urgent need for socio-economic and political change. The main catalyst that made the political crisis into a revolutionary crisis was the rise of mass movements and the revival of political struggle during the second half of the 1970s, as well as the spread of guerrilla warfare by leftist organizations against the regime.

The precursor of the revolutionary crisis can be located in 1979. On 15 October, young army officials staged a coup d'état, initiating a period of reform in an attempt to weaken the struggle of the democratic and revolutionary organizations. At the beginning of 1980 a pact was signed between right-wing elements of the armed forces and the Christian Democratic Party. In 1980, the United States began its open participation in the conflict, in support of a military, non-negotiated, and conservative solution to the crisis. That year Salvadorean society became polarized. The Frente Democrático Revolucionario (FDR; Revolutionary Democratic Front) was founded in April; the Frente Farabundo Martí para la Liberación Nacional (FMLN; Farabundo Martí National Liberation Front) was formed in October. Between them they led the political and military opposition to the government. In January 1981, civil war broke out.

Between 1981 and 1988 the war manifested itself in various ways. More than 70,000 deaths were reported as a result of political violence. More than 500,000 people were forced to leave the country because of the violence and the economic crisis. Another 500,000 are considered internal refugees: peasants displaced from military conflict areas in the north, east, and western–central areas. The economy collapsed, seriously affecting the popular sectors. El Salvador reached the highest rate of unemployment and underemployment of any economically active population in Latin America: 60 per cent. These are alarming figures if we consider the country's size: 5 million people and 21,000 square km. The United States almost totally supports the government and the armed forces. The US assistance, and its military and economic donations, are now larger than the country's gross domestic product. The aim was to prevent the victory of the democratic–revolutionary option.

316

In the course of the civil war, from 1981 on a new set of political forces appeared. The Christian Democratic Party made great efforts to generate a centrist political force to democratize the system and become an alternative political option. Christian Democracy was institutionalized in power in the 1984 and 1985 elections. Its fall from its position as the main political force began with the parliamentary elections in March 1988. The Partido Alianza Republicana Nacionalista (Arena; Nationalist Republican Alliance) won the elections. This ultra-right coalition, founded in 1981, succeeded in replacing the worn-out Partido de Conciliación Nacional (Party of National Conciliation). Arena represents the oligarchy's historical interest. In the corporate field, peasant and union organizations became the main victims of repression and terror. El Salvador was militarily divided between the FMLN, which controlled approximately one-third of the northern and eastern regions, and the government, which dominated the political situation. Popular democracy became a way of life for people living in areas controlled by the guerrilla army. Also in cities, mainly in corporate organizations, the democratic–popular option was the expression of many sectors' desires for peace.

In August 1987, when the Esquipulas II agreements were signed, real opportunities to put an end to the civil war and to initiate political negotiation were, for the first time, seen as possible. The process of dialogue between the government and the FDR–FMLN led to three meetings: in October and November 1984, and in October 1987. The government and the armed forces displayed a total lack of desire to work towards a real process of peace negotiation.

In El Salvador, the popular–democratic is expressed in the struggle of the political, of unions, peasants, religious groups, students, mothers of missing people, etc., pressing for a peace agreement. At the end of 1987 a new political alliance, the "Democratic Convergence," formed by two FDR political parties – the Revolutionary National Movement and the Social Christian Popular Movement – and the Social Democrat Party tried to channel democratic–popular discontent into the limited arenas of formal democracy. The goal was to merge the revolutionary democratic, the popular democratic, and the formal democratic. The main formulation of the "Democratic Convergence" was to push for peace, for the rescue of national sovereignty, for a democratization process, and for an economy for the people.

Arena won in the May 1989 presidential elections. Thus, the military polarization already in existence was transferred to politics. One factor that might explain the ultra-right electoral victory is fatigue generated by war and the desire of the neediest sectors for immediate solutions to their very pressing problems. At the same time, a dispute arose between the two poles of the political spectrum: Arena and the FMLN.

The civil war's future and the possibility of achieving peace depend on many things. Important are the policies of the United States, which are the main support for the economy and the regime. Another factor is a negotiated solution and respect for people's democratic expression in future electoral processes. A third consideration is that the conservative and counter-revolutionary pole, headed by Arena, may not want to defeat the popular–democratic pole through total war – which could mean massive genocide. A fourth is the possibility of the FMLN's military victory over the armed forces; this is not very likely in the short term, however. Of all these options, undoubtedly the most humane, the one that would faithfully express the wishes of the majority, would be the ending of civil war through the recognition of all political and social forces in the country, through a negotiated political solution to the conflict. Otherwise, civil war may become more widespread and prolonged.

V. Regional struggles and negotiations

1. The main inter-state conflicts

Inter-state conflicts in Latin America originated during the national independence processes at the beginning of the nineteenth century. The main causes were border demarcation between the nascent countries and struggles for natural resources in border areas. From the end of the nineteenth century, territorial ambitions began to grow; in the twentieth century, expansionism acquired a geopolitical dimension.

Among the many wars waged in Latin America, three are noteworthy: the Triple Alliance War (1865–1870), in which the Alliance, composed of Argentina, Brazil, and Uruguay, fought Paraguay; the Pacific War (1879–1883), in which Chile fought Peru and Bolivia, and in which the latter two lost a considerable part of their territory, particularly Bolivia, which lost its maritime territory; and the Chaco War (1932–1935) between Bolivia and Paraguay.

Historically, important anti-colonialist and anti-imperialist wars are at the root of current conflicts. There have been Latin American confrontations with European powers, mainly the United Kingdom and France, and with the United States. This sort of conflict constitutes a struggle for national and territorial sovereignty on the part of the affected countries against the hegemonic ambitions of the imperial powers trying to extend their territory and spread their influence. The fight between Argentina and the United Kingdom over the Falkland Islands is outstanding. The struggles between Guyana and Venezuela for the Esequeibo territory and between Guatemala and the United Kingdom for Belize are now being resolved as Guyana and Belize gain independence from the United Kingdom. Tension with the United States dates from the end of the last century and the beginning of this one, when the United States often resorted to a general interventionist policy. Conflicts in the Caribbean Basin are also important; this area is considered by the United States to be within its zone of influence and a priority for "national security." Direct military interventions in Nicaragua, Panama, Puerto Rico, Haiti, the Dominican Republic, and Grenada were some of the most aggressive since the end of the nineteenth century.

Since 1960, the most important conflicts in Latin America have been the following:

(1) The July 1969 war between El Salvador and Honduras, when El Salvador invaded Honduras and took possession of disputed border territory. This conflict is being disputed in the International Court of Justice in the Hague.

(2) The dispute between Chile and Argentina, which escalated in 1977 to the point of pre-war tension over possession of the Beagle canal. A clash was averted through the direct mediation of the Vatican.

(3) The fight between Guatemala and the United Kingdom for Belize, which in the 1970s escalated into the threat of direct invasion by Guatemala of Belize. This event put off Belize's independence until 1981, and, moreover, a British military contingent remained in Belize to prevent the possibility of a Guatemalan invasion.

(4) A very important territorial dispute between Colombia and Venezuela over sovereignty and possession of part of the Gulf of Venezuela.

(5) A dispute between the Guyana Cooperative Republic and Venezuela, which is claiming possession of the Esequeibo. There have even been threats of a military confrontation. One of the problems complicating this territorial conflict is that the Esequeibo makes up two-thirds of Guyana's whole territory.

319

(6) A military clash between Peru and Ecuador in 1981 over possession of the Cóndor range of mountains.

(7) Dating back to the time of the Pacific War, a claim by Bolivia, involving Chile, to an exit to the sea.

(8) A dispute between Nicaragua and Colombia over possession of the San Andrés and Providence islands and the Roncador bank. The negotiated solution to this conflict turned out favourably for Colombia.

(9) Sharp border conflicts between Mexico and Guatemala. Between 1980 and 1983, Guatemala staged more than 60 border attacks violating Mexico's territory.

(10) Border conflicts arising from aggression against Nicaragua. The confrontation with the United States was settled by the International Court of Justice in the Hague in favour of Nicaragua, but high tensions with Honduras and Costa Rica remain unresolved.

(11) Finally, the conflict between Argentina and the United Kingdom for possession of the Falkland Islands. Between April and June 1982, the Falklands War was fought; this was the most important confrontation in Latin America for many years. Argentina tried to recapture the islands by military force, but failed. The levels of international tension that this conflict gave rise to turned out to be a very important test for the inter-American system, whose pillars are the Inter-American Treaty of Mutual Assistance (ITMA, drawn up in 1947) and the Organization of American States (OAS, set up in 1948).

Inter-state conflicts in Latin America acquire another dimension when we consider economic and demographic phenomena, which are outside the sphere of government attitudes and capabilities. At this level, conflicts that result from migration are very important. The main migratory flows, and the tensions deriving from them, are basically resolved and settled through bilateral and multilateral agreements. Migration from Cuba, Mexico, and the Caribbean islands to the United States is potentially highly conflictual and a significant component in the politics between those countries. In the 1980s, Central American migration to the United States – particularly from El Salvador – increased markedly as a result of the regional crisis. There is also migration from Latin American countries in which the level of conflict is high, such as the migration of Guatemalan and Salvadorean refugees to Mexico in search of new economic opportunities, or that of Salvadoreans to Honduras (which is what caused the 1969 war between the two countries). Other examples are Haitian migration to the Dominican Republic, Colombian to Venezuela, and Chilean to Argentina. Brazil is on the receiving end of immigrants coming from neighbouring countries in search of a more promising economic future.

Confrontations resulting from foreign interventions are also notable at the inter-state level. Interventions occurred in the Dominican Republic in 1965, and in Grenada in 1983. Other highly conflictual situations that could often have led to open military conflict were the recurrent tensions between Cuba and the United States, particularly after the Bay of Pigs (Giron Beach) in 1961, and between Nicaragua and the United States. At a less conflictual level, we might look at the historical conflict between Mexico and the United States arising from the very strained border relations since the 1846 war (when Mexico lost more than 50 per cent of its territory). Over the last 20 years this problem has manifested itself at different levels and pitches. From trade disputes, resulting from illegal Mexican migration, to open meddling in Mexican politics and the antagonistic American foreign policy in relation to the Central American crisis, there are sources of tension that deserve attention, as well as those arising from disputes over energy resources – oil and gas – and, more recently, from drug trafficking. In Mexican–American relations, these conflicts have typically been settled through negotiations between the two governments.

A different sort of conflict that is increasingly prominent in Latin America has to do with the definition of geographical areas of influence. These conflicts basically occur between the area's larger countries, or between them and the powers that have traditionally had influence in the continent. Geopolitical rivalry occurs at the level of economic, political, and military spheres of influence. It is sometimes very difficult to assess the real objective of a dispute, owing to pressure or influence from big Latin American countries. In South America there has been constant competition between Brazil and Argentina over control of the South Atlantic. Even the development of naval military forces in both countries is oriented towards controlling that area of the sea. The United Kingdom and South Africa are also involved in that conflict, as are to a lesser extent the United States and the Soviet Union. The principal cause of the conflict is the control and possession of the enormous ocean resources such as foodstuffs and minerals. In the short term, Antarctica will no doubt become an important conflict zone (because of the definition of the countries that will settle down there). In 1989 the Antarctica Treaty expires, and struggle for geographical control may break out. Argentina and Chile claim territories, as do the other treaty signatories: the United Kingdom, France, Australia, New Zealand, and Norway.

In the geopolitical sphere, Brazil has unquestionably the strongest presence. It has influence over countries it shares borders with, economically as well as politically and militarily. This influence is particularly notable in the cases of Bolivia and Paraguay, and to a lesser extent in Uruguay and Guyana. There is a latent conflict between Colombia and Brazil over the "Amazonian Trapezeum," which is at present a part of Colombia. Brazil attaches great geopolitical and economic importance to this conflict, and accordingly has adopted a helpful attitude towards the Colombian people.

In the Caribbean Basin, there is a dispute that has lurched on from independence times in most of the islands, mainly involving the United States, the United Kingdom, Mexico, Venezuela, and Cuba. In some instances, geopolitical matters are crucial, for instance, control of the so-called Líneas Maritimas de Comunicacion (Maritime Lines of Communication), in which Panama and the Canal are the centre of attention. The struggle over political stages of influence has also been striking, especially on the part of Cuba, Venezuela, and Mexico. The military balance in the Basin is another factor to be considered. The United States, which has the strongest military presence (with facilities in Panama, Puerto Rico, and Honduras), intends that the political crisis experienced now by other countries in the area should not affect its hegemony, and perceives Cuba's great defensive capacity as a threat. However, many countries are involved in preventing an escalationist outcome, and have made efforts toward the signing of demilitarization agreements. The struggle against an arms build-up and for peace has mostly developed in Mexico, Panama, Colombia, and Venezuela; it was this movement that gave rise to the formation of the Contadora Group (see below).

Lastly, it is essential to bear in mind that, in solving these interstate conflicts, bilateral and multilateral negotiation must prevail if a solution is to be found, and that only in a very few cases have military clashes been let loose.

2. Non-intervention and peace in Central America

The acute socio-political and military crisis in Central America has led to a series of actions by different countries and political forces, all with the intention of preventing external intervention in the conflict and generalized war.

The causes of the Central American crisis are of a structural nature. A dependent capitalist development and the exclusion of popular sectors from the benefits of development are at the centre of the conflict. In addition, there has been a chronic absence of democratic mechanisms in the political systems, with the sole exception of Costa Rica. Popular protest regularly emerges. During the 1970s a revolutionary alternative arose, taking power in Nicaragua, while at the same time in El Salvador and Guatemala a revolutionary popular movement developed.

Though the causes of the crisis are internal, the US intervention has contributed to intensifying and prolonging the conflict. The United States has integrated Central America into its geopolitical orbit, trying to make it part of the so-called "East–West conflagration." Many actors – for various reasons, similar or different, either openly expressed or dissimulated – want to see the end of the Central American crisis. To achieve this, they have built up autonomy in decision-making in order to neutralize the threat of external intervention.

It could be said that there is a confrontation between two blocs. The US government and its allies would like to see, whatever the cost, a military defeat of the insurgencies in El Salvador and Guatemala and the overthrow of the Sandinista government in Nicaragua. Another bloc – made up of some European and Latin American governments – would like to see dialogue and negotiation as the principal mechanism to solve the problem. The persistence of Latin American countries' encouragement of negotiation in Central America is a microcosmic expression of the struggle of all third world countries to find more favourable frameworks for negotiation in the new global context.

The essential efforts at pacification and negotiation are based on the Contadora Group's work and on compliance with the numerous elements of the agreement signed by the Central American presidents on 7 August 1978, known as Esquipulas II.

The Contadora Group's work

Accepting an invitation from Panama's chancellor, the foreign relations' ministers of Panama, Colombia, Mexico, and Venezuela met on Contadora Island on 8 and 9 January 1983. The purpose of the meeting was to analyse the complex political position in Central America. From that time, the Contadora Group became solidified as those four countries. Its goal was to facilitate the peace process in the area in view of the remarkably increased tensions and the accelerated process of militarization in the region.

On 17 July 1983, the presidents met in Cancún, Mexico, as a result of intensifying conflict in Central America. That meeting was one of the most important in the group's history. Concern was expressed over the rapid deterioration in the Central American situation, the progressive rise in tension, particularly in Nicaragua's relations with the United States, Honduras, and Costa Rica, the increasing number of border incidents, and the threat of a war that could generalize itself and spread beyond the isthmus borders.

The years 1983, 1984, and 1985 were active ones for the Contadora Group. They energetically sought to work out a text for a Peace Act that would satisfy the demands and needs of the five Central American countries. To that effect, a Statement of Purpose (Documento de Objetivos) was drawn up in September 1983; it contained 21 points and principles regarding the achievement of peace. A year later, on 7 September 1984, the first version of the text was published, and on 7 June 1986 the final version of the Contadora Act for Cooperation and Peace in Central America was ready. These proposals did not succeed for several reasons, the main one being the reservations of Costa Rica, El Salvador, and Honduras over what they considered to be unsatisfactory security aspects. These countries accused Nicaragua of being responsible for the arms race in the area, a point of view that coincided with the American outlook on this problem.

Esquipulas II Agreement
During the second half of 1986, the winds of war seemed to prevail over the winds of peace. Surprisingly, from the moment President Oscar Arias of Costa Rica made his peace plan public, on 15 February 1987, a speedy reconciliation, dialogue, and negotiating process began, leading, on 7 August of the same year, to the signing of a document called "Proceedings to establish a firm and lasting peace in Central America," better known as "Esquipulas II." The peace negotiating process between the Central American governments initiated as a result of the Arias Plan's presentation did not hinder the work of the Contadora Group. They formed two parallel, complementary lines of action that would eventually lead to the signing of the Esquipulas II agreement.

President Arias's proposal won him the 1987 Nobel Peace Prize. Concerning the merits of his proposal, it is interesting to note that his starting point was a dead end in the Contadora's negotiating process: security. Arias's formulation is less ambitious and more pragmatic: he assembled the area's presidents and chose a negotiating strategy that departed from the idea that regional governments should initiate dialogue with opposition forces, positing instead national reconciliation as the central axis.

Other points considered were: to cut off aid to irregular forces (counter-revolutionary) or insurrection movements (FMLN in El Salvador and URNG in Guatemala), and not to allow national territory to be used as a base for aggression against other states. These measures would have to have been complied with within 90 days; 120 days later the International Committee for Verification and Follow-up (Comisión Internacional de Verificación y Seguimiento, CIVS), made up of representatives of the five Central American countries, the Contadora Group, the Apoyo Group, the UN, and the OAS, would assess the progress of compliance with agreements stipulated in the document. This point was reached by mid-January 1988, at a meeting of the five Central American presidents.

On 10 January 1988, the tour of inspection by the CIVS came to an end. The CIVS chancellors met in Panama on 12–13 January. The purpose of this meeting was to write up the report to be submitted to the Central American presidents on 15 January in San José, Costa Rica, an evaluation of the situation five months after the signing of Esquipulas II. The CIVS report tended to commend Nicaragua's compliance with the agreements and was critical of the measures adopted by El Salvador. In this report, the central problem of verifying the security aspects of the peace plan was dealt with: on-the-spot inspection. Point 30 of the report specifies: "The need to investigate *in situ* is a requisite *sine qua non* of verification if it is going to be objective, independent, and efficient."

The most important aspect of the presidential summit in January 1988 was that it happened, despite the strong diplomatic opposition of the American government to the Esquipulas agreements. On that date, only the CIVS report was received and it was invalidated because Costa Rica, Honduras, El Salvador, and Guatemala, urged on by the United States, claimed that the report was biased towards Nicaragua. This represented a significant step back. From then on, verification and follow-up would depend on the Central American chancellors, which meant the disappearance from the scene of the

Contadora Group, the Apoyo Group, the UN, and the OAS. These organizations ceased to play any role of great significance.

As we review the presidents' meeting, it is necessary to emphasize that compliance with the Esquipulas II commitments has not been satisfactory. It is undeniable that Nicaragua was the country that most thoroughly complied with the agreements. Later on, the five presidents committed themselves to expedite the agreement, but, contenting themselves with formal compliance, Esquipulas II remained frozen, delaying the peace process.

To counterbalance the propaganda that tends to isolate Nicaragua, and to demonstrate his will for peace, Daniel Ortega made a presidential declaration at the end of the presidents' summit in which he promised to continue with the peace process. The political will for negotiation led to a meeting, at the highest level, between the Sandinista government and the counter-revolutionaries on Nicaraguan territory, in Sapoá, between 21 and 23 March 1988. In spite of many obstacles, an agreement was arrived at that consisted, primarily, in the cessation of offensive military operations throughout the national territory so as to begin a process of integrated negotiating, having as a goal a total cease-fire. Its actual implementation was intended to occur together with the rest of the commitments established in Esquipulas II designed to put an end to war. It is informative here to single out what is said in the CIVS report about Nicaragua: "it is evident that, despite the seriousness of the military harassment common in this country, concrete steps have been taken to begin a democratic process."

In El Salvador, despite the fact that the government encouraged a meeting with the FDR–FMLN in San Salvador on 4 and 5 October 1987, and that it supported an amnesty law and decreed a unilateral cease-fire for 15 days, these measures have not had the pacifying effect envisioned in Esquipulas II, nor have they led to an agreement with the opposition. In general, it can be said that the government only formally and superficially complied with the spirit of these measures. More importantly still, it did not succeed in making them effective. A very important moment for the peace process in Central America was during January and February of 1989 in El Salvador, when, as a result of the peace proposal issued by the FMLN on 23 January, for the first time in 10 years of conflict the FMLN committed itself to stop the armed struggle and try to integrate itself into the democratic–electoral process. Though this proposal was not accepted in the end and the electoral process followed its own agenda (with the elections of 19 March 1989, in which ultra-right-wing candidate Alfredo Cristiani was victorious), it was, at least, widely discussed at every level – by political parties, the National Assembly, unions, peasants, students, entrepreneurial groups – and it opened the possibility of a future political negotiation between the government and the FMLN.

Guatemala was the country where the Esquipulas II commitments were least respected. The reason for this lies in the refusal of the high command forces to make any effort at dialogue or negotiation with the insurgents, and the pressure placed on President Cerezo to do the same. The Guatemalan army puts its trust in the counter-insurgency measures used against the URNG – often genocide in Indian villages. Opposition and government had only one round of dialogue, in Madrid in October 1987, out of which came little reconciliation and no positive results.

Lastly, it is necessary to mention that a peaceful future or the continuation and intensification of the war depend on: (1) the will to overcome the conflict's structural causes; (2) the introduction of conciliation measures in Nicaragua, Guatemala, and El Salvador; (3) the participation of foreign powers in the conflict, mainly the United States' willingness not to intervene, and Europe's willingness to reinforce the non-intervention principle with economic and technical aid to Nicaragua, for this country still suffers from intervention in he form of destabilization and "low-intensity warfare."

3. The battle against drug trafficking

Historically, consumption of plants having psychotropic effects is an old tradition for large sections of the Latin American population. It is interesting to note the daily consumption of coca leaves among the Andean Indians, who descend from the now-extinct Incas and other cultures, and who live in rural areas in Bolivia, Peru, and Ecuador. The custom of consuming coca leaves unintentionally helps them to tolerate exploitation. In recent times, cultivation of other plants such as marijuana and poppy has also developed. Large sectors of the peasantry find the huge profits generated by this trade a strong incentive. Misery dating from time immemorial is the main reason for the preference for these crops.

During the 1980s, drug trafficking in Latin America saw an unprecedented rise. The expansion of rural areas set aside for the cultivation of narcotic plants, the substantial resources involved in their production and trade, and the political power generated through drug trafficking were the main spurs that can be identified. To the last of these we must add the international dimension that the struggle for and against its production and trade has taken on, and the way this phenomenon has become a priority in inter-American relations.

Political conflict caused by drugs is increasing. Some countries' relations with the United States are dominated by the pressure and negotiating agenda concerning drug trafficking, and efforts for its deterrence and control. Drug trafficking has become part of the United States' "restraint" strategy. The government includes it in its new doctrine of conflict response in the third world: "low-intensity war." It is perceived as a threat because of its repercussions on American society; it generates an underground, clandestine power, opposed to government control, which tends to consolidate a set of power relations similar or superior to those of the Mafia when it smuggled alcohol in the 1920s. Seen in this light, it is easier to understand the efforts at dismembering the network formed around the famous Medellín cartel in Colombia (which has a yearly income of $1 billion). Another reason governments fight drug trafficking is the potential danger of broad sectors of society becoming deprived of any motivation and alienated by the consumption of narcotics. This danger looks more real if we consider that drug consumption has become a part of the "American way of life"; furthermore, there are even new cultural and artistic forms developing around it.

However, a significant degree of ambiguity is evident in the United States' efforts to deter drug trafficking, and this can be seen in the military resources supposedly used only for that end. American "anti-narcotics" aid is taken advantage of and used for counter-insurgency campaigns in Colombia and Peru. In addition, resources apparently intended for this end have been more obviously present and influential in the Bolivian, Ecuadorian, Mexican, Jamaican, Venezuelan, and Columbian armies.

In terms of economics, it is important to note that there has been a very significant qualitative change since the end of the 1970s, owing largely to the expansion of cocaine consumption. Formerly, the principal narcotics consumed in the United States were opium, heroin, and marijuana, which came mostly from Asia. With the Chinese revolution and revolutionary conflicts in South-East Asia in the 1960s and 1970s, exports of these products to the United States were impaired because they had mainly been channelled through the Golden Triangle of Burma, Laos, and Thailand. Latin America had mostly exported marijuana, especially Mexico, Colombia, and some Caribbean islands such as Jamaica. Only later, in the 1970s, did large-scale cocaine production begin in Andean countries by processing coca leaves for export.

Most of the estimates of the financial dimension of narcotic imports to the United States agree that the business raises $80–$120 billion a year (equal to Mexico's or Brazil's external debt), which is one-third of the total world trade (calculated at $300–$400 billion). Some alarming data are available on how drug trafficking has modified the economies of Latin American producer countries. The cocaine trade in Colombia puts $6–$9 billion into circulation annually. It has been estimated that approximately 300,000 Bolivians and 1,100,000 Peruvians are involved in cocaine production and distribution. Similarly, land given over to cocaine production is estimated at 25,000 hectares in Colombia, 50,000 hectares in Bolivia, and 75,000 hectares in Peru.

The profits from drug trafficking are deposited in the international finance system, mainly controlled by American, Swiss, and Japanese banks. During the 1970s, bank branches were opened on Caribbean islands, and some countries became true "financial paradises," where profits from cocaine sales could be deposited. These banking havens are located in Panama, the Bahamas, Grand Cayman, the Turks and Caicos islands, Trinidad and Tobago, Bermuda, Puerto Rico, and the Virgin Islands.

Since the beginning of the 1980s it has been known that drug trafficking had permeated the political élites of some Latin American countries. In Bolivia, after the coup d'état that put General Luis García Meza in power, the economy being almost entirely pervaded by contraband, cocaine became just another commodity and members of General Stroessner's government became involved in its marketing. In Colombia, there is evidence of the widespread involvement of many politicians with drug cartel chiefs. This is the origin of a new concept in Latin American and international political relations: "narcopolitics."

As implied by the name, narcopolitics is the use of drug traffic's profits for political ends, as a means of enrichment, and as a means of exercising pressure or blackmail. Narcopolitics is also used by the US government as a means of putting pressure on Latin American countries. It is worth noting the way some governments and countries are accused of not helping in the struggle against drug trafficking. This has been an important aspect of US policies towards Mexico and

Panama. Narcopolitics is determined more by politics and strategy than by will and the actual ability to control the distribution of narcotics. Hence, it is very dangerous to allow the war against drug trafficking to upset and distort inter-American relations to the detriment of solving Latin America's true problems.

Evidently, important confrontations and disputes over spheres of power occur around drug trafficking. Some countries are trying to create special military units made up of forces from several Latin American countries to eradicate cocaine production in Colombia and the Andes. The attempt to transform the anti-drug battle into a war in which agreements must be signed between different armies creates a new type of interventionism: when the war against narcotics becomes substantial external pressure, it makes sovereignty vulnerable.

VI. Popular advances and weaknesses

1. Signs of backwardness in popular attitudes

Amid recurrent pressure and aggression, which have tried to eliminate for good any risk of popular mobilization, it would seem that the most overt imperialist counter-revolutionary intervention has declined, and mechanisms are being sought that could lead to negotiation. One sign of this has been the abandoning of pure authoritarianism and its gradual integration into negotiating mechanisms in the form of controlled democracies.

This trend has meant the revival of centrist tendencies, which try to take over this alternative. The left has provided the best opportunity for the renovation of domination strategy, maintaining as it does a sort of analytical stagnation, which, however, translates into the inability to adopt changes, particularly of the popular kind or those arising as some of the most typical features of the new capitalist process. Nevertheless, people still get organized and spontaneously struggle using their own inspiration and experiences.

The left traditionally searches for orthodox conceptual validity rather than for the real conditions of phenomena, an approach that sets boundaries to scientific and political imagination. This, in turn, has led to a significant conformist trend that in effect invalidates revolutionary theory and replaces it with intellectualizing the "possible" within the framework of abstract capitalist relations. No doubt, as long as there is exploitation, domination and dominated classes, and their international correlate, imperialism, there cannot be a complete crisis in Marxism. Yet most of the left demonstrate a proven inability to translate their view of reality into an image of the future that could lend content to popular struggles. It has not taken up the confrontation with the dominant ideological structure, and it relinquishes the masses to the influence of today's trends of reconciliation with and justification of conformist values.

A debate that assists setting the democratic struggle can be used as a clear example of this. The prevailing trend is for reconciliation and social agreements that guarantee dominant readjustments, and the sacrifice of egalitarian demands in exchange for the granting of basic liberties. In relation to this, there has not yet appeared a leftist discourse that coherently deals with this problem in depth and outlines, as a motive for struggle, liberty's limitations, which are principally reflected in blatantly increasing inequalities.

Unquestionably, the struggle for democracy, as a participative system that rescues popular sovereignty, must strive to eliminate inequalities and place itself strategically within the anti-capitalist and national liberation battle. In fact, the democratic struggles of Latin American peoples are a great reservoir of future anti-imperialist confrontation. This possibility is clearly recognized in the dominant sectors and in the heart of the empire, whose response has been a systematic political, social, and ideological campaign to defend an apparently just democratic scheme, but only within the framework of conservative maintenance of the status quo. One cannot respond to this strategy merely with a profound and convincing demonstration of its falsity.

In countries where the process of democratic recovery has begun, popular movements face internal contradictions that imply serious risks. To some extent, political opening means a considerable broadening of arenas for political and corporate work, and it is difficult for democratic–popular organizations to coordinate these participatory bodies. This in turn stresses the economic claims of sectors that have suffered the sharpest decline in their purchasing power; such claims lead only to indefinite strikes, factory and supermarket seizures, and national lockouts. A heightening of these struggles could mean clashes with a system that has encouraged leftist politics and governmental prospects. Native and transnational conservative forces thereby succeed in exercising increasingly authoritarian pressure on the popular movement; they tend to reduce the participatory opportunities that had been revived. Where they do not directly appeal to dictatorship, they restrain labour rights, exercise greater control over communications and the media, resort to "emergency" situations, etc., eventually imposing a new type of constitutional regime dominated by big capital, a new – constitutional – dictatorship whose juridical and democratic form has not been sufficiently studied in its actual intercessions or in its contradictions and currently emerging rifts.

There are still considerable omissions in the left's thought and political pronouncements concerning the failure to assume jointly the advantages of both currents of popular expression: the political organic and the corporate organic. The left dissociates itself from and despises corporate expression as a generator of political facts. Dominant bourgeois politics, on the other hand, understands and strives to deepen dissociation; this allows for separate negotiations with different groupings, at different levels and over different claims and political projects. In moments of crisis such as now, material claims affect the system more than political challenges.

The left's discourse has generally tended to be defined and realized in the spheres already constituted as the organization's social base. It is rarely constructed to transcend national dimensions. If the dominant classes' "national" discourse turns out to be increasingly less credible, and if the defence of the national depends on the people, the orthodox left's weakness, outdatedness, and trouble adopting the "national" as an essential struggle prevent revolutionary thought from giving meaning to the masses. Rather they contribute to the struggle's tendency to fall within liberal or neo-liberal orbits.

The domestic–national outlook on problems tends to prevail, relegating the regional dimension to a secondary function. Neither in theory nor in practice do consciousness and will correspond to that level. And all this happens while the empire forges a unified regional project with internal allies and with ideological principles and dimensions that serve their plans for regional domination. Progressive movements and parties, in general, make pretty weak forums; some are even dependent upon the will of governments.

2. The new actors

From a different standpoint, the left's inability to understand the emergence of a new and varied spectrum of new social actors, with an equal variety of capitalist contradictions, appears as another form of failing. The conformist perspective pretends to grant these new social actors a hegemonic role corresponding to their heterogeneous nature or their corporate behaviour and origin. The left has in some ways devalued the concept of the proletariat and its role, which historically, in qualitative and quantitative variations, expresses capitalism's fundamental contradiction. It is therefore not a contradictory grouping before the new actors. The unity of the exploited is also undertaken through a hegemonic process in which they represent the most important part.

There has been a tendency to schematize the complex dialectic of class struggle, which is simultaneously the result of a contradiction and a strategic component of change. New groups, such as urban settlers or the Liberation Theology movement, take up a perspective of class struggle. The forms expressing dynamics may vary greatly owing to the diversity of groupings, and are expressions of consciousness. The task then is to integrate them. It has traditionally been thought that the unification of fractions emerging in the exploited regions of underdeveloped capitalism, in other words, class identity, is achieved only in so far as a more organic development is attained, that is, when economic functions give a clearer profile to salaried workers. However, a large exploited group gradually acquires a unitarian identity in the process of repressive displacement, socially and economically manifesting itself in the country as well as in the cities. In this process, employees (urban and rural), settlers, and students, young and old, Indian and Ladinos, etc. are identified among themselves. The identity of the "pueblo" has slowly become more important than that of the "class." This phenomenon has tended to materialize in several important countries as a result of the present economic situation.

Theoretically, exploited factions that arise from subordinated modes of production are supposed to be organized and expressed through and around factions deriving from prevailing modes of production. This has been the hope over many decades and in several revolutionary currents. None the less, this principle has not operated in reality, leaving large groups abandoned to the manipulations of groups and factions, and thus playing into the hands of the system and the dominant classes. The problem has been transposing theory to a reality where a low-profile working-class structuring prevails. On the other hand, this has often implied a disdain for political facts re-

333

sulting from the behaviour of less developed factions, such as the peasantry, and the avant-garde that springs from or is involved with them.

The inexorable crisis of the economy and domination make it easy to predict the many different expressions of discontent, either with or without a class sense, whether short-lived, organic, of micro dimensions, or having a broader scope. Their variety needs a revitalized discourse capable of containing the multiple and uncontrollable scope of the opposition to the status quo.

Stressing exploitation in a process that tends to deepen differences (going as far as to contemplate a dual society in which most of the population lacks access to even basic services) has generated numerous associations in the popular field that are both spontaneous and autonomous in relation to the rest of society. These are forms of organization that deal with survival and the replacement of services that used to come from the state. This phenomenon can be observed in health care, housing, education, and food supply, etc. In some cases highly structured communal forms of organization arise; they have an administrative function in popular society, and sometimes they even have their own codes of behaviour and means of administering punishment.

Corporate organization being a form of social linking of the base, beginning with essential social needs, it passed from being historically an organization of "resistance" to become a form of "claim negotiation" to the extent that capitalist political systems allowed for greater opennesss. In several countries, the trend has been for a return to a "resistance" union situation and a reduction in the scope for negotiating.

Popular basic claims are a subject that should be thoroughly studied. The experience of the most highly repressive periods in several countries has demonstrated that popular expression survives, through organic articulations of strong resistance in relation to labour problems. Conflicts in the area under study have reached a degree of maturity that allows them to justify struggles and their organizations (which are the most stable and resistent manifestations), rearticulating social life and popular politics. We are speaking not only of claims originating in the workplace and related to matters of pay. It is important to re-evaluate the significance of this phenomenon because of its potential political dimensions and its relation to exploited civil society.

3. The processes of consciousness in struggle

When there is a breach in the development of popular organic structures, a coherent link between corporate and communitarian political processes with different circumstances is obscured, in particular in processes with specific dynamics and spheres. Different levels of awareness about problems of confrontation and prospects of struggles tend to appear.

From a union standpoint, the term "collective" involves a sense of class, as a working class; for the settler, it is something vaguer and corresponds generically to "the poor." On the other hand, for the settler, the demand for democracy is expressed by his actual and immediate claims, which include services, shelter, and work, whereas for the worker it constitutes an instrumental space for improving the circumstances in which claims materialize in relation to the boss, the chiefs, and the leaders. It may only be a matter of exercising power in both cases, without being aware of the reasons for its authoritarian origin.

The concepts of "objective politicization" and "subjective depoliticization" are helpful in explaining the situation, for they give an account of real enrichment and impoverishment. On the one hand, it is an "objective politicization" because different situations of different groupings and the conflicting difficulties resulting from their claims arise from specific political and economic conditions. At the same time, a devaluation of the conflict may thus happen in terms of "class," assuming the corporate or community particularities do not speak of class struggle as a whole. This prevents class consciousness from developing as a generator of an attitude in relation to power and exploitation.

From the masses' standpoint, at the level of primary consciousness there are elements of great value that also lack political representation: the massive identity of exploited and subjugated individuals, popular solidarity in a broad sense, autonomy for subsistence and defence, the ability to resist, the recognition of strength, and anti-authoritarian consciousness. However, these qualitative steps do not necessarily generate the full adoption of autonomy as a joint destiny, neither are they the response to a perspective of and for society.

In general, it could be claimed that exploited groups have continued to develop consciousness and a defensive capability in the face of overexploitive trends; at the same time, their political representatives' capacities have decreased, particularly as a result of generalized repression. For this reason, it is possible to find highly structured spontaneous expressions with very little organic direction.

4. The direction of popular politics

Today there is discussion about the conditions under which could be constructed a hegemonic popular political subject that could materialize in an organic formula, able to pass through the elementary forms of struggle to the more elaborate ones; this would be the passage from the corporate and communal to the political, strategically integrating different forms of struggle in the confrontation of ideological alliances. This would be the transformation of contradictory manifestations and crucial potentialities into social forces for change in an area of great force accumulation that requires consciousness and will. Latin American reality exhibits a great variety of political formations and organizations that work to interpret the popular and yet differ in many ways: they have different views on socio-economic reality, social forces, political circumstances, strategies, etc. It is, then, within the framework of a broad political, ideological, and religious pluralism that the avant-garde must arise; this means a long process of overcoming differences and, most of all, of overcoming antagonistic sectarianism, or dogmatic and authoritarian ways of thinking.

Some revolutionary parties have gradually lost their political presence, and therefore have had to look for support among only the most advanced fractions of the working class, expressing a very coherent discourse when it comes to doctrine but not being very significant for the exploited sector or, naturally, for the rest of society either. In many cases, this sort of isolation has led them to processes of internal mutual support. Self-indulgence and denial of the truth make them search for greater external cohesion and support, starting from a minority or small group dynamics.

Liberation processes in Central America and the Caribbean, as well as the parties that always tried to act in the diverse popular sector, have imposed the need for a revision of the concept of political organization in that part of the world. An analytical and synthesizing task that assumes the importance of these processes would be a contribution to a workable concept of political organization. Therefore, this should not be a discriminatory mode of an exclusionary dichotomy of either parties, in the classical sense, or movements with ill-defined historicity. These experiences correspond to multiple conditions and different social histories where class struggles have had qualitative differences, in class composition, in peasant participation, in capitalist development, and in state construction.

Two different types of process can be observed in the rise of political organizations. One is the organization that arises from an ideological formulation and a planned political programme, with which it tries to get support from factions or groups that might be interested. In fact, this has been the traditional emergence of popular parties everywhere. Another form is gradually taking steps towards a sort of self-mobilization arising from the basic identity of essential claims of subordinate factions, which then succeed in formulating a political project by means of a gestating avant-garde becoming involved with them or springing up within them.

We must undoubtedly go deeper into the analysis of popular organizations, into their history and efficiency, and particularly into the different forms of development of their leading avant-gardes or co-ordinating organisms. It is imperative to accept the existence of a generative process of a new popular political culture that has been developing at the margins of thought and scope of Latin American classic revolutionary formulations.

To some extent, a real avant-garde and compliance with the classical principles of a revolutionary organization are still valid when a revolutionary perspective is presented as a means of solving the problems affecting popular majorities in Latin America.

VII. Postscript (February 1990)

This essay was concluded in mid-1989. Since then, events in Latin America of great relevance for the continent's future have occurred, and it is therefore pertinent to mention them. On the one hand, in South America, the consolidation of the Chilean political transition, the electoral "juntas" in Brazil and Uruguay, and the severe crisis in Argentina are worth mentioning. Similarly, in Central America, the consolidation of neo-liberal style governments and a rightist political tendency profoundly question the possibility of evolution towards a true solution to the subregional crisis, for these regimes are moreover imposed by indiscriminate military force, as happened in Panama after the US military intervention of December 1989.

A typical phenomenon that can be clearly observed in the south of Latin America is the consolidation of democracy through electoral processes and the restoration of political forces that military governments had tried to silence. The left returns to important spaces in the political spectrum, challenging one of the premises of "arranged" and "controlled" transitions, in which progressive forces are thought to be displaced by repression or history's "inertia" (a current political trend that considers leftist options to be no longer viable, and to have no reason to exist). The Brazilian case is the clearest refutation of this notion, but there is also the rise of the Frente Amplio in Uruguay and the expected revival of political activity in Chile, legality having been reintroduced as Patricio Alwin took office as president of that country.

Brazil is an example of the political polarization taking place in Latin America: a worker, "Lula" Da Silva, face to face with a young businessman, Fernando Collor de Mello, disputes the presidency in a second round of voting because no one had won an absolute majority in the first round. This happened because of a collective condemnation of corruption and a radical questioning of the greatest inequalities and injustices that a Latin American economic system – supposedly the most modern and developed – can sustain. Economic indicators can be summarized in the inequality of income distribution where 10 per cent of the population holds 50 per cent of produced wealth while 8 million peasants work for $1.50 a day. The great defeat in the last elections was of the representative of the old political class, the leader of the Brazilian Democratic Movement Party (PMDB) and the Liberal Party, which respectively got only 4.4 per cent and 0.8 per cent of the votes.

Lula's government platform brings to mind progressive movements that existed before the coup: the withholding of external debt payments and the formation of a Latin American debtor club, breaking off relations with South Africa, joining the "non-aligned" movement, and, in economic policy, restoring the state's idea of welfare for income distribution.

The second round of voting resulted in a sort of destabilizing polarization. Lula won the big cities such as São Paulo, Río de Janeiro, and Minas Gerais despite the media's – the O Globo chain, for instance – obvious preference for Collor. Collor won in the most depressed areas, relying on a rightist populist discourse, making promises that are easy to utter, but impossible to keep.

The election's final result, though favouring Collor, turned the popular movement into a political actor capable of influencing policies that may be adopted by the future government (for instance, the possibility of undertaking a structural adjustment in the economy).

Thus, the political and social forces sympathetic to Lula speak of new popular political actors, with a revitalized discourse, closer to mass needs and aspirations.

In Uruguay, the general elections of November 1989 reflected the critical balance of society on the new democratic stage. Overall, the presidential victory of the Partido Nacional (37 per cent of votes), and the defeat of the government of the capital by the Frente Amplio (21 per cent in the country and 34 per cent in Montevideo, where half of the total population lives), dealt a blow to the Partido Colorado, which had intended to reorganize representative arenas, tightening the links of economic–social negotiation within a framework of anti-popular neo-liberal politics. The electoral results also reflected the polarizing tendencies generated by the system: the growth of rightist trends within traditional parties, a weakening of the central forces, and the growth of progressive forces that challenge neo-liberal economic policies.

The Frente Amplio's victory in the Montevideo mayoral race was due largely to the popular masses having learned from their dramatic lesson in survival; at the same time, it was due to their deliberate exclusion from political control of the reorganization planned by the centre–right forces. For this political force, it represents an unprecedented experience as well as a challenge, because of its potential as a source of support at the national level. This fact greatly worries the Uruguayan right.

On the other hand, elected president Lacalle has promoted economic and social policies that basically continue those of the previous government, including union regulation and control of the middle sectors. Under such conditions, Uruguayan democracy is still far from being firmly established. The popular representatives of the Frente Amplio have a great responsibility in this effort, for now all of them hold political and administrative responsibilities at every level.

In Chile, the transition to democracy has occurred between attempts by the army command, economic monopolies, and leaders of rightist political parties to maintain a "tutored democracy," through a rigid, carefully planned schedule designed to maintain "governability," and attempts at participation on the part of political and social sectors excluded from the system during the Pinochet dictatorship. Indeed, the transition has not diverged from the 1980 Constitution and the laws derived from it, in spite of the 1988 plebiscite that paved the way for the elections of 14 December 1989. Alwin's victory (with 55.2 per cent of votes) shows a tendency to favour political forces at

339

the centre of the political spectrum. However, the results of parliamentary voting favour conservative political forces, with only 36 per cent for the centre. The right, strengthened by the measures taken by the dictatorship, got 40 per cent and the left 20 per cent. These figures express the people's lack of access to polls over 16 years, progressive parties being illegal and deprived of the conditions to present candidates in every area and district.

This electoral battle is the beginning of a long transition. The right wants to condition it in such a way that major economic groups do not see their exceptionally advantageous situation affected and remain able to dictate economic policies to a weak state and a government lacking the scope to make far-reaching decisions. On the one hand, they have to agree to a democratic opening; on the other, they want to keep their "wild capitalism" status. As for the left, it must grow as popular movements recuperate, struggling for a democracy ever more profound and materially effective, constantly evaluating the extent of its commitment against the future government's centrist policies. Is it possible to realize democracy at the same time as highly concentrated capitalism? Will the Chilean model resist popular pressure to save their basic conquests?

Argentine democratic recovery, which has already lasted for more than one presidential term, does not seem to have progressed. It is paradoxical that such a rich country finds itself in such a state of bankruptcy and economic chaos. Deterioration has led to a crisis of the authority system, and to an undisguised lack of belief in the government. To face this, challenging and essentially individualistic behaviour on the part of the individual becomes imperative. A palliative was sought by bringing forward by six months President Menem's taking of office by making Alfonsín "resign." Menem assumed office with 85 per cent of public support; five months later, this percentage had halved. Power literally slipped through his fingers, and his team is highly unstable: he has replaced a top official every 14 days.

Two power factors loom as fundamental actors in this crisis: the armed forces and the great economic monopolies, neither of them having any great interest in democratic consolidation. Rather, they have been conspicuous as the protagonists of the authoritarian option. Meanwhile, three out of five Argentinians are informal workers; almost 30 per cent of the population lives below the formerly non-existent poverty line; inflation and devaluation records have all been broken. The social pact the new government imposed on the unions has discredited the leaders, who are now unable to control the grass roots. Social eruptions could occur at any moment, speeding up the collapse of the political stability that is already out of Menem's control; the heavy pressure of the armed forces and the oligarchy still weighs upon the frail democratic system.

Looking at Central America, the events of 1989 are not promising for those in search of peace and democracy. In El Salvador, great repression was unleashed after Cristiani's ascent to power in June 1989, diminishing hopes for a peace settlement. Furthermore, two rounds of talks between the FMLN and the government have concluded in Mexico and San José with no results. The open support of the United States for Cristiani and the unchecked activity of the regime's security forces have transferred the total war doctrine to the political conflict, which implies that any progressive political force, union, or religious organization is explicitly allied to the insurgents and must be annihilated. This in turn forced the FMLN to start the November military campaign that led to heavy fighting in the capital and even led the armed forces and United States to question the way they saw the war. The FMLN regained credibility as a powerful army, which makes the military inclined to press for favourable conditions for a real negotiation.

While negotiation is open even to institutions that had not participated as mediators in the conflict, such as the United Nations, the country's internal situation hardens and repression increases, even of ecclesiastical sectors, such as the Jesuits, that had always kept their distance from the conflict's protagonists. Similarly, the activities of the centrist political parties (for instance, the Christian Democratic Party) have been curtailed, as have those of leftist parties (for instance, the Democratic Convergence Coalition, whose leaders have been repressed). The Salvadorean situation has become one of the main axes of the Central American conflict because of the increasing military participation of both armies.

In other Central American countries, such as Guatemala, Honduras, Costa Rica, and Nicaragua, conservative political forces, representing traditional oligarchies, have recaptured significant ground in the political spectrum. In the Honduran and Costa Rican presidential elections, rightist candidates Callejas and Calderón Fournier both won. They both share the view that American hegemony is unchallengeable in Central America, and they would participate in regional convergence processes only as long as the Nicaraguan government is questioned and the FMLN is excluded from dialogue and negotiation in El Salvador. In Guatemala, Vinicio Cerezo's government is in-

341

creasingly trapped by the military and a powerful oligarchy, amid repeated violations of human rights that nobody tries to spotlight or prevent. In Nicaragua, after the failure of military aggression, the United States has changed its destabilizing strategy for a political one, supporting the Unión Nacional Opositora (National Opposition Union), and has increased support to some sectors, using reasoning that takes advantage of the country's serious economic crisis; thus a conservative political force is being reborn.

This picture is unquestionably darkened by the United States' intervention in Panama. Though the intervention was carried out with a simple "justification" – namely to capture General Noriega and bring him to trial in Miami – the real aim was to overthrow a government that opposed American strategic intentions so as to make compliance with the Torrijos–Carter treaties impossible. This military invasion, violating all the juridical principles of the international system on non-intervention and state sovereignty, was accompanied by what was to all intents and purposes genocide through the use of massive and indiscriminate bombardment. This called into question the American claim that the United States is willing to participate in a new climate of harmonious coexistence with its neighbours. The United States considers its position in the world to have been strengthened by the socialist crisis, and that it may, therefore, undertake any action without regard for the principles accepted by most countries about peaceful coexistence and mutual respect. At the same time, this has revealed the great fragility of Latin American unity. Some countries' attitudes – influenced by their bilaterally negotiated relations with the United States, dealing with issues such as external debt – have been merely lukewarm diplomatic condemnation, effectively clearing the way for the unchallenged show of hegemonic force and power.

Bibliography

Books and journal articles

Aguilera, Gabriel. *El fusil y el olivo: la cuestión militar en Centroamérica*. San José, Costa Rica: DEI, 1989.

Alape, Arturo. *La paz, la violencia: testigos de excepción*. Bogotá, Colombia: Planeta, 1985.

Arrosa Soares, María Susana. *Os Intelectuais nos processos políticos da América Latina*. Porto Alegre, Brazil: Editora da Universidade, CNPq, 1985.

Aznar, Luis, et al. *Alfonsín, Discursos sobre el discurso*. Buenos Aires, Argentina: FUCADE–Eudeba, 1986.

Benítez Manaut, Raúl. *La teoría militar y la guerra civil en El Salvador*. San Salvador: UCA Editores, 1989.

Bermúdez, Lilia. *Guerra de baja intensidad. Reagan contra Centroamérica*. Mexico: Siglo XXI, 1987.

Boron, Atilio. "La socialdemocracia europea y la transición democrática en Argentina." EURAL, Working Paper No. 10-85, Buenos Aires, Argentina, 1985.

―――. "De la política a la guerra. Notas sobre los orígenes de la militarización de la cultura política en Argentina." EURAL, Working Paper No. 14-86, Buenos Aires, Argentina, 1986.

Brigagao, Clovis. *A militarização da sociedade*. Brazil: Jorge Zahar Editor, 1985.

Burdeau, Georges. *La democracia*. Barcelona, Spain: Ariel, 1970.

Calderón, Fernando, ed. *Los movimientos sociales ante la crisis*. Buenos Aires, Argentina: CLACSO, 1986.

Camacho, Daniel, and Rafael Menjívar. *Movimientos populares en Centroamérica*. San José, Costa Rica: EDUCA–UNU, FLACSO, 1985.

Cardoso, Fernando H. *Autoritarismo e democratização*. Rio de Janeiro, Brazil: Editora Paz e Terra, 1983.

Carrera Damas, Germán. *La necesaria reforma democrática del Estado*. Caracas, Venezuela: Grijalbo, 1988.

Castillo Rivas, Donald, ed. *Centroamérica. Más allá de la crisis*. Mexico: SIAP, 1975.

Castro, Fidel. *Informe Central. Primer Congreso del Partido Comunista de Cuba*. Havana, Cuba: Editora Política, 1975.

―――. *Informe Central. Segundo Congreso del Partido Comunista de Cuba*. Havana, Cuba: Editora Política, 1980.

CECADE–CIDE, *Centroamérica. Crisis y política internacional*. Mexico: Siglo XXI, 1983.

Cepeda Ulloa, Fernando, et al. *Democracia y desarrollo en América Latina*. Buenos Aires, Argentina: CEL–RIAI, 1985.

CLACSO (Latin American Social Sciences Council). *Los límites de la democracia*. 2 volumes, Buenos Aires, Argentina: CLACSO, 1985.

Cordera, Rolando, Raúl Trejo Delarbre, and Enrique Vega, eds. *México: el reclamo democrático*. Mexico: ILET–Siglo XXI, 1988.

Cueva, Agustín. *El desarrollo del capitalismo en América Latina*. Mexico: Siglo XXI, 1977.

―――. "La democracia en América Latina: ¿novia del socialismo o concubina del imperialismo?" *Estudios Latinoamericanos*, 1(1), year 1 (Mexico, CELA, FCPyS, UNAM, July–December 1986).

―――, ed. *Tiempos conservadores. América Latina en la derechización de Occidente*. Quito, Ecuador: El Conejo, 1987.

Degregori, Carlos Iván. *Sendero Luminoso: 1. Los hondos y mortales desencuentros, II. Lucha armada y utopía autoritaria*. Lima, Peru: Instituto de Estudios Peruanos, 1986.

DESCO. *América Latina 80: democracia y movimiento popular*. Lima, Peru: DESCO, 1981.

343

Dreifus, René. *1964: A Conquista do Estado*. Petropolis, Brazil: Ed. Vozes, 1986.

Fundación Pablo Iglesias. *Caminos de la democracia en América Latina*. Madrid, Spain: Ed. Pablo Iglesias, 1984.

García, Alan. "Deuda o democracia. La alternativa de América Latina." *Cuadernos Americanos*, no. 1, year XLV (Mexico, January–February 1986).

García, Pío, ed. *Las fuerzas armadas y el golpe de Estado en Chile*. Mexico: Siglo XXI, 1974.

García Cantú, Gastón. *El desafío de la derecha*. Mexico: Joaquín Mortiz–Planeta, 1987.

Garretón, Manuel Antonio. *Dictaduras y democratización*. Santiago, Chile: FLACSO, 1984.

Gaspar, Gabriel. "Propuestas programáticas de la Democracia Cristiana en Centroamérica. Guatemala, Honduras y El Salvador." *Avances de Investigación*, no. 3 (Mexico, CINAS, 1986).

Germani, Gino. "Democracia y autoritarismo en la sociedad moderna," In: CLACSO, *Los límites de la democracia*. Buenos Aires, Argentina: 1985.

Gómez, Pablo. *La izquierda y la democracia*. Mexico: Ediciones de Cultura Popular, 1984.

González Casanova, Pablo, ed. *No intervención, autodeterminación y democracia en América Latina*. Mexico: Siglo XXI, UNU–UNAM, 1983.

——. *El poder al pueblo*. Mexico: Océano, 1985.

——."Cuando hablamos de democracia, de qué hablamos." Mexico, mimeo, 1986.

——. *Los militares y la política en América Latina*. Mexico: Océano, 1987.

Heller, Agnes, and Ferenc Feher. "Cromática Política: del rojo al verde." *La Jornada Semanal*, Mexico, 12 April 1987.

"Informe del Grupo Trilateral sobre la gobernabilidad de las democracias al Comité Ejecutivo de la Comisión Trilateral." *Cuadernos Semestrales*, nos 2–3 (Mexico, CIDE, 1978).

Krauze, Enrique, ed. *América Latina: desventuras de la democracia*. Mexico: Joaquín Mortiz–Planeta, 1984.

——. *Por una democracia sin adjetivos*. Mexico: Joaquín Mortiz–Planeta, 1986.

Labastida, Julio, ed. *Dictaduras y dictadores*. Mexico: Siglo XXI–IIS, 1986.

Leal Buitrago, Francisco. *Estado y política en Colombia*. Bogotá, Colombia: Siglo XXI, 1984.

Lechner, Nobert. *La crisis del Estado en América Latina*. Caracas, Venezuela: Cid, 1977.

——. ed. *Estado y política en Colombia*. Mexico: Siglo XXI, 1981.

——. *La conflictiva y nunca acabada construcción del orden deseado*. Santiago, Chile: FLACSO, 1984.

Leis, Raúl. *Comando Sur. Poder hostil*. Panama: CEASPA, 1985.

Maira, Luis. *Chile: autoritarismo, democracia y movimiento popular*. Mexico: CIDE, 1984.

——. ed. *El sistema internacional y América Latina. ¿Una nueva era de hegemonía norteamericana?* Buenos Aires, Argentina: GEL-RIAL, 1986.

Méndez, Candido. *A inconfidencia brasileira. A nova cidadania inierpela a Constituyente*. Rio de Janeiro, Brazil: Forense-Universitaria, 1986.

Nuncio, Abraham. *El PAN (alternativa de poder o instrumento de la oligarquía empresarial)*, Mexico: Nueva Imágen, 1986.

Ominami, Carlos, ed. *La tercera revolución industrial. Impactos internacionales del actual viraje tecnológico*. Buenos Aires, Argentina: GEL-RIAL, 1986.

Peeler, John A. *American Democracies (Colombia, Costa Rica, Venezuela)*. Chapel Hill, NC, USA: University of North Carolina, 1985.

Rodríguez Beruff, Jorge. *Los militares y el poder. Un ensayo sobre la democracia militar en el Perú: 1948–1968*. Lima, Peru: Mosca Azul Editores, 1983.

Rouquié, Alain. *El Estado militar en América Latina*. Mexico: Siglo XXI, 1984.

Rovira Mas, Jorge, ed. *Costa Rica hoy: la crisis y sus perspectivas*. San José, Costa Rica: EUED, 1984.

Slater, David, ed. *New Social Movements and the State in Latin America*. Amsterdam, Netherlands: CEDLA, 1985.

Sonntag, Heinz R. "Venezuela: un futuro incierto." *Nueva Sociedad*, no. 84 (July–August 1986).

Stepan, Alfred. *Os militares: Da abertura a Nova Republica*. Rio de Janeiro, Brazil: Paz e Terra, 1986.

Therborn, Göran. "La contradictoria democracia capitalista." *Convergencia*, no. 10 (Santiago, Chile, December 1986).

Torre, Cristina de la, ed. *Reformas políticas. Aperturas democráticas*. Bogotá, Colombia: Oveja Negra, 1985.

Torres-Rivas, Edelberto. *Centroamérica. La democracia posible*. San José, Costa Rica: EDUCA–FLACSO, 1987.

Torres-Rivas, Edelberto, and Julio C. Pinto. *Problemas en la formación del Estado nacional en Centroamérica*. San José, Costa Rica: ICAP, 1983.

Varas, Augusto, ed. *Transición de la democracia*. Santiago, Chile: ACHIP–FLACSO, 1984.

———. "Fuerzas armadas y transicion a la democracia en América del Sur." Santiago, Chile: FLACSO, Discussion Paper No. 91, 1986.

———, ed. *La autonomía militar en América Latina*. Caracas, Venezuela: Nueva Sociedad, 1988.

Various authors. *México mañana*. Mexico: Nexos–Océano, 1986.

Various authors. *El Salvador: guerra política y paz, 1979–1988*. San Salvador: CINAS–CRIES, 1988.

Various authors. *Elecciones y democracia en América Latina*. Costa Rica: CAPEL, 1988.

Weffort, Francisco. *Por qué democracia*. São Paulo, Brazil: Brasiliense, 1984.

Wolfe, Alan. *Los límites de la legitimidad*. Mexico: Siglo XXI, 1980.

Zavaleta Mercado, René. *Lo nacional popular en Bolivia*. Mexico: Siglo XXI, 1986.

Journals

Comercio Exterior, Banco Nacional de Comercio Exterior, Mexico.

———, vol. 37, no. 2, "La conferencia extraordinaria de la CEPAL" (monographic issue), February 1987.

Convergencia.

———, no. 10, Santiago, Chile, December 1986.

Crítica y Utopía, Buenos Aires, Argentina.

———, nos. 10–11, "La Argentina en transición" (monographic issue), November 1983.

Cuadernos Americanos.
———, year XLV, no. 1, January–February 1986, Mexico.
David y Goliat, Latin American Social Sciences Council (CLACSO), Buenos Aires, Argentina.
El Caribe Contemporáneo, Área del Caribe, Centro de Estudios Latinoamericanos, Faculty of Political and Social Sciences, UNAM.
———, no. 11, article by Gérard Pierre-Charles, "La lucha democrática en Haití," December 1985.
Estados Unidos. Perspectiva latinoamericana: *Cuadernos Semestrales*. Centro de Investigación y Docencia Económica (CIDE), Mexico.
———, no. 14, "América Latina en el proceso electoral norteamericano," 2nd semester 1983.
———, no. 15, "América Latina–Estados Unidos: la agenda política," 1st semester 1984.
Estudios Latinoamericanos, Centro de Estudios Latinoamericanos, Faculty of Political and Social Sciences, UNAM.
———, year 1, no. 1, July–December 1986.
Estudios políticos, Faculty of Political and Social Sciences, UNAM, Nueva época.
———, vol. 4–5, no. 4-1, October 1985–March 1986, Mexico, issue devoted to "El movimiento urbano popular" (the popular urban movement)
Monexico, magazine published by the Council of State, Managua, Nicaragua.
———, no. 6, "Ley Electoral".
Nueva Sociedad, Caracas, Venezuela.
———, no. 84, July–August 1986.
Pensamiento Iberoamericano, Instituto de Cooperación Iberoamericana, Madrid.
———, no. 6, July–December 1984, issue devoted to "Cambios en la estructura social" (Changes in the social structure).
Polémica, Instituto Centroamericano de Documentación e Investigaciones Sociales (ICADIS) and Latin American Faculty of Social Sciences (FLACSO).
Revista Mexicana de Sociología, Institute of Social Research, UNAM.
———, no. 1-1985, "Número conmemorativo del XX aniversario de la publicación de 'La democracia en México'" (monographic issue).
———, no. 2-1985, "Uruguay en la transición" (monographic issue).
———, no. 4-1985, "Actores sociales y política" (monographic issue).
Revista Mexicana de Ciencias Políticas y Sociales, Faculty of Political and Social Sciences, UNAM.
———, no. 120, "México 1985: elecciones, partidos y reforma política," April–June 1985.
Sociológica, Department of Sociology, Universidad Autónoma Metropolitana–Azcapotzcalco.
———, no. 2, autumn 1986, "Politología Contemporánea" (monographic issue devoted to democracy and politics).

Documents

CEPAL/ECLA (Economic Commission for Latin America). "El desarrollo de América Latina y el Caribe: escollos, requisitos y opciones." Basic document of the Extraordinary Conference of ECLA, Mexico, 19–23 January 1987.

Vusković, Pedro, "La crisis económica y sus proyecciones en América Latina."
United Nations University (UNU), Advance report, PAL Project, February 1987.
Nicaragua, *Constitución Política*, Asamblea Nacional de la República de Nicaragua,
El Día, Testimonies and Documents Section, 13–16 April 1987.
"Procedimiento para Establecer la Paz Firme y Duradera en Centroamérica"
(Esquipulas II). Esquipulas, Guatemala, 7 August 1987.

Monographs on conflicts and political struggles in Latin America, elaborated for the Latin American Perspectives Project, United Nations University

Aguilera, Gabriel. "Conflictos y movimientos sociales en Guatemala 1982–1987."
Balve, Beba. "Acerca de la relación legalidad–legitimidad. Argentina 1987."
Benítez Manaut, Raul. "México 1982–1988. Los conflictos políticos en la crisis."
Córdova Macías, Ricardo. "El Salvador: guerra, diálogo y negociación."
Gómez Calcaño, Luis. "La adaptación de un sistema distributivista consensual frente la crisis: el caso venezolano."
Ianni, Octavio. "A nova república do Brasil."
Lara Castro, Jorge. "Paraguay: crisis política y desafíos del tiempo político."
Laserna, Roberto. "Procesos políticos y cambio institucional en Bolivia (1982–1986: Conflictos y perspectivas)."
Maríñez, Pablo. "Movimientos sociales y cambios políticos en la República Dominicana (1982–1987)."
———. "Movimientos sociales y crisis política en Haití (1984–1989)."
Martínez, Milton. "El proceso democrático y la crisis política en Panamá."
Martínez Heredia, Fernando, "Conflictividad y profundización del socialismo: la rectificación cubana" (unpublished).
Molina Chocano, Guillermo, and Marcos Carías Chaverría. "Honduras: proceso político y conflicto constitucional (1931–1987)."
Palacio, Germán, and Fernando Rojas. "Procesos políticos y cambio institucional en Colombia: algunas hipótesis sobre el impacto y el manejo politico del narcotráfico."
Ruíz Contardo, Eduardo. "Chile, proyecto derechista y alternativa popular."
———. "Presentación."
Stolowitz, Beatriz, Raúl Latorre, and Esteban Elizalde. "Las intenciones democráticas en Uruguay: confrontaciones y conflictos."
Vega Carballo, José Luis. "Los movimientos populares bajo control político-institucional: clave del reformismo pacífico en Costa Rica."
Verdesoto, Luis, and Julio Echeverría. "Las coyunturas de la modernización en el Ecuador: democracia social política y autoritarismo" (unpublished).
Vilas, Carlos M. "Guerra y revolución en Nicaragua. El impacto de la guerra contrarrevolucionaria en la estrategia sandinista de transición revolucionaria" (unpublished).

347